My Life in the North

Volume I

By Daniel Allaire

Dedications

In this book, dedicated to my late son Danny Allaire and my late father in law and mother in law, Gabe and Mary Cazon, I share the stories that live in my memory and in my heart. Danny brought a gentle light into my life, a softness and joy that still stays with me no matter how much time has passed. Gabe and Mary welcomed me with warmth and treated me like their own, passing down their strength, their respect for the land, and the quiet wisdom that shapes the North. I have also included stories of my father in law and his older brother, the late Baptiste Cazon, whose skill in the bush, calm nature, and deep knowledge of the old ways taught me lessons I still carry today. May their souls rest in peace.

Contents

Chapter 1: My Upbringing 2

Chapter 2: My Journey to Fort Simpson 15

Chapter 3: My First Day on the Job 98

Chapter 4: My First Girlfriend 115

Chapter 5: Return Trip to Ste-Adele 132

Chapter 6: Return Trip to Fort Simpson 149

Chapter 7: Return Trip to Ste-Adele, Quebec 181

Chapter 8: Return Trip to Fort Simpson 188

Chapter 9: Working at the River Between Two Mountain Camp Surveying 205

Chapter 10: Trip Up the Mackenzie River 262

Chapter 11: Setting a Rabbit Spring Pole Snare Line 270

Chapter 12: Fishing Under the Ice at Reid Lake 285

Chapter 13: Breaking Trail with Snowshoes 352

Chapter 14: Spring Hunt *1976* 377

Chapter 1:
My Upbringing

I was born, in St-Jerome, Quebec, ten years after World War ll ended. Canada's birthrate expanded from the end of the Second World War until 1965. People born between 1946 and 1965 are referred as the Baby Boomers Generation.

I've always been intrigued in learning about my ancestors; who were they? Where they came from? How they lived when they first arrived in Canada? I've heard many stories about my ancestors from my grandparents on both sides of my family.

Many years ago, while looking at family photo albums with my mother, I saw a picture of me and my great grandfather, Laurent Rocheleau, from my mother's side. The picture was taken at his farm, a year before he died, I was then a toddler. It is amazing that in my lifetime, I've met someone born in 1869.

I've been working on my family tree for a few years. However, I've not completed it yet. Nevertheless, I've now added well over eight thousand ancestors to my family tree. My ancestors migrated from France in the 1600s and were some of the first European migrants in New-France, which is now Quebec.

Between 1535 and 1763, approximately 10,000 French migrants, including 2,000 women, are believed to have settled in New-France. From those migrants, the French-Canadian population was born.

My eighth great-grandfather, Jean Allaire migrated to New-France in 1658, contracted to clear land on the Island of Orleans near Quebec City. My seventh great-grandfather,

Jean Beaune migrated to New-France in 1665 as one of the 1,300 soldiers sent by King Louis XIV to assist the colony in New-France from marauding Iroquois who killed and plundered the settlers of New-France.

Jean Beaune married Marie-Madeleine Bourgery who was abducted by the Iroquois at the age of eight. She was assigned to an Iroquois family, where she became a full member until her release at the age of sixteen.

My eleventh great grandfather, Dr. Louis Hebert migrated to New-France in 1604. He was the first European apothecary in New-France, as well as the first European settler to farm and support himself from the soil. Dr. Hebert prepared and sold medicines to the settlers and included Indigenous traditional medicines in his work, as a specialist in pharmacology. He treated sick settlers and Indigenous alike.

Dr. Hebert cultivated enough wheat for the making of flour to support the 300 colonists in Quebec City. Bread represented 70% of the settler's diet. In primary school, I learnt about Dr. Louis Hebert in Canadian history class. At that time, I did not know that he was my eleventh great grandfather.

My seventh great grandfather, Martin Foisy, migrated to New-France in 1665 to clear land and farm. In 1683, he became a Coureur de Bois (trapper, fur trader) and formed a small fur trader company with twelve other companions. In 1684, 200 Iroquois attacked their seven canoes loaded with furs. After pillaging the canoes, the Iroquois captured the entire group.

After nine days of marching to Fort Saint-Louis de Illinois near present city of Chicago, the group of Coureur

3

de Bois was released without provisions, canoes, arms other than two old muzzle loaders with little powder and lead. The group survived the long journey back to Quebec City.

When I was a young boy, every Sunday, we would visit my maternal grandparents Rocheleau at their home in Lesage, a small village north of St-Jerome. On one of these Sundays, three ladies came to visit my grandmother and my mother. I had never seen the ladies before. My mother introduced me and my two sisters to the ladies, who were her cousins. They hadn't seen her since she was a teenager, before she married my dad.

One of the ladies, I do not remember her name, had some fingers missing on both hands and appeared to have a soft spot on her forehead. Being a young boy, I feared the lady with missing fingers and kept my distance. My mother and her cousins were laughing lots and seem to have had a good visit.

A few years later, while at my grandmother, I asked her about the lady with the missing fingers. The lady was my grandmother's niece, a daughter from one of her six older sisters. In the year 1936, when her niece was 16 years old, she was diagnosed with bone cancer. The doctor told her that he could not do anything for her and said that she had less than a year to live.

My grandmother was related to Brother Andre Bessette, who was known as the "Miracle Man of Montreal". Thousands of miraculous healings were attributed to his intervention. Brother Andre's mother was born a Foisy and was a grand-aunt of my grandmother.

My grandmother and her niece went to Montreal's Oratoire St-Joseph to meet with Brother Andre. He lived in

4

a small chapel near the Oratoire. Brother Andre blessed and rubbed some St-Joseph oil on the niece's forehead and hands while praying for her.

It was said that one year later, the niece was still alive. The doctor could not understand how she survived the cancer. Her fingers and forehead remained unchanged. She had married and had five children and lived to be 65 years old.

Brother Andre died on January 6, 1937, at the age of 91 years. Over a million people attended his wake and burial. Brother Andre's first Vatican-confirmed miracle was the healing in 1958 of a Quebec man, Giuseppe Carlo Audino, who suffered from cancer. This miracle was cited in Andre's beatification by Pope John Paul ll in 1982. He was canonized on October 17, 2010, by Pope Benedict XVl, making Saint Andre the first male Catholic Saint born in Canada. Saint Andre cured over 10,000 people in his lifetime according to estimates.

Mom and Me 1956

5

My parents were Paul-Andre Allaire (1930-2017) and Pierrette Rocheleau (1933-1998). They were married on August 5, 1950 in Lesage, where my mother was raised. My father was 20 years old, while my mother was 17 years old when they married. Prior to my birth, my mother had two miscarriages, a boy and a set of twin boys. Following my birth, my sister Johanne was born in 1956 and my second sister Josee in 1959.

The hospital in St-Jerome was inaugurated in 1950. I, along with my siblings were born there. Prior to the hospital's inauguration, most newborns in the St-Jerome and surrounding areas were born at home under the care of a doctor or mid-wife. Both my parents and two of my grandparents passed away at this hospital.

In 1955, the village of St-Jerome had a population of about 8,000 people. Meanwhile, today St-Jerome is a city with a population of 80,000 people. Located about 45 kilometers northwest of Montreal on the Riviere du Nord (North River), it is the gateway to the Laurentian Mountains.

I attended my first four years of elementary school in St-Jerome. From grade one to three, I attended a boys-only school named St-Louis. The school next door was named Ste Marcelle, it was girls only, and the one my sister Johanne attended.

The discipline at school was rigid, all boys wore uniforms, black trouser, white shirt, a tie, and a blue blazer. At the end of the school day, the class of thirty, had to stand in line two by two. We walk side by side from the classroom through the school grounds without breaking rank. Only when we reached the street, could we break rank and head to our homes.

Every morning before class, we had to stand and sing the Canadian National Anthem O Canada. If you're caught talking to another student in class, you were sent to the principal's office and receive the strap inside your right hand. The older you were, the thinner the strap was, making it sting more. I must have been a good student, I recalled being given the strap only three times.

There was a lot of bullying in the school, by older students preying on younger students. The word bullying did not exist back then. It was getting beat up or fight back. I choose to fight back when I am put into such situations.

I do not have too many fond memories living in St-Jerome. Most of the people in St-Jerome were Quebecer, with a few Irish people, who were descendants from orphans of Irish migrants during the potato famines in the 1800s. The Irish orphans were adopted by Quebec families and were able to keep their Irish's family names.

My 4th grade was at the Dubois school managed by nuns. All teachers and the principal were nuns. The school was mixed with boys and girls and had rules like the first school I attended. The nuns did not allow any students using their left hand to write, it was deemed by the nuns as a sign of evil. If they did, they would be hit on the knuckles with the metal edge of a large wooded ruler.

I remember the nuns walking in the class, tapping their ruler in their hands, looking over the student's shoulders to see if they were making spelling mistakes. Now and then, I'd hear a hit on someone's knuckles and a loud ouch! I've had a few of these hitting on my knuckles, I was not so good at spelling.

From St-Jerome, our family moved to Ste-Rose on Laval Island near Montreal, where I finish my 4th grade. There again, the bullying and fighting continued. I remember in grade four, I could count the days on one hand, I did not get into a fight. I did not look for fights but was a target by other boys and had to fight back to defend myself.

I did my 5th grade to part of my 8th grade in Ste-Rose. Not far from where we lived, I met Charles Landry, who became my best friend in Ste-Rose. Charles was a year older than me. He was short, slightly under five foot and four inches, with small built. His brown hair was combed in the style of Elvis. My mother was adamant that my hair was kept very short in the Hollywood brush cut hair style.

Charles, who I nicknamed Charley, was the youngest child in his family. He had two older brothers and a sister. Charley's family came from a small town, Mount Joli, located near the south shore of the Saint-Lawrence River. Charley's mother was a generous and amicable woman.

I never met Charley's father in the four years I lived in Ste-Rose. Many photos of his father wearing World War ll pilot attires adorned the walls of their living room. Mr. Landry was a decorated pilot in the war and had many aerial victories. I was told that his father was working in Northern Quebec in a bush camp, not sure what kind of job he did there.

Due to his small stature, Charley was often picked on by bigger kids. After many beatings, Charley signed up for Judo class. He became a black belt and won many tournaments in his weight class. Charley may have been small, but he was quick as lightning, "you blinked, you missed it."

I remember Charley practicing Judo moves that he learned on me. He would ask me to charge and try to grab him. Before I could grab him, he would flip me to the ground and put me into a choke hold. I'd try my best to get out of the choke hold, but couldn't. I was bigger and stronger than him and just could not catch him, that's how fast he was. While he was practicing his Judo moves on me, he taught me a few of them.

My parents separated when we were living in Ste-Rose. My mother was a manager at a large restaurant and bar in Ste-Rose for a few years and then opened her own bar a couple streets from our home. The bar was named "Le Cochon Qui Tousse" (The Coughing Pig).

My mother had wooden barrels made into chairs. The inside of the bar was decorated like it was barn. My grandfather helped my mother with the decorations. The bar was in the basement of a large building. The door to get in the bar was made of old weathered planks that came from an old barn.

My mother had a large pig head mounted on the wall above the stairs. Once the door was opened, a recording of a pig coughing would play. The local kids would come to the door and open it to hear the coughing pig. Eventually, something went wrong with the recording and my mother did not get it fixed.

Roger Rocheleau was my mother's older brother; she made Uncle Roger build a twelve-foot-tall pig of wood and stucco to promote her bar outside in the parking lot. My mother was very creative and had innovative business ideas.

The bar was successful and I even got to work a few times at the bar, when I was only twelve years old. My mother knew the Chief of Police in Ste-Rose. She would call the chief to let him know that I'd be working at the bar, the day before I was scheduled to work.

The bar could hold about 200 people and had a steak house restaurant inside the bar. There was a stage large enough for people to dance and musicians or comedians to entertain.

My mother hired a honky-tonk piano player named Bob Langlois. He was an interesting character, standing at six feet and seven inches tall, very thin with a dark brown mustache. Bob could play any genres of music on the piano. He couldn't read one note of music and played by ear. Bob would listen to a song or even a classical piece of music and was able to play it.

I remember him playing a prelude by Chopin, which is a challenging piece of music to play. Years later, I learnt the same prelude on the piano while studying classical music.

Bob would have been a perfect extra in a Wild West movie, playing the honky-tonk piano player in a bar scene in a gunfight. I could picture him with a tall mad hatter hat and long coat, sitting on a piano stool set too low for his long legs, playing a fast honky-tonk tune. He would play nonstop during the gunfight scene. Bob's piano playing inspired me to learn the piano.

I've many fond memories living in Ste-Rose. Unfortunately, the owner of the building where my mom operated the bar did not renew her lease after December 1968. The owner wanted a discotheque as an alternative to a bar. Discotheques were becoming popular in Quebec. The discotheque was a failure. After a year, the owner begged my mom to come back to Ste-Rose to start up her bar again. We had moved to Ste-Adele in the Laurentians, where my mother operated a restaurant.

Long story short, the owner lost his building and later declared bankruptcy.

We moved into an old house with a restaurant on the first floor in Ste-Adele that had been closed for a couple of years, between Christmas and New Years 1968. The owner of the restaurant was found dead by the police. He passed away in his room on the second floor above the restaurant. He was known as a heavy drinker and from time to time, he wouldn't open his restaurant for business.

The house was in disarray and infested with rats. I remembered the first night I slept in my room, a rat tried climbing on my bed. I kicked the blanket before he got into the bed.

My Family Christmas 1959

The rat went flying against the wall and fled into a hole in the wall. There were a lot of clean up to do before my mother could open her restaurant.

After the owner of the restaurant had died, a local businessman purchased the house that was converted into a restaurant. The first floor was the restaurant and kitchen. The upstairs was the living quarters, which had five bedrooms and a bathroom. The house and the restaurant were left as they were since the day the owner passed. The rats moved in and took over the house. None of the previous owner's personal effects were disposed of. The house looked as if it had been vandalized.

The previous owner, known as Nicolas, was born in Russia before the 1917 Russian Revolution. He was a Cossack. We found several old-time photos of him riding a horse, dressed in the traditional Cossack's clothing and fur hat.

The current owner allocated to my mother made the first six months of a one-year lease free of charge.

My mother opened the restaurant named "Chez Nicolas" in the spring of 1969. My mother purchased a commercial rotisserie for the cooking of barbeque chickens. On the menu were assorted dishes made from chicken. One of them was my favorite, called "Chicken in the Basket," which was chicken cooked with honey and spices.

The restaurant did well until Rotisserie St-Hubert restaurant, a well-known chain of restaurants in Quebec, opened its door down the hill from my mother's restaurant. Once the restaurant was opened, my mother closed her restaurant. Stiff competition.

At that time, my mother had a boyfriend named Norman Belair. He was in his late thirties. He was six feet tall, with a full head of light brown hair combed back, and had the looks of a movie star. He was a contractor for interior decorators, who hired people to sew curtains, install carpets, and interchange used fabrics from sofas and chairs to new fabrics.

Chapter 2:
My Journey to Fort Simpson
NT-1973

Tom, Denis, Stu, and I, the four Musketeers, lived together for two months before Tom and Denis left hitchhiking to Northern Quebec to look for work. After that, Stu and I were the only ones left at the house.

After some time, Stu and I decided to go to British Columbia to look for work as well. We stored all of our worldly possessions at my mother's home. Before leaving, I gave my mother a big hug and kisses and told her that I'd keep in contact to let her know that I was okay.

Stu Eason - October 1973

15

I could see in her eyes that she didn't want me to leave. I'm her eldest child and only boy. My two sisters said that I was my mother's "chou-chou," meaning her favorite. Nevertheless, she understood that I was determined to travel and experience what the world had to offer.

Stu and I walked to the bus terminal in Ste-Adele from my mother's house with only our backpacks on our shoulders. Our journey started to who knows where or how it will end. I was excited; I needed a change in my life. I was tired of washing dishes in fancy restaurants. I wanted to hit the road and see where it would take me.

Upon our arrival at the Montreal bus terminal, Stu phoned his friend, Michel, and asked him to pick us up at the bus terminal. I had met Michel a few months before. He was a Quebecois with shoulder-length thick dark brown hair and a hairline that nearly covered half his forehead. Michel was over six feet tall with broad shoulders. He was in his mid-twenties.

Michel did not live very far from the bus terminal. He then gave us a ride to the junction of Highway 401 in Ontario, not far from Montreal. From the junction, Stu and I hitchhiked to Kitchener, Ontario, to visit his parents. Once at the junction, we thanked Michel for the ride and then he left for Montreal.

Back then, hitchhiking was commonplace and practiced all over Canada. Nowadays, there are rules and restrictions as to where you can or cannot hitchhike. Highway 401 is a very busy highway with a lot of traffic. This highway is the main road between Montreal and Toronto. Kitchener, our destination, was located one hour west of Toronto, which is a six-hour drive from Montreal.

We both stuck our thumbs out and began hitchhiking. Fifteen minutes later, an older model car stopped by the side of the road near where we were standing. Stu opened the door and asked the driver, "How far are you going?" The driver replied, "Toronto." "We are going to Kitchener," said Stu. "Get in," said the driver.

Mom 1976

Stu sat in the front seat while I sat in the back seat behind the driver. The backpacks were put on the backseat. Back then, most vehicles did not have seat belts. The driver was Anglophone in his early twenties. His hair was blondish and very short, which was uncommon back then for a male of his age bracket. He said that he was happy to have company for the long drive to Toronto.

17

I was tired and made myself comfortable in the backseat using my backpack as a large pillow. Stu and the driver spoke non-stop while I took a nap. About halfway to Toronto, the driver mentioned that he had heard a story about a hobo with long white hair and a full white beard with raggedy clothing that hitchhiked at night on the 401. He said that people would see him on the 401 at night hitchhiking, then twenty minutes later would see him again hitchhiking.

The story was that the hobo was a ghost, and people were afraid to pick him up. About five minutes later, he spoke out loud and said, "There he is!" I jumped up and looked outside. I couldn't see anyone outside, as it was dark. I asked Stu, "Did you see him?" He said, "I did."

I believe that the driver did not want to stop and pick him up, as he was shocked to have seen him. He had heard the story many times, and this was the first time he saw the hobo himself.

We arrived at the junction where our driver was to exit. He stopped the car, shook our hands, and told us good luck with our trip. It was early morning by that time, still dark. Stu and I stood on the shoulder of the 401 and stuck our thumbs out with the hope someone would stop. It was hazardous hitchhiking in the dark. Drivers only see you at the last minute, making it unsafe to stop.

It was a very busy highway, and most drivers were driving over the speed limit. As the sun started to rise, a car stopped on the shoulder of the 401. Stu and I walked to the car and opened the door. A man in his mid-thirties asked, "Where are you going?" Stu replied, "Kitchener." "I'm going there too. Get in."

Stu asked the driver, "Can you drop us off at the Leon's store? My dad works there." "Yes, I can," said the driver. The Leon's store was near Highway 401. The driver did not speak much; he was quiet and focused on the road.

I was tired, as I had not slept much since leaving Montreal. An hour later, I could see the Leon's store from a distance. It was around 8:00 a.m. The sky was cloudless, and the morning warmth indicated that it would be a very warm day. We were fortunate it did not rain while we were hitchhiking.

The driver dropped us off in front of Leon's store. We picked up our backpacks from the trunk of the vehicle, thanked him, and walked away. When we walked up to the main entrance of the store, we saw that the opening hour was at 9:00 a.m.

I rested my backpack against the building and dozed off. I was awakened by a car door being closed and the sounds of Stu talking with his dad. I quickly stood up, rubbing my eyes, trying to wake up from my slumber. Stu introduced me to his dad, John. I shook his hand using my best English and told him, "Good to see you." He smiled and replied, "Yes, good to see you."

John was an older version of his son without the long hair. He was six feet tall and looked strong. John was a World War II soldier stationed in England; he met and married his wife shortly after the end of the war. I believe that he was involved with the liberation of the Netherlands.

Stu's dad was a salesman at Leon's store, where he worked for many years. From what I was told by Stu, his dad was a very good salesman and made a good living selling furniture and appliances. Stu had been away from his family for over a year, and it seemed they had a very good relationship.

John phoned his wife, Mary, to let her know that we had arrived in Kitchener. He then took us to his house in what seemed to me to be a luxurious car. Their home looked new and well-kept. I was most impressed by the large swimming pool in the backyard with a diving board.

John introduced me to his wife, Mary. I shook her hand and said, "Good to meet you." She smiled and said, "Yes, good to meet you as well." Mary bore a strange resemblance to Queen Elizabeth; both were about the same age at the time. She looked to be in her mid-forties, tall, and gracious with a hairstyle like the Queen. Mary even sounded like the Queen Elizabeth.

Although she had been in Canada for over half her life, she still had her thick British accent. Mary had cooked breakfast for us and asked Stu and me to sit at the kitchen table. I was starving. We hadn't eaten since we left my mom's house in Quebec, the breakfast smelled wonderful.

Mary asked if I would like some coffee. I said, "No coffee, milk please." I devoured my breakfast. Stu and I had not had a proper meal in 24 hours. Stu was a tall, slim guy, but can he eat! He had a second helping.

John sat at the table with us and chatted with Stu for a long time. They had a lot of catching up to do. After breakfast, Mary asked me if I'd like to sleep for a while. Mary showed me to a room in the basement and gave me a towel and soap. The mattress was to die for. My body sunk into the mattress, when my head hit the pillow, lights out!

I was very tired when I went to bed; I woke up just before dinner in the same position as I fell asleep. I made my way upstairs; Stu had gone to bed later than I had and he was still asleep. Mary introduced me to her daughter, Emily who was a year older than I was; Mary asked me to sit down at the table and offered me some of the lemonade she just made. The lemonade was delicious, I drank two large glasses which was very cold, just the way I liked it

Stu and I created our own way to communicate between ourselves. We'd use both French and English phrases and words as well as expressions while communicating. We were teaching each other's language. Although I could not understand all of the conversations between Stu and his family, I could feel the love and respect they had for each other. The vibe in the house was joyful and relaxed. It was like I was a member of the family. That was something I was not used to. My parents separated when I was nine years old. I do not have any fond memories of my childhood particularly while living in St-Jerome. I was relentlessly bullied at school and the few friends I had were also victims of bullying. The memories I most cherished were the visits and overnight stays at my grand-parents and aunts and uncles' home.

Stu's mother asked me to help her and her daughter with carrying the food to the backyard, it was a very hot and sunny day; I helped Stu's mom and sister move a large umbrella which was inserted into the middle of the picnic table. The umbrella provided much needed shade from the sun. We returned to the kitchen to find Stu walking into the kitchen rubbing his eyes, still waking up. He looked at me and said, "*on va manger des T-Bone* steaks for dinner". "Cooking T-Bone steaks on barbeque" I said. Stu said, "*oui*". I was hungry and looking forward to eating T-Bones steaks. Stu and I could not afford T-Bone steaks. To save our money for our trip, we were frugal in purchasing food and household items. Our dishes consisted of margarine containers used as

21

bowls and plates. We only had one set of utensils and plastic cup each, a cast iron frying pan and a couple pots. While working at the Totem restaurant, I was able to bring home left-over food such as spaghetti sauce and boeuf bourguignon which is a French dish consisting of beef stew meat, red wine, garlic, mushrooms and spices.

Stu's dad arrived at the house shortly after 5:00pm, his mom had marinated the T-Bone steaks early in the morning. Mr. Eason fired up the barbeque and started to cook the T-Bone steaks. Once back in the backyard, Stu jumped on the diving board and dove into the swimming pool. He was a good diver and swimmer much better than I was; I went back to my room after I dried myself and changed. When I came back to the backyard, Stu's older sister Evelyn and her husband John had just arrived at the house, I was introduced to both. Stu gave a hug to his sister and shook hands with John who did not know that Stu was back for a visit.

Mr. Eason announced that the steaks were cooked and asked us to gather at the picnic table for dinner. The dinner was fit for a king, after the main course, Mrs. Eason had made some apple pie for dessert.

After dinner and desert, Mr. Eason asked if I played darts, I told him no. Mr. Eason explained how the game was played and score kept. The game we played was 301. The objective of the game is to be the first player to reduce the score from 301 to zero. The last dart thrown must land in a double or the bullseye. Mr. Eason won the first game, he was impressed by my playing; to his amazement, I won the second game, he couldn't believe that I won. He asked if we could have a tiebreaker. The third game was close; I could not hit the double number I needed to win. After a few throws, Mr. Eason won the game.

Before bedtime, Stu asked his dad if he could give us a ride to their cottage on Lake Huron. Mr. Eason bought the cottage when Stu and his sisters were in primary school. The cottage was near the town of Listowel where Stu was raised and went to school. He still had several friends there.

Next morning, after a delicious breakfast, we headed to the cottage which was about one and half hour drive. Mr. Eason opened the door of the cottage and gave me a tour. The cottage was open concept and shaped like a large barn with high ceilings There were enough beds to sleep eight and a bathroom at the end of the room. The cottage was facing Huron Lake it was like you were on a beach by the ocean. Lake Huron is the second largest of the Great Lakes and 4th largest lake in the world. The sand on the beach is brownish in color with very little rocks or peddles, the water was clear and cold. The cottage also had running water and electricity.

Stu's friends, Joe and Bobby, were to meet us and spend the weekend at the cottage. Joe had a car; Stu had planned for us to drive to London and spend the day there to visit some friends. Stu and I went for a swim in Lake Huron after which we cooked dinner. It was dark when Joe and Bobby arrived at the cottage. Joe was small in stature and had long dirty blond hair halfway down his back. He had a thin blondie beard and mustache. He spoke English too fast, I could not understand what he was saying. Bobby was the opposite; he was tall and thin with dark brown hair. Bobby was friendly and easy-going and took the time to talk with me as well as teach me a few words and phrases in English.

I went to bed early and fell asleep immediately. Stu and his two friends were talking and laughing very loud. While I was sleeping, I felt a finger tapping on my shoulder, I was not sure if I was dreaming or not. When I opened my eyes, I saw a hideous thing just above my face; It took me a couple seconds to realize that someone was standing over my face, I took a swing at the hideous face and missed. It was Joe playing a prank on me that he called "the freak-out face". Stu explained that when they were kids, they had scared the person sleeping by making a hideous face two inches away from their face and slowing waking the person by gently tapping a finger on their shoulder. At one time, Stu enacted that prank on his father at the cottage when he was 10 years old, that lead to a black eye and broken glasses; his dad was quicker than he was. Stu never played that prank on his dad again.

The next day, we drove in Joe's car to Listowel which was about a half hour drive from the cottage and spent the day visiting some of Stu's other friends. Stu was born and raised in Listowel, a town like the one I was born and grew up in. The dissimilarities I noticed was the culture and language which was obvious and secondly the impression of being in a prosperous town. The homes were well kept with manicured lawns adorned with beautiful flowers and trees.

We spent the night in Listowel visiting with Stu's friends. I felt left out from their conversations in English and could not understand all that was being said. We set up our tents and spend the night in Stu's friend's backyard as it was very hot and humid. Back then, there were no air condition, only fans provided some relief from the heat and humidity. I could hear Stu and his friends having a good time and laughing out loud into the wee hours of the morning. While sitting outside my tent, I wrote my first letter to my mother, letting her know that I was learning new English words and phrases.

Stu wanted to spend the day in London, Ontario to visit his friend Steve. Joe drove us there in his old sixtyish reddish car the following morning. Music blaring from the eight-track player, we made our way to London. I sat on the backseat leaning on my packsack enjoying the music while Stu and Joe talked one hundred miles per hour as if they were trying to catch up with all that had happened in the past year. Joe dropped us off at Steve's apartment near London's downtown. Stu and I walked upstairs to the second floor, as we walked down the corridor, I could hear loud music which sounded to me coming from some type of piano. Stu knocked at the door; the music stopped abruptly; I could hear through the door people talking in a low whisper. Someone came to the door and asked, "who's there?". Stu said, "It's me, Stu", the door quickly opened and there stood in full view a tall slim guy with long black straight hair to his waist looking like a rock star. The tall guy gave a big hug to Stu and said, "you scared the hell out of me, I taught you were the cops". Stu introduced me to Steve who told us to come in.

As I walked into the apartment, an intense aroma of hashish filled the living room area. An acoustic upright piano stood against a wall near the entrance. Stu introduced me to another tall and slim guy with long wavy light brown hair who also looked like a rock star. His name was Sandy.

Steve and Sandy were both musicians playing in the same band. Sandy was the drummer, and Steve was the keyboard player. "We're smoking a spliff when you knocked at the door. I just about flushed my hash down the toilet," said Steve, who was high as a kite.

"Do you guys want to smoke a spliff? It's very good black hash from Afghanistan," said Steve. Stu looked at me and quickly replied, "Yes!"

Steve cut the sticky black hash into small pieces with his long nails and mixed the pieces of hash and a sprinkle of

25

tobacco inside a piece of rolling paper. He rolled the spliff with both hands, licked the edge of the rolling paper from one side to the other, and then gave the spliff one last roll to secure the glue of the rolling paper.

Stu grabbed the one-quarter ounce chunk of black hash from the kitchen table and gave it the once-over by smelling and squeezing it. "Smells like good black hash," said Stu.

Steve lit the spliff, inhaled the smoke, and then gave it to Stu. The spliff made about three to four rounds between the four of us. We all sat at the small kitchen table, each sitting at each side of the table, taking our turns on the spliff until it had expired.

I had smoked hashish from various countries before, including Afghanistan. This was one of the most potent hashish I'd smoked.

We all sat at the table looking at each other without saying a word until Steve got up and said, "want to hear a new tune I'm working on?". I got up and walked to the piano. Steve turned on his amplifier and played the black and ebony keys with his fingers into a progressive rock type tune that was up my alley. Steve played a chord progression that included at least six chords and then got into a solo like he was playing an electric guitar sounding like Jimmy Hendrix and Jimmy Paige. I had goosebumps all over my body listening to Steve playing, he had a microphone plugged into the amplifier which was positioned into the inside of the piano; the guitar pedals were hooked up to the amplifier giving an electrifying sound to the piano like I've never heard or imagined. I could tell by his playing that Steve must have learned classical music. His tunes had a mixture of progressive rock, jazz and a touch of classical. After listening to Steve's tune, I felt

26

inspired by his music. I had not played piano for a couple months and had the urge to play.

After Steve finished his tune, Stu said to him, "Daniel plays piano, he learned classical music". Steve's face lit up, he looked at me and pointed to the piano bench for me to sit. Like a good friend of mine, Lyn Anderson, would say, "I was feeling no pain", I was high as a kite on the black hash. I sat on the piano bench and started to play Bach's Invention Number 13th in A minor as fast as I could. The piano sounded like an electric guitar but played like a piano. I gave a few squeezes on the pedals to intensify the sounds of my playing. From there, I played a few tunes from my repertoire and then finished my concert with Bach's Prelude in D minor mixed with an improvisation that I made on the spot. Steve looked at me very impressed with my playing and sense of music. We both shook hands and had a good laugh. Steve walked me through how he came up with the idea of hooking up an amplifier to an acoustic piano. We could not communicate with each other that well but understood each other as musicians. Before we left Steve's apartment, we smoked another spliff which was about twice the size of the first one. Steve gave Stu a sizeable chunk of the black hash for our train ride to Vancouver. We shook hands and said our goodbyes. Stu and I, with our backpacks, walked to the downtown area of London, Ontario.

Stu wanted to check a few stores and meet with his dad at a rendezvous location that he and his dad had set up. We were to return to his parents' home where we would spend one more night and the following morning his dad would drive us to the CN train station in Toronto, Ontario to catch the train to Vancouver, British Columbia.

FINAL DAYS IN ONTARIO

27

As Stu and I were walking downtown London we heard an elderly women screaming "the Queen! the Queen!". Stu and I turned around and saw several elderly women running on the sidewalk screaming "the Queen! the Queen!". A large black convertible limousine slowly drove by us with Queen Elizabeth II smiling and waving at the crowd, while her husband Prince Phillip smiled and waved at the crowd as well. I had no idea that the Queen was in London, Ontario on that day. June 28th, 1973, I stood on the sidewalk and watched the Queen go by just like I was watching the news on the television. I was surprised and couldn't believe Queen Elizabeth was only a few meters from me, I must say that Queen Elizabeth was a beautiful woman, she was forty-seven years old at the time. What a day, it was full of surprises, and excitement, I met and heard a very talented musician, got to play on an acoustic-electric piano; saw Queen Elizabeth II and Prince Phillip and not to mention smoked some of the best hashish ever.

The evening at Stu's parents felt like coming back home. Stu's mom cooked us another meal fit for a king. Mr. Eason asked me to play darts after dinner while Stu help his mother and sister clean up the kitchen. While sharing a home with Stu in Quebec, he always ensured that the kitchen was clean; as soon as a dirty bowl or utensil was put into the sink, he'd wash, dry and put it away. Mr. Eason's dart playing was at its best that evening, as if he was playing for first place at a tournament, I did not have a chance. After two humiliating games, I surrounded myself and called it quit. "We better call it a night, we've to be at the train terminal in Toronto early in the morning", said Mr. Eason beaming with pride, he was a very serious dart player.

Early the next morning, still dark outside, I could hear Stu and his mom laughing and cooking breakfast. The sound of cracking and mixing eggs in a glass bowl gave it away that scrambled eggs was on the menu. He looked at me and said, *"bonjour, as tu bien dormi?"*. I replied with my best English, "Good morning, I sleep good". Stu smiled and asked me, *"as tu faim?"*, I replied, "yes, I hungry". "Please sit down", said Ms. Eason. The table was loaded with food. After breakfast, we said our goodbyes and Mrs. Eason gave me a big hug and said, "You come back again" with a smile.

The drive to Toronto was about one hour, the traffic in the city reminded me of the traffic in Montreal. Mr. Eason stopped at the entrance of the terminal and shook our hands, "have a safe trip", said Mr. Eason. Stu and I walked into the CN Train Terminal; the interior was buzzing like the inside of a beehive. People with suit cases, cardboard boxes taped with duct tape and backpacks were roaming like they did not know where to go. Stu located the ticket counter to purchase our tickets. "Two coach tickets to Vancouver, please", Stu asked the elderly man, "It will be $39.25 for each ticket", said the elderly man. I misunderstood and though he said that the tickets were $39.25 for both. I reached into my wallet and gave $20 to Stu. He looked at me puzzled and gave me back the $20 bill and said "$39.25 for each ticket" pointing his right index finger signaling one. I reached for my wallet and pulled out one of my $50.00 American Express Travel Cheque. I signed the cheque in front of the elderly man. He looked at me and said, "here's your change $10.75", and handed me my train ticket. He added, "the train is leaving in one hour and twenty minutes at gate twenty" and pointed with his right hand to the direction of gate twenty. "Thank you, sir!", I said. Thirty-nine dollars was a lot of money back then; that was nearly one week's wage washing dishes at $1.50 per hour. I managed to save $500 for our trip over a four-month period.

Our plan was to travel to Vancouver searching for a good paying job which I considered at the time to be $3.50 per hour or above. Back in the early seventies, the thing to do for people looking for good paying jobs was, "Go to Van man". "Van" meaning Vancouver. I was told several stories from people I knew that there were good paying jobs in British Columbia. A friend of a friend told me that he made two thousand five hundred dollars after tax working for three months as a fire fighter on forest fires near Golden, British Columbia. The work was hard and dirty with long hours from sunrise to sunset, nevertheless it was a good paying job. Stu and I had planned to find a good paying job, work for a few months and save enough money to travel to England where Stu had an uncle on his mother's side that owned a large pharmaceutical factory outside London. Stu's uncle invited him a few years earlier when he visited his sister in Canada, Stu was certain that I could also get a job at the factory working with him. The plan was to work for his uncle for about one year then travel all over Europe and make our way to India and Nepal.

ON THE TRAIN OUT WEST

Stu and I boarded the train quickly and made our way to the coach section to get choice seats. In those days, seats were not assigned. We stored our backpacks on the metal rack above our seats. I was excited to begin our journey to Vancouver, B.C. People were gradually making their way to their seats; most of the passengers seemed around our age or little older also with backpack. The trip to Vancouver was expected to last three nights and four days. "All aboard!", said the train conductor out loud, he was a frail elderly gentleman who wore a black hat, and had a white mustache; his uniform was black with a white shirt. "Ticket please", said the train conductor holding a hole punch to make a small hole in the tickets. "Keep your ticket with you until you arrive at your destination", he instructed. Stu and I turned the seats in front of us so we could rest our feet on them. The train began moving slowly then jolted forward for a few meters then abruptly stopped; a few seconds later, the train jolted for a second time. The train started to move slowly at first then increased in speed of about 15-20 kilometers per hour. The train is now moving from the terminal and crossing the city' streets. I laid back into my chair and stretched my legs on the seat in front of me.

All that could be seen now were the vehicles stopped at the train crossing waiting for the train to pass by. I decided to take a nap; it was still early in the day but not time for lunch. Sleeping on the train takes some time to adjust. The constant rocking noises of the train and people around you kept me awake. The car was about half empty, there will be more people getting on and off at each stop. We're heading north to Sudbury, our first stop.

We decided to take a walk and explore the train. Each train car had a bathroom at each end; Each car had a door with a large window at each end. A platform with a metal floor connected to the next car. We walked down a few cars and located the dining lounge and bar car. Inside the car was a booth connected to the kitchen that sold sandwiches, hamburger, hot dogs, French fries, snacks, bottled pop, chips and chocolate bars to name a few; we purchased our food while on the train. The restaurant was too pricey for our budget. At each stop, we would purchase food at the grocery store or fast-food stores if there was one near the train station. We put in a lot of mileage on the train walking back and forth up and down the cars; after a while, I felt and walked like I was inebriated so did everyone else, even the staff working on the train. Stu and I met several interesting people on the train, discussions were mainly about where are you headed, where you are from, what kind of work you do and with people our age, do you want to smoke a joint or do you have anything to smoke.

At our first stop in Sudbury, we purchased fresh fruit, juice and pop along with snacks at a nearby grocery store. More passengers boarded the train with fewer getting off. Not to lose our seats to new passengers, we placed our backpacks on our seats when we got off the train to stretch our legs and purchase snacks. The stops were anywhere from one to four hours. The longer stops were to fuel, replenish goods, cleanup and add more cars. These stops allowed passengers explore the towns or cities and to purchase food from the local grocery stores.

Our next stop was Capreol which is a major divisional point on the Canadian National Railway line. The train that departed from Montreal was merged into the Toronto train. The population on the train nearly doubled. Looking out the window as we travel the countryside throughout northern Ontario was a blend of endless Canadian Shield, muskeg and numerous lakes and rivers of all sizes. We stopped at numerous small communities along the way, many were small Indigenous communities such as Longlac, Armstrong and Sioux Lookout. At each stop, we got off the train and socialized with the local population. This was my first experience being in small towns populated mostly by Indigenous people. Where I was born and raised, I seldom had any interactions with Indigenous people apart from a police officer in my hometown of Ste-Adele who was a Mohawk.

Claude St-Aubin, the Police Officer in question was the biggest and strongest man I ever saw. He stood six feet, eight inches and weighed about three hundred and fifty pounds of muscle. He had a full head of hair which was trimmed very short. His face was squared like a box with a set of mean looking dark brown eyes as if to warn you "do not mess with me, you'll regret it". His body fill up a whole door frame. Once I shook his hands with him after I played piano at a school concert, I was sixteen years old at the time, my hands disappeared in his hand which was twice the width of my hand. The first time I saw him; I was walking to the bus stop to catch the school bus. I was only thirteen years old and was new in town. I saw a police car parked in front of the post office. This huge man came out of the police car; I couldn't believe a man that size could fit in the police car. The Police Officer bent down and grabbed the back bumper of a Volkswagen Beetle car that was improperly parked. I stopped across the street from the post office and saw this huge man pick up the back of the car off the ground almost effortless and moved it closer to the curb; keep in mind that the Volkswagen Beetle's motor is located at the back of the car. I was the only witness of this tour de force, he looked at me from across the street and emitted a loud grunt that made me jump out of my skin, I quickly vacated the site and made my way to the bus stop. I've heard many stories about Mr. St-Aubin's exploits; he was a legend in Ste-Adele.

I met a few francophones after the Montreal train was hitched to the Toronto train. Most of them were going out west seeking jobs. Some of the Francophone's English-speaking abilities were less than mine; I was fortunate to travel with an Anglophone and between to two of us, we were bilingual.

On the second day, we cross over into Manitoba, the countryside changed from Canadian Shield to forested areas near the Ontario-Manitoba border and then into the prairies. It was quite a contrast, one bend of the railroad the forested countryside blended into prairies countryside.

WINNIPEG

A few hours later, we arrived in Winnipeg. The conductor advised us that the stop will be four hours. It was early evening, the date was July 1, 1973. The Train Terminal in Winnipeg was massive, I felt like I was at the Saint Joseph's Oratory in Montreal which is built like a smaller version of the Basilica in Vatican City. The place had a *"je ne sais quoi"* which translates to "I don't know what". It was peaceful but at the same time buzzing with people. The sounds of the people's footsteps were deafening. We went outside to look for a grocery store; however, all the stores were closed due to the holiday. We found ourselves in a bar loaded with people. The bar smelled like a dirty ashtray; the smoke was like a London's fog that you'd see in a Jack the Ripper movie. A local band was playing on a small stage next to a dance floor. We stood next to the bar as there were no empty chairs and ordered two beers. Stu and I were both under age. We both looked older than our ages. While we enjoyed our drinks, the band played some Neil Young songs which were popular in the early seventies. Stu and I enjoyed the music and the ambiance of the bar which was rocking that night. We lost track of time and nearly missed our train. It was a race to make it back to the Terminal in time.

"All aboard", said the train conductor. We reached the train just in time and settled into our respective seats. We both had a few beers at the bar and were feeling somewhat intoxicated. The race and drinking of beers made us hungry, we were out of store-bought food and opted to have a meal at the restaurant. Making our way down the hallway heading to the restaurant, we were bouncing wall to wall as the train was gaining speed. The effect of the beer drinking and movement of the train made me a tad nauseous. A tall, young black man showed us to our table and handed us a menu. I read the menu and could not believe how expensive the

35

meals were, it reminded me of the menu at the restaurant I worked at in Quebec. I had my eyes on a New York steak with potatoes and vegetables worth at least two to three days wage washing dishes if it included a tip and a dessert. The cheapest item on the menu was egg sandwich and *soupe du jour* translated *"soup of the day"*. We both ordered an egg sandwich and soup. I asked the waiter for extra crackers. We sat at the table enjoying our sandwich and soup and acting like we had money. The side effects of the beer were fading away; the food settled my stomach.

We returned to our seats and had a much-needed sleep. Sleeping on a seat for three nights being bounced and rocked from side to side is a challenge and takes time to get comfortable. West of Winnipeg, there were lots of post-card like fields of wheat and barley as well as other types of crops that wasn't familiar. The fields went as far as the eye could see. A few trees here and there stood as if they were watching over the fields.

The following morning, we arrived in Saskatoon, Saskatchewan. The train conductor advised that our stop would be two hours. Stu and I made our way to the Train Terminal that was a fraction of the size of the Winnipeg terminal. A grocery store across the street from the terminal had just opened, we purchased some groceries and split the cost. Back in those days, twenty dollars of grocery went a long way. "We should have enough groceries to last us until Edmonton, Alberta", Stu said. As I was walking on the sidewalk, I felt like I was still riding on the train, my body was moving side-to-side, it was like learning to walk all over again.

"All aboard", said the train conductor. We quickly made our way to our seats. The train started to move slowly at first with jerking motion until it gained speed; The train was sounding like someone groaning as if it was in pain. Stu and I made a decision to stay away from the train restaurant, we had purchased enough food for the remainder of the trip. There were five stops remaining between Saskatoon and Edmonton, the countryside looked the same.

Stu pulled a wrinkled booklet from his backpack which listed the locations of Youth Hostels throughout the Province of British Columbia and Alberta. Stu had mentioned the Youth Hostel prior to our departure. We both looked at the booklet which showed the locations of the Youth Hostels. Stu pointed at a Youth Hostels in Vancouver. The hostels offered a cot to sleep on and a bowl of porridge with brown sugar for breakfast at twenty-five cents per night. The booklet also specified that the hostel had limited space and food and operated on a first come, first served basis "our money would go a long way at that price", Stu said. If we cannot find a hostel, we can sleep in our tent", replied Stu. "I'm sure that we won't be able to put up our tent while in the city, the police will arrest us", I said. "As we hitchhike, we will try to make it to a Hostel for the night, if not we'll setup our tent", said Stu. He had done some research and had heard about the Youth Hostel which was very popular in the sixties and seventies. A lot of the young people back then made their way around by hitchhiking across Canada and staying at Youth Hostels; it was an inexpensive way to travel. A friend of mine in Ste-Adele, travelled from Montreal to Vancouver catching rides on the trains hauling cargo across Canada. There were no coach or luxury room on the trains, not even a seat to sit on. He would go at night to where the cargo trains were being loaded and hop onto one of the cars where he would sleep on the floor; he called this method of travel 'jumping train". Back then, it was easy to get on the cargo train, there was less security. My friend left Montreal for Vancouver with twenty dollars in his pocket and a backpack.

Stu also mentioned that he had a friend from Ontario working for the summer as a busboy at the Banff Springs Hotel, accommodation and food was provided. The money and tips were good, however one of the hiring conditions was that the employee must be clean-cut, no hair below the ears and no facial hair. Neither Stu nor I would make the cut with our long hair and facial hair; I was the only one with facial hair; Stu couldn't grow a mustache or let alone a beard if his life depended on it. We were not willing to cut our hair; it took me a long time to grow my beard. If we did not find a job in British Columbia, Stu wanted to hitchhike to Banff, Alberta to look for his friend. We had planned to explore the area and hitchhike in British Columbia and Alberta before looking for a job.

NEW PEOPLE ON TRAIN

New people boarded the train while a few arrived at their destinations. Many of the new faces were young people our age or little older, most of them had backpacks, very few with suitcases. In my mind, the people with backpacks were hitchhikers and traveled easy on the pocket. There are now limited empty seats in our car, more people to chat and socialize with. At each stop, between Saskatoon and Edmonton more people boarded the train than getting off. Before long, there were no empty seats available; we were all crammed into our seats bouncing and rocking from side to side in unison, it was a sight to behold! The only thing missing was music playing to the beat of our rocking. From my seat by the window, I could see high-rises and buildings. "Next stop Edmonton! We'll be stopping for two hours", said the train Conductor. A young couple in their early twenties, in front of us were getting off in Edmonton. The young woman with long curly brown hair and pretty face from Saskatchewan; she had a waitress job waiting for her in Edmonton. Her boyfriend, a tall broad shoulder, clean cut looking fellow was hoping to find a construction job. He had mentioned that there was a lot of new homes and buildings being built in Edmonton. Stu and I were not interested in looking for a job in the city. On the other hand, we were interested in jobs in a small community or better yet, in a bush camp; where we were told would pay the most per hour. Hard work did not scare us if the pay was good. The train stopped in Edmonton.

Stu and I got off the train at the CN Rail Station to stretch our leg on solid ground. we started walking. The city was buzzing with people going in all directions, it was the mid-morning rush. West of the train station, we saw a large sign above a building, it was the Greyhound Bus Station. Stu and I headed to the bus station for a hamburger and French fries.

The bus station was full of people some purchasing tickets or waiting for their bus. The food was particularly tasty, must have been Alberta beef. We couldn't locate a grocery store to purchase snacks for the next leg of our trip; we settled for the small convenience store; it was expensive as opposed to a grocery store. We walked back to the Station.

THE ROCKY MOUNTAINS

"All aboard", the train Conductor said as we boarded the train heading to our seats. The train Conductor was a younger man in his mid-thirties. There were a lot of empty seats now; must have been the availability of jobs in Edmonton. A panoramic car was added to the string of cars. The large windows to the sides and ceiling of the car are designed for passengers to experience the scenery and the journey through the Rocky Mountains. We're only a few hours from the edge of the Rocky Mountains which began west of Hinton, Alberta. I was excited to finally experience the Rocky Mountains that I learnt about in High School. Music and geography were my favorite subjects in High School; I excelled at both with the highest marks in class. Stu and I made our way to the panoramic car to secure seats for the journey through the mountains. I felt more like a tourist than a traveler with a backpack, seating in a luxury seat looking at the sky through a window above my head. Stops were made in Edson and Hinton, Alberta. From Hinton, I could see the Rocky Mountains at a distance. The sight of the mountains seems surreal as if I was watching a movie. The mountains were majestic with their snow-white tops looking like an ice cream cone in July. We still had a few hours of daylight left; we were scheduled to arrive in Jasper before sunset. The mountains increased in size and appeared to be heading our way. The panoramic car quickly filled up until there were no more seats. A few people stood in the aisle taking photos. Stu and I did not own a camera, it was a pity we did not have a single photo of our train trip. I was in awe at the sight of the mountains and could not believe I was viewing them at close range. Making our way through Jasper National Park, I saw herds of elk and bighorn sheep near the railway and at higher elevations. This was my first time observing elk and bighorn sheep in their natural habitat, the only elk or sheep I saw was in the zoo.

"Next stop Jasper, fifteen minutes; the stop will be one hour", said the train Conductor. The train slowed down until it stopped at the Jasper Train Station. The postcard view of the town of Jasper was breathtaking. Stu and I quickly disembarked the train to explore the town and purchase groceries. We both stopped near the terminal to enjoy the view. I was feeling a bit light-headed and a tad out of breath from walking along the railway. A sign near the entrance of the train station indicated that Jasper's elevation is 3,478' (1,060 m) above sea level. I had never been at that elevation before and felt as if the air was thinner affecting my breathing. Stu and I looked at the sign and understood why we both felt light-headed. The gift shops were enticing with their pricey souvenirs. I told myself, "You're here to work and make money not spend money like a tourist". We found a small grocery store and purchased enough food for the remaining part of our train trip. The sunset over the peak of the mountains was surreal, once the sun set behind the mountain tops, darkness fell quickly.

"All aboard, the panoramic car will be closed for the night and will reopen at first light tomorrow morning", said the train Conductor. We returned to our seats for the night. Sleeping on a bench is not comfortable, let alone being bounced and rocked side-to-side all day and night. "This will be our last night on the train", said Stu. He added, "we should be in Vancouver tomorrow evening". "Where are we staying in Vancouver?", I asked. "At a Youth Hostel in Gastown", Stu answered, "it's about a ten minutes' walk from the train station". It was dark outside with a moonless night, looking outside the window of the car only the reflections of the inside lights and people sitting and walking by could be seen. There was nothing to look at, better to have an early night and be up at first light and back in the panoramic car. I felt excited, I wanted to see more mountain scenery and wildlife. Where I came from in Quebec, the only mountains I saw was the Laurentian Mountains which paled in size and height compared to the Rocky Mountains. Nonetheless, the Laurentians Mountains are amazing in their fall colors.

At first light, I made my way to the panoramic train, there were a few passengers either sitting or standing taking photos with their expansive cameras. The mountains were massive; seemed like they'd fall on the train. The train was following the rivers along the base of the mountains and travelling through multiple tunnels, it was like the mountains had swallowed the train. I marveled at the resourcefulness and hard work of the surveyors, engineers and laborers who built the railway blasting tunnels through the mountains.

Our next stop was Kamloops, "our stop will be 45 minutes" said the train Conductor, enough time to stretch your legs and get some fresh air. The day was beautiful, sunny and hot with a wisp of wind. The rolling hills and open forest and grasslands made me think of a place where cowboys lived raising their livestock and riding their horses. The scenery looked beautiful and inviting. Prior to our departure from Quebec, an acquaintance told us that there were good paying jobs in British Columbia as a forest fire fighter. He was hired with his friend in Kamloops as a fire fighter in the summer of 1972. Both worked fighting forest fires for about three months and made good money; the hourly pay was $3.50 per hour. Both made their way to Kamloops by jumping trains from Montreal with twenty dollars in their pockets. At the end of the fire season, they returned to Montreal by train. They had made good money and were able to afford the price of a train ticket.

Five hours later, we arrive in Vancouver, our destination. I was looking forward to getting off the train and seeing Vancouver's city lights. I have heard so much about Vancouver and wanted to experience the saying "Go to Van man". Stu and I were still in tourist mode, we enjoyed seeing the forests of northern Ontario, the prairies and Rocky Mountains and the west coast. We still had a few hundred dollars each in our pockets; we felt like we were rich, there were still so much more to explore. We had already planned that once in Vancouver, we would start looking for work and hopeful of getting a job on a boat or at a bush camp. Working in the city would be expensive with too many distractions. Working on a boat or in a bush camp would be a better choice to save money.

VANCOUVER

"Next and last stop, Vancouver", said the train Conductor. I was excited to have finally arrived in Vancouver; we hitchhiked and traveled by train from Montreal to Vancouver. It was late afternoon when we arrived, the city was buzzing like a beehive collecting nectar and pollen, people and vehicles were all around. Stu asked the first person we saw after getting off the train directions to Gastown. A young man with blond shoulder length hair looking as if he was high as a kite; he reeked of weed and asked us if we had any change to spare. Stu dug in his pocket and gave him a quarter; the young man pointed a finger muttering directions on how to get to Gastown. Stu picked up his backpack and headed in the direction the young man pointed, I followed Stu, we walked for about fifteen minutes until we reached Gastown, there were a few guys who approached us with the same question, did we have any change to spare. I took a quarter from my pocket and give it to one of the men. I quickly realized that I should pretend that I was as broke as they were, otherwise, I would be penniless in no time. My money was hidden in my socks; I then pulled out both side pockets of my jeans and let them both hang down so that everyone could see that I had no money. I started asking for spare change before they asked me. In an hour, I had at least thirty plus people asking me for spare change. When asked for change, I would point to my hanging pockets. The Gastown area back then was overcrowded.

We made our way to the Youth Hostel to check in. We were told that the Hostel was full, no cots available. Most of the people going in and out of the Hostel were some of the same people asking us for spare change. There was no space to set up our tents, surely the local police would have told us to take down our tents and get out of town. Disappointed, we decided to stay at a cheap hotel for the night, we were both tired and wanted a good night sleep in a bed without the motion of bouncing and rocking side-to-side.

We walked on the sidewalk until we came up to a grungy looking hotel that looked like something out of a horror movie, "Bates Motel". A lot of people hanging around the entrance looking for spare change and drugs. The hotel clerk, an older gentleman who must have been in his late sixties to early seventies must have seen it all and then some registered us and told us that the room is ten dollars per night which included taxes. Stu told the clerk that we were staying for one night. The clerk then handed us our key; as we made our way to our room, there were people talking out loud and arguing with each other that echoed throughout the hall and rooms; the hotel smelled like an ashtray; back then there were no restrictions on smoking in restaurants and hotels rooms. We finally made it to our room, the door looked like it was kicked in a few times. Stu and I looked at the door and just about burst out laughing. I sat on my bed which felt like a piece of plywood. There was no television or radio in the room. The hotel clerk had said, "there's no television or radio in the rooms, most of them were stolen for drug or alcohol money. Stu suggested that we go to the restaurant for dinner, and that we should take our backpack because they may not be in the room when we get back.

There was a small Chinese restaurant that was still open; we ordered several dishes and ate every piece on our plate; the food was delicious and not overpriced. Back in our hotel room, we could hear voices and door slamming all through the night. I was so tired that I finally fell asleep. In the middle of the night, I got up and went to bathroom walking from side-to-side and bouncing like I was still on the train.

46

The next morning, Stu and I decided to leave Vancouver, the city wasn't for us. We were both eager to hit the road and decided to hitchhike to the Tsawwassen Ferry Terminal from there we would board the Ferry inbound to Swartz Bay on Vancouver Island. We then made our way to Granville Street with our backpacks on our shoulders like we knew where we were going; Stu had a map of Vancouver and the surroundings; he was the navigator, and I was the follower when it came to speaking English. I didn't mind; he spoke and read in English much better than I did. I was terrible at asking for directions, once I open my mouth, people would look at me and ask if I was from Quebec and to go back to where I came from or just plain ignore me.

VICTORIA

Stu and I stuck out our right thumbs by the side of the road. There was a lot of traffic speeding by us until a sixtyish beat-up old station wagon stopped a short distance in front of us on the shoulder of the road.

"Where are you guys going?" asked the driver, who was a couple of years older than us, with shoulder-length brown hair and a patchy beard with several bald spots in it.

"Victoria," Stu replied. I didn't say anything because I was worried that the driver would change his mind and drive away, leaving us by the side of the road eating his dust.

"That's where I'm going, jump in," said the driver. I sat in the backseat while Stu sat at the front. I was happy that we caught a ride. The driver asked our names. Using my best English accent, I said, "Daniel," and waited for him to ask me if I was French.

The driver asked Stu what his name was and where we came from. "Ontario," Stu answered. The driver looked over his right shoulder, looked at me, and said, "You're French? My mother is French, but I don't speak French."

"Yes, I'm French," I said. I was relieved the inquisition was over and that I could be myself and not pretend that I was someone else.

The driver was a cool guy, very funny and friendly. It was a beautiful, sunny, and hot day. I opened the window and leaned my shoulder against the door. The warm air felt good on my face, and my hair was blowing in the wind. I didn't comb my hair often back then; I was always looking like I just got out of bed.

Stu and the driver were talking a mile a minute and laughing out loud. I only understood a few words here and there.

The driver slowed down until we reached a lineup of cars and trucks waiting to board the ferry. The cars and trucks slowly moved forward to the ferry for boarding. We ended up on the upper vehicle deck.

The driver paid the fee for the ferry crossing. Looking at us, he may have thought that we didn't have much money. The trip to Vancouver Island was about three hours and thirty minutes. I spent this time enjoying the view and the smell of the saltwater.

It was hot, but being on the water, it felt cooler. People on the ferry were friendly, a more relaxed atmosphere than Gastown, Vancouver. There was no one asking for spare change or eyeballing our possessions, which in our case were our backpacks. If left unattended, I'm certain our backpacks would have grown legs and walked away.

Stu and I still had some money stashed in our socks, enough to be on holiday for a few more weeks. I didn't want us to run out of money before getting a job, I didn't want to become a beggar asking for spare change so I could eat. Stu and I went out west to make money to travel to England then Europe and India, well that was the plan, and we all know that plans sometimes change. After we reached the Swartz Bay Ferry Terminal, the driver dropped us off in downtown Victoria. We shook hands and thanked him for the ride and then started walking around exploring downtown Victoria, it was quite a contrast to Vancouver's downtown.

No one was asking for spare change, the streets and sidewalks were clean free of garbage and broken bottles. Stu pulled out his Youth Hostel booklet to look for the address of the Hostel. The Hostel was a five minutes' walk. The people waiting at the Hostel to register were friendly and welcoming, a young man holding a guitar came up to Stu and I and started singing American Pie, which was a very popular song in the early 70's, it made it to number #1. I've heard the song on the radio many times; he sang the song like the record; In my mind, he was the singer on the record. We waited outside the Hostel until it opened; I tried very hard to converse with the people on the sidewalk; no one made fun of my accent or mistakes I made while trying to speak English; Instead, some helped with the correct words to use in English phrases. Most were young travelers hitchhiking across Canada eager for adventure and new experiences.

The Hostel door opened, everyone rushed inside to register for a cot. The inside of the hostel was well maintained and cozy; it was a large room containing numerous cots enough for approximately sixty or more people. The eating area had large tables and chairs used for meals. An upright piano rest against the wall in the eating room that was also used to socializing. Stu and I were assigned a cot each and a ticket for an oatmeal breakfast at twenty-five cents. There was a bathroom for men and another for woman they were equipped with showers. The Manager told us that we could leave our backpacks under our cots; and that it will be safe. The only meal the Hostel offered was breakfast. The Hostel opened at 5pm each day and close after breakfast around 7am. If we wanted to spend another night, we had to register the next day. Stu and I stored our backpacks under our cots and went exploring.

We saw a double-decker bus just like the ones in London, England, we went on a tour downtown. The bus had a guide on board recounting the history of Victoria. I was and still am a history buff.

We boarded the bus and went up to the second deck, pretending we were tourists. It was very interesting and informative and made me appreciate the City of Victoria more. The Parliament Buildings near the Victoria Harbor were impressive; I marveled at the details on the buildings as if they were sculptured from one large piece of metal. It gave me the impression that I was in Rome, Italy.

From the photos and films, I've seen, it sure felt like I was in Italy. Not far from the Parliament Buildings, the Empress Hotel stood facing the harbor with beautiful and expensive boats of all shapes and sizes.

Stu suggested that we have dinner at the Empress Hotel. I looked at him and said, "Too expensive, you crazy!" Stu was determined to have dinner at the hotel, so he headed there to eat.

I was curious to see what would happen, so I followed Stu to the hotel. Once at the hotel, I took a deep breath and stepped inside, expecting a large bellboy to grab me by the scruff of my neck to show me the door. To my surprise, that didn't happen.

We made our way to the restaurant; it was the fanciest hotel we had ever seen. The restaurant was jam-packed with men in suits and tuxedos and women in very expensive dresses. Everyone stopped what they were doing and stared at us with their mouths open. Stu and I stood there with our mouths open as well.

At any second, I was expecting the security guard to ask us to leave. In contrast to the well-dressed people, we were dressed in worn-out jeans with patches to cover the holes and tears, which was the style back then.

Stu and I looked at each other and said in unison, "Let's get out of here." We were both famished, so we found a hamburger and hot dog booth near the harbor and ate our fill, just like hungry wolves.

After eating, we made our way back to the Hostel. The dining area was full of young boys and girls talking, laughing, and having a good time. Stu sat at a table, and I headed to the piano. I sat on the piano bench and put my hands on the keys.

I started with my mother's favorite piece, Beethoven's Moonlight Sonata. I played the piece at a slower tempo with passion. All through my playing, I couldn't hear anyone talking or laughing. I was thinking that everyone must have left, not wanting to listen to classical music.

Once I finished the last chord of the Sonata, I turned around and saw everyone sitting in their chairs, applauding and asking me to play some more. I played a few more classical pieces and then switched over to improvising my rock-type music, which was well received by the audience.

It felt good to play the piano again. I used to practice after school for three to four hours per day and then eight to ten hours a day on the weekends and holidays. Playing the piano revived my passion for music.

I doubted whether I made the right decision in quitting school and the opportunity to attend the Vincent D 'Indy Music Conservatory in Montreal. Instead, of hitchhiking on the west coast, hoping to find a good-paying job to finance my trip to England with Stu.

I went to bed thinking of returning to school and getting back into music. The following morning, after having a great sleep and a large bowl of oatmeal with brown sugar, I decided to carry on with my adventures and travels.

Stu and I decided to stay another night in Victoria. Stu met a girl from Sweden at the hostel we were staying at, they were close in age; she had flown from Sweden to Canada with the intention of traveling across Canada on her own. She was a university student on her summer break.

Stu liked Linda, she was as tall as Stu, six feet, with long blond hair to her waist and deep blue eyes. Linda spoke English well with a slight Swedish accent, which made her sound exotic.

She had mentioned to Stu that there's a beautiful park named Beacon Hill in Victoria, near the ocean, where you can rent a bicycle for the day. All three of us walked to the park. We made arrangements with the manager of the hostel to keep our backpacks at the hostel.

It was another beautiful and hot day. We all rented a bicycle each; the rental fee for the day was five dollars, which was a lot of money back then. The park attendant gave us a map of the park. The bicycle trails were all paved with direction signs.

Stu wanted some private time with Linda, so, we agreed to meet at the park's entrance at 4:00 p.m. I headed in the opposite direction on my bicycle. The park was incredible, arrays of flowers of all colors adorned the side of the trails and small fields. I pedaled over an old stone bridge and paused to enjoy the scenery. I sat on a bench and watched the ducks and geese feeding and swimming. The tall trees provided much-needed shade from the sun. I continued

53

down the trail until I reached a beach, small rippling waves landed on the beach making a whooshing pleasant sound. I got off my bicycle and walked to the beach to taste the water; I had promised myself that given the chance, I would taste the water of the Pacific Ocean. I used both hands as a cup and plunged my hands into a wave; the water was colder than I had expected and it was very salty.

I sat on a nearby bench and enjoyed the scenery for some time. Stu showed up after a while alone, I asked him where was Linda was, apparently Linda told him that she had to go somewhere. From the look on his face, he was disappointed. We took one more spin around the park before we returned our bicycles. On our walk back to the Hostel, Stu said that we should leave Victoria tomorrow and hitchhike to Long Beach, I then asked how far away was Long Beach from Victoria, Stu replied, that it was approximately 3 to 4 hours. We spent our last night in Victoria, B.C. at the Hostel. I played the piano at the Hostel for a couple hours that evening to the delight of the crowd and they requested that I play Beethoven's Moonlight Sonata a second time. I didn't know when I would have a chance to play the piano again so I was delighted.

After our oatmeal breakfast, Stu and I made our way walking towards the outskirts of Victoria. It was a hot and humid day; we were both sweating while walking on the sidewalk with the sun directly over our heads. We were now getting very thirsty, so we stopped at a small convenience store and purchased something to drink, it was good getting out of the sun for a bit and it felt good. We continued on until we reached Highway 4 (Pacific Rim Highway). We both stuck out our right thumbs and began our journey to Long Beach. About half-hour later a Ford pickup stopped on the shoulder of the road. The passenger, was a young girl in her late teens with long wavy blond hair, asked us where we were going, Stu told her that we were going to Long Beach then the driver said that they were going to Port Alberni, he looked to be in his mid-twenties with shoulder length brown hair and a small scruffy beard. He said that they had no room in the cab, but that we could ride in the box of the truck. We immediately jumped in the box with our backpacks resting on the cab of the truck. The breeze felt good and helped us cool off. I closed my eyes and took a nap. The drive to Port Alberni was just under three hours. The driver stopped at a gas station in Nanaimo for fuel, while he was fueling his truck, Stu, and I purchased some drinks and snacks at the gas station; we were both getting dehydrated. We arrived at Parksville about half-hour later, the truck driver dropped us off at the junction leading to Port Alberni and Long Beach.

The highway from Parksville to Long Beach goes through rolling hills and mountains. The view was spectacular and scary at the same time. Some sections of the highway were adjacent to steep cliffs.

We stopped at one of those sections to have a better view. Stu and I walked in the ditch for about fifty feet, then saw the drop straight down the mountains, which must have been at least one thousand feet down. There was no room in taking the ditch on the right side of the highway; no one could survive such a drop.

"A few years ago, the driver of a large fuel truck lost control of his truck on the icy road and ended up rolling his truck down the mountains," said the driver. From there on, his story made me nervous. I'm not a fan of heights. In my mind, if the driver was to lose control of his truck, I'd jump out of the box to my left. Better land on the road than one thousand feet down the mountains.

55

We arrived at Port Alberni mid-afternoon where our ride ended. We said our goodbyes, thanked them, and stuck our right thumbs out hitchhiking, "on the road again."

A station wagon, a few years old but still in decent shape, stopped at our side. "Where are you heading, man?" asked the front passenger, a good-looking young girl. I found out her name was Janet, in her early twenties with perfect teeth, dark brown long hair, and eyes.

Stu replied, "Long Beach." "Get in, man, we still got some room inside. We're heading to Long Beach too," said Steve, the driver, who looked like he just came back from Woodstock and didn't sleep for three days or wash or comb his shoulder-length tangled dirty blond hair since.

I opened the back door of the station wagon to get in and saw a couple with their enormous St. Bernard dog, black as coal. The couple had hitchhiked all the way from California with their dog.

John was from Boston and had John F. Kennedy's accent to prove it. He was in his mid to late twenties with short brown hair, balding at the front, and a short grubby beard that he must have grown for the past three years. John was an army draft dodger who refused to join the armed forces in the United States and go to war in Vietnam, which is why he was in Canada.

Mary, his girlfriend, was red-haired with freckles on her face. She was very beautiful. Mary was only eighteen years old, born in San Diego, California. She had never seen snow and was excited to see snow.

I was thinking to myself, "It's going to be a few months yet before there's snow; we're in mid-July." I guess John hadn't told her that yet. She was talking like there would be snow any day now.

Bear, the dog, was friendly and scary at the same time. He was in the backseat of the Volkswagen and came jumping over the seat to greet Stu and me.

Stu wasn't expecting an enormous black St. Bernard jumping on him. As he let out a loud yell, I saw his knees buckle, and he nearly collapsed to the ground.

We managed to all fit inside the VW just like sardines in a can. Mary sat on the front seat, sandwiched between Steve and Janet, while Stu, John, and I sat on the backseat. Bear, the dog, laid on top of our backpacks behind the backseat.

John rolled a big fat joint, lit it up, then passed it to Stu then to me. Mary reached over to take the joint from me and then passed it to the couple. The fat joint made a couple of rounds from the front seat to the back seat, then expired.

Everyone was talking a mile a minute, then silence. The weed made its impact. The inside of the VW smelled like a mixture of everybody's body odors, dog, and weed.

The scenery was spectacular with rolling hills and a beautiful forest, with majestic trees towering over the landscape.

We arrived at the junction to Long Beach. "Let's get some fresh salmon from the fisherman and some beer and wine," said Steve. We drove to the dock at Ucluelet, where a fisherman had just docked his boat with his catch of the day.

Stu, John, and I exchanged a twenty-dollar bill for two large spring salmon. "We'll cook the salmon on an open fire wrapped in tin foil with onion and mushroom inside the salmon," said Stu.

We stopped at the grocery and liquor store to purchase a small roll of tin foil, two large onions, mushrooms, a couple of cases of beer, and four bottles of sake (Japanese rice wine). Stu drank sake before and said, "Sake is to be drunk warm."

I could smell the salty water and feel the cool breeze from the Pacific Ocean. Although it was very hot and humid, the cool breeze felt like outdoor air conditioning.

LONG BEACH

We all climbed back into the station wagon and carried on to Long Beach, Pacific Rim National Park. Twenty minutes later, we arrived at the beach, which, just like its name, was long. I could see hundreds of people laying on the beach like beached whales, and only one person in the water in a wetsuit surfing. It was a very hot day, and I couldn't understand why no one was swimming in the beautiful, inviting ocean.

I'd been waiting for this moment for a long time and had promised myself that the first time I saw the ocean, I'd put my swimming suit on, run to the ocean like I was in a movie, and then jump into the salty water.

I quickly hid behind the VW and put on my swimming suit. Next, I ran to the ocean, which was quite a way from where the VW was parked. As I approached the ocean, I ran as fast as I could and made my way up to my waist and dove into the ocean, only to realize that the water was very cold.

As fast as I entered the salty water, I was just as fast to get out. I made my way back to the VW, shivering from the cold water. Steve and Janet laughed at me and both said, "That is why the people are laying on the beach and not swimming."

The vibe on the beach was amazing. It was hard to believe that a little over two weeks ago, I left Ste-Adele, Quebec, and now I was looking at the Pacific Ocean as far as I could see.

The smell of the saltwater and the breeze from the ocean energized me like I had never felt before.

Stu and John stuffed the inside of the salmon with onions, mushrooms, salt and black pepper. The nippy abrupt swim I had, and the fresh salty air awoken my appetite. Both salmon were wrapped in tin foil and slowly cooked on an open fire on the beach. Stu laid the Sake bottles on the beach in plain view of the sun. Everyone grabbed a cold bottle of beer waiting for the salmon to cook. I've eaten salmon before but never cooked on an open fire, I couldn't wait to taste the salmon. All six of us gather around the campfire drinking our cold beers as the sun quickly disappeared behind the horizon. The scenery of the ocean with the background of the sun setting was breathtaking. I regretted not having a camera, "A picture is worth ten thousand words".

"The salmon is cooked," said John. Bear, the jet-black dog, was sniffing and exhaling, getting at the head of the line.

"Bear, get back and sit," said John. Bear was in a trance, his sight on the two pieces of tin foil. He had become deaf to his master's commands.

"You better feed him now, he won't leave us alone when we eat," said Mary, John's girlfriend. John went to the VW to fetch Bear's bowl. The sound of the bowl being filled with dog food caught Bear's attention. John tied Bear to the VW.

I was relieved that he was tied up. I didn't want to have to wrestle him for my portion of the salmon; I would have lost the battle. The salmon was delicious. I couldn't get enough of it. We all had a good portion of the salmon, enough so that no one went hungry.

By the time we finished eating, it was very dark and getting cold. "The evenings and nights were cold on the beach," Steve said. He and Janet had been to Long Beach many times.

Stu opened the bottles of Sake and shared them with our new friends. The Sake was warm and tasted like no other wine I had tasted before.

Steve asked Stu and I if we would like to go clam digging early in the morning. We both said, "Yes, for sure." The best time to go clam digging is at low tide, just before sunrise, Steve said.

A loud rock music played from Steve's 8-track tape player in his VW, while we drank Sake and beers. John lit up a few joints that we all shared.

An Indigenous girl joined our party. She was hitchhiking across Canada on her own, she was Ojibway from the town of Sioux Lookout. It was the same town we had stopped at to buy groceries while on the train.

Her name was Lucy. She was a year or so older than me. Lucy had long black hair halfway down her back, tied into a ponytail, and dark brown eyes. She was friendly, and somehow, we were able to communicate. She knew a few words in French.

Lucy introduced herself to our group. Mary and Lucy became friends immediately, as if they had known each other for years.

We all sat around the campfire, enjoying each other's company, some Sake and beers, and a few joints.

The effect of the Sake, beers and weed got everyone in a dancing mood. Everyone stood up and followed the lead of Lucy around the campfire. With music blaring with a heavy bass drumbeat, Lucy danced by stepping forward and lightly jumping on her feet side to side to the beat of the bass drum, Mary followed Lucy by mimicking her dance then everyone joined in, including me. I'd never seen a dance like that; it was so cool and moving to see; it gave me goosebumps. Dancing around the campfire made me feel like I was in a trance, it was hypnotic.

We danced, laughed and told stories of our journeys and where we hail from. The story that stood out in my mind was John's story; he was a Vietnam Draft Dodger who deserted the US army in 1972 and ran away to Canada. "I didn't want to be shot at and didn't want to shoot anyone, I didn't believe in the Vietnam War", John said. As the night grew old, one by one our group disperse and headed to their sleeping shelters. It was early morning hours and very dark, not even a sliver of the moon in the sky. Stu had set up his tent before we had our feast of salmon, I didn't, I laid by the campfire on my ground sheet and used my backpack as my pillow. Bear was also laying near the campfire; he was close enough from the campfire to keep warm. The night was cold; I put on my heaviest sweater and soon fell asleep. A few hours later, I woke up with my arm around Bear. The fire had died; Bear and I must have move closer to each other to keep warm. I could feel Bear's body heat; he was a big dog and out weighted me by at least thirty to forty pounds; he kept me warm.

I felt someone poking me on my shoulder. I thought that I was dreaming, then I heard Steve saying, "Wake up, we're going clam digging."

I opened my eyes, not sure what time it was. I could see that it was dawn.

"Where's Stu?" I asked.

"I tried to wake him up but no luck," Steve said.

"I got my shovel and bucket, let's go," Steve said.

I stood up and followed Steve heading to the beach.

"Take the bucket, I'll carry the shovel," Steve said. The shovel was short and narrow at the head.

The sounds of the waves beating against the shore of the beach sounded like music to my ears.

As we got closer to the beach, I couldn't believe what I was seeing. That wasn't the same beach I saw yesterday. Large rock formations and rocks were exposed from where the water had been. I'd heard about low tide but had never experienced it.

Steve walked to one of the rock formations and started to dig with his shovel. It was getting lighter by the minute; the sun would be rising soon.

I wasn't sure what to look for, but Steve did. He dug into the mud and bent down to pick up a clam. He washed the clam with saltwater and handed it to me.

I took a closer look at the clam and dropped it in the bucket. Steve kept digging and handing me the muddy clams, which I washed with saltwater, then put into the bucket.

We moved to another location, and Steve started digging again. I could tell that he'd done it many times before.

Once the sun was in full view, the temperatures gradually got warmer until I started to sweat. An hour or so later, our bucket was well over three-quarters full.

"Let's go back to camp, pass me the bucket", Steve said. He filled the bucket with saltwater. "I'll use the saltwater to boil the clams, that's our breakfast", Steve said. Everyone at the camp was still sleeping including Stu. Steve and I gathered some firewood from the pile we'd used yesterday. Steve made a fire and put the bucket on the fire. "The clams have to boil for about 10 minutes or until the shells open", Steve said. Although, I couldn't speak English that well, I understood most of what Steve was telling me. It was getting hot outside; I exchanged my heavy sweater for a light t-shirt. Steve woke up his girlfriend, Janet. Steve and Janet slept in their station wagon. John and Mary spent the night in their tent while Lucy set up her tent next to their tent. Everyone was slowly waking up. I could hear Stu unzipping his sleeping bag, "man it is hot in this tent", Stu said. Steve announced to the group, "the clams are cooked, if anyone is interested". I grabbed my plate and took a few clams from the pot, they were delicious. I've eaten clam and oyster before.

We spent three more days exploring the beaches, rainforest and the two communities nearby; Tofino to the north and Ucluelet to the south where we purchased more salmon from the same fisherman. We spent the evenings having a good time with our newfound friends, eating salmon cooked on an open fire, listening to music, talking, laughing, smoking a few joints and clam digging early in the mornings at low tide. The scenery was gorgeous and breathtaking, something I'll never forget. The weather was fabulous, sunny every day with no rain and very hot in the daytime and very cold in the evenings and nights. The

Pacific Ocean was very cold nevertheless; I swam every day in the evening to cool off.

Our friends made plans to spend more time at Long Beach, we had such a good time, and met some awesome people, it was difficult to leave. Stu and I talked it over and decided that it was time to hit the road in search of a job. At this time, it was already mid-July, the summer will be over in a couple months, we had plans to be in England no later than October. Steve offered to give us a ride to Ucluelet where we'd hitchhike to Banff to look for Stu's friend, Dave who worked as a busboy at the Banff Springs Hotel. Stu believed that his friend would be able to help us in getting a job at the hotel.

We had a going away party that night after our meal of salmon. We said our goodbyes and thanked everyone for the good times and wished them all good luck with their trips. Steve dropped us off on Highway 4 at the outskirts of Ucluelet. We were the only ones on the road hitchhiking, it was not long before a sixtyish pickup truck stopped on the shoulder of the road, the driver asked us where we were going. "Banff" answered Stu. "Well, I'm not going that far but I can give you a ride to Nanaimo", said the driver. "That would be great man", said Stu. We put our backpack in the box of the truck and got in the truck. "How far is Nanaimo?", asked Stu. "About two and half hours", said the driver. "Would you be able to give us ride to the Ferry Terminal?", asked Stu. "No problem, I'm going not far from the Ferry Terminal anyway", said the driver. This was the same highway we travelled to Long Beach. The driver drove above the speed limit; I was nervous, the road was in the high country with rolling hills, the road was approximately one thousand feet deep ditches. Stu laid against the passenger door and had a snooze; we partied late into the night so he was very tired. I kept my eyes on the road and felt like I was driving along with the driver, although I didn't have a driver license then. The driver dropped us off at the Ferry Terminal.

The ferry was at the harbor, vehicles and passengers were making their way onto the ferry, the fee for the crossing to the Horseshoe Bay Ferry Terminal in Vancouver was $4.00 each, the crossing was one hour and forty minutes. We perched ourselves on the deck to have the best view of the crossing. Stu approached a guy who appeared to be with his girlfriend, and asked him where they were going, he told us they were heading to Kamloops, I told him that my friend and I were going to Banff. We introduced ourselves to the couple, the guy's name was Jeremy and his girlfriend was Martine.

I pick up on Martine's accent and asked her in French, *"Parle tu Francais?"*. She looked at me a bit surprised and smiled, *"Oui, je parle le Francais"*. We both started to speak in our mother tongue, she was happy to speak French, with me it had been a while since she had spoken French; her boyfriend didn't speak any French. Martine was petite with light brown wavy hair with dark brown eyes; she undeniably dressed like a hippie. Martine was from northern Ontario where there were many francophones. We both had a long discussion during the crossing about picking mushrooms and our plans to go to England. Stu and Jeremy bonded right away, they were both from Ontario and lived not far from each other. Jeremy and Martine lived as hippies in Kamloops with other hippies, both were in their mid-twenties and had been together for five years. They met in the Okanagan while picking morel mushrooms; Jeremy and Martine were happy to give us a ride to Kamloops. We followed Jeremy and Martine and got into their Ford Pinto car which were very popular in the seventies. The car only had 2 doors; we put our backpacks in the back of the car and squeezed ourselves in the back seat. There was not much room for our legs, *"this is going to be a long three and half hour's ride to Kamloops"*, I told myself.

The trip from Vancouver to Kamloops followed a similar route to the train trip. I made myself as comfortable as I could and drifted off to sleep.

I had short nights at Long Beach, staying up late and getting up early in the morning to go digging clams. Stu sat behind Jeremy, debating about the best-paying jobs in BC.

I woke up not knowing where I was. My foot was completely numb, and I didn't want to complain or ask the driver to stop. I moved my feet into a different position and did a few ankle pumps. The sensation in my feet began to return.

We stopped in Merritt for a bathroom break. It felt good to get out of the vehicle and walk. Finally, the circulation in my feet returned.

It was mid-afternoon, and Stu asked Jeremy how far it was to Banff. Jeremy said it was about six to seven hours.

We arrived in Kamloops an hour later. Jeremy dropped us off on the highway at a gas station, where Stu and I bought some hot dogs and something to drink. We were both famished; the last time we ate was at Long Beach.

We walked to the shoulder of the road and saw a few hitchhikers also heading in the same direction as we were. Courtesy in hitchhiking dictates that you should hitchhike behind the hitchhiker(s) that were there before you.

Two groups of hitchhikers stood about fifty feet apart ahead of us. We were third in line. About twenty minutes later, two girls with their backpacks walked by us and stuck out their thumbs behind us. Less than a minute later, a car stopped by the two girls and picked them up.

The two groups of hitchhikers ahead of us were all males. We waited about an hour and a half before the hitchhikers ahead of us got a ride. We were next in line for a ride.

It was getting dark when Stu told me that most people do not pick up hitchhikers when it's dark. We might have to spend the night in Kamloops.

A few minutes later, a car stopped on the shoulder of the road about one hundred feet from us; Stu and I ran to the car with our backpacks, as soon as Stu put his hand on the door handle, the driver floored the gas pedal and the car shot up like a rocket leaving pebbles flying in the air. About five minutes later, another vehicle stopped on the shoulder of the road, this time, Stu and I just walked to the vehicle. When we reached the vehicle, Stu touched the handle on the passenger side; in case the driver pulled away suddenly. The driver was alone and waited for us to open the door, the driver asked where we were going, Stu told him Banff; the driver then told us that he was going to Golden and that he could give us a ride Golden. "That'll be great, thanks," said Stu.

I sat on the back seat and Stu sat in the front seat. The driver was in his mid-thirties with very short brown hair and not much of a talker.

"How far to Golden?", asked Stu.

"About four hours", said the driver.

"Would you be able to drop us off at the Young Hostel in Golden?", asked Stu.

"Yes, I'll be driving right by it before going home", said the driver.

"That would be great, thanks", said Stu.

The vehicle was a four door and a lot roomier in the backseat; there was enough room for our backpacks, I used my backpack as a pillow. It was just past sunset, was thinking we should be arriving in Golden at about one in the morning, hopefully the Hostel would be still open, if not we'll be camping in the ditch".

Banff, Alberta is well known as a tourist town alike my hometown, Ste-Adele. Stu's friend, James, worked as a busboy at the Banff Springs Hotel which is internationally recognized as a prime location for its natural beauty, wildlife, surrounding lakes and mountains. James was a student at a University in Toronto; this would have been his second summer working at the hotel. James told Stu that accommodations and meals were provided by the hotel at no cost. What enticed James to return to work for a second summer was the tips. Stu believed that Banff was the place to find a good paying job, my wish was to find a good paying job at a bush camp.

Both Stu and I would have to cut our hair short and me shaving my beard before getting a job as busboy.

I dozed off for a while until I felt the car slowing down to a stop. I open my eyes not sure where we were.

"Get up! we're at the Hostel in Golden", said Stu.

I grabbed our backpacks and stepped out of the car and thanked the driver.

"Good luck with your trip to Banff", said the driver.

It was very dark; you couldn't see your hands in front of your face. We were at the bottom of a small hill and the Hostel was at the top of the hill. The person in charge of the Hostel never gave us his name, he came down the hill with a flashlight to light our way to the Hostel which was essentially made up of large army tents and outdoor latrines one for the boys and one the girls. The person in charge told us there would be porridge for breakfast and that we could pay the Hostel fee of twenty-five cents in the morning.

The tent where we slept had two openings at each end and could accommodate about twenty-four people, twelve on each side of the tent. I walked into the tent on the left side to find a spot to lay my sleeping bag on the floor of the tent, it was a large tarp. It was very dark outside and even more so inside the tent. I took a couple steps before stepping on someone's leg nearly tripping on top of him. The person let out a loud scream as if I broke his leg.

"You, ok?" I asked.

"You scared to living **** out of me, I thought that a grizzly bear was attacking me in my sleep", said the person.

He then said, "a couple nights ago, he was told by one of the other campers that a grizzly bear walked into the tent during the night, it walked from one end of the tent to the other end, one of the other guys sleeping in the tent woke up and heard and smelled the grizzly bear walking by the foot of his sleeping bag".

After hearing his story, I couldn't fall asleep for a while.

Golden's elevation is 800 meters or 2,600 feet above sea level. It was very cold in the tent the whole night. At 7am, someone used a frying pan and a metal spoon to make noises to alert us that it was time for breakfast.

After getting up, I rolled up my tarp and went outside. There was dew on the tents and picknick tables so much so that it looked like it rained during the night. Stu and I walked over to the table that had a large pot of porridge and a small woman wearing an apron, she was waiting with a large metal spoon to fill our plastic bowls. After getting my bowl filled, I sprinkled some brown sugar on top and a dash of milk made of powder milk and water and ate. "We better get to the highway and start hitchhiking", said Stu. The highway to Banff wasn't very far. The morning was cool and humid.

A few groups of hitchhikers stood in line along the highway. There were at least 4 groups ahead of us. "It's going to be some time before we catch a ride", said Stu. More hitchhikers got in line behind us. We spent three hours with our thumbs out and finally got a ride to Banff. The driver was in his early twenties with long wavy brown hair looking like a rock star.

"Where are you going man?", asked the driver.

"we're going to Banff man", said Stu.

"Get in man", said the driver.

It was a beautiful day; the sun was shining in its full glory. The sixtyish ford pickup truck had seen better days; it was amazing that it was still running. I'd never seen a vehicle with so much rust on it. I could hear the motor making a clicking sound. I told myself, "Hopefully, we'll make it to Banff before the truck kicks the bucket". The backdrops of the Rocky Mountains were breathtaking, from one place to another it was another postcard photos. The driver was a musician playing guitar in a rock band, hence why the look of a rock star. He was on his way to Calgary to meet with his band, they had a four-week gig at a bar in Calgary. The truck

71

was a single cab; I was sitting in the middle between the driver and Stu. I looked at the floor between my feet and noticed something odd on the floor; it was moving. I asked myself "what's that"? and realized that I was looking at the ground. There was a hole through the floor the size of a Lonnie. From time to time, I'd look at the floor thinking that the hole would get bigger and that I'd fall through the floor. The driver noticed that I was looking at the hole and said, "there're a few more holes, don't worry you'll not fall through the floor". "Can you drop us off at the Banff Springs Hotel?", said Stu.

BANFF

The driver started to laugh out loud and said, "you guys are hitchhiking and you're staying at the Banff Springs Hotel". "No, I've a friend working there, we're looking for a job at the hotel", said Stu." ok, that makes sense, I'll drop you off there", said the driver. We shook hands and thanked the driver and wished him luck with his band. The Banff Spring Hotel is stunning; it bears a resemblance to a large castle. I'd seen photos of the hotel before but seeing it in person was something else. We entered the hotel and asked where we could find James. We were told that he was on a break at the staff quarters on the first floor. We made our way to the staff quarters.

Stu said, "Hey, James". There he was dressed in his busboy uniform standing tall, little over six feet, short dark brown hair above his ears and clean shaved.

"Hi Stu, good to see you", said James.

Both shook hands and laughed. I could see that both were good friends. Stu introduced me to James.

"I'm sharing a room with another busboy, I can sneak you in the room, you guys will have to sleep on the floor," said James.

"That will be great, when are you done your shift?", asked Stu.

"In a couple hours", said James. "

Can we leave our backpacks in your room?", asked Stu.

"Sure, let's do that now", said James.

73

We made plan to meet James at a local bar not far from the hotel, in the meantime, we had something to eat at a Chinese restaurant and explore Banff's downtown. Everything was expensive, there were a lot of tourists walking on the sidewalks and in the gift shops.

As we were walking down the sidewalk in Banff, I saw a payphone and decided to call my mom, it had been a while since I spoke with her. Once a week, I wrote her a letter to let her know that I was ok and enjoying my trip. I called her collect, she was happy to hear from me, she was worried that something may have happened to me. I told her that we were in Banff looking for a job and that I'll be calling her back in a week or so. It was good to talk to my mom; we were very close.

We met James at the bar, the drinking age was 21 years old, I was four months shy from my eighteen birthdays. The long hair and beard made me look older, never once I was asked for my ID. James ordered a tray of draft beer which was twenty-five cents a glass. The tray held 40 glasses, I couldn't believe it, there was no way the three of us could drink all 40 glasses that only cost ten dollars; talking about an inexpensive drunk.

Both James and Stu were hung over the next day and didn't hear the roommate clearing his throat. James's shift started at 11am,

"Let's go have breakfast at the staff kitchen", said James.

Only employees of the hotel could eat at the staff kitchen. James was good friends with the cooks who served us a big breakfast of bacon, eggs and pancakes.

"What will you guys be doing today?" asked James. Before Stu had a chance to answer, James said,

"You guys should rent a bike each and go for a swim at the Upper Hot Springs; it's a pretty cool place, the water is great, good for hangover". Stu's eyes lit up and said, "good idea, let's do that".

"There's a bike rental shop a couple streets from here", said James. After breakfast, Stu and I grabbed our swimming trunks and headed to the bike shop. When we walked into the bike rental shop, an employee asked if he could help us, he was tall and thin with blond wavy hair well below the ears and a mustache. I told myself, "I thought that guys with long hair could not get a job in Banff". We asked to rent two bikes for half-day, at the back of the store, another employee was working on bikes, putting air in the tires and making sure that the bikes were in good order "How much for half-day?", Stu asked. "Rental for half-day is $5. "How do we get to the Upper Hot Springs?", asked Stu. "Just head north on Spray Avenue then turn left on Mountain Avenue then head south to the base of the mountain. The Upper Hot Springs is near the end of Mountain Avenue".

With our swimming trunks pretending to be tourists, we climbed on our bike and headed to the hot springs. It felt great being on a bike with the wind blowing in my hair. We were not the only people pedaling, this reminded me when we rented bikes in Victoria. The scenery around Banff was stunning, no wonder millions of tourists visit every year. The hill to the Upper Hot Springs was quite steep to pedal, I worked up a sweat pedaling up the hill and was looking forward to bathing in the hot springs. I had never been at a hot spring; this was my first time. Huffing and puffing, we made it up the hill. I could feel the heat from the hot spring as we walked inside the building. We were asked to take a shower before getting into the hot springs; it cost $3 to bathe and $1 for a towel.

75

There were a few people bathing in the warm water, mostly people old enough to be our grandparents. The smell of the hot spring had a sulfur eggy odor which smelled like somebody let one go. I eased myself into the hot springs, it was much hotter than a hot bath. Stu and I sat in the hot springs relaxing and enjoying the warmth of the springs. We both stayed in the hot springs a little too long, I felt like a dried-up prune, it was time to step out and take a break. After our mini break, we went back in the hot springs for a second time and made sure we didn't bathe for more than twenty minutes. I enjoyed the bathing and felt rejuvenated and relaxed. We dried ourselves with the towel and headed down the hill back to town.

Riding a bicycle down the hill, I didn't have to pedal, I just let the bike do the work. We cruised around town and found a pizzeria, we were both famished, the hot springs made us very hungry. After eating our pizza, we went back to the hotel to change and meet up with James after his shift was over.

We were not employees of the hotel and were not allowed in the staff quarters, no one stopped us from going in and out. James had just finished his shift and was eager to go out and have a few beers. I drank Ginger Ale while Stu and James drank copious amounts of draft beer, I just sat at the table listening to Stu and James talking, I didn't participate in the conversations as my English was not up to par in keeping up with their conversations.

As I was observing the room, I heard someone speaking French, I looked over to my right and saw a guy with scruffy long hair and beard, as a matter of fact, we looked alike. He was talking to another guy with scruffy long hair and beard. I walked over to their table and introduced myself. Both guys were from Quebec City playing tourist like I was. They both had worked a few months as forest firefighters in Central British Columbia. They had also travelled to Kamloops, BC by hitchhiking from Quebec City to look for jobs and ended up fighting fires instead and making good money. When we came to BC, "we were down to our last $10 when we got our jobs", said Michel; "we're now on our way back to Quebec City, this time, we're going back by train".

I told Michel that my friend and I were looking for a job, at the moment we're playing tourist and now it was time to find a job before we run out of money. Michel told me that he had friends that went to Yellowknife, Northwest Territories to look for jobs last year, they all found good paying jobs. You should go to Yellowknife; you'll find good paying jobs there for sure. His words struck me like a lightning bolt; it was Deja vu. I had heard of Yellowknife and the Northwest Territories in my geography class in high school. I didn't realize it then, but my life was about to change. Michel and his friend Jacques took the bus to Calgary later that evening and then on to Edmonton where they will be boarding the train to Montreal.

"How far is it to Calgary?", I asked. "About one hour and half, there's six bus a day from Banff to Calgary", said Michel.

I had a beer with my two Quebecois newfound friends.

"I will be heading to Calgary tomorrow with my friend Stu and then we will make our way to Yellowknife from there".

"From Calgary take a bus to Edmonton then to Hay River, Northwest Territories, from there you can catch a bus to Yellowknife, after you arrive in Yellowknife, go to the Manpower office that would be the quickest way to find a job", said Michel. "That sounds like a plan, thanks for the information", I said. It was time for Michel and Jacques to make their way to the bus station.

I made my way back to Stu and James who were talking a mile a minute and having a good time. I thought that I'd wait until the next day before telling Stu that we were heading to Yellowknife to look for a job. I believed that we had enough money left to pay for a bus ticket to Yellowknife.

Most of the hitchhikers were about our age. Hitchhiking to Yellowknife, NT may take days, we could sit and relax or sleep while travelling by bus. We had hoped that there would be a Youth Hostel north of Edmonton. Most likely we would be spending our nights in our pop-up tents at a campground or in the bush by the side of the road.

I sat at the table staring at the wall mulling over my options and concluded that travelling to Yellowknife by bus would be the way to go. "Daniel let's go back to the room" Stu said, while lightly tapping on my right shoulder. I was lost in thoughts, "are you ok?", Stu asked. "Yes, I'm ok, I was just thinking".

The following morning, James' roommate woke me up at 5:00am getting ready for work, I laid awake in my sleeping bag on the floor reflecting on how I should tell Stu that we were heading to Yellowknife today by bus to look for a job. I was determined to be on the bus heading to Yellowknife with Stu or by myself. So far, Stu had been overseeing our journey making all the decisions as to where we were heading and staying and how long. We had been on the road for three weeks playing tourist and having a good time, now it was time to get serious about finding a job to fund our trip to England. I was worried that we'd run out of money before finding a job, I didn't want to be begging for money so we could have something to eat.

James got us in the cafeteria for breakfast for a second time, the cooks made us a hearty breakfast. Stu and I ate like it was our last meal, we didn't know where and when our next meal will be. I told Stu that I met a guy from Quebec in the bar the day before; he said that we should be able to find good paying jobs in Yellowknife, Northwest Territories. He also said that he had friends that went to Yellowknife last year and found good paying jobs. I suggested that we take the bus from Banff to Yellowknife as opposed to hitchhiking.

"When do you want to leave?", Stu asked. "This afternoon, the sooner we get to Yellowknife, the sooner we will find a job", I said. Stu didn't know anything about Yellowknife; he was intrigued about heading north. Stu told me that "Dennis and Tom left last spring to Northern Quebec and found good paying jobs. "We should have enough money left for the bus tickets to Yellowknife", I said. "I've about hundred dollars left", said Stu. "I have one hundred and fifty dollars left, that should be enough to get us there" I said. "I'm tired of hitchhiking, there're too many hitchhikers on the road. Taking a bus to Yellowknife sounds like a good plan", said Stu. I was happy to see that Stu agreed with my plan. I was expecting him to say that he wanted to spend a few more days in Banff, he was having such a good time with his friend, James. We both understood that we did not get a paying job in Banff, and it was time to hit the road.

Before we leave Banff, we should do our laundry at the laundromat, there is one not too far from here. We made sure that all of our laundry was done and packed away. Both Stu and I shook hands with James and thanked him for letting us stay in his room and letting us eat in the cafeteria unnoticed.

79

"I hope that you guys find a good paying job in Yellowknife, safe travels. You'll be travelling in style on a bus and not hitchhiking", said James.

The sky was greyish looking with heavy clouds threatening to rain at any moment. We headed to the laundromat with our pack sack laden with dirty clothes. We each put on our swimming truck at the laundromat so we could wash all our dirty clothes including the ones we wore.

Once the laundry was dried, I put my laundry into my backpack. Dressed in clean clothes and our backpack on our shoulders, we headed to the bus terminal, Stu asked the ticket agent the time of the next bus to Calgary, "You just missed the bus but there's another one in two hours", said the ticket agent, "how much to Calgary?" I asked. The ticket agent looked at me and said in French, *"quatre dollar et cinquante"* (four dollar and fifty). I didn't expect him to reply to me in French. *"Ton accent ma dit que tu parle le Francais"*, (your accent told me that you speak French), said the ticket agent.

We boarded the bus to Calgary mid-afternoon; it had rained quite heavily and there was more downpour ahead. We sat at the back of the bus and stored our backpacks on the rack. Most of the people on the bus appeared to be tourist with a few people tired of hitchhiking. I could see along the Trans-Canada highway in both direction groups of hitchhikers in their raincoat with their thumbs out hoping to get a ride to their destinations. The clouds were low hiding the tops of the mountains and their beauty. Now and then, the rain came down like a torrential deluge. I felt for the hitchhikers and was sure glad that we were in the bus, dry and comfortable and not worrying about being in the rain and trying to hitch a ride. "Today is not a good day to hitchhike, better being in a bus travelling than sticking our thumbs out", said Stu. I sat in my seat feeling good that I'd made a good decision. The Oxford Languages' definition of destiny is, the hidden power believed to control what will happen in the future. I become aware of this so-called destiny a few months later and how meeting a stranger in Banff changed my life and took it in a new direction.

We arrived in Calgary an hour and half later. The sky had cleared up, the sun was shining, it was hot. We checked with the ticket agent at the terminal, "what time is the bus leaving for Edmonton?", asked Stu. The overweight balding ticket agent in his fifties looked at us over the top of his slouching glasses as if to say, "why aren't you guys hitchhiking?". He pushed his glasses with his right index finger to his forehead and said, "the Edmonton bus is leaving at 8:00pm, it will be arriving in Edmonton at 11:30pm". "How much is the ticket?", asked Stu. "It is $9.50 one-way, including taxes", said the ticket agent. I reached in my wallet and gave the ticket agent my last $10.

"Let's find a restaurant nearby and have something to eat", said Stu. We walked a block down from the bus terminal and located a steak house restaurant. "Let's have a T-bone steak", said Stu. "That will be very expensive, we have to be careful with our money", I said. "Let's buy one T-Bone steak and one burger and fries, we'll share it half and half", said Stu. I agreed. We stepped inside the restaurant and waited to be seated. The host, a tall man with a cowboy hat in his mid-twenties looked at us from head to toes and looked at us right in our eyes and said, "we don't serve hippies in our restaurant, you'll have to leave". Stu and I turned around and stepped outside. "Let's try another restaurant, across the street was a Chinese restaurant. We crossed the street and stepped inside the restaurant expecting to be told to leave. An elderly Chinese woman directed us to a table and gave us a menu each. "Well, I guess they don't care that we have long hair and looked like hippies", said Stu. Let's order a dinner for 4, whatever we don't eat, we'll take it as a takeout", said Stu. The food was excellent, and the portions were generous. To our surprise, we almost ate everything, the leftover was placed into one container; food for the bus ride. We wobbled back to the bus terminal and patiently waited to board the bus to Edmonton.

It was finally time to board the bus; we made our way to the back of the bus and stored our backpacks on the rack above. The bus was jam-packed with luggage and individuals from all walks of life; there were no empty seats left. The driver was an elderly gentleman in his sixties with hair as white as snow. Prior to our departure, the driver walked down the aisle to verify that all passengers had a bus ticket. Using a single hole punch, the driver made a hole on each ticket so that it couldn't be used again. The driver announced over the intercom that the restrooms were located at the back of the bus and our estimated time of arrival in Edmonton was 11:30pm. Sunset was about an hour away; the sky was blue with a few puffy clouds. Shortly after our departure, Stu laid his head against the window of the bus and quickly fell asleep.

I stayed awake, my brain sketching our next move. The whole trip thus far was day by day. I would like to know or at least have an idea of what tomorrow will bring. I was determined to get to Yellowknife as soon as possible. I didn't want to get to a point where we had to beg for money to eat. I'd seen too many people in Vancouver begging for money to eat or to support their drugs or alcohol habit.

I could see the sun disappearing below the horizon. We were halfway to Edmonton. I rested my head on the back of the seat and dozed off, I was tired of thinking and worrying.

I felt the bus slowing down; we had arrived in the city. Twenty minutes later, the driver parked the bus at the terminal. Stu woke up, not knowing where he was.

"We're in Edmonton. I'll check what time the next bus to Hay River is," I said. We grabbed our backpacks and walked inside the terminal. I remember eating at the terminal when we stopped in Edmonton on our way to Vancouver by train.

I walked to the ticket counter and asked the ticket agent the time for the next bus to Hay River. He replied, "Twenty minutes." I looked over my right shoulder and saw Stu still trying to wake up.

"The bus to Hay River is leaving in twenty minutes," I said.

"Let's find a hotel and spend the night in Edmonton," said Stu.

"No, I want to take the bus to Hay River," I said. Stu looked at me with an angry look, which was odd for him to do.

Before he had time to reply, I said, "I'm taking the bus," and then I purchased my ticket to Hay River. Stu looked like he didn't know what to do.

I was determined to get on the bus. I walked to the line where people stood waiting to board the bus. A minute later, Stu stood in line behind me. He didn't look so happy.

There was a long line ahead of us, it would be another jam-packed bus ride. The ticket agent had told me that the bus was stopping in Peace River at 6:00 am for about two hours to refuel and change drivers.

The price of the bus ticket to Hay River was $29.50, including taxes. I was down to my last one hundred dollars.

Stu and I were the last ones to board the bus. There were two seats left near the front of the bus. I sat on the first available seat next to an elderly woman who wasn't interested in talking with a hippie, let alone a French hippie.

Stu, on the other hand, sat beside a young woman who was holding a baby in her arms. The driver was a short, middle-aged man in his late forties, wearing his Greyhound Lines suit. The driver walked down the aisle, punching a single hole in our ticket and telling us to hang on to our ticket for the passengers traveling beyond Peace River.

The driver backed out of the terminal and made his way out of the city. It would be a long ride. I made myself comfortable and dozed off.

The first stop was in Whitecourt, Alberta. It was a forty-five-minute stop to stretch our legs. The mother and baby sitting next to Stu cried most of the way to Whitecourt and once got sick all over Stu's lap.

To Stu's delight, the woman with the baby got off the bus at Whitecourt. The bus was still jam-packed. We departed Whitecourt bound for Fox Creek.

I dozed off again and woke up at Fox Creek, where we had a twenty-minute stop.

"Next stop Valleyview!" said the driver of the bus. Forty-five minutes later, we stopped in Valleyview for another twenty minutes. It was still dark and cool outside.

"Next stop Peace River!" said the driver. As we were heading to Peace River, the sun began to show its rays above the horizon to the east.

One hour and a half later, "Next stop Peace River! everybody will have to get off the bus," said the driver.

The steep rolling hills before we arrived in Peace River were picturesque. I saw a few deer staring at us from the bushes along the highway as if they were waiting for us to go by before crossing the highway.

We got off the bus with our backpacks and headed to a small restaurant for breakfast close to the bus terminal. It was cool outside. I recalled the heavy dew on the green grass and the windshield of parked vehicles along the sidewalk.

Stu was in a better mood; we were both tired and in needs of a good breakfast. We sat at the restaurant eating our breakfast and speculating on what types of jobs were available in Yellowknife. One of Michel's friends was hired on a barge travelling between Hay River and Inuvik on the Mackenzie River delivering supplies to the smaller communities along the river throughout the summer. "That would be a fun job and would see a lot of interesting things along the river, that would be the job to get", said Stu. We made our way back to the terminal and were told that the bus wasn't ready for boarding. Half-hour later, an announcement over the intercom saying that the bus was now ready for boarding. We were first in line this time and made our way to the back of the bus. There were less passengers on board, a few seats were empty.

"Ticket please", said the driver who was a middle-aged man dressed in his Greyhound bus driver suit. The driver put the bus in gear then headed to the highway leading to the bridge across the Peace River. The crossing of the bridge over the river impressed me. The river was over one kilometer in width and fast flowing, we climbed a steep hill on the other side of the bridge, the driver had to gear down the bus as it struggled a bit climbing the hill. There were rolling hills after rolling hills, we plateaued over an area of level high ground where wheat fields adorned the landscape. The Peace River valley reminded me of the Laurentian Mountains where I came from with their rolling hills and deep valleys. The sun had risen over the horizon and heated the ground which had cooled when we arrived at Peace River in the early morning hours. "Next stop, Manning! we will be stopping for half hour", said the driver over the intercom. We got off the bus to stretch our legs and inhaled some fresh air. The town was relatively small, giving it an inviting and friendly countryside feel where everybody knows everybody. A small river named Notikewin runs through the town.

A few passengers boarded the bus while others disembarked. As we travelled further north, there were less and less passengers remaining in the bus "Next stop, High Level!", said the driver while driving away from the bus terminal. The bouncing around in the bus slowly but surely rocked me to sleep. My mind went blank, lights out! Next, I felt the bus slowing down and heard the driver say, "High Level! we will be stopping for half hour". I woke up from my slumber as the driver parked the bus by the terminal where most of the passengers disembarked. Stu and I went outside to stretch our legs and get some fresh air. We'd been on a bus for twenty-four hours; I could see in Stu's face that he had enough of riding in the bus.

A few passengers heading to Hay River boarded the bus. There were about seven or eight of us remaining. The new driver's name was Jim. He was a tall man with a head of thick curly brown hair. He spoke with a very thick accent that I didn't recognize.

Stu did right away and said, "He's Australian, I'm sure."

The driver checked our tickets, and Stu asked him where he was from.

"Sidney, Australia, mate," said Jim.

"How many hours to Hay River?" asked Stu.

"About four hours, mate," said Jim.

It was late afternoon, the sun was way up in the blue sky, and it was a hot July day. I was looking forward to arriving and seeing the Northwest Territories.

As we traveled north, I noticed that it was getting later for the sun to set. A short drive out of High Level, the paved road turned into a gravel road.

I could hear the little rocks on the gravel road hitting the frame underneath the bus, sounding like a cacophonic out-of-rhythm beat. The road was dusty, just like a fine powdering dust hanging in the air, reducing visibility ahead that could be smelled and tasted with the bus's window open.

A large rig ahead of us roused a lot of dust on the road, preventing Jim from safely passing the rig. Attempting to pass the rig under those conditions would be risking your life and that of the passengers.

A few vehicles and rigs drove by us on the opposite lane, seemed like they were throwing rocks at the bus. A few rocks struck the bus's windshield, causing rock chips and elongated cracks across the windshield.

The rig ahead of us slowed us down as it was driving under the speed limit. The gravel road was made from a mixture of crushed and pit-run gravel, some of which appeared to be the size of boulders.

Two hours later, Jim stopped the bus by a large sign indicating that we'd reached the 60th Parallel, the border of the Northwest Territories.

I felt like an explorer, though not the first one; I was late exploring by one hundred and eighty-four years. I guess I missed the canoe!

Jim asked us to sit at the front of the bus so Stu and him could carry on with their conversation. The dust on the road had settled, the rig was way ahead of us. We carried on to Hay River. "We'll stop at Alexandra Falls for fifteen minutes or so", said Jim. The Falls was about thirty-five minutes from Hay River. We'd been travelling for hours on the dusty road with no sight of houses or buildings along the road apart from a few buildings in a place called Indian Cabin, Alberta, located a few kilometers south of the Northwest Territories. We stopped at Alexandra Falls where we walked a short distance to the falls. I could hear the water rushing down the falls and landing below and into the Hay River. The view and sounds of the falls were magnificent and looked as if the river had been fractured into two pieces and put back together one piece above the other.

The next stop was Enterprise, a smaller community adjacent to the junctions leading to Hay River and Yellowknife. The view of the plummeting Hay River Gorge by Enterprise is impressive. Jim slowed down so we could have a better view of the gorge. "I was a tour guide back home in Sidney, Australia driving a bus. That's how I made my money to travel all over the world, I've been on the road for two years", said Jim. Listening to his stories travelling all over the world inspired me to travel even more. I was looking forward in getting a job, saving money and then embarking on my journey beginning in England.

At last, we arrived in Hay River, the sun was still up and the sky was still blue, it was around 9pm. I couldn't believe that it was still light. The streets were made of gravel, it was a hot day, each time a vehicle drove by, dust hung in the air and slowly settled down on the streets. I could smell and taste the dust. Jim dropped us off at a hotel called the Zoo in the old town in Hay River. "I'll be driving the bus to Yellowknife leaving tomorrow morning at 8:00am, I can pick you up at the hotel tomorrow", said Jim. "How many hours by bus from Hay River to Yellowknife?", asked Stu. "About 8 hours' drive", said Jim. "We'll be waiting for you", Stu said, even though he wasn't keen on getting in a bus again.

There was a flight the next day to Yellowknife. We checked in at the hotel and split the cost of the room; we were both tired having travelled and sleeping in a bus for nearly a day and a half. "How much is the flight to Yellowknife?", Stu asked the hotel clerk. "$29 one-way", said the hotel clerk. The bus ticket to Yellowknife was $15 including taxes. I told Stu that I'll be taking the bus tomorrow morning, it was up to him if he wanted to fly to Yellowknife or take the bus. I was determined to get to Yellowknife as soon as possible. I was going to get there with or without Stu, we were both getting low on money and in need of a job.

The following morning, Stu and I had breakfast at the hotel and waited for Jim to pick us up from the hotel. At 8am sharp, Jim opened the door of his bus to let us in. "I'll stop at the bus depot to pick up the other passengers, you guys can buy your bus tickets there", said Jim. I reached for my wallet to pay for the ticket and counted what was left in my wallet. I had Sixty dollars and some change left. "Let's hope we find a job in Yellowknife or else, we'll be begging in the street for money so we can eat", said Stu while smiling at me. He knew that I was worried about running out of money.

Stu was the type of guy who didn't worry about the future. He had more experience than I did when it came to hitchhiking and being broke without a job. Along with his friends, Dennis and Tom, Stu hitchhiked to Quebec from Ontario with no job waiting for them and with next to nothing in their pockets. They succeeded in finding low paying jobs, making barely enough money between the three of them to rent a small two-bedroom house and pay the bills.

I met Dennis, Tom and Stu, in December 1972, they rented a small house a couple's street down from my mother's house. They invited my friend Yvon and I to their house. They'd lived in Ste-Adele for about one month and wanted to make friends as well as learning French; Stu and Tom didn't speak French; Dennis had worked in northern Quebec for one year to make a living and learn French.

In January 1973, my mother had broken up with her boyfriend and was offered a job in New-Brunswick; her boyfriend and I didn't get along. As soon as my mother left for her new job. "You have four hours to pack up and get out of this house", my mother's boyfriend told me. I was now homeless but had a job as a dishwasher in a fancy restaurant. I'd only worked for a few days and was expecting my first weekly pay cheque in a couple days. It was a cold night, with my backpack on my shoulder, I walked a couple of streets down from my mother's house to ask my new friends from Ontario if I could sleep on their couch for the night. When I knocked on the door, Stu opened the door and asked me to come in. I told Dennis about my situation; he spoke with Tom and Stu. Dennis smiled and told me that I was welcome to stay with them and then he said that I would have to pay my share of the rent and bills. I was relieved, I felt a weight lifted off my shoulders, I now had a roof over my head. Five months later, Stu and I left Ste-Adele to look for a good paying job in British Columbia.

A few passengers from Hay River boarded the bus, Stu and I sat at the front of the bus listening to Jim's stories of his travels around the world. "Do you guys have a place to stay in Yellowknife?" asked Jim. "In our pop-up tents at the local campground", said Stu. "I stay at the Greyhound's bunk house in Yellowknife Old Town; I'm currently the only person staying there. You guys are welcome to stay there for a couple days, there are a couple beds, shower and kitchen in the bunk house", said Jim. "That'd be great, thanks man", said Stu.

Along the way to Yellowknife, we stopped at Lady Evelyn Falls located on the Kakisa Lake's access road. We walked down to the Kakisa River to have a view of the Falls. From a distance, I could hear the roaring of the falls and the river. The falls were majestic like postcard scenery, we spent about half-hour looking at the falls, the other passengers didn't mind the stopover. Less than an hour later, we boarded the ferry on the Mackenzie River crossing near Fort Providence. Here it was, the river that Stu and I hoped to travel by barge all the way to Inuvik. It was a beautiful hot July day, the winds on the river felt cool. "That would be an awesome job getting to work on a barge travelling the Mackenzie River up to the arctic", said Stu.

I leaned against the rail of the ferry looking at the river daydreaming about travelling by barge down the river. We made a quick stop in Fort Providence to pick up the mail and carry on to Yellowknife. Jim drove by the Manpower building downtown Yellowknife where tomorrow we'd look for a job. Jim gave us a tour of the bunkhouse and told us that we could cook ourselves something to eat. Stu and I cooked some eggs and bacon with toast, I was hungry, the last meal I had was in Hay River. We said our goodbyes and thank Jim who had to leave early the next morning back to High Level.

The following day after having the same meal like the day before, we headed to the Manpower building, which is now called Service Canada. I was excited and at the same time nervous, this was a gamble travelling all the way from Banff to Yellowknife for the sole reason that a stranger told me that there was a lot of jobs in Yellowknife and that we will get a job there for sure.

The Manpower office had just opened its doors. We spoke to the first person we saw in the office, a man of average height with short brown hair in his early thirties.

"Are there any jobs open on the barges?" asked Stu.

"No, all jobs on the barges were staffed in April. Most of the employees working on the barges are seasonal employees who return to work each year," said the employee.

He added, "Currently, there are jobs available in Fort Simpson laying sewer and water lines for the Village of Fort Simpson."

"Where's Fort Simpson?" I asked.

The employee pointed to a large map on the wall and indicated where Fort Simpson was.

I was disappointed; I was hoping that we would get a job on the barge. However, at this moment, beggars can't be choosers.

"How far is Fort Simpson by road?" Stu asked.

"About seven hours driving," said the employee.

"Is there a bus to Fort Simpson?" Stu asked.

"No, if you accept the job, we'll pay for the flight to Fort Simpson," said the employee.

Stu and I looked at each other, not believing what we heard.

"Did you say that our flight to Fort Simpson will be paid?" said Stu.

The employee looked at us as if to say, "Are you guys deaf?"

"Yes, the flight will be paid for, and there's a house where you can stay for $1 a day each, including utilities, which will be deducted from your paycheck. Food is not included," said the employee.

Stu and I looked at each other again, this time smiling from ear to ear.

"How much is the pay per hour?" asked Stu.

"The pay is $3.50 per hour and $5.25 per hour for overtime. The project is behind schedule. You'll be expected to work overtime on the weekends and holidays as well as during the week," the employee informed us.

"When can we start?" Stu asked.

"There's a flight leaving for Fort Simpson in three hours. You start work tomorrow morning. You will have to leave today," said the employee.

We can leave for Fort Simpson today said Stu. "Good, your plane tickets will be at the airport, you will need your ID with a photo". "Someone will be picking you up at the airport in Fort Simpson and will drive you to the house where you'll be staying". After completing our hiring forms, Stu and I made our way outside the building, cool as cucumber, but as soon as we were outside, we couldn't hold our joy any longer. We both jumped up like little kids opening their Christmas gifts. I was so happy, the gamble paid off, we didn't travel from Banff to Yellowknife by bus for nothing; we both couldn't believe that we got good paying jobs, a place to stay and a paid flight to Fort Simpson, I felt like we hit the jackpot, both Stu and I worked in Quebec for $1.50 per hour which was the minimum salary then. The minimum salary in the Northwest Territories was at that time $2.00 per hour.

We walked around downtown looking for a pay phone, I finally found a payphone in the lobby of a hotel. I called my mom collect at the business she owned; she accepted the call right away, she was so happy to hear from me and surprised that I was calling from Yellowknife, Northwest Territories. I told her about the job in Fort Simpson that Stu, and I signed up for. I told her that I'll keep in contact with her once a week.

After my call to my mom, Stu and I got a taxi and made our way to the airport,

On the way to the airport, we saw two young men about our age with their backpack walking fast on the shoulder of the road in the direction of the airport. One had long dirty blond hair down to his waist like Stu and the other shoulder-length black hair. Both were struggling carrying their backpacks, the young man with the waist length hair was also carrying a medium size suitcase that he dropped on the ground because he was walking so fast.

Stu and I checked in at the airport and boarded the plane, the hostess was about to close the door of the airplane when someone on the tarmac said, "there's two more passengers", The hostess stood at the door and directed the two passengers to their seats they were both breathless and winded; I looked and recognized them as the two guys walking fast towards the airport. Both sat across the alley from Stu and I. Catching their breath, the guy with the black hair said to the other, "*on n'est arriver juste a temps*", which translates from French to English to "we arrived just in time". I introduced myself and Stu to the two guys, their names were Alain and Raymond. Alain was the fellow with the waist length hair and Raymond was the fellow with the shoulder length black hair. To my surprise, both were hired in the same job as Stu and I, as well as staying at the same house. I asked both if they both spoke English, Raymond said that he knew a few words and understood basic phrases. Alain didn't speak or understood any English. At the time, I could get by in English although with a few mistakes here and there. Both asked me when needed if I could translate for them. I told them yes. Alain and Raymond had taken the train to Edmonton then hitchhiked from there to Yellowknife. They both had heard that there were jobs in Yellowknife from friends. Both went to the same Manpower building that Stu and I did.

An hour later, we landed at Fort Simpson Airport, it was July 25th, 1973. A taxi driver came in a van to take us to the bunkhouse in town. Prior to arriving in the town, we drove over a causeway, which is a raised road made of dirt and gravel to an Island where the Village of Fort Simpson was located. Driving over the causeway, we came to the junction of the Liard and Mackenzie Rivers that could be seen in all its grandeur. At the bunkhouse, we met Sandy who was not feeling well and had taken the day off. Later we found out that Sandy was from Ontario and had just started working for the Village of Fort Simpson. Sandy was average height with short light brown hair; he had a speech impediment. Sandy also had a cousin living in Fort Simpson, that is how he found out about the job. He flew from Ontario to Fort Simpson, he didn't travel by train, bus or hitchhike like we did. Most of the time, I couldn't understand what Sandy was saying, it was challenge working with him.

Sandy gave us a tour of the bunkhouse that had three bedrooms, one bathroom, kitchen, living room, including a basement. The house was a good size with plenty of room for all five of us. There was no washer or dryer machines in the house.

Sandy said that there was a laundromat across the street from the Sub-Arctic restaurant just as you drive into town. He told us that there were three grocery stores in town, Stu and I purchased our groceries at the Hudson Bay store. I asked Alain and Raymond if they wanted to go to the store with us, they both gave me a sad looking face and told me that they were flat broke and they did not have enough money to take a taxi to the airport in Yellowknife, that was the reason for walking to the airport. I lent Raymond one of the twenty dollar bills I had left.

All four of us made our way to the Hudson Bay store to purchase groceries. Sandy showed us the shortcut to the Hudson Bay store. At the time, the community of Fort Simpson had a little over seven hundred residents; it didn't take us long to learn how to get around. Everything at the store was expensive compared to the grocery stores in Quebec. There was no other option but to pay the high prices. Fortunately for us, back then, we could purchase quite a few grocery items with twenty dollars.

The four of us shared the house with Sandy, Stu and I shared a decent sized bedroom with a view. Alain and Raymond had a bedroom the same size as ours and Sandy's bedroom was the largest in the house. I was excited to start my new job; I wasn't afraid of getting dirty and working hard. I had never worked laying water and sewer lines. The only outside job I did before was being a caddy at a golf club.

Our first evening in Fort Simpson, NT, Stu and I sat by the riverbank to watch the colorful sunset over the Mackenzie River which left an impression on me to this day.

Chapter 3:
My First Day on the Job

It was a beautiful sunny day, and it felt like a hot one was ahead. Around 8:00 a.m., a truck pulled up to the house to pick us up. The five of us climbed into the box of the truck since the cab was already full of other workers.

The driver dropped us off at the water plant, where we met the town foreman. He was a tall, slim man in his late thirties, with short blond hair and piercing blue eyes. He spoke with a thick Australian accent—much like Jim, the Greyhound bus driver who had let us stay at the bus bunkhouse in Yellowknife.

The foreman was eloquent and clear in explaining the tasks assigned to each group of workers.

Alain, Raymond, and I were assigned to work with a backhoe operator. Our task was to connect a water and sewer line to the Igloo Building, which was a hardware store at the time. Sandy was assigned to continue working with the same crew he'd been helping near the post office, laying water and sewer lines.

Stu, on the other hand, was sent to work with a man named Jim Venable, who was running the water supply operations for the Village at Spring Hills, located on the mainland south of Fort Simpson Island.

Jim was around six feet tall and very slim—he couldn't have weighed more than 140 pounds. He had long, perfectly straight dirty blond hair that reached halfway down his back, tied into a ponytail. Jim was a true hippie in both lifestyle and personality.

Stu and I rarely worked together. He spent most of his time with Jim out at Spring Hills, where Jim lived in a small shack. The spring itself emerged from the ground near the top of a hill and formed a small pool, which was then channeled through a pipe down to the community. This spring supplied cold, pure water to part of the town from May to September.

Back at our job site, our foreman, the backhoe operator, and the three of us got started on the line from the main to the Igloo Building. The backhoe began digging when suddenly an employee from Canadian National (CN) arrived and shouted, "Stop digging! There're telephone lines just a few feet away. If you cut the line, the whole Village will lose phone service."

The foreman looked at the backhoe operator and said, "Keep on digging."

"No, you can't do that!" the CN employee barked, then quickly left in his truck.

A few minutes later, a big man—clearly someone you didn't want to mess with—pulled up in another CN truck. He stepped out, followed by the same employee who had told us to stop.

"What the hell are you doing? I said stop digging!" the big man shouted.

The foreman didn't respond. The big man grabbed him by the shoulders and repeated, "Stop digging, I said."

The foreman turned to the backhoe operator and said, "Keep on digging."

And then—crack—the fractured telephone lines surfaced through the dirt.

I was on the opposite side of the trench, right in the front row, watching what was turning into a full-on wrestling match. The CN employee lunged at the foreman. Then the backhoe operator jumped in and grabbed the big man.

They were all yelling, swearing, and grabbing at each other, but no punches were thrown. Still, they clung to one another like they were in some bizarre square dance—like they were doing the "Do-si-do."

Alain, Raymond, and I looked at each other, jaws dropped. We had no idea what to do. Not that we wanted to get involved—there were already more than enough "dancers" on that stage.

Eventually, the big man and the CN employee stormed off, furious. The foreman looked at the backhoe operator and said, "Shut down the backhoe."

"I assumed we'd find the telephone line without severing it," he added, "then dig around it with shovels." Turning to us, the foreman said, "You guys can go home for the rest of the day. You'll be paid for eight hours. I'll see you tomorrow morning at the water plant."

Alain turned to me and asked what the foreman had said. I translated, letting him know we could head home and would still get paid for a full day's work. Alain and Raymond were in disbelief. "We worked one hour, watched a wrestling match, and now we get the rest of the day off with pay—and still keep our jobs."

"I like this job," I said, laughing.

Later that day, I decided to take a walk around town to get a better sense of the layout. It was a hot July day, but the heat wasn't humid like back in Quebec. On some summer days there, you could be sweating just sitting in the shade doing nothing.

It was still early. As I walked down the main street, I was stopped twice by two different men driving trucks, both asking if I was looking for a job. I told them I was already working for the Village.

I wandered toward what the locals call "downtown" until I reached the Fort Simpson Hotel and Turner's Store, one of the town's groceries. Inside, the shelves were mostly bare— just tea, coffee, flour, sugar, lard, oatmeal, tobacco, a few bottles of pop, chips, and a handful of chocolate bars. I bought a pop and stepped back onto the dusty street.

All the streets were dirt mixed with gravel. Each time a vehicle passed, a cloud of dust rose, hanging in the air so thick I could taste it.

On the next block, two Indigenous boys, maybe four and six, ran up and asked for a dollar each. They were hilarious— especially the younger one, a born comedian. Even though I missed half their words, their timing and expression cracked me up. I was getting better at English, just not yet tuned to the local accent.

I handed each boy a dollar bill. They jumped for joy, thanked me, and bolted toward Turner's Store. I marveled that they sprinted barefoot over dirt and gravel while I would have tiptoed, muttering "ouch" with every step. I did not know then that both boys would someday become my brothers-in-law.

101

From there I headed to the river and followed its edge back toward our house.

The riverbank was postcard-pretty. Wooden boats with outboard motors bobbed at their moorings. A small board-plank cabin sat nearby, and beside it an upside-down wooden boat lay drying in the sun—silent, weathered, and surely full of stories.

Further along I heard piano music drifting from a building marked "Anglican Church." I knocked. A man in his early forties, average height and build, short wavy brown hair, brown eyes, opened the door. I told him I was new in town, working for the Village, and that I played piano.

"Come in," he said, leading me to the instrument. "What kind of music do you play?"

"Classical," I answered. His eyebrows rose in surprise.

I sat down and played two Bach Inventions, then Beethoven's Moonlight Sonata. He pulled up a chair and listened. When I finished, he smiled. "You can use the piano anytime. I'll show you where I hide the church key."

I thanked him and shook his hand. After that, whenever I had free time, I walked to the church to play. When I told Stu, Sandy overheard and said he played piano too. A few days later we visited the church together. Sandy sat down and, to my amazement, belted out Elton John's "Your Song," sounding almost like Elton John.

That evening, after relaxing on the riverbank for what felt like hours, I cooked dinner for Stu and me. Sandy burst into the house, breathless. "There's a girl with dirty long blonde hair in our yard, she's sexy!" he gasped.

102

Curious, I followed him outside—only to find Alain hanging washed clothes on a makeshift clothesline. When Sandy realized his "sexy girl" was our buddy Alain, he groaned, "Oh man!" and pulled a face like he'd smelled something foul.

Alain had strung the line facing the river. He washed his clothes by hand in the basement sink and hung them to dry. A moment later Jim, Stu's co-worker, rolled up in a late-'50s pickup, the bed stacked with large bottles of spring water. We hauled them inside—river tap water tasted silty and chemical, so we cooked and drank only spring water.

For the rest of the summer Alain, Raymond, and I worked together. I think the foreman grouped us because Alain and Raymond struggled with English, and I could translate—more or less. I kept learning new words daily. Raymond tried to practice English, but Alain preferred I handle the talking.

Sandy worked on another crew, doing the same trench work—laying water and sewer lines. Our trench work was risky. We depended on the backhoe operator to watch the walls and keep them from caving in. He was a Frenchman from a small Alberta town. One day he told me a trench wall had once collapsed on him. Only his head stayed above ground while coworkers dug him out by hand. The weight on his chest nearly suffocated him.

He finished the story, looked me in the eye, and said, "That's why I run the backhoe up here, not down in the trench."

Once the trenches were dug to a depth of about twelve feet and there was enough space to work, a ladder was lowered to allow us to go down. My first day in the trench was rough. I felt like I was being buried alive—this

103

claustrophobic sensation stayed with me for a few days until I got used to it.

The trenches were narrow, and when I looked up, all I could see were steep walls of dirt and the sliver of sky above. We spent long hours down there laying water and sewer pipes. These pipes had to be buried deep to reduce the risk of freezing.

Each pipe was 3.9 meters (13 feet) long with an inside diameter of about 10 centimeters (4 inches). They looked like they were made of concrete and were heavy to handle. One end of each pipe had a collar with a rubber gasket, while the other end was slightly tapered. Grease was applied to the tapered end so it could slide into the collared pipe.

Sewer lines were laid at the very bottom of the trench. Water lines were laid in the same trench but several meters (feet) above to avoid contamination in case of a sewer leak.

The pipes were lined up along the trench edge, sorted by collared and tapered ends. If the wrong ends were sent down into the trench, it was nearly impossible to turn them around in that tight space. I remember standing one pipe upright, making sure the correct end was facing the wall, and then carefully lowering it down without breaking it.

We used two ropes to lower the pipes—one tied to each end. The top ends of the ropes were secured to a truck on the surface, while the bottom ends were passed underneath the pipe with no slack. One person on each end would gently lower the pipe in sync. It was crucial that both ends were lowered evenly, otherwise, the pipe could hit the trench floor too hard and crack or shatter.

Even though they were concrete, the pipes were prone to cracking or breaking. I'll admit, at first, we broke a few pipes during unloading or lowering them into the trench. Every time we did, the foreman or the backhoe operator would give us that look. But after a few days, we got the hang of it, and the breaks stopped.

To connect each pipe, we'd grease the tapered end. Two of us would hold each end of the pipe between our legs, count to three, then swing the pipe into position. The tapered end was carefully lined up with the collared end of the pipe already laid on the ground.

We'd place a small piece of 5-by-15 centimeters (2-by-6 inches) board on the collared end to protect it, then tap it in with a short-handled sledgehammer to secure the joint.

Once a section was installed, a surveyor would check the slope using a level and rod. One of us in the trench would hold a 4.8 meters (16 foot) rod on each collared pipe. The surveyor would call out how much to raise or lower it—or confirm if it was just right. We'd shovel dirt out or add it in until he was satisfied with the inclination.

The sewer line was always laid and packed first. A hand packer and a motorized packer were used to compress the soil along both sides of the pipe and over the top. Then the backhoe operator would cover the line with about 30 centimeters (1 foot) of dirt, which we leveled and packed again. We repeated this until about 1.2 meters (4 feet) of dirt covered the pipe.

Once that was done, we installed the water line on top of the packed dirt, following the same process. I spent a lot of time operating the packers—honestly, it was my favorite part of the whole job.

The next morning, we returned to connect the sewer and water lines from the Igloo Building to the main line.

Meanwhile, the CN crew was still busy repairing the telephone lines we had accidentally damaged. They braced the repaired lines using ropes and boards placed above and below the cables.

The CN foreman—the same big man from before—stood at the edge of the trench, watching us work. Our foreman was nowhere to be seen. Later, I overheard a backhoe operator telling a coworker that our foreman had been fired for damaging the CN telephone lines.

Because of that, any work near the repaired lines had to be done by hand. The big man made sure no backhoes came anywhere nearby.

A Village employee handled the connections between the building and the main line, while Alain, Raymond, and I did the spreading and packing of dirt with shovels. It was a brutally hot, sunny day. I remember being drenched in sweat, my face streaked with dust.

Now and then, I'd pull off my hard hat just to wipe the sweat off my forehead.

Raymond, Alain, and I worked well together. We were the "Quebec crew," always chatting in French, making jokes, and occasionally poking fun at whoever happened to be supervising or watching us work.

And we had quite the audience—people with nothing better to do than watch us shovel, sweat, and hustle in the dirt.

A few days later, we were introduced to our new foreman—a short, bald man in his late forties or early fifties. He was a chain smoker, and I rarely saw him without a cigarette hanging from his mouth. Unlike our previous

106

foreman, he wasn't friendly at all. He had these evil, beady eyes, and every time he looked at you, it felt like he was sizing you up. He swore constantly, using profanity like it was punctuation—swear words for subjects, verbs, and objects.

He looked like the kind of guy you wouldn't want to run into in a dark alley.

On his first day, he told us firmly that we must always wear our hard hats. He also laid out our schedule—fifteen-minute breaks in the morning and afternoon. Alain didn't understand what he had said, so I translated it for him. That's when the foreman snapped.

"Speak English! We're in Canada!" he shouted at the top of his lungs.

I was offended, and by the look on his face, I could tell he was hoping I'd argue back. But my inner voice told me to stay quiet and not start a fight. Then he looked at Alain and said, "I don't want any girls on my crew."

Alain turned to me, confused. I leaned in and said quietly, "He thinks you're a girl."

Alain just looked away. He was used to being mistaken for a girl because of his long, thick, dirty blond hair—hair that would have made any woman jealous.

A couple of days later, while I was in the trench packing dirt around the sewer pipes, the foreman yelled at me and threw a small short-handled sledgehammer into the trench, landing a couple meters (feet) in front of me.

"Go down the manhole and bust the sewer pipe with the hammer," he barked.

The manhole had been installed earlier that day.

I asked, "Is there any sewer in the pipe?"

"No," he snapped.

I leaned a ladder against the manhole and climbed up to the top, then lowered the ladder inside and climbed down. I wasn't thrilled about going in there—it was tight and claustrophobic.

"Hurry up, bust that pipe!" the foreman yelled again.

I gripped the sledgehammer and swung with all my strength. "Go faster, go faster!" he screamed.

Suddenly, the pipe shattered—sewage exploded all over my face and into my mouth.

I could hear the foreman laughing hysterically from the edge of the trench.

I hadn't expected there to be sewage in the pipe since it was newly installed. Clearly, the foreman knew and sent me down there on purpose. It was a cruel joke, and I was the punchline.

I gagged and spat the foul stuff out of my mouth.

"How's the sewer taste?" he called out, still laughing.

I didn't answer. I climbed out of the manhole, walked up to him, and said, "I'm going home to clean up."

"Yeah, you stink like sewer. See you tomorrow morning at the water plant," he said, still chuckling.

I was furious, but I kept my emotions in check. I walked home, spitting constantly. The taste was salty and disgusting. It was a good thing I had a strong stomach—otherwise, I would've puked all the way there.

At the house, I took a long, hot shower and hand-washed my clothes. Everyone else was still at work, so I had the place to myself. I skipped dinner—I had no appetite. The sewer taste had killed it.

The foreman constantly picked on the three of us Quebecers, mocking our accents or our limited English. A few days later, on a side street near Main, a new manhole was installed. The crew set up a jackhammer hanging sideways by a rope into the trench. The plan was to drill a hole into the side of the manhole.

The foreman called me over and told me to use the jackhammer.

"I've never used one before," I said.

"Just pull the trigger and aim the bit where the black mark is," he replied.

I climbed into the trench, grabbed the jackhammer, and squeezed the trigger. I tried to steady the drill bit against the manhole, but I wasn't doing a great job. The jackhammer jumped and jerked.

"Stop! Stop!" the foreman shouted. Then he let loose a string of curses and called me a greenhorn.

He climbed down into the trench, and I climbed out. Alain, Raymond, and I stood at the edge, watching as he tried to drill the hole. He was struggling just like I had. And he wasn't wearing a hard hat—something he constantly yelled at us about.

I wanted to shout, "Where's your hard hat?" but I kept it to myself.

The foreman kept cursing the jackhammer, calling it every name in the book. I noticed a few small rocks in the dirt by my feet. Without thinking, I kicked a bit of dirt down the trench. Then I stepped back.

Seconds later, the foreman exploded in a storm of swearing. Alain saw me kick the dirt and smiled, nodding in approval. The foreman looked up and saw all three of us standing there. I'm sure he knew I was the one who kicked the dirt.

He had a small cut on his bald head, and the backhoe operator yelled, "Where's your hard hat?" Everyone burst out laughing.

The foreman gave up on drilling the hole, climbed back up the ladder, and walked past me. I braced for him to explode, but instead, he gave me a strange look, like he was saying, okay, you got me. We're even.

From that moment on until he left a few weeks later, he stopped picking on the Quebec crew.

The weather was hot and dry. Because of that, we were able to work after dinner, pulling twelve-hour days and even working weekends.

The first Monday in August is a statutory holiday in the Northwest Territories. Our backhoe operator asked if we wanted to work over the long weekend. He didn't have to

110

ask twice—we were in. That's exactly why we'd come to Fort Simpson.

Those first couple of weeks were all about work, work, and more work. The dry spell continued. Dust was everywhere, even inside our clothes. I could smell and taste it.

Aside from hard hats, we weren't given coveralls, gloves, ear protection, goggles, or boots. We worked in whatever we had in our backpacks. After work, we took turns showering. The fourth and fifth guys often ended up with cold water— and it was cold.

To be fair, we rotated the order so that everyone got a hot shower at least three times every five days. Skipping a shower wasn't an option. The mix of sweat and dirt would make sleeping impossible.

By mid-August, it started getting dark around 11:00 p.m., just enough to see a few stars.

One night, as I was getting ready for bed, Stu burst into the house.

"There're Northern Lights in the sky!" he shouted.

We all rushed outside. It was the first time I'd seen auroras so vivid and colorful. I had seen faint, colorless Northern Lights once before in Ste-Adèle, Quebec, but nothing like the breathtaking display above Fort Simpson.

The sky was on fire, shimmering with green, red, purple, and blue lights dancing overhead. I was in awe. What a natural show; the experience gave me goosebumps. The Northern Lights covered a huge portion of the sky, moving like waves of color across the heavens.

I could hear Stu, Alain, Raymond, Sandy, or myself blurting out, "Wow," "Ha," "Look at that," and "Look at the color!" We stood there for a good hour, necks craned upward, completely captivated. Eventually, my neck started to ache from staring so long, but I didn't care. I still remember it like it was yesterday.

The following morning, the brilliant sky was gone, hidden behind a thick layer of low, grey clouds. There was a light drizzle drifting from above, just enough to cut down the dust.

The Village truck came to pick us up and dropped us off at the water plant for our morning meeting. The Quebecer crew was assigned to a new area near the Fort Simpson Hotel. A fresh trench had been dug the day before. The backhoe operator, a few years older than us with slick black hair combed back like Elvis, continued the job he had started.

We lowered a few pipes into the trench to begin installing the sewer line. The rain had dampened the area, and the bottom of the trench was quickly turning to slippery mud. We had to watch our footing to avoid falling or getting hurt.

I was about to pick up a pipe with Raymond when I suddenly heard the backhoe operator shout, "Watch out!"

I spun around and saw a large crevice forming on the left side of the trench. He frantically motioned for me to move. I stepped back just in time; a massive piece of the trench wall collapsed in front of me.

The chunk of earth was at least twice my height and must have weighed several tons. It slid down and buried my feet up to my knees. I was stuck. Alain and Raymond rushed over to help dig me out.

112

The trench filled with dirt nearly twelve feet high. It was a close call. Had I not moved when I did, I would have been buried alive.

Then the rain came down fast and hard. Within minutes, the dirt became thick mud. We climbed out of the trench, pants soaked and caked in mud.

The backhoe operator looked down at his boots and sighed, "I got mud all over my brand-new cowboy boots."

He told us to hop in the truck, then added, "Let's go back to the water plant and check in with the foreman."

All the workers were gathered there, sipping coffee. The foreman took one look at the weather and said, "Looks like it will be raining all day. You guys can head home. I'll see you tomorrow morning."

"Are we getting paid for the rest of the day?" asked Joe, a salt-and-pepper-haired Dene man with a French last name, Villeneuve. Joe was friendly and hardworking. I had worked with him in the trenches a few times.

"Yes, you'll all be paid for eight hours today," the foreman confirmed.

The rain continued on and off for the next twenty-four hours. The dusty streets and trenches turned to slush and sludge. It would take at least a couple of sunny days to dry everything out.

"You guys take the weekend off and come back Monday morning," the foreman told us at the water plant. "The trenches should be dry enough by then."

That Friday was our first payday, and we were all excited to see how much we had earned since arriving. The foreman called our names one by one and handed us envelopes containing our pay cheques.

I took a deep breath, opened my envelope, and was shocked at how much tax had been deducted. The deductions alone were more than what I used to make net as a dishwasher in Quebec. Still, my take-home pay was higher than I had ever earned for the same amount of time back home.

I walked to the CIBC bank, which at the time was located in the same building as the post office. It was tiny, more like an office that had been turned into a bank than an actual branch. The waiting line started inside, but the bank could only hold a couple of people at a time, so most folks waited in the hallway or even outside.

There were quite a few people ahead of me. It felt like I waited forever. Eventually, I made it inside, opened an account, and deposited my entire cheque, keeping only a single twenty-dollar bill to cover food until next payday.

Back then, I didn't have a credit card. In the early 1970s, credit cards were still limited-use, mostly accepted in department stores. Debit cards didn't exist yet. Our only payment options were cash or cheque, and most businesses wouldn't even accept a cheque.

As I walked out of the bank, I heard one of the tellers announce, "We're out of cash! Deposits only now."

The Fort Simpson bank was notorious for running out of money on payday. People still in line turned around, frustrated. For some of them, it meant a weekend with no cash in their pockets.

Chapter 4:
My First Girlfriend

My first Girlfriend, Pheobe

The next day after dinner, Sandy, Stu, Raymond, and I headed to one of the bars in the village, the Fort Simpson Hotel. The sky was blue, and the sun had started to dry up the streets and trenches. We followed the road along the riverbank until we reached the street that led to the hotel.

Raymond, Sandy, and I were all under the legal drinking age, which at the time was nineteen years old. Stu was the only one of legal drinking age. I walked into the bar wondering if someone would ask how old I was. No one asked. We each ordered a beer and sat at a table in the far

115

corner of the bar, where a door stood open, letting in fresh air.

The inside of the bar smelled like an ashtray. A heavy cloud of smoke lingered like fog. Back then, people could smoke indoors. The bar was busy and loud, with country-western music blaring from the speakers. It was so loud that to have a conversation, you had to speak very loudly or lean close to the person.

Raymond was sitting closest to the door while I sat furthest away. From my seat, I could see a couple of young Dene girls peering inside. Both were very pretty, with tanned skin, jet-black hair, and dressed in tight jeans and T-shirts. They asked Raymond if they could have a drink from his beer. He handed the bottle to the girl nearest to him, and within seconds, it came back empty.

The girls asked for more beer. I didn't like the taste of mine and I've never been a beer drinker. I gave my bottle to Stu, who passed it to Raymond. Four Dene girls were now standing at the door, smiling and laughing.

I could tell all four of them were drawn to Raymond. He was good-looking and had a natural friendliness and honesty about him. The girls each took a swig from my bottle. I had only taken one sip of that Pilsner and didn't like it anyway.

They lingered near the door, keeping an eye out for the barmaid. They chatted mostly with Raymond and Stu, though I couldn't hear much of what was said over the music.

Eventually, Stu nodded to us—it was time to leave.

We met the girls outside and introduced ourselves. I shook hands with each of them. Their names were Tracy,

Elizabeth, Sara Jane, and Phoebe. Tracy had long, wavy jet-black hair and brown eyes. She was the shortest. Elizabeth was the tallest, also with jet-black hair and brown eyes. Sara Jane, the second tallest, had shoulder-length hair and a look in her eyes that could get a guy in trouble. Phoebe was just a couple inches taller than Tracy, with shoulder-length hair and almond-shaped brown eyes. She was the shy one.

All four had tanned skin and were very pretty. Stu and Sandy led most of the conversation. They asked the girls if they wanted to come over to our house. The girls looked at each other and spoke briefly in their language, South Slavey, then giggled and said yes.

We walked back together along the riverbank. On the way, another Dene girl named Sally stopped to chat with the group, then joined us. When we arrived at the house, the girls asked if we had any beer or alcohol. Stu told them we didn't. They looked a little disappointed.

Alain came out of his room, saw what was going on, and went right back in. He had a girlfriend in Quebec and was deeply in love with her.

Sally said she had to leave. Again, Stu and Sandy carried the conversation. I was still struggling to understand the girls. They spoke English, but very quickly and with accents that were new to me. I caught some words here and there.

Every now and then, they would switch to their own language. Most likely, they were talking about us. They'd laugh and giggle, and we would laugh along with them, shrugging our shoulders.

We sat in the living room, talking and laughing as the evening wore on. Stu and Sandy told the girls we were working for the Village, installing sewer and water lines.

One of them said, "We noticed you guys working in town a week ago."

Soon, the group began to pair off. Raymond with Sara Jane, Sandy with Elizabeth, and Stu with Tracy.

Phoebe stood up and went outside. I followed her.

She pointed up to the sky. The Northern Lights were dancing again, even more stunning than the first time I saw them. We walked to the riverbank and sat on the grass side by side.

I didn't know it then, but my life was about to take a new turn.

She spoke to me in a low, soft voice. She did most of the talking. I tried my best to keep up and answer her questions. She told me she had just returned to Fort Simpson from Fort Smith, where she had gone to school for the past two years. She had arrived in the village about two weeks earlier.

She asked me how old I was, and I asked her in return. She said she had turned sixteen on August first, just ten days ago. I was three months away from my eighteenth birthday.

I was nervous and unsure of what to do next. I had never really had a girlfriend before—just girls who were friends.

Back then, I was very shy. In high school, some of my female classmates would ask me to go to school dances with them, but I always made excuses. My sister Johanne used to tell me some of those girls had crushes on me and wanted to go out with me. I never believed her.

Johanne is thirteen months younger than I am and had her fair share of boyfriends. She used to tease me, saying it was about time I had a girlfriend. I avoided that subject completely. Talking about it made me uncomfortable.

Back then, I was all about music. I played the piano and was learning music theory.

Phoebe and I laid back on the grass to watch the Northern Lights. I slowly reached over and kissed her. That kiss lasted—who knows how long. I think the sun was starting to rise when we finally stopped.

Tracy and Elizabeth had already left. It seemed they hadn't clicked with their pairings. But Phoebe stayed, and something new had begun.

Sara Jane stayed the night with Raymond in the room he shared with Alain.

In the early hours of the morning, I walked Phoebe to the hotel where I had first met her. The sun was just beginning to rise, promising a warm and beautiful day. Phoebe said her house wasn't far from there. She didn't want her dad to see her with a guy.

I gave her a quick kiss before she headed home and asked if I could see her next weekend. She didn't say anything, just nodded, and I took it as a yes.

At that hour, the village was still asleep. The streets were quiet, empty except for a few ravens and seagulls.

On Monday morning, the village truck picked us up from the house and drove us to the water plant. The hot weekend temperatures and sunshine had dried up the streets and trenches. It was time to get back to laying sewer and water pipes.

We returned to the area where the sidewall of the trench had collapsed. The backhoe operator told us he would remove as much of the dirt as he could, but we would need to dig out the pipes by hand using shovels.

"The pipes may have broken when the dirt fell on them," he said.

We knew we had our work cut out for us.

The backhoe operator did a solid job clearing most of the dirt. We climbed down into the trench with our shovels and began filling the backhoe bucket with soil. Once full, he would swing it up and dump it into a growing pile along the street.

After a few bucket loads, we found the pipes. They were intact. I gave the backhoe operator a thumbs up, and he smiled and returned the gesture.

We laid the sewer pipes, had them checked by the surveyor, and packed the dirt. That street was completed in a few days. I spent most of my time in the trench, only coming up for lunch, dinner, or to help lower pipes. We took our breaks right there in the trench, drinking cold water from a large cooler.

There were still many pipes to install. The foreman asked if we wanted to continue working after dinner and on weekends. Though he never said it outright, it was clear he was pleased with our performance. We had made great progress and worked seamlessly with the backhoe operator. The foreman had even stopped picking on us, no longer commenting when Alain, Raymond, and I spoke French.

We never missed a day of work and were always punctual, ready at a moment's notice. The three of us were fully committed and happy to work as many hours as we could.

A couple of days before the weekend, I saw Phoebe walking with another girl who looked like she might be her sister. She was a bit shorter than Phoebe, had slim build, shoulder-length black hair, and wore glasses. As we were lowering pipes into the trench, I waved at Phoebe.

She looked right past me and kept walking. I knew she had seen me, and it stung. I felt invisible. Maybe she didn't want to see me again. Maybe I had kissed her for too long or came across as strange. I couldn't stop thinking about her. In my mind, she was my girlfriend. I told myself to just forget about her.

The weather remained hot and dry. We often worked long hours, sometimes until 11:00 p.m., just before the sun dipped below the horizon. Working in trenches was risky, but I trusted our backhoe operator to keep a close eye on the trench walls. He had already saved me once, and I was grateful.

That Saturday evening, after showering and getting ready for bed, Stu called my name. He said a girl was at the door for me, though he couldn't remember her name.

To my surprise, Phoebe stood there, smiling. My heart skipped a beat. I was so happy to see her.

I walked out to meet her, and we made our way to the riverbank for some privacy. I asked if she had seen me wave at her a couple of days earlier.

Looking down at the ground, she said softly, "Yes, I saw you. I was with my sister Florence and didn't want her to

121

know I knew you. She had asked me why I came home so late last Saturday and if I had a boyfriend."

"I thought you didn't want to see me again," I said.

"Yes, I wanted to see you again," she replied.

I hugged and kissed her. She hugged me back.

We sat together in the grass along the riverbank. It was still light out, even as the sun slowly sank below the horizon.

The sunset was dazzling, and we had front-row seats. The sky was clear, and the Northern Lights were getting ready to close the show. We lay on the grass, watching the lights, talking, and kissing. I had to work the next day and needed to get some sleep. The workdays were long and demanding.

Following the road along the river, I walked Phoebe to Turner's store and asked her where she live.

She pointed to the next street across the road and said, "A few houses down that street, that's where my dad's house is."

"Do you have two little brothers?" I asked.

She smiled, half-laughing, and said, "Yes, Melvin and Allan are my two youngest brothers."

"A couple of weeks ago, I met two boys, maybe four and six years old. They asked me for a dollar. The youngest one was hilarious," I said.

Phoebe laughed and said, "That sounds like my brothers. The youngest one is Allan."

"Can I see you again next Saturday?" I asked.

Phoebe smiled and said, "Yes, I'll come see you next Saturday at your house."

I made my way back to the house, following the road along the riverbank. It was the early morning hours. The Northern Lights were dancing across the sky, lighting my way home.

Everyone was up by 7:00 a.m., having breakfast and their coffee. Everyone except me. I don't drink coffee, so I had my usual morning glass of milk. At 8:00 a.m. sharp, the village truck pulled up at our door. The sun had been up for a couple of hours. The sky was clear, with no sign of rain clouds. The past few days, temperatures had been in the high 20 Celsius (high 70 Fahrenheit), and it looked like another hot day ahead.

Since our weekend off due to heavy rain, the weather had turned hot and dry. We had been working twelve-hour days, seven days a week. The work was physically demanding. Digging with a shovel and moving heavy pipes took a toll on our backs. But I didn't mind the hard work or getting dirty. Summer was ending in a few weeks. Fall was around the corner, bringing frost and snow. The cold weather would mark the end of the pipe-laying season. That meant we would be laid off. So now was the time to work as many hours as possible.

Our foreman assigned us to a new area, a large empty field across the street from LaPointe Hall and Bompas Hall. A three-story apartment building and six duplexes were scheduled to be built there starting in October. Stu was assigned to our crew. We had only a few weeks to complete the project before construction began.

We worked through mid-September, laying the sewer and water lines needed for the apartment building and the six duplexes. The infrastructure would be ready for connection once the buildings were completed.

By the third week of August, the leaves began to change color from green to yellow, red, and brown. Every day, I looked across the Mackenzie River and watched the forest change shades. Barges were still traveling up and down the river, some going as far as Inuvik. A few of them stopped in Fort Simpson to drop off or pick up cargo.

At that time, the highway along the Mackenzie River ended at Fort Simpson. Supplies were trucked in, then loaded onto barges to be delivered farther north. Every time I saw a barge, I couldn't help but imagine what it would be like to work on one. But I guess a job on a barge wasn't in the cards for me.

Destiny had brought me to Fort Simpson for a reason. I'm a firm believer in destiny, meaning the purpose or path that guides us through life. I couldn't wait for Saturday. Phoebe was on my mind constantly. Whether I was shoveling dirt, laying pipes, or eating lunch, I thought about her. Saturday couldn't come fast enough.

One morning at the water plant, we were told we had a new foreman. He introduced himself and shook everyone's hand. He was a tall, slim man in his late thirties with short, light brown hair and blue eyes. He was polite and friendly, the opposite of our previous foreman.

We were making good progress in the large field, but there were still many pipes to install. Thankfully, the weather was on our side. Even though it was hot and dry, it allowed us to work long hours without worrying about unsafe, muddy trenches.

All good things must end sooner or later, two days of intermittent rain fell over the Fort Simpson area and brought our labor to a standstill. Puddles formed at the bottom of the trenches, and some of the sidewalls had collapsed. The streets were muddy and slippery again.

The foreman gave us the weekend off and said, "The rain should stop on Saturday, and things should be dried up by Monday."

I was a little disappointed to have the weekend off, but at the same time, I welcomed the rest. I needed it. All five of us in the house didn't know what to do with ourselves. There was no television, only a small AM/FM radio.

Because of how the satellite orbit passed over Fort Simpson, there were only four hours of television each day. Only one channel—CBC Vancouver—was available from 4:00 p.m. to 8:00 p.m. During those hours, most people either watched TV at home, if they owned one, or visited neighbors who did.

I had grown up with two televisions in our home. My dad was a television repairman, so as far back as I could remember, I was always sitting in front of a TV, watching my favorite shows.

The rain stopped late Saturday afternoon. The sun pushed its rays through as the clouds began to break up. I couldn't wait any longer. I headed toward Turner's store, following the road along the riverbank, hoping to find Phoebe.

From a distance, I saw two girls walking toward me. As we got closer, I recognized Phoebe and noticed she was with her sister Florence. Phoebe smiled when she saw me. I walked up and gave her a hug and a kiss on the cheek.

Florence gave me a strange look, as if what I had done was inappropriate. In Quebec, it's customary to hug and kiss someone of the opposite sex on the cheek if you know them well or are good friends. Phoebe looked surprised. She clearly hadn't expected me to do that in front of her sister.

It was an awkward moment, but short-lived. I quickly offered my hand to Florence and introduced myself before she could say anything. She looked at me with a half-smile from the corner of her mouth and said nothing. She shook my hand quickly.

I took her silence and reaction as confusion. I figured she didn't understand what I was saying and thought I probably came across as a strange guy. I was likely the first French hippie, with long hair and odd mannerisms, she had ever met.

Phoebe, Florence, and I walked to my house. From there, Florence continued on to visit with cousins uptown.

Phoebe and I decided to walk to the Flats, along the shore of the Liard River. On the way, we stopped at the Anglican church.

Phoebe looked surprised. "Why are we stopping here?" she asked.

"I want to play the piano for you," I said.

I reached for the hidden key and unlocked the church door. She followed me in and sat beside me on the piano bench. Before I began playing, I gave her a kiss.

I played Bach Inventions as fast as I could, hoping to impress her. I believe I did. Then I played Beethoven's Moonlight Sonata, a slow and passionate piece. When I finished, she softly asked, "Play it again."

We left the church and continued our walk to the Flats. I reached for her hand, but I could feel she was uncomfortable. I asked, "Are you okay?"

"My cousins might see us holding hands," she said.

To make her feel more comfortable, I let go of her hand, and we continued walking side by side.

As we walked along the river, Phoebe shared stories from her childhood.

"Before we moved to Fort Simpson, we lived at the mouth of Trout River on the Mackenzie River. My family would travel by boat to Fort Simpson at the beginning of summer and stay in a tent at the Flats. We'd visit my uncles, aunts, and cousins. A lot of families would stay in tents during the summer. There was drum dancing and hand games," she said.

"At the end of summer, we'd travel back to Trout River by boat."

We continued along the Liard River shoreline. She pointed toward the junction of the Liard and Mackenzie Rivers.

"This is the Liard River, and this is the Mackenzie River," she explained. "That high riverbank at the junction is called Gros Cap. That's where my dad sets fish nets for Coney in the spring after breakup."

I didn't catch every word, but I understood enough. I had a pretty good idea of what she was telling me.

The water of the rivers was calm but fast, I could see a bald eagle flying overhead. The evening was peaceful; the sun was getting ready to set over the Mackenzie River. As we walked on the beach of the Liard River, Phoebe stopped and said, "Bear tracks", I'd never seen a bear track in the wild just in a zoo not far from where I used to live. "Bear is close to town", I said. "Sometimes, bears are walking down the streets looking for something to eat", said Phoebe. I was captivated and drawn hearing her telling me stories of her childhood and being raised in the bush as a child. We both had such an unalike upbringing.

We walked back to the house as the sun had just set. Although the sun was below the horizon, it was still light enough to read a book outside for at least another hour. I was getting used to the long daylight hours. We sat in the grass by the riverbank, held hands and kissed under the Northern Lights. In all the fifty plus years I lived in the north, the end of summer and fall of 1973 was the year I witnessed the most stunning Northern Lights. In the early hours of the morning before the crack of dawn, I walked Phoebe to her house. Much like two thieves wishing to stay incognito, we both tiptoed our way to the door of her house.

"You better go before my dad wakes up," said Phoebe.

"When will I see you again?" I asked.

"I'll be at your house next Saturday after you finish work," said Phoebe.

Slowly, the door was being pushed open, I froze in my tracks and didn't dare to move. My heart was pounding in my chest. I was expecting to see Phoebe's dad behind the door, mad at his daughter for coming home so late and mad at me for being her new boyfriend. Phoebe froze like a deer caught in the headlights. Florence emerged behind the door. Both Phoebe and I exhaled a sigh of relief. Florence had stayed up waiting for her sister to come home.

"Is mom and dad sleeping?" asked Phoebe.

"Yes, everybody is sleeping," said Florence.

"You better go," said Phoebe to me.

"Ok, I'm going," I said.

I was expecting a goodbye kiss before I bolted home, but I assume Phoebe was too bashful to kiss me in front of her sister.

As I walked home, the sun was midway behind the horizon in line with the junction of the Mackenzie River and Liard River. What a sight. The cool air became warmer air. It was going to be another beautiful day. I went to bed to catch a few hours of sleep before going to work. The new foreman had us starting work at 9:00 am on the weekend.

My roommates and I, along with one backhoe operator, worked on the weekends. Sandy was planning to return to Ontario at the end of the week. He was accepted at a college near his hometown. I made it known to everyone at the house that I was laying claim to Sandy's room. Stu was happy to have a room to himself, and Alain and Raymond were happy with their room. I had plans for the upcoming weekend.

The week lingered on as if hours were added to the days. Saturday wasn't coming fast enough. The week was spent working twelve hours a day in the trenches, with a short half-hour for lunch and dinner. We were getting close to completing the sewer and water lines at the large field. We had a few showers here and there but not enough for us to shut down work. Our foreman was a great guy, praising us for the good work we did and even bringing us sandwiches and pops for lunch.

Being nice to people you work with goes a long way. Everyone is productive and happy. It doesn't hurt to throw a joke here and there as well. Between Alain, Raymond and I, we had some fun times laughing and telling jokes or funny stories, as well as scary ones. We were the only ones laughing because the jokes were in French. Our co-workers and people who stood by the trenches watching us shovel dirt and sweat must have come to the same conclusion—that the three of us were losing it, maybe spending too much time in the trenches. When I'm tired, I have a tendency to act giddy and sometimes laugh hysterically, particularly when I was young. A good belly laugh is good for the body and the soul.

We at last completed the lines at the large field the day before payday, which was on a Friday. I needed a change of scenery. The trenches at the large field all looked deep and dusty. At the morning meeting at the water plant, our foreman said, "Alain, Raymond and Daniel, for the next few days, you'll work on the wooden sidewalk repair and paint them, starting on the main street."

The sidewalks were made of 10-by10 centimeters (four-by-four inches and 5-by-15 centimeters (2-by-6 inches). The sidewalks were in dire need of repair and painting. On my first day in Fort Simpson, after we were sent home because the backhoe operator had severed the phone lines, I took a walk on the main street and made my way to Turner's store. While I was walking on the wooden sidewalk, one end of a board wobbled and made me lose my balance. The front of my body was bent over trying to regain my posture. I took half a dozen steps running in that position, still on the wooden sidewalks, looking like an airplane getting ready to take off, until I made a crash landing on my belly.

While on my belly, I took a quick glance to see if anyone saw me falling.

"Are you ok?" asked an elderly Dene gentleman.

I said that I was ok. I didn't feel any pain, only my pride was hurt. That was my introduction to the Fort Simpson sidewalks. I witnessed a few people hit the dust a few times too. Those sidewalks were like a trap just waiting for someone to come along and then crash—you were down for the count or trying to take off like a plane on a wooden sidewalk as a runway.

At coffee time, the foreman took us to the bank to deposit our pay cheque and get some cash. We were lucky, there were a few people ahead of us. We did not have to wait very long before we deposited our pay cheques and got some cash enough to purchase groceries until next pay cheque. I gave the teller my signed cheque and bank book. She gave me two twenty-dollar bills and my bank book back. This was my third pay cheque; I could not believe how much I had in my bank account more than I had saved in six months in Quebec as a dish washer. Stu couldn't believe it either he had a big smile from ear to ear and said, "A few more pay cheques like that, we should have enough money for our trip to England. I was not so sure about England anymore. Phoebe and I had spent only three Saturdays together thus far; I was falling in love with her and could not imaging leaving Fort Simpson without her.

Chapter 5:
Return Trip to Ste-Adele
September 1973

Our foreman informed us that our work in the trenches was coming to an end in a couple of weeks. Alain, Raymond, and I were scheduled to finish work on September 28th. Stu had two more weeks of work to help Jim wrap up summer operations at Spring Hills. We were told that once we were laid off, we could no longer stay at the house and had to find our own accommodation. Winter was just around the corner, and there would be no more laying of sewer and water lines by the end of September.

We were also informed by our foreman that the construction of a three-story apartment complex and six duplexes would begin at the end of October. The buildings were to be constructed on the large field where we had laid sewer and water lines earlier in the summer. He added that a large construction company had been awarded the contract to build the apartment complex, and a Winnipeg-based construction company had secured the contract for the six duplexes.

Going to England with Stu was no longer in my future. Phoebe had registered to attend Thomas Simpson High School at the beginning of September. She attended classes for a few days before deciding to quit school. I was in love with Phoebe and asked her if she wanted to come live with me in Quebec. Since there was no more work available with the Village after September 28th, I decided it was time for me—hopefully with Phoebe—to leave Fort Simpson so we could be together and truly get to know each other. While in Fort Simpson, Phoebe and I only saw each other on Saturdays.

"I'll have to ask my parents if I could go to Quebec with you," said Phoebe.

I had not yet met Phoebe's parents and had asked her to introduce me. One week before I was scheduled to leave, Phoebe told her parents she had a boyfriend from Quebec named Daniel. She didn't tell them that I had asked her to come live with me. Phoebe told me, "You can ask my parents if you'd like me to live with you in Quebec."

The last Saturday before I was scheduled to leave, Phoebe asked me to come to her house on Sunday after work to meet her parents. I had a lump in my throat, and my legs suddenly felt weak, as if they could no longer support my weight. Phoebe had told me that her dad was older than her mom— he was forty-nine years old, and her mother thirty-four. She had four brothers, the two youngest I had already met, Melvin and Allan, as well as Michael and Gilbert. She also had two sisters: Florence, whom I had already met, and Jane, the youngest girl in the family.

Sunday after work, I took a shower and put on my best and cleanest jeans and shirt. I made my way to Phoebe's home. On the way there, I kept thinking about the best way to ask her parents for their consent to take their daughter to Quebec. I didn't think they would give it. Phoebe had just turned sixteen less than two months and had returned to Fort Simpson from Fort Smith two months prior, after being away for two years. My chances of their consent felt close to none.

I nervously knocked on the door. Phoebe's mom, Mary, answered and said, "Come in!" I felt at ease right away—she was welcoming and smiling. I shook her hand and introduced myself. Mary was my height, with long, straight black hair that reached halfway down her back. Phoebe bore a strong resemblance to her, especially her smile. Mary

133

asked me to sit at the kitchen table. She called in Slavey for her husband Gabriel, known to everyone as Gabe. He was lying in bed in the bedroom next to the kitchen. It seemed to take a while before he came out, which gave me the impression that he wasn't in any rush to meet me.

Gabe walked into the kitchen as if he had just woken from a nap. He had salt-and-pepper hair and a toothbrush mustache like Charlie Chaplin. He was a few inches shorter than Mary, with a slim but muscular build. His hands were large and strong for a man his size. I could tell he was a hardworking man. I stood up, shook his hand, and introduced myself. I sat at one end of the table while he sat at the other. Gabe lit a cigarette, poured himself a cup of tea, and waited for me to talk. Mary offered me a cup of tea and a piece of freshly baked Bannock. It was the first time I had ever tasted Bannock; it was delicious.

Phoebe, Michael & Florence from right to left with their mother Mary Cazon in the background. Photo taken at Spence Creek along the Mackenzie River in 1962.

134

Melvin and Allan walked into the house, both looking at me with surprise. Melvin said, "That's the guy who gave us a dollar." I looked at them both and acknowledged them. Mary asked them to step outside and play while their dad and I talked. Phoebe and Florence were in their room, and I didn't see Phoebe until after I had finished speaking with her dad.

Instead of beating around the bush, I asked Gabe if his daughter Phoebe could come with me to Quebec for a couple of months. I caught Gabe off guard, judging by his facial expression, he hadn't anticipated that question. Although my English wasn't the greatest, he understood me.

"I spent eight years at the Convent in Fort Providence. The nuns taught me how to speak and write in English, count, and even some French," said Gabe.

He didn't answer right away. He seemed to need some time to digest the question and think it over. I told Gabe that I would take care of his daughter and that if she didn't like it in Quebec, I would bring her back to Fort Simpson.

"I will think about it," said Gabe.

Phoebe came out of the room, clearly glad that her dad and I had spoken. Mary seemed to be in favor of her daughter going to Quebec with me. Michael, Phoebe's brother, walked into the house. He was thirteen at the time and the oldest boy in the family after Phoebe and Florence. He was tall for his age and looked timid but at the same time jovial. He had jet black, thick hair down to his shoulders and covering his ears. He looked like someone who could easily pull a prank on you. Gilbert and Jane weren't at the house.

After I had finished talking to Gabe and Mary, I said good night and thanked them for listening and talking with me.

135

Phoebe and I went for a walk along the river to talk about the discussion I had with her parents. I felt confident that Mary was in favor of her daughter coming with me to Quebec. On the other hand, I didn't know what to make of Gabe's response.

"My mother will talk with my dad about it. I'll give them a couple of days and then ask them," said Phoebe.

I had only four days of work left. Friday would be the day we left Fort Simpson. I felt confident that Phoebe would be coming to Quebec with me, so I bought two one-way tickets from the local travel agent from Fort Simpson to Yellowknife. From there, we would spend the night and then board a flight to Edmonton the next morning and hopefully catch the train the same day to Montreal.

Two days later, Phoebe came one evening to visit me at the house.

"Daniel, Phoebe is here to see you," said Stu.

I came out of my room as if Stu had told me the house was on fire. In the few steps it took from my room to the door, my mind kept racing, she's coming with me or she's not coming with me. Phoebe stood at the door with a smile from ear to ear. Before she even said anything, I was ecstatic.

"My parents said yes. I can go with you to Quebec," said Phoebe.

We hugged and kissed each other.

"My mom spoke with my dad and convinced him that I should go with you to Quebec. My dad would like me back for Christmas," said Phoebe.

"No problem. We'll come back for Christmas," I replied. "I bought our tickets to Yellowknife. We're leaving Friday afternoon for the airport to catch our flight."

"Before we leave, I'd like to spend some time at my house with my little brothers. They don't know that I'm leaving," said Phoebe.

"I'm taking the day off Friday. I'll withdraw my money from the bank and go to the Village for my last paycheck. I'll come to your house two hours before we leave for the airport," I said.

Friday morning, I said my goodbyes to Stu before he left for work.

"I guess we're not going to England then," said Stu.

"No. Phoebe and I will be spending two and a half months in Ste Adele and then coming back to Fort Simpson for Christmas."

"After I'm done work in a couple of weeks, I'll visit my parents for a week or so and then return to Ste Adele. Can you ask your mom if I can stay at her place until I find one of my own?" said Stu.

"That should be no problem. I'll ask her," I replied.

We shook hands and said, "See you back in Ste Adele."

I cashed my last pay cheque and withdrew the money I had earned in the past nine weeks. My wallet was loaded with fifty-, twenty- and ten-dollar bills. I could barely fold my wallet into one piece due to the thickness of the bills. I never had this kind of money in my life. I felt like I was a millionaire, my wallet was loaded with cash. I was happy that the bank had not run out of cash at the time of my withdrawal.

I made my way to Phoebe's house, my pack on my shoulders, looking like a hitchhiker, but this time I wouldn't be hitchhiking. I would be travelling in comfort with my girlfriend by plane and train. I was looking forward to travelling with Phoebe and getting to know her. I knocked at the door. Florence answered and asked me to come in. Phoebe's two youngest brothers, Melvin and Allan, asked me, "Are you my sister's boyfriend?" I replied, "Yes, I am." Both Melvin and Allan were sad to see their big sister leave again.

"We'll be back home for Christmas and will have gifts for you both," said Phoebe.

"I have a gift for both of you," I said. I reached in my wallet and gave each brother a ten-dollar bill. Both looked at Phoebe and me and said, "Thank you," while jumping up and down.

I reassured Mary that I would take care of her daughter and bringing her back for Christmas. Gabe was away at work. I asked Mary to thank Gabe for letting his daughter come with me to Quebec.

"I will write you letters when I'm in Quebec," said Phoebe.

I gave Mary a piece of paper with my mother's phone number, where we would be staying. Phoebe's parents did not have a phone at their house. I told Mary she could use the pay phone at the hotel and call collect at the number I gave her.

The taxi was beeping his horn outside. It was time to go to the airport. Phoebe hugged her sister Florence, her two little brothers, and her mom. The taxi beeped his horn once more. Phoebe's mom started to cry and said Phoebe should stay at home. Phoebe looked at me and said, "Let's go." We hopped into the taxi and asked the driver to take us to the airport. It was getting late. I was worried we might miss our flight. We made our flight in the nick of time.

I had not told my mother about my new girlfriend, Phoebe. As a matter of fact, she was my first girlfriend. I wanted to surprise my mother. She did not know that I was on my way back to Ste Adele. The last time I called her, I told her I would be working until at least the end of October. My mother was still under the impression that Stu and I would be heading to England once our jobs were done in Fort Simpson.

We took a taxi to the Yellowknife Inn in downtown. The hotel was very busy. I did not have a reservation for a room. I waited in line to speak with the desk clerk to book a room for the night. In my state of eagerness, I left my wallet on the front desk to talk to Phoebe who was at the back of the line. There were several people near the front desk. Once I realized that I had left my wallet there, I quickly returned to find it still laying on the counter. I was amazed that no one took it. That would have been disastrous. All the money I had was in that wallet. I did not have a credit card or debit card, which did not exist yet. I had a good scare, and from then on, I was more careful.

The following morning, we caught a flight to Edmonton. I purchased the airplane tickets at the airport. Back then, you were able to buy airplane tickets at the airport in cash. We landed at the municipal airport in Edmonton. There was no international airport in Edmonton yet. From my previous train trip to Vancouver, I remembered that the CN train station was at the CN Tower building in downtown Edmonton.

We took a cab to the train station. I did not know the train schedules as I didn't have access to that information. I walked to the ticket desk and asked the agent, "When is the next train to Montreal?"

The agent replied, "The train to Montreal will be leaving in one hour."

I could not believe my luck.

I asked the agent, "Two coach tickets to Montreal, please."

If I recall correctly, a one-way ticket from Edmonton to Montreal was thirty-nine dollars.

We settled in our seats by turning around the seat in front of us before someone else could use it, so we could stretch our legs while sleeping. I purchased a grey-colored blanket from the train conductor to keep us warm. This was Phoebe's first trip on a train. Sleeping on a bench for three nights and being rocked from side to side for the entire trip is not the best way to get restful sleep. This was a new experience for Phoebe.

During the train trip, I asked myself how Phoebe would handle being around people who did not speak English but only French. Most of my friends and family from both sides did not speak English. Communication would be a challenge. She would feel at times left out of conversations, just as I did when I traveled out west and to Fort Simpson. I promised myself that I would do my best to translate conversations and any questions she might have.

My ability to understand and speak English was improving slowly but surely, enough that I could carry a basic conversation with Phoebe. My mother had been bilingual since the age of five and spoke English significantly better than I did. I could rely on her to help me communicate with Phoebe. The contrast between Dene culture and French culture might also be a challenge for Phoebe. I too had experienced this while working with people in Fort Simpson and spending time with Phoebe's family. The French culture and English culture, which is what Phoebe had been exposed to while attending school in Fort Simpson and Fort Smith, are both distinct.

For the next three days, we sat and slept in our uncomfortable seats and communicated with each other, learning more about one another. We ate our meals at the restaurant on the train and purchased some food at the stops throughout our journey. We both felt more comfortable with each other and with being our true selves. We had just met on August 11th, seven weeks ago, and had only spent time together every Saturday during that time. We had actually only been together for seven full days. There was still so much to learn about each other.

At last, we arrived at the Montreal CN train station. We made our way to the Greyhound bus terminal via the underground subway. It was late evening. I asked the ticket agent, "When is the next bus to Ste Adele?"

"The last bus for today to Ste Adele will be leaving in twenty minutes," said the ticket agent.

We made the bus just in time. We boarded with our suitcase and backpack, feeling like we were in a race against time. The ride to Ste Adele took one hour. I asked the bus driver to drop us off near the streetlights by my mother's house. We only had to walk about 60 meters (200 feet). It was a few minutes past midnight. Knowing my mother, I was sure she would still be up, most likely reading a book.

We entered the house via the kitchen door on the first floor. I knew where the key was hidden. I signaled to Phoebe to be quiet by holding my right index finger to my lips. We made our way to the bottom of the stairs, where we left our suitcase and backpack. Quietly, we started up the stairs, one step at a time, as if we were tiptoeing.

Halfway up, a step let out a loud squeaky sound, and we both stopped in our tracks.

"Who's there?" said my mother with a concerned tone in her voice.

My mother wasn't expecting me until the end of October. She knew I had a girlfriend but wasn't expecting me to show up in Quebec with her. We continued up the stairs.

"Who's there? I'm calling the police," she said with urgency in her voice.

We carried on until we reached the entrance of her bedroom. My mother was sitting up at the head of the bed with a book in her hands. The only light in the room was from a lamp on her night table next to the bed. I half-expected her to throw the book at me, followed by the lamp or anything else she could get her hands on. My mother was a fighter and wouldn't have gone down without a fight.

I slowly walked to her side of the bed.

"Daniel! You scared me to death. I thought I was going to be robbed," she said.

I gave her a hug and a kiss. She was very happy to see me. For a moment, I had forgotten that Phoebe was standing behind me. She stood at the bedroom entrance, likely wondering why I had just given my mother a heart attack.

I introduced Phoebe, and my mother stood up, walked over, gave her a big hug, and welcomed her into the house. A few seconds later, my sister Johanne appeared behind us and gave each of us a big hug.

We were both exhausted and hadn't had proper sleep in three days. Phoebe wanted to take a shower and go to bed. My mother asked my sister to move into my old bedroom so we could stay in her room, which had a queen-size bed.

Before arriving in Ste Adele, I had wondered if my mother would approve of me having my girlfriend in her house. Phoebe was sixteen, and I was one month shy of turning eighteen. I was relieved to hear that my mother didn't have a problem with it.

My mother and I stayed up for a few hours talking about my trip out west and Fort Simpson.

"When you told me you had a girlfriend, I knew she would be coming back with you to Quebec," she said.

I told her that my plans to travel to England with Stu and then throughout Europe, India, and Nepal were no longer happening. I could tell by her facial expression that she was happy to hear that I wasn't going to India or Nepal.

"I made a promise to Phoebe's parents that she'll be back in Fort Simpson for Christmas," I said.

"Will you be looking for a job?" asked my mother.

"No, I've got one thousand dollars, which is enough to take care of myself and Phoebe and get us back to Fort Simpson, where I'll look for a job. Two construction companies will be starting a large apartment complex and six duplexes at the end of October," I replied.

"I'll need you to help Adrian with the pickups and deliveries of sofas and chairs. Some of the sofas are too heavy for Jean-Marie," she said.

"I'll be available anytime you need me, just let me know ahead of time," I said.

Adrian was an employee at my mother's business. He picked up and delivered the sofas and chairs that my mother and her team reupholstered. He also removed the old material and helped reupholster furniture under her mentorship. Adrian was in his early thirties, with short, combed-back light brown hair. He was a tall man, built to move heavy furniture. Aside from working for my mother, he was also a part-time police officer and a bouncer.

During my time in Quebec, I made numerous sofa and chair pickups and deliveries with Adrian and got to know him well. Adrian was an honest and hard-working man who didn't seem to realize how strong he was. One time, while picking up two large sofa beds from a client, Adrian tried to push me into a snowbank. At the last second, I quickly moved out of the way and pushed him instead. He lost his balance and landed on his stomach in the wet snow. He wasn't too happy. He got up, grabbed me in a headlock, and lifted me off the ground as if I were a ragdoll. Adrian was at least 15 centimeters (6 inches) taller than me. He held me in that headlock for what seemed like an eternity. There I was, unwillingly caught in a wrestling match with someone much taller and at least fifty pounds heavier. I thought he was going to break my neck. Eventually, he let me go and tossed me into the snow. We were both soaked, but we carried on as if nothing had happened and walked to the client's home to pick up the two heavy sofa beds.

The walkway from the house to the driveway was at least 100 meters (300 hundred feet) long. We had to take a couple of breaks carrying the sofa beds to my mother's van. The house was nestled in a large clump of trees. The owners didn't speak French, only English. Judging by their accents, I could tell they were Jewish. The husband mentioned that the house was their chalet, a retreat from the city of Montreal where they lived. The house was huge and beautifully decorated with very pricey furniture. I could only imagine what their home in the city must look like if this was their getaway place.

Most of my mother's clients were Anglophones or Jewish and wealthy. Adrian showed the couple some material samples for the upholstery. His English was good enough for him to communicate effectively. After they selected the fabric, he gave them an estimated cost for upholstering both sofa beds and a date for completion. Most clients were courteous and easy to deal with, but a few were rude and eager to remind you that they were wealthy and you were beneath them.

Some of my mother's clients were well-known celebrities in Quebec—singers, songwriters, film and TV actors, comedians, and even the Bronfman family, former owners of Seagram Company Ltd. One of the most surprising names among her clients was Frank Cotroni, the head of the Cotroni crime family.

Jean-Marie is like family to us. He's not related by blood, but he's lived with us since I was ten years old. He stands

145

about 149 centimeters (4 feet 11 inches) tall and weighs around 41 kilos (90 pounds). He has light brown, balding hair combed back. His nickname was "Biscuit," which translates to "Cookies" in English. Though he was small, Jean-Marie was incredibly strong for his size. He worked for my mother and helped Adrian with furniture pickups and deliveries, as well as removing the old materials from sofas and chairs.

Jean-Marie loved to have fun and clown around. If he had an audience, he'd crack jokes and act silly. One time, without thinking, he grabbed a hard rubber hammer—the kind used to drive in staples securely—and hit himself hard on the forehead. His little legs nearly buckled, and he almost knocked himself out. Even though he was in pain, he still managed to laugh at himself.

A couple of weeks later, Stu arrived at my mother's house. I had asked my mother if Stu could stay with us for a while until he found a place to live, and she was okay with it. Phoebe and I decided to move to a small motel called "Moulin Rouge" across the street from my mother's house. Johanne got her bedroom back, and Stu slept in my old room. My mother didn't want us to move out, but I told her we would move back after Stu found a place. She insisted that Phoebe and I have dinner at the house every day.

Phoebe and I wanted some space to ourselves. The motel was small, with only a few rooms, and we rented the one room with a kitchenette. The price was $35.00 per week or $5.00 per night. I wouldn't have been able to afford it if I had still been working as a dishwasher. My weekly salary after taxes would have just covered the rent, leaving no money for food. I had no intention of working in Ste-Adele. The only jobs available were in hotels and restaurants—as a busboy or dishwasher. I would have had to cut my hair and shave my beard for a busboy position, which paid the same hourly rate as dishwashing but with tips.

I had saved $1,000 after paying for our trip from Fort Simpson to Ste-Adele, and I felt like a millionaire. I deposited more than enough money in my bank account to cover our return trip to Fort Simpson. We took the bus to St-Jerome, where I was born, a few times to shop for clothes for Phoebe and me and eat at restaurants. I didn't have my driver's license, so I couldn't drive my mother's car.

I remember going to see "The Exorcist" at the movie theater in Ste-Adele. The movie was in English, so I didn't need to translate for Phoebe. Poor Phoebe was somewhat traumatized by the film. I knew she liked horror movies, but The Exorcist was in a league of its own. After the movie, we made our way back to the motel. It was very late. Once we lay in bed, I started imitating the voice of Regan, Linda Blair's character. I must say, I did a pretty good job and nearly got a slap across the face from Phoebe. She told me to stop—and I did.

Stu found himself a job and a small apartment. He worked in the kitchen at "Le Bistro d'la Butte" in Val-David, about 13 kilometers (8 miles) north of Ste-Adele. The Bistro was owned by the famous jazz upright bass player Charlie Biddle. I had the pleasure of listening to Charlie and Nelson Symonds, a well-known jazz guitar player, perform together as a duo at the Bistro.

Once Stu moved his things out of my old room, Phoebe and I moved back into my mother's house. We spent most of our time together, apart from when I assisted Adrian with deliveries and pickups of sofas and chairs. In a short time, we got to know each other very well. I could see that Phoebe was beginning to miss home, especially her two younger brothers, Melvin and Allan. She wrote a few letters to her parents and received some in return, asking when she would be coming back to Fort Simpson.

Weeks turned into months, and December was just around the corner. It was time to plan our return trip to Fort Simpson.

Chapter 6:
Return Trip to Fort Simpson
December 1973

My good friend Pierre Chouinard was not working, so I asked him if he'd be interested in coming with us to Fort Simpson. I had known Pierre for about five years. He was the kind of guy who would give you the shirt off his back. Pierre stood around 167 centimeters (5 feet 6 inches) tall, built with a small frame. His thinning dark brown hair hung straight down to his shoulders, and his piercing dark brown eyes matched the color of his hair. His face was round, and a thin mustache along with a goatee accentuated his jawline.

Pierre and I met in high school while attending grade 10. On occasion, we would skip school by sneaking out of the schoolyard and following a well-worn trail up the mountain behind the school that led to Ste-Adele en Haut. From there, we'd walk down to Pierre's parents' house, where we'd listen to Alice Cooper's album *Killer*. We had the house to ourselves since his parents were away at work. We would lie on the floor of the living room between the speakers, playing the album at full blast after smoking some hashish or weed.

Pierre was very interested in traveling to Fort Simpson with us, but he didn't have any money for the train and plane tickets. Hitchhiking was out of the question—it was wintertime, and I didn't want Phoebe hitchhiking. Pierre was an old hand at hitchhiking. He and a friend once left Ste-Adele without telling anyone, not even their parents, and ended up in Boston, USA. They crossed the US border by jumping a train, and back then, Canadian citizens didn't need a passport to enter the States. Pierre had left with only ten dollars in his pocket and managed to get a job at the historic Suffolk Downs racetrack in Boston, cleaning horse stables.

Eventually, he was caught working without a permit and was deported back to Canada. He returned home after eight months away—my guess is he had grown tired of shoveling horse manure.

I figured Pierre would be an experienced travel companion in case we couldn't find work in Fort Simpson and needed to head somewhere else. As promised to Phoebe's parents, my plan was to take her to Fort Simpson and make sure she got home safe and sound. I offered to pay for Pierre's tickets and lend him some money for travel expenses. Pierre was a heavy smoker, going through about two packs of cigarettes a day. I had saved enough money to cover the cost of our return to Fort Simpson and had enough left over to buy Pierre's tickets.

In the first week of December, Phoebe and I packed up our gear into our suitcases and backpack. We had purchased some clothes and gifts for Phoebe's family and needed an extra suitcase. My mother understood that I had to return to Fort Simpson to keep my promise, though she still wished I would stay in Quebec and work for her. She even mentioned to both Phoebe and me that she could teach Phoebe how to sew cushions for sofas and chairs.

I also understood that in Fort Simpson, Phoebe and I wouldn't be able to stay together unless I rented a house or an apartment, which would have been far more expensive than what I could earn working as a laborer. Pierre packed up his gear in the same backpack he had used to travel to Boston.

Phoebe and I said our goodbyes to my mother and sister. My mother had tears in her eyes—I was leaving again, and no one knew when I'd be back. Years later, she would tell me she had always believed I'd eventually come back home and settle down in Quebec.

Pierre, Phoebe, and I met at the bus terminal in Ste-Adele and boarded a bus to Montreal. From there, we made our way to the train station via the subway. This time, I had made reservations for three tickets to Edmonton. We had a two-hour wait before boarding the train. This was my third trip by train, so I knew my way around and what to anticipate.

I had mixed emotions about returning to Fort Simpson. On one hand, I was keeping my promise to ensure Phoebe would be back with her family before Christmas. On the other hand, I felt a bit apprehensive about finding a job and a place to stay in Fort Simpson. I kept asking myself, "Will I find work and a place to live?" The first time I went to Fort Simpson, I had both a job and housing waiting for me. Now it was winter—how would I handle the cold temperatures working outside? Would Phoebe be able to stay with me? Her parents' house was already small, with nine people living there. I knew there'd be no room for Pierre or me to stay. These thoughts and questions stayed with me the entire trip, though I didn't share them with Phoebe or Pierre. I didn't want to worry them.

Three days later, we arrived at the train station in Edmonton, tired from a lack of restful sleep. We headed inside the terminal and called for a taxi. I knew there was a flight to Fort Simpson departing in a couple of hours. It was bitterly cold and windy in Edmonton. The taxi took us to the municipal airport, and I purchased our plane tickets at the counter using cash. We landed in Fort Simpson as the sun was setting. Back then, there was a direct flight from Edmonton to Fort Simpson.

As soon as I stepped off the plane, the northern wind and minus 30 Celsius (minus 22 Fahrenheit) temperatures chilled me to the bone. We took a cab and dropped Phoebe off at her parents' house. Everyone was home and happy to see her. Her two youngest brothers jumped up and down, eager to see what their big sister had brought back. I briefly spoke with Gabe and Mary. They both smiled and shook my hand. They seemed happy I kept my promise, and I had faith I'd earned their trust.

Pierre and I checked into the Fort Simpson Hotel. I requested a room with two double beds for two nights and gave the front desk clerk two twenty-dollar bills. My change was one five-dollar bill. After the payment, I had two twenties and one five left in my wallet.

Pierre had already spent most of his money on cigarettes. He smoked nearly two packs a day. He kept insisting he could quit if he had to—but he couldn't go more than a couple of hours without lighting one. He'd become miserable and constantly talk about how badly he needed a smoke. I wasn't a smoker and never have been. In my opinion, nicotine addiction is as strong as heroin or cocaine addiction. Pierre understood some English and could speak a few words, but while he was in Boston with his friend, he hadn't learned much. His friend was bilingual and did most of the talking.

Phoebe came to the hotel later that evening and spent the night. She and I went for a walk to where the three-story apartment building was being built—on the same large field where we had once laid the water and sewer lines. It was late, and no one was on site. The frame of the first floor was completed, and work on the second floor had started. It was bitterly cold and windy.

"I'll come look for a job tomorrow morning," I said.

"My dad told me the company building the apartments is hiring local laborers," said Phoebe.

That lifted my spirits. There was clearly a lot of work left to do, so I felt certain Pierre and I could both get hired.

The next morning, after breakfast at the hotel, Pierre and I went to the construction site. We walked into a small building that looked like where the crew hung out. Inside was one man—the foreman. His white hard hat had a large sticker that said "Foreman." He looked to be in his mid-to-late thirties, with a brown mustache and brown eyes. He was tall, well over 182 centimeters (6 feet), with broad shoulders and a look that said, *don't mess with me.*

I walked up and asked, "Are you the foreman?"

He looked at me like I had a screw loose. "What, you can't read?" he asked, pointing to his hard hat.

I smiled. "I just wanted to make sure I was talking to the right person."

"Yes, I'm the right person," he replied.

"My friend and I just arrived in town yesterday. We're looking for work," I said.

"Are you French?"

"Yes, we're French from Quebec," I answered.

"I could tell by your accent. My wife is from Quebec. What are you guys doing in Fort Simpson? You're a long way from home."

"I worked here this past summer laying sewer and water lines—right where your apartment project is going up."

"Well, right now, we don't have any jobs available. Come check back in about a week—we might have something then."

Pierre and I shook his hand.

"What's with him—can't he talk?" the foreman asked.

"His name is Pierre. He doesn't speak English—just a few words," I explained.

I was disappointed. I had hoped the foreman would hire us on the spot so we could start working that day. A week felt like a long time to wait. We only had one more night at the hotel, and after that, we'd have to find somewhere else to stay.

Next to the apartment building, construction on six duplexes had just started a few days ago. Piles of construction materials were stacked on the ground where the duplexes were being built. We saw workers organizing the materials. I walked up to one of them and asked, "Can I speak with the foreman?"

The worker, who didn't seem to be a local, looked up and said, "The foreman is in the trailer over there."

Pierre and I walked to the trailer and knocked on the door. The foreman answered and asked, "What do you want?"

He was of average height and build, with thinning hair on top. He looked to be in his forties and was clearly not in a good mood.

"Hi, my friend and I are looking for a job," I said.

"I don't have any jobs available," he snapped, slamming the door in our faces.

It was bitterly cold and windy, making it feel even colder. Pierre and I walked back to the hotel with our tails between our legs.

"Let's warm up at the hotel and then check the campground. There are small buildings there with woodstoves. Maybe we can stay in one of them," I said.

On one of my days off this past summer, I'd walked to the campground and met a couple staying inside one of those buildings. They had a fire going in the woodstove. It was drizzling and cool outside. The couple appeared to be in their late forties or early fifties. Judging by their appearance, they must have lived hard lives. They were friendly and could have easily been my parents. They told me they had hitchhiked to Fort Simpson, though I wasn't sure if they were just passing through or looking for work. I never saw them again, so they must've left the village before fall set in.

Pierre and I headed toward the campground, following the road along the river. As we passed the house where I had stayed a few months ago, I walked up and knocked at the door. No one answered. There were no tracks leading in or out of the house, so it seemed vacant. I'd been hoping someone would be there.

We continued walking until we reached the campground. The buildings were open, but there were no woodstoves inside. My heart sank. We couldn't stay there without heat— we would freeze to death.

We made our way back toward the hotel, following the same road, until I spotted the small Anglican church where I used to play the piano. We walked to the minister's house and knocked on the door. No answer.

"Looks like no one's home," said Pierre.

I knew the minister—he was friendly. I figured he might have let us stay in the church. I knocked again and waited, but still no answer.

"Let's check the church," I said.

We walked the short distance to the church. The back door was unlocked, so we went in. There was no heat inside.

"It's too cold to stay here," I said.

"We should check if we can get inside the house," said Pierre.

I wasn't comfortable with the idea of breaking in, but Pierre had done this before during his trip to Boston when he had no place to stay. He found an unlocked window facing the river, crawled through it, and opened the main door from the inside.

I stepped inside and immediately felt the warmth from the furnace. Every window had thick dark blankets blocking the natural light. We walked through the house from top to bottom. It seemed no one had lived there for a while.

Pierre and I looked at each other and smiled.

"I guess we're moving here tomorrow," said Pierre.

We checked for any food, but the pantry and fridge were completely empty—not even a single can of sardines. In the basement, we found dozens of large jars of dill pickles stacked neatly on shelves.

"Someone must be checking on the house while the minister's out of town," I said.

"We don't have a choice. Starting tomorrow, we don't have a place to stay," said Pierre.

I felt stressed. Breaking into someone's house wasn't my style, but we didn't have any other option. I wasn't about to ask Phoebe's parents if Pierre and I could stay with them—I didn't want to look like I couldn't take care of myself. The little money I had left needed to last until we found work.

The sun had already set, and it was getting dark. I stepped outside while Pierre locked the front door and crawled out the same window he came through. We returned to the hotel and had dinner—an order of fries and a hamburger split between the two of us. Phoebe stayed with her family that night.

It was the first night we'd been apart since we left Fort Simpson at the end of September. I told myself, "Better get used to being alone."

The following morning, we dragged our feet and checked out of the room as late as possible, then had lunch at the hotel. Pierre drank a few cups of coffee after we ate. Phoebe stopped by and sat with us in the restaurant.

I told her, "We found a way into the Anglican minister's house yesterday. I think the minister must be out of town. There's heat in the house and lots of dill pickle jars. Come see me at the house later, just knock at the door."

"I'll come see you after dinner," said Phoebe.

We waited for the sun to go down before moving into the house. Before heading there, we passed by the apartment construction site to check again about jobs. The foreman was outside talking to a worker. He looked over his shoulder and said, "You guys, I told you to check in a week. I don't have any jobs right now."

"We'll check again in a few days, thanks," I replied.

As the sun was setting, we made our way toward the house. The temperature was brutally cold in the high minus 30 Celsius (minus 31 Fahrenheit). With the wind blowing from across the river, the wind chill made it feel like minus 50 Celsius (minus 58 Fahrenheit). Pierre crawled through the window and opened the main door. Inside, the house was warm and cozy.

I turned on the lights in the kitchen and living room, then stepped outside to check if any light could be seen from outside. There were no signs of it—everything was covered well.

A couple hours later, Phoebe knocked at the door. She brought a large piece of freshly made Bannock and a small stick of butter. Pierre had never tasted Bannock before. He devoured half of it in no time.

"That tasted good, the only thing missing was peanut butter," said Pierre, who was a big fan.

Phoebe spent the night with me at the house. There were four bedrooms to choose from. Early the next morning, while it was still dark, she made her way home and returned in the evening to stay the night again. I was grateful that we had a warm place to stay, even though I felt guilty for breaking in.

We stayed inside during daylight hours and only went out at night when we needed to. We didn't want to get caught— if we were, we'd probably end up in a holding cell at the RCMP Station. At least it would have heat and three meals a day.

We ate a few jars of dill pickles until we couldn't stomach any more. I was down to my last ten-dollar bill. Pierre was starting to lose it. He'd been out of cigarettes for a few days, and that was all he could talk about—how badly he wanted one. I couldn't take it anymore.

"Let's go to the Hudson's Bay Store and buy a pack of cigarettes, a jar of peanut butter, and a loaf of bread," I said.

Pierre's eyes lit up. "Let's go," he said quickly.

I bought a pack of Du Maurier cigarettes and handed it to Pierre. He tore it open and lit one up right there in the store. Back then, you could still smoke indoors. I could tell how much he was enjoying it by the way he puffed.

"You buy the bread, and I'll steal a jar of peanut butter," Pierre said. "The bread is cheaper, and stealing the peanut butter will be easier than trying to sneak out a loaf."

We were both starving and tired of dill pickles. I bought a loaf of white bread and walked out of the store to wait for Pierre. He came out still puffing the last of his cigarette and smiled at me.

We walked back to the house like thieves in the dark. Inside, we each had a few slices of bread slathered with a thick layer of peanut butter.

"That tasted so good," I said. "The only thing missing was a cold glass of milk to wash it down."

I drank a few glasses of tap water so I wouldn't choke on the peanut butter.

Later, Phoebe returned to the house with another large piece of Bannock. Her mother had baked a fresh batch, since the one from the day before had disappeared so quickly. We split it in half and covered it in peanut butter, filling our stomachs. At that point, we had already eaten more than half the jar.

We were counting the days until we could return to the construction site to ask for a job. I had only one five-dollar bill and a few coins in my wallet, just enough to purchase another loaf of bread and a pack of cigarettes. Pierre was smoking the cigarettes like there was no tomorrow.

A couple days later, we heard someone opening the main door with a key. Pierre and I froze in our tracks, nowhere to run. I stood by the door, expecting to be arrested by the RCMP. As the door opened, I saw a frail older man whom I recognized as the local postmaster. We both looked at each other, stunned. For a moment, it looked like he was about to step back out of the house. Judging by his facial expression, I could tell he was scared.

I identified myself. He looked at me and recognized me.

"Hi, I worked for the village this past summer and used to play the piano at the church," I said.

"Yes, I remember you. How did you guys get into the house?" he asked.

Pierre, who had been half hiding in the living room, stepped beside me.

"This is my friend Pierre. We got in through the front window, it wasn't locked," I said.

The old man looked Pierre up and down. "I've never seen this guy before."

"This is his first time in Fort Simpson. We traveled together from Quebec to look for a job," I explained. "We didn't have a place to stay. The foreman at the Mackenzie Manor construction site said he might have a job for us in a few days."

"I'm looking after the house while the Anglican minister is away in Ontario. He should be back in a couple weeks. I'll give him a call this evening to let him know that you are staying in the house. Come and see me at the post office tomorrow morning," said the old man. "I don't want you guys to have parties in the house or other people."

I replied, "No, we won't. Thanks."

"If there's a problem with the furnace, let me know right away," he added.

"I will. Thanks," I said.

The old man left without locking the door.

Pierre hadn't understood the conversation and asked, "What did the old man say? Is he calling the police?"

I looked at him somberly and said, "Yeah, he's calling the police to arrest us. They should be here soon."

Pierre was nearly in a panic. "We should get our stuff and leave before the police arrive."

I looked away, trying not to laugh, but couldn't hold it any longer. I burst out laughing. Pierre realized I was messing with him. I could see the relief on his face.

"The old man's not calling the police," I said. "He's calling the Anglican Minister to let him know we're staying in the house. He knows me, I met him last summer. He works at the post office. I told him we're waiting for jobs at the construction site. He asked me to come by tomorrow morning."

"Do we have to move out of the house?" asked Pierre.

"We'll find out tomorrow morning," I said.

The following morning, I walked to the post office to meet the old man.

"I spoke with the Minister yesterday evening. He said he's fine with you guys staying at the house as long as you don't make a mess or have parties. He's coming back in two weeks with his family and would like you out of the house by then. He also said there are dill pickle jars in the basement—you can help yourself if you want," said the old man.

I was so relieved.

"Take the key. Once you're done with the house, give it back to me," he said.

We didn't have to hide anymore, but we needed to find a job before the Minister returned.

We ran out of bread, peanut butter, and cigarettes. We went back to the Hudson Bay store and repeated our previous actions—bought a loaf of white bread and a pack of cigarettes and stole a jar of peanut butter. Pierre even had the audacity to ask the manager if they had larger peanut butter jars since the ones they sold were medium-sized.

"Sorry, those are the only sizes we have," said the manager.

We ate the entire loaf of bread and jar of peanut butter in just two meals. By then, Pierre had made a serious dent in his pack of cigarettes. I kept telling him to ration them, but it was pointless. He kept puffing like each one was his last.

Phoebe had to take care of her two little brothers and didn't come to the house for a couple of days. I had only a few coins left—not enough for a pack of cigarettes or a loaf of bread. We hadn't eaten in two days.

We were both starving and decided to walk back to the construction site to see if the foreman had any good news. It was another cold, windy day. We followed the road along the river, walking against the ice-cold wind. I couldn't stop thinking about the situation we had gotten ourselves into. We were in dire straits—no money, no food apart from dill pickles, and we'd be homeless in a few days. It wasn't exactly the kind of situation that lifts your spirits.

I walked into the foreman's office; he was sitting at his desk looking at a blueprint. He looked up at me and said, "Two of my local guys didn't show up to work this morning. Are you guys ready to start working right now?"

"Yes, we're ready to work," I said.

163

"There are a few lifts of plywood to move from the ground floor to the second floor. Come with me, I'll show you," said the foreman.

Pierre and I followed him to the stairwell at the main entrance. There were no stairs, only a ladder connecting the first floor to the second floor.

"You guys move the lifts of plywood to the second floor, then let me know when you're finished. I'll work on your hiring papers," said the foreman.

Pierre climbed the ladder to the second floor, and I handed him one sheet of plywood at a time by raising the plywood sheet above my head. The plywood was 1.9 centimeters (3/4 of an inch) thick, tongue and groove, meant for the flooring on the second floor. Each sheet weighed 34 kilos (75 pounds).

Once a lift was moved upstairs, I climbed the ladder to help Pierre move the sheets to the carpenters who were working on the second story. There was quite a distance between the plywood and where the carpenters were working. Pierre and I carried two sheets at a time, one stacked over the other, with each of us on either end like we were carrying a stretcher.

By the time we finished moving the first lift of plywood to the carpenters, the foreman yelled, "Lunch time." The workers came down the ladder single file and got inside various pickup trucks.

The foreman looked at us and said, "You guys look tired."

"My friend and I haven't eaten anything in the last two days," I said.

The foreman replied, "You guys don't have any money?"

"We ran out of money two days ago," I said.

He pulled out his wallet and said, "Here's twenty dollars. I'll deduct it from your first paycheck. You can come with me to the restaurant for lunch. I'll set you up with an account so you guys can eat."

"By the way, how much are we making an hour?" I asked.

"Four dollars an hour for regular time and six dollars an hour for overtime," said the foreman.

I told Pierre how much we'd be making. He smiled and said, "My feet are freezing."

As we were making our way to the restaurant, the foreman said, "Looks like you guys are good workers. I didn't expect you to move the lift of plywood before lunch."

Pierre and I were starving and weak, working purely on fumes. I knew the owner of the restaurant, a Chinese fellow named Harry Yee. The foreman asked him to set up an account for us and told him we'd pay on each payday.

Pierre and I sat at a table and ordered double orders of deluxe hamburgers each.

"My feet are freezing," said Pierre.

I told him, "Take your boots and socks off and give them to me."

Lunch was at one o'clock in the afternoon, after the lunch rush. The workers were eating and talking loudly. Pierre handed me his boots and socks. I took the black pepper shaker from the table and sprinkled pepper into both. As I was doing this, the whole restaurant went quiet. I looked around and saw everyone staring at me.

Then, someone said, "Are his boots and socks that smelly?" and everyone burst into laughter.

"That's an old nun's trick to keep your feet warm in the winter. I used to put black pepper in my socks and skates to keep warm," I explained.

They all laughed and went back to their conversations. The black pepper worked for a few hours until I heard Pierre complain again that his feet were freezing.

We went back to the restaurant for dinner and worked a couple more hours afterward. We moved all the plywood sheets for the flooring to the second story. Pierre and I were dead tired and chilled to the bone. The combination of sweating and freezing temperatures while moving the heavy plywood gave us the chills.

Back at the house, I sat in the bathtub soaking in hot water to warm up my aching body.

For the next few days, we moved plywood sheets and 5-by-15 centimeters (2-by-6-inches) boards cut to size for building the walls of the second story. Each day was as cold as the one before. I had never experienced or worked in such freezing temperatures. The work was physically demanding and took a toll on our bodies.

On December 21st, the shortest day of the year, there were only five hours and twelve minutes of daylight. Our working hours started in darkness and ended in darkness. Temperatures stayed in the minus 30 Celsius (minus 22 Fahrenheit) and even dropped into the minus 40 Celsius (minus 40 Fahrenheit) for a few days. I was impressed with Pierre. He didn't look very strong, but he kept up with the heavy workload without complaining.

Twice a day, we took coffee breaks in the small office where the foreman worked. Inside, there were wooden benches built along the walls, like in a hockey dressing room. The office was cozy and warm. Pierre would take off his boots and socks to warm his feet by the small oil furnace. All the workers, mostly from the south, gathered in that space to drink coffee and smoke cigarettes.

One of the workers, who was Italian, made some offensive comments when he heard Pierre and me speaking in French. He looked straight at us and made it clear he didn't like French people, calling us lazy and stupid. I was furious. Pierre and I had been nothing but respectful to everyone. We worked hard to make sure the carpenters had the plywood and two-by-sixes when they needed them.

Growing up, between the ages of eight and twelve, my neighbors were Italian families. They were my best friends. We played soccer in the summer and street hockey in the winter. Italian and French are both Latin-based languages. After a few months, I could understand a fair bit of Italian and speak a few words.

This guy looked like he could have been an actor or a hitman in a Mafia movie. He looked at me and said we shouldn't speak French because this was Canada, and we should go back to Quebec.

I looked him in the eye and said, *"Fongool,"* which translates to "f*** you" in Italian. He shot up from his seat and started walking toward me. I stood up too. Right then, the foreman walked into the office and said, "Hey you guys, stop that. What happened here?"

I told him that the Italian guy told us not to speak French and called French people lazy and stupid.

The foreman was upset and said, "My wife is French and she's not lazy or stupid." He made the guy apologize to Pierre and me and told us to shake hands. The guy apologized, and we all shook hands. No one understood what I'd said in Italian, and the guy didn't bring it up. From that point on, we had no more issues. Later, we even worked together on the roof of the apartment building and got along fine.

The Postmaster came to the house one evening to let me know that the Minister would be arriving in Fort Simpson in the next couple of days. Good thing Phoebe wasn't there that night.

The following morning, I asked the foreman if there was a vacant room in the trailers where the workers stayed. The trailer camp was set up next to the restaurant.

"Yes, there is one room vacant. The rent is ten dollars per day," said the foreman.

"Is that for two people?" I asked.

"Yes, for two people. There are two beds in the room. There's also a trailer with showers, toilets, washers and dryers."

"When can we move in? I asked"

"This evening after work."

There wasn't a kitchen or eating area in the trailers, just a few coffee pots and tea kettles for making hot drinks. Pierre and I cleaned up the house and packed our gear into our backpack. I was elated — we were just a few days away from having to move out of the Minister's house, so the timing was right. We moved in that evening. I returned the key to the Postmaster and thanked him for letting us stay at the house.

Every second Friday, the foreman gave us our pay cheque in an envelope. We went to the bank during coffee break to cash our cheques, and I deposited some money into my account. Pierre would give me some money, paying me back for the plane and train tickets from Quebec; I had purchased. for him. He finally had enough money to buy himself a much-needed pair of winter boots, which he found at the Hudson Bay store. After that, I didn't hear him complain about freezing feet again.

A couple of days before Christmas, the whole crew and the foreman left for the South to be with their families over the holidays. Only one worker stayed behind to look after the trailer camp and work site. Pierre and I were asked by the foreman to assist him. We worked every day except Christmas and New Year's Day. The foreman and the crew were scheduled to return a few days after the New Year.

During that time, I was able to bring Phoebe into my room so she could spend the night with me. The worker's name was Sandy. He was in his mid-twenties, with short dirty blond hair and blue eyes, and he didn't mind that Phoebe stayed with me. He was single and had met a local woman in the village who became his girlfriend. She visited him during the holidays and spent the night in his room as well. The foreman wouldn't have allowed our girlfriends to stay at the camp if he had been there.

It was extremely cold throughout the Holidays. The thermometer hovered in the minus thirties and dipped into the low forties. Sandy measured and sawed boards for the floor joists and walls of the third floor. Our work revolved around bringing him boards to cut and moving the sawn pieces to the second floor. Pierre and I kept warm by carrying loads from the ground floor. Even in those temperatures, we were both sweating. My frosted beard and mustache turned white, and the frost on my eyelashes had to be plucked off just so I could see where I was going.

By the end of each day, the clothes next to our skin were soaked with sweat. But each day we grew stronger and had more stamina. We didn't need a gym — the construction site was our gym.

For Christmas Day, Pierre wanted to drink some wine. At our afternoon coffee break the day before Christmas, we walked to the local liquor store and bought a case of Baby Duck wine — twelve bottles for around twenty dollars. It was the cheapest wine they had. With a 7% alcohol content, Baby Duck was fruity, sparkling, and easy to drink.

After work and a warm shower, we opened a bottle. One was enough for me. I didn't want to get drunk. But Pierre kept drinking bottle after bottle. He got so drunk, he could barely stand. I hid what was left of the case — which wasn't much. Then we headed next door to the restaurant for dinner.

As we walked, Pierre was behind me, swearing and talking to himself. A tall, broad-shouldered Indigenous man heard Pierre and thought he was being insulted. He grabbed Pierre by the scruff of his neck and asked, "What did you say to me?" I turned around and saw this huge guy, wearing just a t-shirt, holding Pierre up by his neck. I stepped in and said,

"He doesn't speak English. He drank too many bottles of Baby Duck and is just swearing at himself, not at you."

The man let go and asked me, "Are you French?"

"Yes. My friend and I are French from Quebec," I replied.

He smiled and said, "My grandfather was French from Quebec too." Then he laughed and shook my hand.

Pierre, barely able to stand, was babbling like a baby trying to talk. I grabbed him by the arm and led him into the restaurant. If I hadn't intervened, he would've taken a bad beating that might have landed him in the hospital. Once he sobered up, he didn't even remember being grabbed by the neck.

Pierre spent Christmas Day nursing a terrible hangover. The restaurant was closed for the Holiday, so we didn't have anything to eat except some snacks we'd picked up earlier at the Hudson Bay store.

A large truckload of shingles arrived at the work site between Christmas and New Year. There was no forklift or other piece of equipment available to unload the pallets of shingles. Sandy, Pierre, the truck driver, and I unloaded the shingles by hand, one shingle bundle at a time. Each bundle of shingles weighed 36 kilos (80lbs). The bundles were stacked on wooden pallets and covered with large tarps. I recall that day being very cold and windy. The wind felt like a slap on my face, and I developed frostbite on both cheeks. Pierre also had matching frostbite on his cheeks. I felt pins and needles in my skin as the affected areas turned white.

Many people in Fort Simpson used to say that the best thing to do for frostbite was to rub snow on it. I later learned that rubbing snow on frostbite is a terrible idea. It only causes further damage to already compromised tissue. Still, we were both getting used to the cold temperatures and the demanding work conditions.

This was my first time working in construction as a laborer. Doing that kind of work in the winter months made it more challenging, especially compared to my past jobs washing endless piles of dishes in the warmth of a kitchen for only one dollar an hour.

On New Year's Day, Pierre and I were invited to Harry Yee's home for a turkey dinner. Harry was the owner of the restaurant where we had our meals. He was an older Chinese gentleman and a very kind person. He cared about people and often went out of his way to help others, including us. He was short and small in stature, likely in his late sixties, balding, and a heavy smoker. Still, he always welcomed us into his restaurant with a smile. We had a dinner fit for a king, and I deeply appreciated Harry's generosity and his good food.

After dinner, we returned to our room to finish what was left of the Baby Duck's wine. Pierre enjoyed the wine and did not get inebriated this time. I'm certain that if he had more wine, Pierre would have drunk too much and suffered the consequences the following day.

The foreman and the workers were back in Fort Simpson a few days after New Years. The foreman was pleased with the work we did when he was away. Sandy took a couple of weeks off and went south to see his family. Having the workers back increased our workload and pace. The boards that we had moved to the second floor were assembled into the floor and walls of the third floor. Pierre and I were busy moving plywood sheets for the floor and walls. The foreman would ask me, "Are you guys cold?" "Yes," I said. "Then

172

work harder, you won't be cold," said the foreman. He was a hard-working man who wasn't afraid to get his hands dirty. However, he was the type of foreman who turned a blind eye to the working conditions and hazards on the work site.

We worked in extreme cold temperatures well below minus 42 Celsius (minus 43 Fahrenheit) when non-emergency work should cease. There were many days when the temperatures and wind chill factor generated temperatures well below minus 42 Celsius. I recall one day when I was working on the roof of the building, laying plywood sheets with temperatures of minus 40 Celsius and winds gusting to 40 kilometers (25 miles) per hour, generating a temperature equivalent to minus 61 Celsius (minus 78 Fahrenheit). I was holding a 1.5 centimeters (5/8 inch) thick plywood sheet when the gusty wind ripped the sheet right out of my hands while I was laying it on the roof. The plywood sheet flew like a piece of paper into the wind down the three stories and landed 60 meters (200 feet) across the road. It was a blessing in disguise that the plywood sheet was ripped from my hands. If I had held the sheet sturdier, I would have most likely fallen off the roof and landed on a large pile of metal pipes lying below against the building. It was fortunate that no one was in the path of the plywood; serious injuries or even death could have occurred.

I was shaken up, made my way to the first floor, and told the foreman that it was too windy to lay plywood sheets on the roof. I told him about the incident, to which he made a facial expression as if to say, "Tell someone who cares."

Upon his return to work, Sandy worked on installing the rafters. I was working on the third floor when I saw Sandy fall backward and hit the back of his head on the end of one of the rafters, breaking a piece of a 5x10 centimeters (2x4 inches) board. Sandy fell 2.4 meters (8 feet) down and

173

landed on his back on the floor. Before anyone helped him, Sandy got up and put his hand on his neck to see if there was any blood. The foreman was on the third floor supervising the installation of the rafters and saw Sandy's fall. "Are you okay?" asked the foreman. "I don't think that I broke any bones, but I've got a headache now," said Sandy. One of the workers said to Sandy, "You should get yourself checked out at the hospital." "You'll be okay, get back to work," said the foreman. Sandy looked at the foreman, still holding his hand to his neck, and did not say anything. I could tell that Sandy was hurting and upset by the foreman's comments. He went back to work, fixing the 2x4 inches board on the rafter that he broke with his neck. Sandy complained about his headache for the next two days but then did not mention it again. He never did see a nurse or doctor. I believe that an incident report was not completed.

On each pay day, Pierre and I went to the bank to deposit and withdraw enough cash to pay our accounts at the restaurant. We both ate a lot of food to maintain our strength and stamina while keeping ourselves warm. By mid-January, we began to work on the roof of the building. Pierre and I moved a lift of 1.5 centimeters (5/8 inch) plywood sheets, one sheet at a time, from the ground floor to the roof. Once the lift was on the third floor, I climbed the ladder to the third floor.

"Do you want to climb on the roof?" said Pierre. The carpenters had nailed a 60 centimeters (2 foot) wide piece of 5/8 inch plywood sheets along the edge of the rafters. Along the edge of the plywood sheets, 5x10 centimeters (2x4 inches) boards were nailed so workers working on the roof would not slide off. I climbed the ladder and poked my head between two rafters. The strong cold wind was blowing on my back. I nearly panicked when I looked down; it was at least 9 meters (30 feet). down.

174

I told Pierre, "I'm scared of heights, I do not think that I can stand on the edge of the roof piling up plywood sheets." "That's okay, I'm not scared of heights, I'll go on the roof," said Pierre. The carpenters had built a platform on the edge of the roof where the plywood sheets were to be stacked. I was thankful to Pierre for volunteering to climb on the roof and stand on the edge. If the foreman had known that I feared heights, he would have surely told me to get on the roof and made fun of me.

Once the first layer of plywood sheets was nailed along the two-foot-wide plywood, I could then tolerate climbing and working on the roof. I was afraid that I might be fired because I was afraid of heights. By the end of the day, I became less fearful of climbing and working on the roof. The plywood sheets on the third floor were handed to Pierre by the end of the day. Outdoor spotlights provided enough light so we could work before and after sunset.

The following day, Sandy, Pierre, and I started to install the plywood sheets and H clips on the roof. The next morning, a coat of thin ice had formed overnight on the plywood sheets, making it very slippery to move around on the roof. I started to slide down and couldn't stop until my foot reached the 2x4 inches boards on the edge of the plywood. If the 2x4 inches boards had not been installed, I would have surely fallen to the ground.

For the next few days, Pierre and I moved lifts of plywood and bundles of shingles from the ground floor to the roof. The bundles of shingles were the most challenging to move while climbing a ladder. Each bundle weighed 36 kilos (80lbs) and had to be properly balanced on my right shoulder. I climbed up the ladder until Pierre could reach the bundle. He would then pull it off my shoulder and stack it. Pierre had to be very careful not to drop the bundle while I was making my way down the ladder. He never did, but came close a few times. On those close calls, he would let out a loud, "Watch out!"

The stairway was built shortly after Pierre and I had finished moving the plywood sheets and shingle bundles to the roof. I wondered why the stairway wasn't built before we moved the plywood sheets and bundles of shingles. It would have been easier and safer to use a stairway as opposed to a ladder. I didn't want to ask questions or make suggestions to the foreman. He would have told me not to tell him how to do his job.

Near the end of January, the foreman told me that "Headquarters in Edmonton has asked him to increase our rent for the room. "How much will be the new rent?" I asked. "Thirty dollars a day for both of you, the deduction for the new rate will be deducted on the next pay cheque," said the foreman.

I quickly calculated in my mind how much we were making per day and how much we were spending for meals at the restaurant and paying the new rent. "Pierre and I are making about one hundred and twelve dollars per day before taxes. After taxes, we've about eighty-five dollars left. Our meals at the restaurant are about forty dollars a day, and the new rent is now at thirty dollars per day, which would leave us about fifteen dollars. We would be basically working for fifteen dollars a day between the two of us," I said.

The foreman looked at me and said, "I was told to increase you guys' rent by headquarters, nothing more I could do."

"I'll have to discuss this with Pierre and get back to you," I said. I was very upset and gave the news to Pierre that our rent would be increased to thirty dollars a day. Pierre looked at me in disbelief. "How much will we have left after paying for our meals and rent?" said Pierre. "About fifteen dollars a day for the two of us," I said. "We should quit and go back to Quebec," said Pierre.

"I will ask Sandy how much he is paying for rent," I said. I asked Sandy, "How much are you paying for rent?" He laughed and said, "Nothing. The company is paying for our room and board. I wouldn't be coming up here to work if I had to pay for my room and board."

Phoebe had travelled with Tracy to Fort Providence about one week ago and had not returned yet. I did not want to leave Fort Simpson without her. I told Pierre that we would quit our job next pay cheque, which was ten days away, and return to Quebec. Once we quit our job, we would have to move out of the camp, as we did not have alternative accommodation. We were basically working for room and board. I had saved enough money for the three of us to return to Quebec. However, we would not have any money left. I did not want to work as a dishwasher again at one dollar and fifty cents an hour. My plan was to return to Quebec with Phoebe and head back north in the spring to look for a job on the barges.

I gave notice to the foreman that our last day at work would be on the next pay day and requested our Record of Employment. The month of January displayed its true color with brutal temperatures of minus 30 to 40 Celsius (minus 22 to 40 Fahrenheit), not considering the wind chill factor. There were more windy days than no-wind days. Like the foreman had said, "Work harder, you won't be cold"; that was our motto. Pierre and I were getting stronger and in better physical shape each day, just like athletes in training for the game that we would never play. At lunches and

177

dinners, we ate heaps of food to replenish our much-needed energy.

A few days before we were scheduled to leave, I walked to Phoebe's house after dinner to ask her parents if she had come back from Fort Providence. On my way to the house, I met Phoebe walking on the main street. I was so glad to see her. I asked her, "When did you come back from Fort Providence?"

"I came back this afternoon. Tracy and I got stuck in Fort Providence. We didn't have a ride to get back to Fort Simpson," said Phoebe.

"Pierre and I will be quitting our job on Friday and are planning a trip to Quebec. I was told that our rent at the camp will increase to thirty dollars per day. We would be working for our room and board and making no money," I said.

Phoebe looked surprised and didn't know what to say. "Would you like to come to Quebec with me?"

Phoebe hesitated for a few seconds and said, "Yes, I would like to, but I will have to ask my parents."

"Can you let me know as soon as possible? I've got to buy the plane tickets in a couple of days for Friday's flight to Edmonton. From there, we will take the train to Montreal. We will come back to Fort Simpson in May," I said.

I walked with Phoebe to her house; it was very cold. The sky was cloudless with millions of stars as the backdrop to the dancing Northern Lights. They were spectacular and colorful. Lately, I had not paid attention to the sky; I was too busy working.

I asked Phoebe, "Do you want me to talk to your parents?"

"No, I will talk to my parents and see you tomorrow after work at the restaurant," said Phoebe. I was not sure if Phoebe's dad would want his daughter to leave again.

The following evening, Phoebe met me at the restaurant. I was anxious to hear what her parents had told her. Phoebe looked at me and smiled. "My parents told me that I can go with you to Quebec. I told them that we will be back in Fort Simpson in May," said Phoebe.

The foreman gave Pierre and me our last pay cheque and Record of Employment at the end of our last day of work.

"This will be you guys' last night at the camp. Make sure that all of your gear is out of your room first thing tomorrow morning," said the foreman.

We shook hands with the foreman. "You guys are good workers. It's too bad that you're leaving," said the foreman.

Pierre, Phoebe, and I had dinner at the restaurant.

"Harry, we'll pay you for our meals tomorrow morning after we cash our cheques. We'll be leaving tomorrow afternoon and would like to close our account," I said.

"No problem, I will see you tomorrow," said Harry.

"Let's not pay him," said Pierre.

"You won't be back in Fort Simpson, but I will be back. No, we will pay him. He was nice to us, even invited us for dinner at his house on New Year's Day," I said.

179

I was upset with Pierre for saying this. The next day, we paid Harry all the money we owed him, thanked him and left.

Chapter 7:
Return Trip to Ste-Adele, Quebec
January 1974

Pierre and I walked to the Esso station to get a taxi. We stopped at Phoebe's parents' house to pick her up. I knocked at the door, and Phoebe opened it. I walked inside to say goodbye to her parents and siblings. I promised Phoebe's parents that their daughter would be back in Fort Simpson in early May.

At the airport, I purchased three one-way tickets to Edmonton. The flight was a direct flight. Once in Edmonton, we made our way to the CN train station downtown by taxi. I was happy to return to Quebec, but on the other hand, I would have kept on working at the apartment complex if the foreman had not raised our rent. I was getting used to the cold temperatures and the physical, backbreaking work. This was my first winter in the north. The winters in Quebec can also be cold from time to time but pale in comparison to the winters in the Northwest Territories, particularly back in the 1970s. The present-day northerly winters are not as austere and cold as they used to be.

During our nine-week stay in Fort Simpson, Phoebe and I did not have much time together. In Quebec, we would have all our time together.

I purchased three coach one-way tickets to Montreal, as we could not afford tickets with a room. We boarded the train in the evening and should have arrived in Montreal late in the night, three days later. Sitting and sleeping on a seat for three days, not to mention being rocked side to side, we arrived in Montreal very tired. The train was behind schedule, and we arrived too late to catch the last bus of the day to Ste-Adele. I had called my mother from Edmonton to let her know that we were on our way back to Ste-Adele and to expect us to arrive in three days.

At the bus terminal, I spoke with a taxi driver who was parked outside and asked him, "We missed the last bus of the day to Ste-Adele. Could you drive us to Ste-Adele?" The driver looked at me in surprise and said, "I will have to call my wife as she is expecting me to be home in half an hour." He was tall and slim, in his thirties, with short hair. He came back and said, "I will drive you to Ste-Adele for forty dollars. I want to be paid before we leave." I gave the driver two twenty-dollar bills.

It was very warm in Montreal. There was a light drizzle of rain, and the snow was melting. It was after midnight, and there was little traffic on the road, which was unusual in Montreal. As we drove north of Montreal, the light drizzle turned into freezing rain, making the road very slippery. The driver was talking a hundred miles a minute and almost drove that speed. I told him more than once to slow down before he loses control of his car. I was sitting in the back seat of the car with Phoebe, and Pierre was sitting in the front seat. Back then, the seats in the car were a single bench in both the front and back. There were no seat belts in the taxi. The driver almost lost control of his car a couple of times, scaring the hell out of us. As I told him to slow down again, the driver lost control of his car and let go of the steering wheel.

We headed straight for the high snowbank dividing the Laurentian Highway. I put my left arm around Phoebe's shoulders and held her tight against my body, bracing for impact. We hit the snowbank dead on, and the car tumbled head over heels three times. I recalled counting the tumbling—1-2-3. One second, we were sitting on the bench

182

of the car, then the next second, we were sitting on the inside of the roof of the car. It happened so quickly that I didn't have time to be scared. On one of the tumbles, I kicked Pierre in the head with my winter boots. The car finally landed in an upright position in very deep, wet snow. I could see Pierre at the front with his head down. My first thought was that he was badly injured.

"Pierre, are you okay?"

"I'll be okay when the bastard lets go of my arm. He let go of the steering wheel and grabbed my arm when we hit the snowbank," said Pierre.

I could see that Pierre and the driver had small bleeding cuts on their foreheads. A window had broken on Phoebe's side of the car. Just like in the movies, I pictured the car blowing up any minute. I kicked the door a couple of times; it didn't open. Then I realized that I should grab the door handle and open the door. I quickly pulled Phoebe out of the car by her right arm. In the process, she and I put our hands on the seat full of broken glass and both cut our hands. Once outside the car, I opened the door on Pierre's side. The driver was in shock, still holding Pierre's arm. Both Pierre and I shouted at the driver to let go of Pierre's arm.

All three of us visually checked each other for cuts and injuries. Aside from a few small cuts and bruises, we all seemed to be fine. The driver sat in the car, holding the steering wheel and said, "We should all sit in the car and wait for the provincial police to show up." It was still freezing rain. I cleaned the broken glass in the back seat, and Phoebe, Pierre, and I sat in the back seat. Pierre was mad at the driver and did not want to sit in the front seat.

"Why did you let go of the steering wheel and grab my arm?" said Pierre to the driver.

"I got scared, I'm sorry," said the driver.

The provincial police arrived at the scene of the accident and asked the three of us to sit in their car. They asked us a few questions about what had happened and took us to the hospital in St-Jérôme, where I was born, to be checked by a doctor. I called my mother to let her know what had happened. Both Pierre and Phoebe had a few stitches on their foreheads and hands. I had a small cut at the base of my thumb on my left hand. The doctor told me that I didn't need any stitches.

Eighteen months later, while working at Anderson's Sawmills a few miles away from Fort Simpson, I began to feel a small lump at the base of my left thumb. At first, I thought that a wood splinter had made its way into my left hand while I was tailing saw at the sawmills. Each time I grabbed something with my left hand, I felt a sharp pain at the base of my thumb. After enough pain, I asked Phoebe to help me remove whatever was inside my left hand.

We used a single razor blade, the old style of blade that I used whenever I was tired of wearing a beard. Doctor Phoebe made an incision at the tip of the lump and started digging inside with a tweezer to see what was in there. Each time she touched whatever was in there, I felt a sharp pain in my hand. We didn't use any anesthetic; we didn't have any. However, we sterilized the razor blade and tweezer with rubbing alcohol prior to the surgery.

Doctor Phoebe almost quit on me, but I pleaded with her to keep going until she saw something shining inside my hand. It was a very warm and sunny day, and we were outside in the sun doing the surgery.

"I think that it's a piece of glass, I saw it shining in the sun," said Phoebe.

I looked at my hand and said, "You're right, it is a piece of glass."

Doctor Phoebe used the tweezer and pinched the piece of glass in the middle, pulling it out of my hand. It was about 6 millimeters (1/4 of an inch) thick and long.

"How did you get this piece of glass in your hand?" asked Phoebe.

"The piece of glass must have gotten into my hand when we had the car accident in Quebec about a year and a half ago," I said.

There was little blood during the surgery. Doctor Phoebe put some spruce gum on the incision and then a band-aid. There was no infection. The incision healed well, and there was no more pain in my left hand. The piece of glass had been inside my hand for eighteen months and made its way out slowly. It just needed a little help.

We were tired from the train trip and shaken up from the accident. We were at the hospital for a few hours and then released. My mother was very scared of driving on slippery roads and did not offer to pick us up. I called for a taxi and asked to be dropped off at the bus terminal. We were in luck; the bus was leaving in less than one hour. I was looking forward to being in my old room and my own bed with Phoebe. We were all very tired. It had been four long days getting back to Quebec.

I asked the bus driver to stop at the streetlight not far from my mother's house. Pierre got off at the bus terminal and made his way home from there. It was still early morning. My mom was happy to see us and cooked us breakfast.

For the next three months, I helped Adrian deliver and pick up sofas and chairs for my mother's business. My mother was very busy; her business thrived with new contracts and customers. She was a workaholic, working six and sometimes seven days a week from morning to late night. I was told many times that I'm a workaholic, but I pale in comparison to my mother.

I applied for Employment Insurance and was elated when I received my first cheque. I saved as much money as possible for our return trip to Fort Simpson in early May. My mother did not ask us for any money for room and board. However, Phoebe and I did some work for her without being paid. That suited us fine; we had a roof over our heads and ate like a king and queen. Phoebe did some sewing of cushions when needed, and I helped with the delivery and pickup of sofas and chairs in the Ste-Adele area and sometimes in Montreal. It seemed like the wealthier the customers were, the heavier their sofas and chairs.

At the end of April, about one week before we were scheduled to leave, my mother said, "I got you a job at the Rolland paper mill in Mount-Rolland. I know a friend who works at the paper mill; he got you a job." The jobs at the paper mill were unionized and difficult to obtain. The paper mill was one of the mills in Quebec that produced the paper to make money. My mother's friend was a foreman at the paper mill. At the time, he had over thirty-five years of service. He would have been my supervisor if I had taken the job.

My mother did not know that I was planning to return to Fort Simpson. She was not happy when I told her that I was leaving in one week for Fort Simpson. My mother tried very hard to persuade me to take the job. The starting hourly rate was in the four to five-dollar range, which was a very good wage in Quebec at the time.

Chapter 8:
Return Trip to Fort Simpson
May 1974

Phoebe's parents and siblings were expecting her back in Fort Simpson by early May. I had no interest in settling in Quebec. Working in the north was much more enticing to me. I decided to move north with Phoebe permanently. Phoebe and I left Ste-Adele the first week of May 1974 by bus to Montreal. I did not want a travel companion with me looking for a job. I decided that I would be doing this on my own. My plan was to travel by train to Edmonton, from there Phoebe would travel by plane to Fort Simpson on her own while I hitchhiked from Edmonton to Yellowknife to look for a job on the barge.

Three days later, we arrived in Edmonton, and we made our way by taxi to the Municipal Airport. The plane was departing in about two hours. I purchased her ticket and gave her some money.

"I will hitchhike to Yellowknife and look for a job on the barge. If I can't find a job, I'll hitchhike to Fort Simpson and look for a job there," I said.

Phoebe was sad and wanted me to travel to Fort Simpson with her.

"If I get a job on the barge, I will see you when I'm in Fort Simpson. The jobs on the barge are seasonal jobs from May to October. I would return to Fort Simpson when I'm done in October," I said.

Phoebe wasn't having it and started to cry.

After the plane departed, I walked to the Yellowhead Highway and started hitchhiking. It was about two o'clock in the afternoon. Twelve hours and sixteen rides later, I arrived in High Level. It was around two o'clock in the morning, and I was tired and in need of sleep. I set up my tent in the ditch across the street from a restaurant. A few hours later, I got up, packed my tent, and walked to the restaurant to use the bathroom and have something to eat; I hadn't eaten anything since I left Edmonton. I went to town and ordered a ham omelet and toast. I devoured my breakfast.

Once my belly was full, I walked back across the street, set my backpack in front of me on the shoulder of the road. A tall and slim fellow came out of nowhere and introduced himself as Leonardo from Switzerland. He was six feet, seven inches tall with a thick brown mustache, shoulder-length curly brown hair, and a pair of glasses Elton John would have worn. He wore a hat that looked like a hat Robin Hood would have worn back in the day. He had also slept in the ditch but without a tent.

"The mosquitoes were really bad, I hardly had any sleep," said Leonardo. He asked me, "Can I hitchhike with you?"

"Yes, no problem," I said.

Shortly after, we both caught a ride in an early seventies black Chevrolet Caprice driven by a young woman from Yellowknife named Angie. She was a couple of years older than me, medium height and build with long black hair. Her dad was a white man, and her mother was Inuit. She was very friendly and happy to have someone to travel with.

A few miles after we left High Level, the paved road metamorphosed into a gravel road with stones the size of golf balls. As the day grew older, the temperature became hotter and drier, and the road became so dusty that Angie could not overtake vehicles ahead of her. There were several large trucks ahead of us generating large plumes of dust. I sat in the back of the vehicle, thinking that I could catch a wink of sleep. The sounds of the gravel hitting the undercarriage of the car kept me awake.

A few hours later, we crossed into the Northwest Territories. The clouds in the direction where we were heading looked laden with rain. We boarded the ferry near Fort Providence, where we stopped to fuel up, stretch our legs, and take a bathroom break. The rain started lightly at first, then, as if someone turned up the faucet, the rain hit and bounced off the ground. The dusty road became the muddy road. It was so slick that Angie had to slow down in the curves of the road.

In one instance, an hour outside Yellowknife, where there were numerous sharp turns, the car slid sideways into the ditch. It was a good thing that the car was only going 48 kilometers (30 miles) per hour. Leonardo and I managed to push the car out of the ditch. Our pants and shirts were coated with mud, not to mention our faces and hands. We looked like two mud wrestlers who had won a battle with a car. Slowly but surely, we crawled into Yellowknife, eluding the ditches.

Angie dropped us off at the campground across from the airport. I took a shower at the campground and washed my muddy clothes.

Leonardo traveled with a small pack and a fiddle. He was not looking for a job but wanted to play his fiddle in the street and make money to travel and eat. He did not have a tent to sleep in and asked me if he could stay in my tent. It was starting to rain again. My tent was small, barely enough room for the both of us. He was so tall that we couldn't close the zipper on the tent entirely; his feet stuck out of the tent. The mosquitoes were out in full force. To make things worse, Leonardo snored like there was no tomorrow.

The following day, I walked to the Canada Services Center hoping to find a job on the barge. No such luck—I was told that all the seasonal positions on the barges were staffed for the season. I was very disappointed; that was the job that had brought me to Yellowknife. Leonardo followed me like a lost puppy. I purchased some food to make sandwiches and went back to the campground, Leonardo in tow. I shared my food with him at the campground.

Leonardo was the type of guy who believed that he could survive in the north with little to no money. In the two days that he spent with me; I didn't hear him once play his fiddle. He spent a second night in my tent, but the next morning, I had enough of him and told him that I was leaving Yellowknife. I packed my tent and gear and walked to the highway, sticking out my right thumb for a ride. There was no need for me to hang around Yellowknife. I decided it was time for me to hitchhike back to Fort Simpson. I was missing Phoebe and told myself that I would find a job in Fort Simpson. I was down to just a few dollars left in my wallet.

Less than twenty minutes later, a pickup Ford truck stopped and the driver asked me, "Where are you going, man?"

"I'm going to Fort Simpson, I can drop you off at the junction, hop in," said the driver.

He was in his late twenties, with long wavy blond hair. He looked more like a hippie than I did. The driver was heading back to Edmonton. He was friendly and spoke most of the way, and I listened and snuck a word here and there. We boarded the ferry a few kilometers (miles) past Fort Providence. The driver dropped me off at the junction to Fort Simpson. I thanked him and shook hands with him.

I stood at the junction brushing off large mosquitoes looking to taste my French blood. It was a beautiful day; the sun was shining with no signs of rain. An hour later, I saw a station wagon coming my way from the Yellowknife direction. I was hoping that he was heading to Fort Simpson and not south. The driver slowed down at the junction and turned in my direction. My heart skipped a beat. I stood there with my right thumb pointing in the direction of Fort Simpson.

He stopped beside me. I opened the door and asked the driver, "Are you going to Fort Simpson?"

"Yes, I am. Get in," said the driver.

He was a salesman selling chainsaws for a living. He was in his early thirties, balding at the top, with a small brown mustache, which was popular back then. The road was dusty, however, there were only a few vehicles on the road.

We boarded the Liard Ferry three hours later. Riding on the ferry made me think about the barges. I guess getting a job on the barges wasn't in my cards. I asked the driver to drop me off at the Fort Simpson Hotel. I wanted to surprise Phoebe by walking to her house and knocking at the door. I made my way to her house.

I could hear Elton John's song "Daniel" blaring from a small cassette player. Florence was helping Phoebe rinse her hair outside in a large tub. Florence turned around, surprised to see me. I put my right finger to my lip to let her know not to say anything. Phoebe had just finished rinsing her hair and wrapped a towel around her head.

I walked towards her until I stood behind her. She slowly turned around with her hands holding the towel and saw me standing in front of her. She put her arms around my neck and started to cry.

"I thought that I'd never see you again," said Phoebe.

"I didn't find a job on the barges and decided to hitchhike back to Fort Simpson. I missed you," I said.

I added, "I will look for a job tomorrow."

Phoebe's parents were at home and happy to see me. Phoebe's mom asked me to come into the house to have something to eat. She gave me a piece of Bannock and soup that she had just made. I sat at the kitchen table and had dinner with Phoebe's dad, Gabe. Gabe and Mary were speaking in Slavey; I didn't understand a word. Mary then spoke to Phoebe in Slavey.

After I finished my meal, Phoebe came to me and said, "My parents said that it's okay for you to stay with me at the house."

I looked at Gabe and Mary and said, "Thank you."

Phoebe and I shared a single bed in a small room facing the street. In lieu of a door, Phoebe installed a small curtain at the entrance to the room. I was happy that her parents let me stay in their home; I felt like they accepted me as a member of the family. I spent the evening drinking tea with Gabe at the kitchen table and listening to his bush stories. I was mesmerized by his stories of trapping and hunting. Gabe had a way of telling stories; he was precise in the details. If he was describing how to make a pair of snowshoes, he would go through the whole process, beginning with the type of birch tree you should select, how to divide up the birch, and ensuring the birch had straight grains as opposed to cross grains. He had a wealth of bush knowledge and skills. He may not have earned a university degree, but over his lifetime, he earned a PhD in traditional bush knowledge and skills.

Later that evening, before we went to bed, Phoebe told me, "I think I may be pregnant." Phoebe was three months shy of her seventeenth birthday, and I was eighteen and a half years old. I was mature for my age and eager to become a father. We decided not to tell anyone until we could confirm that Phoebe was indeed pregnant. Only Florence knew that Phoebe might be pregnant. Phoebe and Florence were very close sisters.

The following day, while walking uptown, I was stopped by two fellows in a pickup truck. Both looked like they were brothers. I recognized the one in the passenger seat; he was the fellow who had asked me if I was a hippie when I first arrived in Fort Simpson. They introduced themselves as Ron and Allan Anderson. Ron was the driver; he was the older brother. Ron was stocky with broad shoulders, reddish short hair, and freckles. He wore a baseball cap. Allan was of average build and height, with brownish-red hair longer than his older brother's.

"Are you looking for a job?" said Ron.

"Yes, I am," I said.

"We own a sawmill up the old Nahanni Butte winter road near the Liard River. We have a camp at the sawmill," said Ron.

"I've never worked in a sawmill before," I said.

"No worries, we'll show you. We're short one guy to work as tailing saw," said Ron. "The work is from Monday to Friday, eight hours a day at four dollars per hour. You will stay at the camp, room and board are free. My mother is the cook; she makes good food."

"Will I be working on the weekend?" I asked.

"There may be some work on the weekends if we're very busy," said Ron.

"I'm interested, when do I start?" I asked.

"Tomorrow morning. I leave at 6 a.m. for the sawmill. Meet me at my house," said Ron, pointing to where his trailer was.

I shook hands with Ron and Allan and told them that I would be at the house tomorrow morning at 6 a.m. I could not believe my luck. I didn't have to look for a job; the job came to me. Four dollars an hour was very good money back then. I was used to working long hours and was hoping to work some overtime. I had been on my way to the Manpower office to look for a job, and I got a job before I even made it to the office. It was good timing. I had only a few dollars left in my wallet, and I was hoping I could get an advance by the weekend so I could purchase some groceries for Phoebe and me.

I went back to Phoebe's house to let her know that I had a job and that I was starting to work the next morning. Phoebe's parents asked us if we wanted to come with them to visit the Saulteaux family at the end of the island. Fort Simpson is located on an island along the Liard River side of the Mackenzie River. The river had cleared of ice a few days ago, and people on the island were boating on the river, setting fishnets, and hunting for ducks and geese. A few families lived year-round down the river and made trips to Fort Simpson for supplies.

It was a beautiful, sunny day, and the breeze along the river felt refreshing. We made our way along the river until we reached the Saulteaux family's house. The family consisted of an elderly woman, which I assumed was the mother, two brothers, and one sister with her young son, about four or five years old. All were outside around a campfire cooking fish that they had caught on the river. A short distance from the campfire, stood a wooden rack with dry fish hanging above a smoldering fire. Phoebe explained to me that the fish was cut into dry fish and smoked. A large tea kettle rested on the open fire, and I could hear the water boiling. The sister threw a few tea bags into the kettle. Phoebe's parents spoke in Slavey with the elderly woman. Phoebe and I sat by the fire, and the sister offered us a cup of tea each. I was not much of a coffee or tea drinker back then but, became a tea drinker.

All four adults in the family were very dark-skinned. Initially, I thought that they were black people but concluded that they were Dene people who made their living from the bush and the river. It was interesting to witness just how Dene people cook, dry, and smoke their fish. After a couple of cups of tea, we shook hands with the Saulteaux family and headed back to Gabe's house.

As we walked along the river, a small-built Dene man with a grey cap, in his mid to late seventies, walked up the bank. Gabe and Mary walked up to the elder and shook hands with him. His name was Joe Boots, and he was from Willow Lake River, he and his three brothers resided at the

196

mouth of the river on the Mackenzie River. Gabe introduced me to him.

"Me Joe Boots," said Joe, tapping on his chest.

"I'm Daniel Allaire," I said.

Gabe and Joe spoke in Slavey for a few seconds and then walked down the bank. I followed them; I was curious to see what they were talking about. Joe's wooden scow was tied up next to the Saulteaux family's wooden scow. Inside Joe's scow was a butchered moose lying inside a large tarp. Gabe translated what Joe had told him.

He shot the moose on his way up the river about two hours earlier," Gabe said.

Gabe reached into his pocket and traded a one-dollar bill for a piece of moose meat. Joe reached for his hunting knife and cut a large piece of moose meat from one of the back legs. Joe went to town to buy some supplies for his brothers and himself. I heard Gabe and Joe say "Mashi" to each other when they traded the one-dollar bill for the piece of moose meat. In my mind, "*Mashi*" must translate to "*Merci*," which is "Thank You" in English. I shook hands with Joe and said, "*Mashi*" and helped him carry his empty ten-gallon drums up the bank. The drums were for his outboard motor's mixed gas.

We had fried moose meat and Bannock for dinner. It was delicious. I had never eaten moose meat before but had eaten deer meat as a child in Quebec. I recalled eating deer meat while having dinner at my paternal grandmother's home in Ste-Jérôme. My uncle Claude had shot a deer and gave some meat to my grandmother. The evening was spent drinking tea and eating Bannock while listening to Gabe's bush stories.

I recall once asking him, "Where do you get your water when you are on your trapline?" Gabe looked at me with a smile and said with a smirk, "You just melt snow in a pot over a fire." I was caught by surprise with his answer and told myself, "Why didn't I think of that?"

The following morning before 6 a.m., I was at Ron Anderson's door waiting for him. He came out of his trailer surprised that I was standing there.

"Good, you're early. My mother will have breakfast ready by the time we get to the mill," said Ron.

"Sounds good to me," I said.

We headed towards the ferry crossing and turned right onto a bush road about halfway to the ferry.

"The mill is about 10 kilometers (6 miles) up the bush road. It used to be the Nahanni Butte winter road a few years ago," said Ron.

The sun had been up for a few hours, and it looked like it would be a sunny and hot day. The mosquitoes were out looking for blood. The road did not have any gravel on it, just natural soil.

"The road must be muddy when it rains," I said.

"Yes, sometimes the road is so muddy that the truck gets stuck. One spring, I got stuck halfway between the mill and the highway and had to walk back to the mill to get our skidder to pull my truck out," said Ron.

After a few bumps and ruts, we arrived at the mill. The layout of the site included two trailers, a wooden shed/garage, a sawmill with a wooden roof, a skidder, a

198

loader, and piles of logs and milled lumber of different sizes and lengths.

I followed Ron into the trailer where breakfast was waiting for us. I was introduced to Ron's parents, the co-owners of the sawmill, Allan and Therese Anderson. Allan was a World War II veteran in his early fifties. He was a millwright and kept the sawmill running, as well as being a sawyer. Allan was average height and build; he wore glasses and a cap, which were popular with men of his age back then.

Therese was slim and of average height. Her brownish-red wavy hair was shoulder length. Therese wore makeup and red lipstick. She looked like she was ready to go out to a fancy dinner, as opposed to serving breakfast to sawmill workers. Both Allan and Therese shook my hands and made me feel welcome.

Ron and I had a hearty breakfast of eggs, bacon, beef sausages, pancakes, and toast. He wasn't kidding, his mother was an excellent cook.

After breakfast, I met Lyn, Ron's youngest brother. He was a year and a half younger than me. He was tall with broad shoulders, and his brown wavy hair was shorter than mine. He shook my hands, just like his parents had, and made me feel welcome.

Allan Junior, Ron's younger brother, was out in the bush with Frank Poulin, the skidder operator. Allan felled the trees with a chainsaw while Frank hauled the trees to the sawmill with the skidder.

Ron gave a demonstration on how the sawmill operated without the engine running. The sawmill was a model most likely from the late forties or early fifties. Three people were required to operate the sawmill: the sawyer determined and

199

adjusted the cuts and sizes of the dimensional lumber pieces, controlled the actions of the carriage, the canter rolls, and secured the logs to be milled on the carriage. The tailing saw removed the slabs and lumber from the carriage as it moved back and forth between the canter and tailing saw positions.

I was assigned to the tailing saw position. Between the carriage and where I stood was a metal platform about 40 centimeters (16 inches) in width, 60 centimeters (2 feet) in height, and 4.8 meters (16 feet) in length. The metal platform had rollers built in every 30 centimeters (12 inches). The platform was used to set down the slabs and lumber.

I quickly learned not to have my fingers under the slabs and lumber before I set them down on the platform. The slabs were pushed over the carriage track once the track was moved back to the canter position. The pieces of lumber were rolled on a platform and then slid down from the sawmill's platform to their piles located on the ground according to their sizes and lengths. The wooden platform of the sawmill was built about 1.2 meters (4 feet) above the ground.

Ron started the motor of the sawmill; the sound was very loud. When the blade was sawing a log, the blade was the most intimidating. I stood ready for the first cut. Lyn rolled and secured the first log of the day on the carriage. Ron pulled on a handle to adjust the cut on the log and then stepped on a pedal on the floor, like a gas pedal, next to him to allow the carriage to move forward towards the 1.2 meters (4 feet) circular blade. Once the log reached the blade, sawdust poured out from the cut and fell into an open space to the ground under the platform of the sawmill. From time to time, sawdust had to be removed from under the platform.

Once the slab was cut from the log, it fell on the metal platform with the help of my hands. The slabs were thrown over the carriage track.

The log was then repositioned with the flat side down and secured to the carriage. Ron adjusted for the cut of the log by pulling on the handle, then stepped on the pedal. The carriage began to move towards the circular blade. A second slab resulted from the cut, which was thrown over the carriage track. The log was repositioned two more times and sawed until it had a square shape.

Six 5 by 30 centimeters (2 by 12 inches) dimensional lumber pieces were sawed from the square-shaped log. Each piece of lumber was green and heavy, with patches of spruce resin and gum scattered along the lumber. The last two pieces of lumber were sawed from the remaining part of the log. The first piece fell into my hands and was placed on the metal platform, while the other piece of lumber was tugged away from the carriage using the bottom of the piece. Both pieces were placed on the platform and slid down to the 5 by 30 centimeters (2 by 12 inches) lumber pile. The pieces had to be lifted by hand for a short distance so I could reach the lumber pile.

One piece was heavy; I struggled a bit with lifting two pieces at the same time. After a week of working as tailing saw, I had no issues lifting two pieces of lumber at the same time. It took me a few sawing of logs to get familiar with the rhythm and timing of the sawmill's operation, as well as keeping up with Ron and Lyn. At all times, I had to be aware of my surroundings and pay attention to what I was doing. In this line of work, an accident could happen in a blink of an eye.

At the end of my first 8hr. shift, I was physically and mentally drained. Before I started working as tailing saw, I was hoping that our daily hours would be in the neighborhood of 12hr. per day. Ron had laughed at me when I asked him if our hours of work would be twelve hours per day. After working eight hours tailing saw, I laughed at myself and understood that 8hr. a day tailing saw was ample.

We had lunch at noon with the Anderson family, Frank, and me. Frank was small in stature but used to say that he was strong and a giant when he operated heavy equipment. He was in his late fifties to early sixties. Frank smoked like a chimney; seldom did I see him without a cigarette between his lips. He was French from Saskatchewan; he could understand French well but was a bit rusty speaking it. Frank walked hunched over, like he was in pain.

I was famished; different sorts of sandwiches, soups, and pieces of cake and pie adorned the table. Ron made a joke about my fast eating and said, "Hey, Mom, better give Daniel extra jam in his sandwiches, he'll need it to keep up with me." After our meal, we sat relaxing at the kitchen table talking about where Allan Junior was harvesting large spruce trees near the Liard River.

The afternoon was non-stop sawing, apart from a short fifteen-minute coffee break. At the end of the day, we had a delicious dinner with desserts. I was running on empty, and the food replenished my tank. After dinner, Ron said, "You can catch a ride with me back to town, pack up some clothes and a sleeping bag, tomorrow you will be staying at the camp with the boys. We may work this weekend; we are behind on the order for Giant Mine."

On the way to town, I asked Ron, "Would I be able to get an advance for the weekend?"

"Friday is payday, I'll make you a check for the hours you worked up to Friday," said Ron.

"Thanks, Ron," I said.

Ron dropped me off at Phoebe's house and told me, "I'll pick you up here tomorrow morning at 6 a.m." Phoebe was at home with her parents and siblings. I told her that I would be staying in the camp at the sawmills starting tomorrow and might have to work this weekend.

Phoebe took me aside and told me with a worried look on her face, "I went to the hospital this afternoon to take a pregnancy test; it was positive, I'm pregnant."

I looked at her with a smile and said, "I'm happy, I'm going to be a father and you a mother." Phoebe's worried look faded away to a happy one. We hugged each other.

I asked her, "Have you told your parents that you are pregnant?"

"Not yet, I will wait for a while before telling them, only Florence knows that I'm pregnant."

I then came to the decision that I would settle in the north and only return to Quebec on holidays to visit my family and friends.

Ron was at Phoebe's house at 6 a.m. on the dot. He gave me my cheque, which I signed and gave to Phoebe to purchase groceries. I spent the weekend and the following week working at the sawmills tailing saw and piling lumber. My jeans had multiple rips on both legs and were coated with spruce resin and gum. I was stung several times by large spruce beetles on my legs and behind. The amount of spruce resin and gum must have attracted the spruce beetles, who must have mistaken me for a spruce tree.

Unfortunately, throughout the summer, the work at the sawmills came with work stoppages due to breakdowns at the sawmills. Parts needed to be ordered from the south, which back then could take weeks or months before the part made its way to Fort Simpson. I recall on one occasion that a part that had been ordered weeks ago arrived in Fort Simpson, only to find out that the part was the wrong one.

During those breakdown days, I was assigned to peel the bark of 12 meters (40 feet) white spruce trees that were to become power poles. The bark was removed with a drawknife. The trees were rested with a loader on two homemade sawhorses, one at each end. Once the top section of the tree was peeled, Lyn would use the loader to flip the tree on the opposite side so we could complete the peeling.

Lyn and I peeled the bark of the forty-foot white spruce trees that were lying on the ground at the sawmills. Many more were needed to fulfill a contract for four hundred power poles that were to be shipped to Frobisher Bay, now named Iqaluit. The skidder was out of commission for several weeks, and parts were needed to repair the skidder.

My pay cheques were getting few and far in between, and winter was just around the corner. Now was the time to look for another job.

Chapter 9:
Working at the River Between Two Mountain Camp Surveying
1974-1975

Weary of not earning a steady wage, one morning in early September, I made my way to the Department of Public Works (DPW) office to inquire about a job at a camp north of Fort Simpson. Construction of the highway south of Wrigley had been going on for a couple of years. Hire North, a company from Fort Simpson, was under contract to build the highway and provide training to Indigenous heavy equipment operators. DPW was under the Federal Government at the time and provided all survey services for the construction of the highway. A large camp capable of lodging and feeding Hire North's and DPW's employees was set up south at the mouth of the River Between Two Mountains, near the Mackenzie River.

As I walked into the office, two men about twenty years or so my senior, one who appeared to be in charge, were discussing an employee who was expected to report to work today after his time off but hadn't. I didn't know the man but had seen him around town. I introduced myself and asked them, "Do you have any job openings?"

Both men looked at each other, and one said, "Do you have any survey experience?"

"No, I don't, but I'm sure I can learn," I said.

"The surveyor in charge at the camp can train you as a Chainman/Rodman. Would you be ready to leave this afternoon at one o'clock?" said the man with the salt and pepper hair.

"Yes, I can be ready," I said.

The man with the salt and pepper hair hired me on the spot, completed the hiring paperwork, which I eagerly signed and dated.

"The hours are 10 hrs. per day, seven days a week. You'll be staying at the camp for a shift of thirty-five days, followed by one week off, then back to camp for another shift of thirty-five days. The wage is four dollars and eleven cents per hour, which includes the isolation post allowance. Overtime hours are at time and a half," said the man with the salt and pepper hair.

I couldn't believe it; I was ecstatic. That was the type of work I had been looking for—working in a camp with long hours per day, seven days a week. With this kind of wage, Phoebe, our child, and I would be able to have our own roof over our heads. I made arrangements so Phoebe could pick up my paycheck at the DPW office. Back then, the paychecks were made in Ottawa and sent by Canada Post.

"How am I getting to the camp?" I asked.

"There's a float plane leaving at one o'clock from the Arctic Air float dock," said the man with the salt and pepper hair.

"Thanks, I know where the dock is," I said.

I shook both men's hands and thanked them.

I was excited and happy. Finally, I had a job in the bush camp working seventy hours a week. I'd be able to rent an apartment at the Mackenzie Manor where I worked this past winter. Lately, the income I was earning at the sawmills was barely enough to buy groceries and non-existent when it came to paying a monthly rent at the manor. We were expecting a baby at the end of January, and Phoebe was now five months pregnant.

All those thoughts were running through my mind as I walked back to Phoebe's parents' house. I announced, "I got myself a job at the River Between Two Mountains camp surveying on the highway south of Wrigley. I have a couple of hours to get ready. I'm flying to the camp in a small plane on floats, leaving at 1 p.m. this afternoon."

She stared at me with a combination of a happy and saddened expression on her face and said, "You're leaving this afternoon."

"How long will you be away at the camp?" Phoebe asked.

"Five weeks at the camp, then one week off," I said.

"That's a long time to be away," said Phoebe.

"I made arrangements at the DPW office for you to pick up my check on paydays. You can deposit the check in our joint account and withdraw money to buy what you need," I said. "The camp receives mail just about every day. We can send letters to each other," I added.

Phoebe's parents did not have a phone at their house. There was access to a mobile phone at the camp, which was mostly used for ordering food and supplies for the camp.

Phoebe and I walked to the Arctic Air dock; it was a sunny and warm day for the month of September. Across the river, the colors of the leaves blended from green, yellow, gold, and a touch of red. The pilot, a man in his late thirties with a baseball cap on his head, was fueling up the small float plane. A local Dene woman with an Antoine last name was at the dock waiting to board the plane. We were the only passengers on the flight. The pilot loaded our gear into the small plane. I hugged and kissed Phoebe and asked her to write me letters, and that I would do the same. This was my first flight in a small float plane; I was excited but at the same time a bit nervous.

The plane taxied on the river; the pilot revved the engine, then all of a sudden, the plane started to pick up speed on the water. I sat in the back seat while my fellow passenger sat at the front next to the pilot. The plane took some time bouncing on the water until it was airborne. What a rush! The view from the air was magnificent. Looking down at the bush appeared as if I was looking at a colorful painting. I could see mountains in the distance to the west. I relaxed in the back seat and enjoyed the view from above.

About forty-five minutes later, the plane started to descend until it landed on the Mackenzie River near the mouth of the River Between Two Mountains. It was mid-afternoon, and a friendly man in his mid-thirties with a baseball cap on his head met us at the dock and gave us a ride to the camp, which was a short distance away. There were two camps; the largest camp housed and fed the Hire North staff, while the smaller camp housed the DPW staff. The small camp was located about 150 meters (500 feet) walk from the larger camp, where our meals were served.

At the camp, I met Louis Tale, a Dene from Wrigley. He was the camp attendant at the DPW camp. Louis was a friendly and happy man, and he gave me a tour of the camp and showed me where my room was. I had a whole room to myself. Across from the trailer I stayed in was the shower/washroom trailer. Louis told me that there were only five people staying at the DPW camp, including myself and him. Next door was another trailer with a pool table, ping pong table, and shuffleboard, along with a small kitchenette for making coffee, tea, and sandwiches. A fridge was loaded with a variety of snacks, juices, and fruits for making our daily lunches. Louis ensured that the fridge was always full of goodies.

Every Friday, two or three movies in large cassette tapes, like VHS tapes but only bigger, arrived at the camp by plane with supplies for the camp. Friday evening was movie night. The movies were the latest, and some of them were still playing in the theaters. What a treat! A large television and several sofas and chairs added the final touch to the trailer, making it comfy.

I met my crew of three at the Hire North camp at dinner. The surveyor in charge introduced me to my two fellow co-workers and himself. David Deneyoua was a Dene from Fort Simpson, a few years older than me. He had jet-black hair with an Elvis-style haircut, combed back with a lot of Brylcreem to ensure that his hair stayed in place. David was short in stature and of medium build. He never wore a hat, no matter how cold it was; he wore only a large ear warmer. I asked him once, "Why don't you wear a hat or a tuque?" He looked at me as if I had told a joke and said, "I don't want to mess up my hair." He combed his hair with a small comb, what seemed like every five minutes. No matter how windy it was, not a single strand on his head moved. David was funny and good to work with; he kept you on your toes.

Eddie Fabian was David's sidekick. The two of them were quite the pair, making jokes and laughing all the time. Eddie was at least ten years older than me. He was a Dene originally from Fort Resolution. Eddie was short like David but had a heavy chest for a man his size. His wavy black short hair was also combed back; I believe that he didn't use as much Brylcreem on his hair as David did. Eddie wore a wool tuque just like I did.

Sandy, the surveyor in charge, was a white guy from Edmonton. He was in his late twenties, at least 182 centimeters (6 feet) tall, and of medium build. Sandy had long wavy dirty blond hair down to his shoulders and blue eyes, just like me. He looked like a hippie, just like me, but older. Sandy was what I called a cool guy; he knew his job well and was also a good mentor to me. Sandy taught me my job as a chainman and rodman and how to drive our standard 4x4 work truck up and down the 19 kilometers (12 miles) of gravel road. I didn't have a driver's license and didn't know how to drive. Within a few days, I felt comfortable driving the truck and changing gears. At the start, I was grinding the gears and getting made fun of. I was the youngest one on the crew and the greenhorn.

The chainman assists the surveyor in accurately measuring distances of land with the use of measuring instruments such as chains and tapes. Most of the measurements were made with a 30 meters (100 feet) chain made of metal. The chain had measurement indicators in the imperial system, feet and inches. The chain was wound up around a metal circular case with a handle. Once the measurements were taken, the chain was wound up around the circular case.

The rodman assists the surveyor with data collection for mapping the elevation of the terrain. A rod, 5 meters (16 feet and 6 inches) in length, was used to collect the elevation of the terrain. The rodman would slowly move the rod back and forth in front of him while the surveyor looked into a survey level to capture the height of the terrain by recording the precise numbers on the rod. My job alternated between chainman and rodman. Sandy taught me how to use the survey level and how to record the elevation of the terrain. A couple of years later, I was hired to survey the elevation of sewer and water pipes, as well as measuring terrain elevation at the Fort Simpson airport when it was paved in 1977.

After making our lunches and thermoses of tea and coffee, the four of us headed to the end of the gravel road south of the camp. From there, we took some elevation data on the right-of-way of the highway. It was a beautiful September day, with temperatures above zero and no mosquitoes or sandflies in sight. The colors of the leaves were at their peak, displaying vibrant colors from green, yellow, gold, and red. large groups of spruce grouse were out along the gravel road, swallowing small stones and grit to aid in their digestion. The grouse were everywhere; we must have seen over one hundred that day.

Hire North's heavy equipment operators were spreading soil hauled from nearby borrow pits along the highway. Several large wheeled excavators, commonly called buggies, driven by the operators at the camp, scraped the dirt from the borrow pits by dragging their underbelly into the dirt, driving forward until the box of the buggies was full. The dirt would then be dispersed on the road for the dozers to spread out. The buggy operators were young Indigenous men being trained on how to operate the buggies. Every other day, a buggy would roll on its side or get stuck in the borrow pit. Some of the operators drove the buggy as if it were a sports car.

Once, coming out too fast from the access road of a borrow pit, a buggy almost T-boned us on the passenger side of our work truck. It was a close call; the operator quickly pressed the brake and stopped just a few feet away from our truck. Sandy was livid. He got out of the truck and started to

211

yell and swear at the operator. The operator of the buggy backed up and then drove around us, speeding away at high speed. The tires of the buggy were about the same height as the truck. The buggy would have crushed us, which could have resulted in serious injuries or even death. It happened so fast.

A few days after my arrival at the camp, I received my first letter from Phoebe. I was happy to hear from her. From then on, I received a letter almost every day. I did not write as many letters as she did. One morning in late September, the ground was white with snow—the winter had prematurely begun. From there on, the temperatures were below 0 Celsius (32 Fahrenheit), along with cold north winds. A couple of weeks later, there was over 30 centimeters (1 foot) of snow on the ground. Early October, our crew was tasked with collecting soil samples on the banks of creeks and rivers north of our camp. Our mode of travel was to be by helicopter.

I recalled seeing an Alouette helicopter landing at our camp. I had never flown in a helicopter, and I was excited about the prospect of flying in one. I met the pilot in an open area behind our camp. Glen was his name. He was in his late twenties to early thirties. He was tall and slim, with very short brown hair, dressed in pilot coveralls and the helmet he wore each time he flew the helicopter. The sun was going down behind the ridge of mountains to the west.

"I have to put the helicopter to bed before dinner," said Glen.

Innocently, I asked him, "What do you mean by putting the helicopter to bed?"

Glen looked at me with a blank expression, as if saying, "Greenhorn alert."

"I have to cover the blades and plug in the helicopter, the same as you would for a car in the winter," said Glen.

I helped Glen by stretching the long extension cord from the helicopter to the nearest trailer. Glen covered the three blades of the helicopter with a custom-sized casing over the blades. Louis, our camp attendant, was on his time off. I told Glen, "There are a couple of empty rooms at the camp; our meals are at the other camp," I said.

The following morning after breakfast, our crew of four received a helicopter safety briefing on what not to do and do around a helicopter. Barrels of fuel were placed next to the helicopter. The pilot fueled the helicopter using a hand wobble pump.

"We should have enough fuel for the day, we're not going very far," said Glen.

It was so cool—what an interesting job, flying by helicopter and getting paid four dollars and eleven cents an hour to boot. We loaded our gear and lunches into the helicopter. David, Eddie, and I sat in the back seat while Sandy sat up front next to the pilot. It was a sunny and near cloudless day, a good day to fly a helicopter. I sat behind Sandy so I could get a good view of the ground.

The pilot fired up the helicopter. The blades began to turn slowly at first, until I could no longer see the individual blades—three blades blurred into one. The helicopter slowly lifted off the ground, and I felt a rush from the bottom of my stomach to my brain. Wow! What a rush. I was instantly hooked on flying in a helicopter. The helicopter raised up above the camp and headed north.

Our first stop was at the River Between Two Mountains. At the time, there was no bridge across the river, only a right-of-way where the highway was to be built. We landed on the right-of-way on the south side of the river. The fluffy snow was about halfway up to my knees. Sandy selected an area near the bank of the river, and snow was removed with a shovel to the ground. Sandy demonstrated how to use the auger to collect the samples.

The first few centimeters (inches) of the ground were frozen, and I struggled a bit cranking the hand auger until I broke through the frozen layer. From there, we collected samples at different depths and put them in sample plastic bags. Using a black felt pen, Sandy wrote information on the plastic bags along with the same information in his notebook. The three of us took turns cranking the auger and collected the samples under Sandy's instructions.

The river was not completely frozen, and the water was too deep for us to cross the river walking. Glen fired up the helicopter and flew us across the river. The samples were taken across the river.

I was enjoying this type of work; we were gathering important samples that would be used for the construction of the bridge across the rivers. We continued to gather samples for a few days, making our way north of the camp. At the end of each day, we returned to the camp at RBTM. The samples were packaged and sent on the daily flight to Fort Simpson.

A couple of kilometers (miles) south of the camp, an airstrip was built on the highway wide enough for a plane to turn around. A contracted Britten-Norman Islander fixed-wing aircraft was scheduled daily, weather permitting, from Fort Simpson to RBTM (camp 1), Ochre River (camp 2), and

Blackwater River (camp 3) to transport staff, groceries, mail, and needed parts for the heavy equipment.

To save on flight time, we relocated to camp 3 at Blackwater River to collect samples north of Blackwater River. The camp was currently closed until the ground was frozen enough to build the winter road. A camp attendant and his girlfriend looked after the camp until it re-opened for the workers to resume work after the winter road was open. The camp was used for cutting trees on the right-of-way of the highway. Cutting the trees on the right-of-way was conducted when the ground was frozen enough to support the weight of heavy equipment.

We landed at the camp as the sun was setting over the horizon. The camp attendant, a fellow with a thick Polish accent, met us at the helicopter pad. He was of average height with large broad shoulders, too large for a person of his size. He had short blond hair and blue eyes.

"We were expecting you, my girlfriend cooked dinner for you, it's ready," said the camp attendant.

Glen put the helicopter to bed, and we made our way to the camp. The attendant's girlfriend was from Fort Simpson; I had seen her before. Her family's name was Tonka. She was short, small-built, with shoulder-length black hair. The food smelled good, and I was famished.

"You guys can sit at the large table, I will bring you the food," said cook Tonka.

The food was delicious, and we even had a freshly cooked blueberry pie with ice cream—just what the doctor ordered after a hard day's work. The camp attendant showed us our rooms after dinner.

The following morning, the weather had turned for the worse. Low clouds to the ground with freezing rain reduced the visibility to near zero.

"We are not going anywhere today. The weather is supposed to be like this for the next couple of days," said Glen.

I told myself a day off would be nice; up to that point, I had worked for about a month without a day off. After breakfast, I went back to bed and relaxed. The cook called us for lunch at noon. The camp attendant was in his tight shorts and a sleeveless t-shirt. He was bench-pressing a heavy-looking dumbbell. The camp attendant was built like a bodybuilder and looked like a mini-Arnold Schwarzenegger. Each time he lifted the dumbbell, he let out a loud groan. I could see a large vein in his neck expanding each time he lifted the dumbbell. He worked out until he was sweating profusely. His girlfriend seemed to enjoy watching him. I guess he had a lot of time on his hands.

The following day, the weather had not improved, and we could see no more than half a mile. The clouds were low to the ground, giving the impression that we were in the clouds.

"We're not going anywhere today, and maybe tomorrow as well," said Glen.

He added, "I cannot fly in freezing rain; it's not safe."

The temperatures were hovering a few degrees below freezing. Sandy was not very happy; he wanted to wrap up the collection of the samples and head back to our camp. Another day was spent sleeping, eating, and taking a walk outside to see if the weather had improved. Glen did not mind staying at the camp; he kept himself busy reading a book. David and Eddie played pool and drank cups of coffee and tea.

The following day was a repeat of the day before, like Groundhog Day. I was getting restless and wanted to get back to work. I learned years later, while working as a forest firefighter, that helicopters and planes should not be flying in freezing rain, which could lead to ice accumulation on the rotor blades and helicopter surfaces. Glen's decision to stay put at the camp and wait for the weather conditions to improve was the right call. Sandy and I believed that Glen did not want to fly unless it was a sunny day with unlimited visibility. If Glen had decided to ignore the weather conditions, I would certainly not be writing this story and book, and we would have most likely been just another aviation accident statistic.

In early November, on a very cold and windy day, while working adjacent to a small frozen lake, our crew found a small duck wandering in the snow along the shore of the lake. The duck must have waited too long to head south. The lake must have frozen overnight, and the duck could not get airborne on the fresh ice. It was incredible that the duck had managed to survive that long in the cold temperatures, wandering in the deep snow.

Sandy and I walked up to the duck, who looked as if he was literally on his last leg. Sandy gently plucked him out of the deep snow and put him inside his winter jacket against his chest. Sandy put the duck on the front seat of the truck. It was nice and warm inside the truck; we kept it running while working, and sat in the truck for our coffee breaks and to warm up.

A few minutes later, the duck began to quack and walk around on the front seat of the truck. He was not afraid of us and seemed to enjoy when we picked him up and stroked his head.

"What name should we call the duck? He's now our pet?" said Sandy.

"I know, we will call him Glen because he does not like to fly," said Sandy.

We all started to laugh.

"Yes, that is a good name for him," I said.

We kept Glen in the furnace room in the trailer next to Sandy's room. The furnace room was nice and warm. Sandy laid some newspapers on the floor and put a bowl of oatmeal and water on the newspapers.

"Glen will be warm in here and hopefully, he will eat the oatmeal," said Sandy.

Every day after work, Sandy and I checked on Glen. I was curious to see if Glen would eat the oatmeal. Sure enough, Glen ate the oatmeal and seemed to be happy in his living quarters. Sandy was getting attached to Glen and said, "I will take Glen with me south on my time off. I have a friend who has a farm raising chickens and ducks just outside Edmonton."

A week passed, and Glen was getting stronger, happily quacking at us when we checked on him after work.

"Where's Glen? I can't find him?" said Sandy one evening after work.

"Maybe Louis knows where Glen is," I said.

Sandy and I found Louis at the camp, who had just returned from an extended time off. Sandy asked Louis, "Did you move the duck that was in the furnace room?"

"I ate the duck; it was nice and fat," said Louis.

"What! You ate my duck? He was my pet! I was taking care of him!" said Sandy. He was furious at Louis and was just about in tears. Sandy went back to his room, slamming the door behind him.

I was cheering for Glen to make it south, where he would have a chance to make it through the winter, hanging around and quacking with the domestic ducks at Sandy's friend's farm.

At last, the weather cleared on the third day enough to complete the collection of samples north of Blackwater River. Glen, the pilot, knew the area and had done some flying in the past couple of years north of Blackwater River.

"There is a large sinkhole not too far from here, large enough to fly the helicopter inside of it," said Glen.

I was curious and wanted to see this sinkhole. I had never heard of a sinkhole before and did not know what they looked like. Ten minutes later, Glen said, "At our three o'clock, there's the sinkhole."

I looked in the three o'clock direction and just saw some tall trees with no sinkhole in sight. A few seconds later, we were hovering over the sinkhole. I looked down and saw clear water at the bottom of the sinkhole; the water looked very deep. The sinkhole was perfectly round, with rocky steep cliffs adorning its inside. The circular cliffs were at least 30 meters (100 feet) in height. The sinkhole was at least 150 to 180 meters (500 to 600 feet) in diameter. Glen was

219

correct—the sinkhole was large enough to land a helicopter inside it.

"There is nowhere to land at the bottom of the sinkhole, only water. The only way to get down or out of the sinkhole would be with ropes," said Glen.

We continued our flight to the next river north of the sinkhole. The scenery was beautiful, with mountain ranges to the east and the Mackenzie River to the west. We flew to a river near the Mackenzie River and landed on the highway's right-of-way. The scenery on the ground was as beautiful as the scenery from above. We collected our samples and headed back to Blackwater River to collect samples on both sides of the river.

The day was getting shorter every day by the minute. The camp was only a few minutes from the Blackwater River. I was coming up on my time off and was looking forward to spending some time with Phoebe. I had not received any letters from Phoebe for the past few days, so there must be a few letters waiting for me at the RBTM camp.

We spent the night at the Blackwater River camp and headed to our camp the following day at first light. The helicopter was loaded to the maximum with sample bags and our gear.

A couple of days later, I boarded a plane at the airport on the highway near the camp with my pack, heading to Fort Simpson. Thank God it was a beautiful day for flying and not a bad weather day. It was a Friday morning; I had the weekend off, then five weekdays, and another weekend off before I had to return to the camp for another thirty-five-day stint. I was happy and excited to see Phoebe and have some time off. She did not know that I was to arrive in Fort

Simpson earlier. We hadn't spoken with each other since I left; our only way of communication was by letters. The plane could not get to Fort Simpson fast enough.

We landed at the town airstrip, and from there it was a couple minutes' walk to Phoebe's parents' house. I just walked into the house; I was family now. Phoebe, Florence, and Mary were having breakfast, surprised to see me. Phoebe got up, walked to me, and gave me a big hug and a kiss. She was much bigger than the last time I saw her at the dock, five weeks ago. Phoebe was around six and a half months pregnant by then.

Mary offered me a cup of tea, and I joined them at the kitchen table.

"Did any of my cheques arrive at the office?" I asked.

"I picked up your first cheque yesterday at the office. They told me that your cheques would be three to four weeks behind," said Phoebe. She added, "I deposited your cheque into our account and withdrew forty dollars to buy food."

Before I left for the camp, we had planned to rent an apartment at the Mackenzie Manor, I had worked building it.

"I went to the manor to speak with the landlord a couple of weeks ago. A two-bedroom apartment is two hundred and seventy dollars a month. Heating and water are included; you only have to pay for power. I had a look at a couple of apartments on the second floor. Nobody has stayed in them yet," said Phoebe.

"Let's have a look later today. I would like for you to move into the manor before I head back to the camp," I said.

At lunchtime, Gabe came home for lunch. He was working at the water plant for the village. While he was having his lunch, he asked me how work was at the camp. We talked until it was time for him to go back to work. Gabe and I were getting along well; we had a connection between the two of us. He accepted that I was young and inexperienced and had a lot to learn. I was the father of his soon-to-be first grandchild. Gabe knew that my heart was in the right place and that I would take care of his daughter and grandchild.

Being six and a half months pregnant, Phoebe was very emotional at times. She was only seventeen years old and scared. She would, on occasion, start to cry and say to me, "I'm too fat, you don't love me anymore." I would reply to her, "No, you are not fat, you are pregnant, and I love you the way you are." I don't think my words consoled her.

Phoebe's friend Tracy Michel and her boyfriend Bill Champion asked us if we would be interested in sharing an apartment at the Mackenzie Manor with them. Tracy was pregnant and expecting in about one month. I had met Tracy when I first met Phoebe in August 1973. I met Bill before I went to work at RBTM, and we both got along well. We were the same age. Bill was from Alberta, had short wavy brown hair with brown eyes. He was the same height as me.

Phoebe and I walked to the manor to look at the apartments. The manager gave us a tour of two apartments on the second floor that had not been rented yet. Both apartments were identical. One was facing the street, while the other was facing the parking lot. The apartments had two good-sized bedrooms, an open-concept kitchen and living room, a bathroom with a bath and shower, and a medium-sized storage room. Everything was brand new, no scratches or stains on the walls or floors. I opted for apartment 207 instead of 205.

Phoebe wanted 205 because it was facing the street. I took her aside and explained to her that while I was working at the building this past winter, the carpenters used to urinate on the inside wall of apartment 205. They were too lazy to walk down to the outhouses near the office. Phoebe looked at me with a disgusted expression and said, "We'll take apartment 207."

Later that day, Bill and I wrote a cheque each for the rent and damage deposit and handed it to the manager. We both signed the lease.

"You can move in on Monday. You will have to notify NTPC and have them switch the power to your name," said the manager.

I registered the power under my name. Bill and Tracy paid half the power bill each month.

Phoebe and I were both excited and could not wait to move into our apartment. I was making good wages at the camp and could now afford to rent the apartment along with anything else needed. On Monday morning, we purchased a bed, pillows, sheets, and two blankets at the Hudson Bay store, along with dishes, utensils, pots, pans, and groceries. As we walked to the cashier, I saw a small fourteen-inch black-and-white television on sale for forty-nine dollars. I looked at Phoebe and said, "The television is on sale. Should we buy it?"

Phoebe looked at me with a smile and said, "If you want it."

I snatched the television off the shelf before someone else took it. CBC Vancouver was the only channel available in Fort Simpson at the time; there was no cable or satellite dish yet. A rabbit ear antenna was included with the television and was required to capture the channel signal.

Phoebe's cousin, Alex, happened to be at the Hudson Bay store. I asked him if he could move our bed and items we purchased in his truck and help me move the bed to the apartment. I offered him ten dollars, and he accepted, helping us move to the apartment. Bill and Tracy moved in on the same day as us. They took the bedroom closest to the bathroom.

In our bedroom, we set up our new bed, and the television was placed in the living room on top of a cardboard box. We didn't have any chairs, tables, or a sofa yet—that was for the next paycheck. We sat on the floor in the living room to eat and watch television. We didn't have much, but we were happy to have a roof over our heads.

My time off flew by quickly, and it was time for me to leave for the camp. I was relieved that Phoebe would not be alone in the apartment while I was away.

"I will ask around town if there is any used furniture for sale," said Phoebe.

Early Monday morning, Phoebe and I walked to the DPW office. The man with the salt-and-pepper hair said, "Your plane is leaving in one hour from the town airstrip."

We walked to the Arctic Air office and sat waiting for my flight. Half an hour later, the Islander plane landed at the airstrip.

"That is your flight. The pilot will fuel up, then you can board the plane. You're the only passenger. The plane is loaded with groceries from Hay River," said the receptionist.

Phoebe and I hugged and kissed; I could see tears in her eyes.

"You will be okay. Tracy and Bill will be with you at the apartment. You can just relax and take it easy," I said.

The pilot signaled at me by motioning with his right hand for me to walk to the plane. I did not know the pilot but had seen him at the Hudson Bay store before. He was tall, at least 187 centimeters (6 feet 2 inches), with a medium build. His name was Glen, and I chuckled a bit when he told me his name. He was the contract pilot for flying employees, groceries, and parts for the heavy equipment for the three camps. Glen was friendly; he was in his late twenties to early thirties and wore a baseball cap with the Arctic Air logo.

"The only seat available is the co-pilot seat next to me," said Glen.

I sat beside him and secured my seatbelt. The plane was loaded with groceries right up to the ceiling, not even room for another small box. Before Glen started the airplane, he said, "Well, if we go down, we won't go hungry. I saw a few cases of T-bone steak somewhere in the back of the plane."

The two engines roared to life. The plane taxied to one end of the airstrip. As we gained speed down the runway, I saw Phoebe waving at me. I waved back at her. The plane must have been very heavy; we used most of the runway before the plane finally lifted off. The Mackenzie River was choked with large ice pieces floating down the river. The river would be frozen solid when I came back in five weeks; maybe the winter road would be open by then.

We gained altitude until I could see the mountains to the west. The clouds were scattered with a few openings, revealing patches of blue sky. A blanket of snow adorned the ground and trees; the lakes were frozen with a layer of snow on top of the ice. I kept my eyes on the ground, looking for moose or any other type of wildlife.

In the third week of January 1975, I flew again with Glen on my way to Fort Simpson during my time off. I boarded the plane at the RBTM airstrip and flew to the Blackwater River camp, where my crew had been stranded for three days due to bad weather in October. The plane dropped off much-needed dozer replacement parts and picked up a couple more passengers. We flew from the Blackwater River camp to Fort Simpson in the dead of the night.

Halfway to Fort Simpson, Glen informed us that there was a major snowstorm in the Fort Simpson area. He was unsure if we would be able to land in Fort Simpson. Once over Fort Simpson, Glen was informed by the Fort Simpson airport that 30 centimeters (1 foot) of snow had fallen so far, and more was on the way. Both airstrips, in town and at the main airport, were shut down until the snowstorm subdued. Glen circled once around the airstrip at the main airport and climbed above the layers of clouds to fly above the storm.

We were heading back to the RBTM camp. I was very disappointed; I was looking forward to seeing Phoebe and spending time with her, she was expecting to give birth in the next couple of weeks. I had planned and notified my supervisor that I would stay with Phoebe until she gave birth to our first child.

As I was sitting next to Glen, I kept my eyes on the fuel gauge on the plane, wondering if we would have enough fuel to make it back to the airstrip at RBTM. The weather north of Fort Simpson was snowless, the skies were clear, and the Northern Lights were in full display, dancing and bouncing in the skies. As we're getting closer to RBTM, Glen radioed the Wrigley airport to request them to contact the RBTM camp via mobile phone to inform the supervisor at the camp that the plane would require lights at the RBTM airstrip in order to land the plane. Back in the seventies, air control staff were on duty 24 hrs. a day, 7 days a week at the Wrigley airport. After a few minutes, Wrigley airport radioed back to Glen to let him know that they were unable to contact the camp. Glen headed to the Wrigley airport, which was located about fifteen minutes away from the camp. Glen landed at the airport and parked the plane next to the terminal. I glanced at the fuel gauge; it was almost empty. I was grateful that we had made it safely to the Wrigley airport. If I would have been alone, I would have kneeled and kissed the ground. Glen used the telephone at the airport and finally contacted the supervisor at the camp. He looked at the three of us and said, "Let's get back in the plane, we will fly to the camp and spend the night there." "Do we have enough fuel to make it to the camp?" I spoke. "No worries, we have enough fuel to make it," said Glen.

We boarded the plane, once again I sat beside Glen. The dual engine roared and woke. The airplane got off the ground effortlessly. Once over the RBTM airstrip, Glen made a semi-circle and lined up the plane between the barrels with small fires inside them on both sides of the airstrip. The plane touched down; Glen headed to the north end of the airstrip where planes were to be parked. About 100 meters (300 feet) from the parking area, both propellers, starving for fuel, came to a sudden stop. That was a close call; if Glen had had to make a second attempt at landing, we would have crashed into the nearby bush. The night was very cold in the minus 30 Celsius (minus 22 Fahrenheit). Glen and us three passengers along with a couple workers from the camp pushed the plane to the parking area. Glen fueled up the plane from a couple of barrels in the back of a truck with a hand wobble pump. We all caught a ride to the camp; it was near midnight.

The following morning, after an early breakfast, we made our way to the airstrip where Glen was warming up the plane with a Herman Nelson heater. The sun was peeking behind the horizon. We boarded the plane and headed to Fort Simpson. The sky was clear with no signs of fallen snow ahead of us. We landed at the town airstrip; Glen parked the plane near the Arctic Air buildings. I stepped out of the plane and immediately headed to the Mackenzie Manor. I rang the buzzer at the front door, Phoebe answered, and said, "Finally, you're home." I made my way to our apartment on the second floor; Phoebe was waiting in the corridor at the front of our door. I was so happy to be home. "I heard the plane flying over last night, I was expecting you back. We had a big snowstorm last night," said Phoebe. "We had to turn around and head back to our camp last night," I said. I did not want to tell her about the plane running out of fuel on landing, it would have added more worries. Phoebe's belly had grown more since I last saw her. I did not mention it to her as she was very emotional about being pregnant.

A couple of days later, Glen returned to Fort Simpson from Hay River with a load of groceries for the camps. He picked up the mail in Fort Simpson for the camps and resumed his flight to the RBTM camp. Glen lifted off near the end of the runway, shortly after both engines stopped, and the plane crashed into dense bush near the end of the island. Glen was the only one on board; he had forgotten to fuel up the plane prior to his departure to the RBTM camp. He had been working long hours flying without proper rest between the flights. Glen was fortunate; he had only a broken leg with a few minor cuts and bruises. I remember seeing the ambulance dropping him off at the Fort Simpson hospital. Glen was carried into the hospital on a stretcher; he was conscious and talking and did not appear to be in pain. Years later, while flying a helicopter in the mountains near the Yukon border, Glen was slinging, under the helicopter, a large dish for a tower at the top of a mountain. The rope that was attached to the large dish and belly hook on the helicopter snapped and sprung up into the main rotor. Alas, Glen was killed in the crash.

Like my first time off, time went by quickly. Phoebe had purchased a second-hand kitchen table and chairs and was on the lookout for a second-hand sofa. Phoebe's parents had purchased a baby crib from the Hudson Bay store. Phoebe's dad set up the crib in our bedroom. Tracy was expecting in early November; she and Phoebe were a couple of months apart from giving birth. Come Monday morning, it was my time to head back to the camp. I caught a ride in a small plane on wheels with two other employees. The survey job was interesting; I enjoyed learning and working on the construction of the highway. However, it was difficult to be away from Phoebe for five weeks at a time. Back at the camp for my second stint, the winter had established itself, and the snow depth was now nearly 60 centimeters (2 feet) deep. Every day seemed like the temperatures were in the high minus 20 to minus 30 (minus 4 to 22 Fahrenheit). The winter did not let up until the month of April. The days were spent surveying ahead of the Hire North's operators.

As we worked south of the current gravel road, we established survey benchmarks every 152 meters (500 hundred feet) on the west side of the right-of-way. The distance between the benchmarks was measured with a chain. A survey benchmark is a permanent mark established at a known elevation and used as the basis for measuring the elevation of the highway during its construction. Once the location of a benchmark was measured, the snow around the chosen tree, which would become a benchmark, was removed to bare ground with a shovel. The chosen tree was approximately 7.5 centimeters (3 inches) in diameter at the base and was cut with an axe about 20 centimeters (8 inches) above the ground. Most of the trees that were made into benchmarks were black spruce, tamarack, poplar, or birch. The stump was blazed with an axe at the front of the stump facing the right-of-way, and the number of the benchmark was written with a carpenter's pencil on the blazed side. A 20 centimeters (8 inches) nail was hammered on the top of the benchmark (stump) with the back of the axe. The top of the nail was used to rest the survey rod while taking elevation measurements. Surveyor flagging, usually orange in color, was hung in the trees nearby to mark the location of the benchmark.

Every morning, I woke up early and made my way in the dark from our camp to the Hire North camp by means of a shortcut trail through a stand of jack pine. The walk got my blood flowing; by the time I walked inside the trailer where breakfast was served, I was fully awake and ready to eat breakfast. I helped myself and filled my plate with eggs, bacon, sausages, and toast along with a large glass of milk and a cup of hot tea mixed with sugar. The snow was deep, and the temperatures were in the minus 30 Celsius (minus 22 Fahrenheit); the food would give me energy and keep me warm. I made note that on my next time off, I would make an appointment with the dental therapist at the hospital. There was no dentist stationed at the hospital year-round. A dentist would travel to Fort Simpson two or three times a year and see patients at the hospital for a couple of days and then leave town, not to be seen for another three to four months, appointments had to be made well in advance. I recalled Phoebe's father telling me that he used spruce gum in the past for toothache.

After breakfast, I made my way back to our camp to prepare for the day. I came across a large clump of spruce gum that I broke off with my hand from a large white spruce tree near our camp. I took the gum to my bedroom to thaw it out. I chipped a small piece and put it in my mouth to chew it and soften it. The spruce gum tasted strong, a taste that I found pleasant. I put the gum inside the hole of my tooth until it was crammed inside the hole of my tooth. The spruce gum blocked the sugar in my tea from reaching the nerves inside the hole of my tooth. Provided that I had spruce gum inside the hole of my tooth, I had no pain when I drank sweet tea or ate sweet desserts. The spruce gum had to be replaced daily; it would eventually break down into little pieces and come out of my tooth. I gathered enough spruce gum and had a good stash of it. I still had about four weeks before my time off, the toothache was painful, but thanks to the spruce gum, I was pain-free. I wrote to Phoebe and asked her to book an appointment for me.

Each day was like a clone of the previous day, setting up benchmarks along the right-of-way, surveying the newly built sections of the highway and the borrow pits to calculate the amount of soil taken out. I used a pair of snowshoes to break trails on the right-of-way; the snow was at least two feet deep. The trails would freeze in no time, and once frozen, one could walk on the trails without snowshoes. Sandy would let me drive our truck to our working areas at the end of the road. A dozer operator made a trail for us to drive, two blades wide. This cut down on the walking and time to set our benchmarks. I was having a good time driving the work truck, getting more confident in switching gears and using the four-wheel drive when I got stuck a few times. After work, I would find Phoebe's letters on my bed. Louis Tale, our camp attendant, would clean our bedroom and make our bed just like at a hotel. One evening, I found a dried squirrel hide in a leg hole trap on the floor near my bed. I had asked Louis to show me how to skin and dry a squirrel just like trappers do. Louis had set some squirrel snares nearby and caught one. He was not busy at the camp as there were five of us. He set a few traps and snares not far from the camp to catch some fur and keep busy. My time after work was spent reading Phoebe's letters and writing letters to her.

At last, I was to board the plane heading to Fort Simpson early Friday morning. I recalled catching a ride to the airstrip that morning. A very large grey wolf with striking blue eyes sat on the side of the road looking at us as we drove by. The driver, who was a Hire North employee, said, "That must be the wolf the cooks are feeding, he is not scared of people." That was my first time seeing a wolf in the wild. The wolf was only a few feet away from us when we drove by; he did not look aggressive or scared at all. The look in the wolf's blue eyes gave me the goosebumps, what a rush. It was a bright sunny day but very cold; I could feel the frost building on my beard and mustache. It was great to be heading home again.

We had another occupant at the apartment; Tracy had given birth to a boy named William, a.k.a. Billy, who was born on November 11th, a week after my birthday. Phoebe and I were Billy's godparents at his baptism. Phoebe had gotten even bigger than the last time I saw her. It was great to be back home. Phoebe did a lot of walking during her pregnancy to her parent's house and the Hudson Bay store and back home. Phoebe had seen the doctor at the hospital a week before. "I should be giving birth around mid-January," said Phoebe. I was looking forward to being a dad; I was still very young, only nineteen years old. Phoebe was seventeen years old in August. We were kids in age but matured in mind. I could tell that Phoebe was a little scared and nervous about being pregnant. We relished our time together at the apartment, taking it easy and relaxing. A couple of days before my return, Phoebe's parents purchased a crib from the Hudson Bay store; it was a nice surprise and much appreciated by both of us. Gabe put the crib together in our bedroom. Phoebe bought baby blankets and had the crib made up, ready for the arrival of our first child.

One cold morning, I walked to Baptiste's house, Phoebe's uncle, to borrow Stanley's car, another cousin of Phoebe; I had spoken to Stanley a few days earlier about borrowing his car to take my driver's license test with the RCMP in Fort Simpson. Stanley was a year or two younger than I was; he wore his hair combed back Elvis-style, which was popular back then in Fort Simpson. He was tall and slim built and always wore a leather jacket year-round, even when the weather was cold or hot. Stanley owned a sixties blue Plymouth Barracuda; he was proud of his car; he made some holes with a hammer and nails in his muffler so it would sound and roar like a sports car. You could hear his car from across town when he started it and stepped on the gas pedal.

Stanley drove me to the RCMP station, I walked inside the station unannounced and asked if I could take my driver's license test. Back then, the RCMP conducted the driver's license test. Two RCMP officers stood near the front desk in a conversation. They ended their conversation and looked at me as if saying, "Look at what the cat dragged in." One of the officers asked me, "Do you want to do the test verbally or written?" I told him, "Verbally, I don't read English that well." I lied to him; I thought that I had a better chance of passing the test verbally. He would read the questions to me, and I would answer them. The officer checked marked my answers on the test. I was nervous and did not think that I had passed the verbal test. After marking my test, the officer stood and said, "Do you have a vehicle for the driving test?" I looked at him surprised and asked,

"Did I pass the verbal test?" The officer looked at me dumbfounded and said, "Yes, you did, that is why we are doing the driving test." I was so happy that I had passed the verbal test. "Do you have a car for your driving test?" said the officer. "Yes, I do, it's outside," I said. "Did you drive the car here?" asked the officer. "No, my girlfriend's cousin drove it here, it is his car," I said. "Good, I won't have to charge you for driving without a license," said the officer. The officer asked Stanley, "Driver's license, registration, and insurance, please." Stanley handed them to the officer.

I sat in the driver's seat, and the officer sat next to me. I was expecting the officer to ask me to do a parallel parking; I had never done a parallel parking at the camp. I started the car, which sounded like it needed a new muffler. The officer told me to drive to the front road, and he had me drive around the block and park at the station. I did my signals and stopped at the one stop sign around the block. "Come in the office, I will give you your driver's license," said the officer. I was ecstatic, like a small child waiting to open his Christmas presents. The RCMP looked at Stanley and told him, "Better get a new muffler on your car." Stanley nodded his head to the officer.

A few days later, I purchased a late sixties Ford Galaxie 500 from Louis Cazon, Phoebe's cousin, for five hundred dollars, which was a lot of money back then. The car was red and could sit eight people inside: four in the back bench and four more in the front bench. There were no seat belts in the car. I was so proud of my first car. Aside from having to put a liter of oil in the engine each time I fueled up and some minor fuel leaks from the gas tank, the car got me where I wanted to go and back.

I had run out of spruce gum, and my appointment with the dental therapist was scheduled the next morning. I was a tad nervous and did not like going to the dentist, but I had to deal with the aching tooth. At the reception desk, I was given directions to where the dental therapist's office was. Unsure if I was at the right office, I knocked at the door and heard what seemed like someone getting their tooth pulled out. "I will be done in a couple of minutes, just have a seat and wait, please," said the dental therapist. A few minutes later, a young Dene man around my age came out of the office holding his jaw with his right hand; he appeared to be in pain. Behind him stood a young woman a couple of years older than me. She had shoulder-length wavy dirty blonde hair with blue eyes. She was wearing a lab coat like what doctors' wear. Back then, I was not fond of seeing a doctor or dentist; I had the white coat syndrome. When I saw a white coat, my blood pressure would go up. The dental therapist introduced herself as Sandy; she was friendly as well as comical.

"What can I do for you today?" said Sandy. "My filling in one of my bottoms back teeth came off; I now have a big hole in my tooth," I said. "Have a seat in the dentist chair; I will have a look," said Sandy. She adjusted the light above her head until the light was shining right into my eyes, blinding me. "Yes, I see the big hole in your tooth, you will require a new filling in your tooth. I'm only a dental therapist; I am not trained to replace dental fillings. I am only trained to pull teeth and clean them," said Sandy. She added, "The dentist will be in Fort Simpson in a couple of weeks; I can book you an appointment if you want."

"I will be at RBTM camp where I work for the next five weeks in a few days," I said. "The dentist won't be back in Fort Simpson until sometime in March," said Sandy. "I cannot wait that long, just pull the tooth out," I said. Sandy looked at me surprised and said, "Your tooth is still good; a filling will fix it." "I do not want any more pain from the tooth, just pull it out," I said. "Okay, I will just do that," said

235

Sandy. I had enough of that tooth and the pain and wanted it out of my mouth. Sandy gave me two or three injections on both sides of my gum.

Sandy leaned toward me with what looked like a pair of plyers in her right hand. "Open wide," said Sandy. She grabbed the tooth with the plyers and started to wiggle the tooth from side to side. The tooth was not having any of it. Instead of having the tooth move side to side, it was my whole head moving side to side.

For a woman her size, Sandy had a good grip on my tooth and was not giving up on it. I could feel her struggling and breathing heavily. "Can I climb on top of you and put my knee on your chest? That way, I will have good leverage to pull your tooth," said Sandy.

I had been to the dentist a few times before but had never heard a dentist say, "Can I climb on top of you and put my knee on your chest?" That sounded like something out of a Charlie Chaplin or The Three Stooges movie. With the plyers still in my mouth, I mumbled a distorted and faint yes.

Sandy proceeded to first climb on the chair, then on top of me. At that moment, if someone had walked into the office and seen us, I could picture what they would have thought. I am certain the story would have made it around town in no time. Once, someone told me in Fort Simpson, "If you do not hear gossip by 11 a.m., make one up."

Sandy put her knee in the middle of my chest and started to pull on my tooth. She was not a heavy woman; nonetheless, she was not a lightweight woman either. The tooth was not budging. Sandy had me pinned down on the chair. I could tell by her heavy breathing that she was getting tired.

236

Sandy let go of my tooth for a bit to catch her breath, still with her knee on my chest, and then took a deep breath with the plyers on my tooth; it was now or never. Sandy gave her almighty push. I felt like my jaw was going to break.

I grabbed both of her arms, which were pulling on the plyers, with both my hands and helped her pull. The tooth started to loosen up until it popped right out of my mouth. It was a good thing that I was holding Sandy's arms when the tooth popped out; otherwise, she would have fallen off me and down to the floor.

During the procedure, I heard my jaw crack a few times. It was a good thing that Sandy had given me enough injections to completely freeze my mouth and jaw. Sandy and I started to laugh out loud.

"You had a strong and stubborn tooth there," said Sandy. "Can I have a look at my tooth?" I spoke. She gave me the tooth and said, "That's a souvenir and a good story to tell." We both laughed again.

My time off was ending, and it was time for me to pack up and head back to RBTM camp. My third shift at the camp was to be a three-week shift, as RBTM camp would be shutting down until the second week of January. The winter road to the camp had just opened, and the ice crossing at the end of Fort Simpson Island was thick enough to support the weight of light vehicles.

The winter road trailed the Canadian National Telecommunications Line (CNT Line). Tripods made of telephone poles with black wires hanging from tripod to tripod could be seen along the east side of the winter road. The CNT line provided telephone services up and down the Mackenzie Valley, and the telephone services were interchanged with microwave towers along the Mackenzie Valley.

The winter road was very narrow in some places, barely wide enough for vehicles to pass each other. My ride to the camp this time was in a pickup truck via the recently opened winter road.

"Are you ready to go?" said Denis, the salt-and-pepper-haired fellow who had hired me in early September.

"Yes, I'm," I said. I helped the driver, who happened to be Denis, load the work truck with surveying equipment and tubes of blueprints for the water crossings between the Camsell Bend Crossing, now called the Ndulee Crossing, and the community of Wrigley.

Denis was excited to get out of the office and drive on the winter road. "I'm always stuck in the office doing paperwork; I miss being out in the field," he said. We stopped at the local gas station to fill up the truck and several five-gallon jerry cans.

Chuckling, Denis said, "There are no gas stations on the winter road." The temperature was in the mid minus 30 Celsius (minus 22 Fahrenheit) with clear skies. As we drove over the ice crossing, I could see behind us the truck's exhaust lingering like a small cloud over the crossing.

We took a left turn once across the river. Tall snowbanks, about 1 meter (3 feet) high, on both sides of the winter road denoted the path of the road. Denis and I bounced in unison on the seat of the truck whenever we hit a bump or a depression on the road. The road was indeed very narrow.

"The winter road will be widened in the next few days. It just opened a couple of days ago," said Denis. We didn't see any wildlife, though there were several big and small game tracks crisscrossing the road.

About three hours later, we arrived at the bank of the Willow Lake River. Both banks of the river were a bit steep. Denis took his time crawling down the bank as the road was very bumpy. There were no seat belts in the truck, so I extended both arms above my head and rested my hands against the ceiling of the cab to avoid hitting my head.

The ice crossing was in poor shape, with chunks of river ice poking through the snow here and there. Before reaching the bottom of the bank across the river, Denis told me, "Hang on," and sped up the somewhat steep bank. As we climbed the bank, the truck started to slow down. Denis stepped on the gas, and the truck bounced a couple of times up the bank. I felt like a cowboy riding on a wild bull.

At last, we made it to the top of the bank without getting stuck halfway up. "There is still a lot of work to do on both approaches and the ice crossing," said Denis.

Forty minutes or so later, we reached the end of the gravel road that leads to the RBTM camp. The sun had set behind the mountains to the west.

"It will most likely hit minus 40 Celsius (minus 40 Fahrenheit) tonight," said Denis. He added, "I'll spend the night at the camp and return to Fort Simpson in the morning."

Denis was an interesting fellow; he had worked most of his adult life surveying on road and highway constructions in the north as well as in the south. He had a lot of experience and was getting near his retirement. I will always be grateful to him for hiring me. Prior to the DPW hiring, I had daily weekday visits for at least one month at the Hire North office in Fort Simpson inquiring for a job. I had heard from several locals that Hire North was looking for employees to work on the highway north of Fort Simpson. Walking around town, I would see the Hire North truck picking up people in the street. In my mind, that meant that they were short of workers for the camps. Each day during the week, like a well-oiled machine, I would show up at the office to talk with the person in charge of the hiring. He was a Dene man from Jean-Marie River, a small community up the Mackenzie River from Fort Simpson. He had short black hair and wore thick glasses. The Dene man; name was Freddie. He was very polite and all business. "No, I'm sorry but we do not have any jobs available at this time," said Freddie. Each day, I showed up at the Hire North office, I heard the same line until one month later, Freddie told me in a gentle, polite voice, "We are only hiring Indigenous people to work at the camps." I was disappointed and wished I was told this the first time I came to the office looking for a job. Without sounding aggressive, I said, "I wish you would have told me this the first day I came to your office looking for a job." "Yes, I'm sorry, I have to follow the rules," said Freddie. "I understand, I won't be coming to your office anymore," I said. The following day, I walked into the DPW office and was hired on the spot. I believe the reason why I was offered a job was because one of the employees did not report to work on the day he was scheduled to. On that day, DPW was short one Chainman/Rodman at the camp. My timing was right; I look at this as my reward for being persistent in seeking a job.

I settled myself back into my room. In anticipation of my return, Louis, the camp attendant, had my room ready with a new set of sheets on my bed and a freshly washed floor. Louis took good care of us at the camp and did his job very well. This time, my stay at the camp was to be for four weeks, the camp was scheduled to shut down for the

Christmas Holidays and reopen the second week of January. Sandy was back from his time off in Edmonton. We continued working at the end of the gravel road ahead of the heavy equipment operators. We surveyed and set up wooden stakes on the right-of-way to denote where the highway was to be built along with how much soil was required for the elevation of the highway. The night shift's heavy equipment operators worked on the area where we surveyed and marked with stakes. The following day, we surveyed the section of the road that was worked on overnight to ensure that the road and its elevation were as they should be. If there were some amendments to be done, we set new stakes for the amendments and the day shift crew would make the required upgrades.

The cold weather did not let up and the days kept getting shorter and shorter, with an average of 5 hours of sunlight per day. We went to work in the dark and ended our day in the dark. In some of the areas where we surveyed, the snow depth was between my knees and my waist. I used snowshoes to break trails along the right-of-way. The cold temperatures and depth of snow made me earn my salary. The temperatures were hovering in the minus 40 Celsius (minus 40 Fahrenheit). Taking account of the wind chill factor, on windy days, temperatures could be an additional ten to twenty degrees colder. We took our coffee breaks inside our work truck to warm up. The truck ran from the time we left camp in the morning until we returned. The winter of 1974-1975 was brutal, nowadays, winters are milder as opposed to fifty years ago.

I was looking forward to returning to Fort Simpson and spending time with Phoebe. She continued writing letters, at times four to five pages in length. My writing of letters was not as frequent as hers. I was counting the days, like an inmate waiting to be released. A few days before Christmas, the exodus began. Only a few employees stayed at the camp for the duration of the camp's closure. These employees were tasked with ensuring the protection of the camp from vandalism and freeze-up. Everyone who was to be demobilized from the camp was ecstatic and longing for their time off to spend time with their family and friends. Some of the heavy equipment operators and cooks had not had any time off since September. I caught a ride in a pickup truck to Fort Simpson. We left shortly after breakfast, everyone in the truck was from Fort Simpson.

The driver of the truck dropped me off at the apartment. I made my way up to the front door and rang apartment 207. Phoebe met me at the entrance of the apartment; she was even bigger than the last time I saw her. I told Phoebe that, "I do not have to return to the camp until after our child's birth." Phoebe looked at me, smiling, and gave me a hug. Due to the upcoming birth of our child, I was granted extra time off after the holidays to ensure that I would be in Fort Simpson for the birth of our child.

The day after my return, Gabe and I went on the search for birch trees with my car to build snowshoes we headed towards the ice crossing on the Liard River. We located a large birch tree big enough to make two pairs of snowshoes. I had been asking Gabe to teach me how to set spring pole snares for rabbits for some time. "Before we set spring pole snares, I will need to make two pairs of snowshoes. The snow is very deep this winter," said Gabe.

Early one morning after breakfast, Phoebe said, "Let's get a Christmas tree from across the syne." We returned to our apartment with our tree and decorated it. The apartment smelled like fresh cut white spruce. The decorated Christmas tree stood in the corner of the living room adjacent to the window facing the parking lot. Phoebe had been busy buying gifts for everyone. Beautifully wrapped gifts lay at the base of the Christmas tree, waiting to be opened on Christmas day.

On Christmas day, we invited Phoebe's parents and siblings to the apartment for a turkey dinner and the opening of the Christmas gifts. Phoebe and Florence cooked the turkey and dinner, which was delicious. Phoebe's parents sat at the small table on the two chairs we had to eat their dinner, and the rest of us sat on the floor eating our dinner and watching an old Christmas movie on our black-and-white fourteen-inch television resting on a cardboard box on the floor. After dinner, we opened our gifts by the Christmas tree. We did not have much to show for back then, nonetheless, we had a good time eating and laughing, enjoying each other's company. We had a roof over our heads, food to eat, and a warm and cozy place to live and sleep. I have fond memories of Christmas 1974, a month prior to Danny's birth.

January 25th, 1975, Phoebe began to experience irregular contractions in the evening. I could tell that she was in pain and very nervous. As time went by, her contractions became stronger and more frequent until her contractions were occurring every 3-5 minutes, lasting up to one minute.

"Phoebe, we should go to the hospital," I said.

"No, no, not yet," said Phoebe.

The contractions became more painful and intense until I said, "We should go to the hospital now." Phoebe held her belly and nodded her head. I helped her put her boots and jacket on.

"Let's walk to the hospital," said Phoebe.

I helped her walk down the stairs from the second floor to the main floor. The hospital was a couple of minutes' walk from our apartment. It was very cold with a strong north wind, which intensified the cold. Phoebe held my arm until we reached the hospital. I rang the buzzer at the hospital, and a nurse opened the door for us. She knew us and said, "It's time, I will call Nurse Maureen." The nurse took us to a room in the maternity ward.

Ten minutes later, Nurse Maureen walked into the room to assess Phoebe. I was asked to leave the room. The nurse came back a while later and said, "Phoebe wanted you to be with her." I spent one hour with Phoebe in the room. She held my hand in her right hand, and each time she had a contraction, she squeezed my hand with all her might for the duration of the contraction. I could not believe her strength; I felt my hand being crushed in her hand.

Nurse Maureen came to talk to us in the room and said, "It will be a while before the birth, you should go home, we will call you when it's time." I walked back to the apartment to call my mother and wait for the call from the nurse. We now had a phone in the apartment, and I called my mother to let her know that Phoebe would be giving birth today or tomorrow. My sister Johanne had given birth to a girl called Pascale on January 24th. My mother's first grandchild, with a second one on its way in the next few hours. I told my mother that I was waiting for a call from the hospital and said goodbye.

A few hours later, I must have fallen asleep and was awoken by the ringing of the telephone. It was the nurse. "Phoebe has been asking for you, can you come to the hospital?"

"Yes, I will be right over."

I practically ran to the hospital. Phoebe was happy to see me. I sat by her, holding her hand, which she squeezed at every contraction. An hour later, she was brought to the delivery room where she gave birth to our son Danny. He was 4.1 kilos (9 pounds and 1 ounce) and 55.8 centimeters (22 inches) in length. Being at the birth of your child is an experience that you will never forget. Our son was healthy and appeared to be normal physically. I was worried prior to the birth that our son may have physical deformities. I was so happy that he was healthy and physically normal. Danny was born January 26th at 6:40 am.

Danny 1975

I returned to RBTM camp a few days after our son Danny's birth. Once again, I caught a ride in a pickup truck heading to the camp on the winter road. The temperatures had been very cold, hovering in the minus 30s and 40s Celsius (minus 20s and 40s Fahrenheit). I had been on time off for nearly five weeks, and it was time to get back to work.

It was a blessing in disguise that my cheques were four weeks overdue as a result of the two-week holdback on the first pay cheque and the belated postal mail from Ottawa to Fort Simpson. This allowed me to receive two pay cheques while I was on time off. Back then, it took about fifteen to twenty days for my mother's letter to make it from Ste-Adele, Quebec to Fort Simpson, NWT.

The end of January and the beginning of February 1975 were brutal, for a full week, temperatures were between minus 40 and 50 Celsius minus 40 and 58 Fahrenheit). On the coldest day, the thermometer read minus 58 Celsius (minus 72 Fahrenheit) It was so cold that we had to run the engine in our truck, twenty-four hours a day, seven days a week. Even plugged in, the truck would not start if it was turned off overnight. A drum of diesel fuel gelled like it was Jello.

Following our extreme cold temperatures week, Sandy, our head surveyor at the camp, asked my co-workers David and Eddie if one of them would volunteer to set up benchmarks from Willow Lake River to the Camsell Bend (Ndulee) crossing using snowshoes. Both looked at Sandy as if he was out of his mind.

"No, it's too cold and too far to walk, are you crazy?" asked David.

"The snow is very deep, I'm having problems with my legs," said Eddie.

David's facial expression was hilarious; his eyes became very large as if he could not believe what was asked of him. Sandy turned his head in my direction, and before he could ask me, I said, "I will do it." Over the holidays, I walked about 40 kilometers (25 miles) with snowshoes checking my father-in-law's snare line.

"When do you want me to start?" I asked.

"We're waiting for our contract helicopter to arrive at the camp, it should be here in the next couple of days," said Sandy.

Later in the day, I heard David telling Eddie that there is a large wolf pack hanging around the right-of-way south of the camp. Throughout our surveying at the end of the gravel highway south of the camp, we saw several large wolf tracks on the right-of-way. I remember seeing one, in fresh snow, as large as my closed fist.

A couple of days later, a Bell 206 Jet Ranger helicopter landed behind our camp. The pilot was in his mid-twenties with short brown hair and no facial hair. He was at least 183 centimeters (6 feet) tall with a medium build. I recognized his accent as French but not from Quebec. I asked him, "Where are you from?"

He said, "New Brunswick."

His name was Jean-Pierre, and his English was much better than mine. We got along well and mainly spoke in French while working together. I was his only passenger. Each day, he would drop me off starting at the Willow Lake River and pick me up where I ended on each day. The following day, he would drop me off where I left off the previous day.

The benchmarks were set up 152 meters (500 feet) apart, along the west side of the Wrigley Highway's right-of-way by travelling by snowshoes, that were like the ones Gabe hand-made, but factory-made. The distance between the benchmarks was measured by counting my snowshoes' steps up to 166 steps. The benchmarks were built from the Willow Lake River up to 8 kilometers (5 miles) north of the Camsell Bend (Ndulee) crossing, which was a total distance of 65 kilometers (40 miles). The setup of the benchmarks took me twenty-one days to complete. I estimated that I set up approximately four hundred and fifty benchmarks.

I never did come across any wolf on the right-of-way, but I saw several wolf tracks as well as big game tracks such as moose and woodland caribou. Once, I saw someone driving a dog team across the right-of-way from a far distance. I believe that whoever was driving the dog team did not see me. Once I reached the dog team trail, I could see a hand-cut trail leading in the direction of the Mackenzie River. I assumed that the dog team driver was from the mouth of the Willow Lake River, where the Boots brothers and the Betsidea family lived.

Almost every day, I spotted Spruce and Ruffed grouse as well as Ptarmigans. Once, I witnessed a marten in hot pursuit of a white snowshoe hare. The marten was slowly but surely gaining ground on the snowshoe hare that was zigzagging, while the marten was moving as the crow flies. The marten and snowshoe hare were heading in my direction and were too engaged to notice me. The marten was a few steps away from reaching the snowshoe hare when all of a sudden, I let out a loud yell. The marten stopped, stood up on its hind legs, sniffed the air, looked in my direction, and then made a lightning-quick ninety-degree turn and ran for cover in the dense bush. The snowshoe hare kept on zigzagging and leaped nearly onto the head of my snowshoe without saying a thank you. If I had not interfered, I would have witnessed a marten killing a snowshoe hare about 5 meters (15 feet) from me. The snowshoe hare escaped death that day, and the marten most likely went to bed hungry. That was my first

248

time seeing a marten in the wild. The fur bearer was beautiful and graceful, wearing its fur coat.

My usual day after being dropped off by helicopter was to walk to the last benchmark I did the day before and then paced with my snowshoes 152 meters (500 feet) to the next benchmark. In a day, I would, on average, make twenty-one benchmarks and walk about 3.2 kilometers (2 miles). Halfway through the day, I made a fire, melted snow for water and tea, and ate my lunch. A lone raven flew over my campfire every day while I was having my lunch, looking for something to eat. I left a piece of my sandwich by the campfire after I had finished my lunch. The raven waited until I walked away from the campfire and then landed where I sat on spruce boughs next to the campfire. The raven grabbed the piece of sandwich and gobbled it down. Flying high in circles above my head, making this exclusive call as if the raven was grateful for the food I had left by the campfire.

The snow was, in some areas, up to my waist. Breaking trail was strenuous and good for the body. It kept me in good shape and was good for my spirit. Prior to sunset, I would listen for the helicopter, my ride back to the camp. Not once did I have to spend the night on the right-of-way due to bad weather or the helicopter having mechanical issues. I was prepared and willing to spend the night under the stars, if I had to. The temperatures were in the minus 20s to 30s (minus 4 to 22 Fahrenheit). On windy days, the temperatures felt much colder. Unfortunately, I could not complete the last 8 kilometers (5 miles) to the Ndulee crossing, the contract on the helicopter expired before I was able to complete the benchmarks. I really enjoyed working by myself and breaking trail by snowshoes. I felt like the work I did was worthy and meaningful. I traveled by helicopter to work every day, which was cool, and got paid for it too.

I had one more week left before my time off. I rejoined my crew and we continued making our way in the direction of Willow Lake River, surveying the right-of-way. The view from the top of the hills north of Willow Lake River was breathtaking. Looking to the west, several chains of mountains adorned the skyline. Looking to the east, the Franklin Mountains range reminded me of the Laurentian Mountains north of Montreal, Quebec. Below the hills, north of the mouth of the Willow Lake River, smoke from several cabins hung low in the cold air as it could not rise any further as a result of the cold temperatures.

At last, I boarded the Islander aircraft at the airstrip near the camp and was on my way to Fort Simpson. The day was beautiful, with bright sunshine and a cloudless sky. It was still very cold, nonetheless, nowhere close to minus 50 Celsius (minus 58 Fahrenheit). I was excited and felt, inside, the same way as the beautiful, bright sunshine and cloudless sky. Our son Danny was a well-behaved baby, he did not fuss much, yet drank milk like a newborn calf. Phoebe's sister Florence helped her from time to time taking care of Danny and eventually moved with us to take care of Danny when Phoebe started to work at the hospital in April.

I was looking forward to seeing Phoebe and Danny, he was at the time five weeks and a couple of days old. The flight was smooth and pleasant; every seat was taken by employees of the RBTM camp. Days were growing longer each day, and the month of March had tiptoed into the calendar. It had been a very long, brutal winter with extreme cold temperatures and heaps of snow. It was great to feel spring in the air.

I stepped out of the aircraft, picked up my backpack, and made my way to the apartment, across the street from the town airstrip. I rang the buzzer at the front door, no one

250

answered. I told myself, "Phoebe must be at her parent's house visiting." We had purchased a small wooden toboggan from the Hudson Bay store so Phoebe could pull Danny from one place to another while doing errands or visiting her parents. Phoebe's parents made a canvas wrapper for the sleigh, making it resemble a small dog sleigh. A warm blanket was used inside the sleigh so Danny would have a cozy and warm ride while being pulled around.

On my way to the house, I saw Phoebe pulling the sleigh on the main street. She smiled when she recognized me walking towards her. We hugged and kissed each other. I looked inside the blanket in the sleigh to find Danny sound asleep and looking comfortable. The bumps on the sidewalks must have given him the impression that he was being cradled. I took the rope from Phoebe and pulled the sleigh to our apartment.

Early 1975 in Fort Simpson, disposable diapers (Pampers) were not available yet. In the first couple of months after Danny was born, Phoebe used cloth diapers that were changed several times a day and washed by hand. Before the snow had melted in Fort Simpson that year, Pampers had finally reached Fort Simpson. Everyone was talking about Pampers around town; from the sound of it, it was a godsend to all the mothers who had babies and young children. Believe me, I was sold on Pampers after changing a few cloth diapers.

Turners' Store, across the street from the Fort Simpson Hotel, was selling Pampers by the case when they first arrived in town. I purchased one case, which contained twelve boxes of Pampers, thinking that it would last for months. The box of Pampers lasted only a few weeks; I could not believe how quickly the Pampers vanished. The Pampers were very popular and became a must-have item. They were a hot-ticket item and were in shortage at the stores many times. During these times, Phoebe would use the good old-fashioned cloth diapers.

I spent my time off relaxing and enjoying the company of Phoebe and Danny. He spent most of his day sleeping and would wake up when he needed to be fed. Danny loved his milk; I was the same as a baby. Once my mother told me that I did not need a mother but a cow for milk. I returned to the camp in mid-March by way of the winter road. The snow was starting to melt during the day while the sun was not hiding behind the clouds. Soon, the winter road would be shutting down for the season.

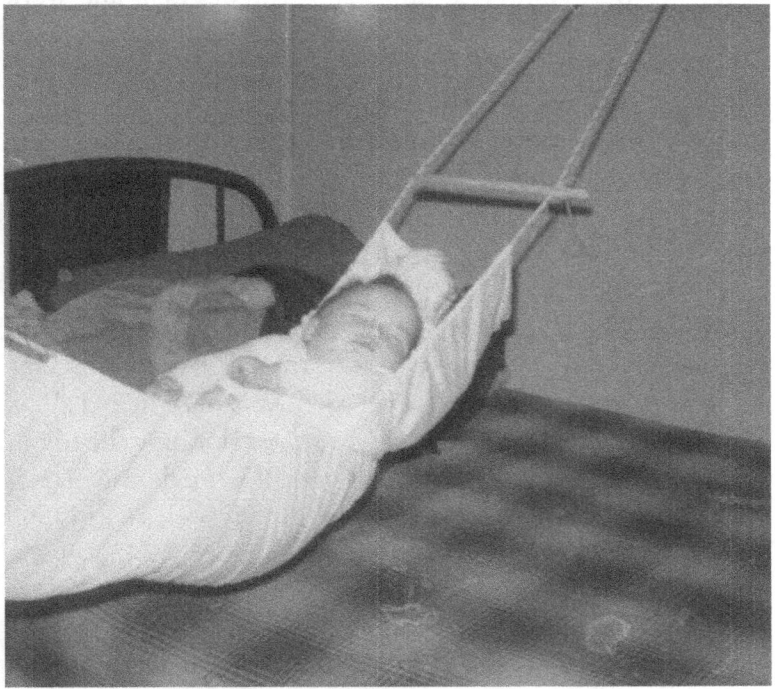

Danny sleeping in a swing 1975

The following day, our new supervisor, Victor Cook, informed us that in a week or so, we would be relocating to a new camp on the south side of the Willow Lake River. Victor was Dene from Fort Good Hope, and he was at least fifteen years my senior. Victor was of average height and build with short black hair. He was knowledgeable in terms of surveying road construction and had many years of experience. He was good to work with and had the distinctive good sense of northern humor. There was always a laugh to be had with Victor.

A company from Fort Nelson, British Columbia, was awarded a contract to build the road from the Willow Lake River to the Camsell Bend (Ndulee) crossing. Once the camp was set up on the right-of-way south of the Willow Lake River, we were to drive to the camp with our gear and work from there. A week or so later, we were informed that the camp was set and ready for us to move in. We packed our work and personal gear and headed to the camp. The winter road was on its last leg; the warm temperatures and sun had created deep potholes and bumps on the road. Several pieces of heavy equipment were working on the road to keep it open until it was no longer safe to drive on. We left after an early breakfast when the road was still frozen from the overnight below 0 Celsius (32 Fahrenheit) temperatures. It was another bright sunny day, looking to be a warm one. The drive to the camp, after the end of the gravel road, was bumpy and slow. Hidden deep potholes in the ice, by water flooding the top of the ice on the Willow Lake River crossing, made it feel as if we were driving on the surface of the water, with intermittent falls into the deep potholes that were hidden by the water. This was my first time being in a truck driving on a river crossing in the spring, covered with water on top of the ice. I was a tad nervous and worried that we might go through the ice.

"At that time of the year, the ice on the river is still solid and thick," said Victor.

At last, after struggling up the bank of the Willow Lake River, we arrived at the camp, which was made of several trailers connected. The person in charge at the camp, was a short and stocky man with a baseball cap and a cigarette hanging for dear life between his lips, said, "There is a small plane coming tomorrow before lunch with the owner of the company. Can you guys' survey and lay out the stakes for the airstrip? My night crew will build the airstrip once you guys are done with the surveying."

"Where exactly do you want the airstrip?" asked Victor.

Victor and the person in charge of the camp took a walk where the snow had been cleared south of the camp for the airstrip while we unloaded our gear and stored it inside the camp. The head cook met us inside and assigned us our rooms. I was to share a room with Victor; David and Eddie also shared a room. The head cook was a woman in her early forties with shoulder-length grayish hair. She was loud-speaking, as if she had hearing problems. Her name was Nancy; she had arrived at the camp the previous evening and was unpacking and storing the food as well as preparing lunch for the skeleton crew.

"I'm the only cook, my helper quit before we left Fort Nelson. I have another helper coming on the plane tomorrow morning," said Nancy.

"I have lunch ready for you guys, come in," said Nancy.

"Let's have lunch first before we start surveying the airstrip," said Victor.

About six weeks ago, I began making the benchmarks starting from the Willow Lake River. The scenery had changed drastically since; I could see some remnants of my snowshoes trail here and there. It was inconceivable that a camp stood on the right-of-way and that an airplane would be landing tomorrow morning on an overnight-built airstrip.

Nancy was a very good cook; her kitchen reeked of the wonderful smell of food. I was famished, and Nancy cooked us a wonderful dinner with freshly baked cakes and pies. The end of the airstrip was only about 150 meters (500 feet) from the camp. Under Victor's directions, we surveyed and laid our wooden stakes where the airstrip was to be built. Nearby, the heavy equipment opened a borrow pit to provide the soil needed for the airstrip. It was a race before darkness; we had to complete the surveying before dark so the night crew could haul the soil and build the airstrip. We all felt the pressure of getting the job done. It was all hands-on deck; we finally completed the survey as the sun had set to the west behind the horizon. The night crew did not waste any time; the buggies were hauling soil from the borrow pit to the airstrip. The camp was not completely set up yet; more trailers were on their way. The winter road was scheduled to close in the next 48 hours. Travel on the winter road was done from around midnight to the early morning hours when the temperatures were colder, and the road was frozen, not slushy.

Early the following morning, I peeked outside and was amazed to see the airstrip being worked on by drum rollers for the compaction of the airstrip. After breakfast, we gathered our work gear and started to survey from the south bank of the Willow Lake River. Victor asked me to take a shot with the rod on the benchmark that I made near the bank of the river. From there, I took a few shots with the rod along the bank of the river. While I was holding the rod, I heard some noises behind me. I looked over my shoulder and recognized the man who had sold a piece of moose meat to Gabe this past summer at the end of the island in Fort Simpson. The elderly Dene man, small in stature and in his

255

late seventies, pointed to his chest with his index finger and said, "Me Joe Boots, me Joe Boots." He extended his right arm in the direction of the mouth of the river and said, "Stay Willow Lake River."

I walked to Joe, shook his hand, and introduced myself, much like how he introduced himself. He smiled at me and slightly bowed his head forward while looking at me.

"Do you remember me?" I asked.

He did not seem to understand what I was saying. Joe was wearing a small hunting bag made of canvas with a strap made of moose hide over one shoulder. He opened his hunting bag and pulled out a dead white snowshoe hare and said, "Rabbit snare." Joe was wearing a pair of snowshoes on his feet and had one axe in one hand and a .22 rifle in the other hand. He was checking his snare line across the river from where he had his cabin. Joe waved at me and headed along the bank of the river in the upstream direction to check his snare line.

An hour later, I heard from a distance an airplane heading in our direction. The plane was a Cessna 185 on wheels. It circled twice around the camp to allow the drum rollers to move away from the airstrip. The plane made its approach coming from the south and safely landed on the airstrip and parked at the northern end. Once the propeller of the airplane had stopped, the owner of the company and the cook helper came out of the airplane. The owner was a tall and stocky man in his early fifties, dressed like he was going on a hunting trip. The person in charge of the camp walked to the airplane and shook hands with the owner. The head cook met the cook helper at the end of the airstrip; she was a young woman in her late twenties with long dirty blond hair tied in a ponytail. They hugged as if they knew each other. The owner took a walk on the airstrip and stomped one foot on the packed soil as if to check the compaction of the soil. Our crew walked to the camp to meet the owner and have our lunch. We introduced ourselves and shook hands with the owner and the cook helper. The owner looked around the camp and seemed to be happy with how things were going.

"There is a convoy of equipment, trailers, and the remainder of the crews on their way from Fort Nelson. They should be arriving early tomorrow morning," said the owner. He was pleased that the airstrip was completed in time for his visit.

For the remainder of the day, using the benchmarks I made a month or so earlier, we surveyed the right-of-way heading in a southerly direction from Willow Lake River. The winter road had been beaten up by the moving of the camp and heavy equipment, making it difficult to get around. Once the construction of the highway begins, we will have a means to travel and carry on with our surveying of the highway.

True to his word, the convoy of equipment, trailers, and the remainder of the crews arrived at the camp in the early morning, safe and sound. Listening to some of the drivers at breakfast, the drive on the winter road was challenging. The drivers who hauled the trailers on their low beds had to drive back to Fort Nelson before the winter road became impassable. The trailers were unloaded and connected to the existing camp. As luck would have it, the weather was on the drivers' side; cold temperatures in the minus Celsius (below 32 Fahrenheit) were forecasted for the next couple of days. The drivers with low beds were scheduled to head south at midnight.

The last two weeks of March and the first two weeks of April went by so fast. The temperatures had warmed up considerably, and the snow was melting at a rapid rate. The daylight hours were ever-increasing each day. We were barely keeping up with the road construction crews and had, on some days, worked extra hours to ensure the night crew had the surveying data to adhere to. It was apparent that Fort Nelson's Road construction company was well organized and experienced. Each day, the gravel road grew in length. Culvert and multi-plate culvert sites were surveyed at each of the creeks and drainage crossings. Once the sites were surveyed, the crews installed the culverts and multi-plate culverts. Once installed, we surveyed the culverts to ensure that they were accurately laid out.

As a result of the workload, I was asked if I could stay at the camp an additional week before my time off. I was on board and stayed the additional week. Mid-April, senior staff from our headquarters flew to the camp to pay us a visit. I knew most of the staff apart from a tall, slim man with clean-cut blond short hair and blue eyes. It was apparent that he was the person in charge. He and Denis took me aside and asked me if I would be interested in furthering my work in surveying. They indicated that they were interested in training me on how to run the surveying level and transit. I enjoyed the work and learning the components of surveying. This could become a career for me. I was very interested in the offer; however, this would mean that I would be away from home for extended periods. The person in charge cleared his throat and said, "There will be another surveying crew assigned to this camp. The crew will be arriving next week." I was happy to hear that we would have another crew to share the workload. He added, "Shifts will be designated for each crew, which means that your days and hours of work will be cut down to five days per week and eight hours per day. Conditional on the workload, working overtime hours may be approved by the camp head surveyor."

I was distraught, the main reason why I wanted this job working in a bush camp setting, seven days a week and ten hours a day, was to earn enough money to support my Phoebe and our newborn son. My working hours of seventy hours per week would be cut down to forty hours per week. My motivation for working at the bush camp was now shattered into pieces. I was very upset.

"What are we supposed to do at the camp on our two days off?" I asked.

"The days off will not be consecutive, you will have the two days off spread out throughout the week," said the person in charge.

"I will work the one extra week and then resign my position. I can find a job in Fort Simpson at 40 hours per week and be home with my family every night," I said.

The person in charge looked at me with a surprised expression on his face but did not comment on my statement. I told myself, "Phoebe will be happy to have me working closer to home. I guess I will have to look for a new job when I return to Fort Simpson."

Upon my return to Fort Simpson, Phoebe announced that Tracy's and Bill's relationship had not been going well lately and that both were on the verge of breaking up. The following day, Tracy moved with her son Billy to her parents' house.

"I will be moving out tomorrow to my uncle's trailer, I am sorry, but Tracy and I are not getting along," said Bill.

Our co-tenants were moving out, meaning that Phoebe and I would be accountable to pay the full monthly rental fee, two hundred and seventy dollars, and the utilities. Fortunately, Phoebe had started to work at the hospital a couple of weeks ago, doing laundry, cleaning rooms, and translating for the elder.

"I will have to look for another job; I resigned my position with DPW. They are cutting down our weekly hours of work from seventy to forty," I said.

Phoebe smiled and was happy that I would not be away for five weeks at a time. A couple of days later, I knocked on Ron Anderson's door looking for a job at their sawmills.

"Good to see you, we will be starting sawing, we have a lot of work for this summer. Will you be ready to start Monday?" asked Ron.

"Yes, pick me up at the Mackenzie Manor, Monday morning," I said.

Danny had grown and was more aware of his surroundings. He was almost three months old. He was a happy baby and rarely cried, only to let you know that he was hungry or hurting. It was good to be home again.

Phoebe & Danny -December 1975

Chapter 10:
Trip Up the Mackenzie River

It was the August long weekend of 1974 when I experienced my first trip up the Mackenzie River. Phoebe and her family (mom and dad, and two younger brothers, Melvin and Allan) left Fort Simpson early Saturday morning on a wooden scow powered by a 20-horsepower outboard motor (kicker). This would also be my first experience on a wooden scow. The scow, which he borrowed, was old and in need of a paint job; quite frankly, it had seen better days. I immediately thought to myself, does it leak? Is it stable? Will it, or us, survive the trip? I kept those thoughts to myself and made no mention to Gabe. Fortunately, the morning weather was nice and sunny with light winds (the summer of 1974 had been mostly rainy with very few warm and sunny days). We were to travel southeast against the current of the river, making it a slow-going journey. Our first stop would be Jean-Marie River for fuel, and then to Crow Nest near the mouth of the Trout River.

After loading the gear and everybody being on board, Gabe gave the old kicker a pull. It sputtered and died. Again, he pulled, and again, nothing. After a few moments, the boat had started to drift from the shore and downriver. While Gabe continued to pull the starter cord, he asked me to paddle the scow towards the shore. Because the Mackenzie and Liard rivers merge approximately 2 kilometers (1.2 miles) southeast of our position, the river's current was extremely strong and difficult to navigate. After some struggle, Gabe and I managed to reach the shore and tied the boat to a large boulder. Once ashore, Gabe worked on the kicker and soon managed to get it started. With the motor now purring like a cat, I untied the scow, gave it a push, and jumped in. Before Gabe took off, he placed his cap on his head, held it in place by the brim, pulled it down to his forehead, then twisted it side to side to secure it in place so that the wind would not blow it away, then gave the throttle a twist. We soon found ourselves heading across the river. No one wore a life jacket, a custom of the time.

While crossing the river, I glanced at the floor of the boat for leaking, and it was dry. Once across the river, I felt more relaxed and started to enjoy the trip. Just after the next bend, a bald-headed eagle dived and scooped a fish near the water surface. We were close enough to see the fish's tail wiggle as the eagle gained altitude with his lunch. Wow! A Kodak moment and I didn't have a camera.

We followed the river shore and crossed over to a small island, where we stopped for a bathroom break. The island was small with very few trees. Gabe called it Ghost Island; he explained that a long time ago, someone camped on the island and, throughout the night, felt the island moving, hence the name. We quickly departed and continued up the river. After a few hours, we arrived in Jean-Marie River. Gabe slowed the boat, cut the engine, and let the boat drift to shore, telling me to anchor the boat to a steel cable secured to the river's bank. Gabe and Mary made their way up the steep bank carrying a couple of empty jerry cans. Behind them, Phoebe and her two brothers followed. I waited at the boat and walked along the shore, stretching my legs. Driftwood and debris littered the shoreline, remnants of the river's spring break-up.

Continuing further, I could see the Jean Marie River, or in Slavey *Tthek'éhdélį* (Water flowing over clay). I remember Mary telling me that Jean Marie River was a very traditional Slavey community, with some of its inhabitants speaking Slavey only. About forty minutes later, the group returned with the jerry cans full. I quickly climbed the bank to help with the containers. Arriving at the top, I noticed an elder and his wife from the community standing with Gabe and Mary. Gabe introduced us, and we shook hands. They seemed very friendly. Once introduced, they spoke to Gabe and Mary in Slavey. At the time, I knew a few words, but not enough to understand their conversation, yet I felt confident that some of it was about me; the word *'Mola'* was said a couple of times (In Slavey, *'Mola'* refers to white man).

We left Jean-Marie shortly after the encounter and arrived at Crow Nest three hours later. We unloaded the boat while Gabe picked a location for the tent. I helped him clear the area with an axe and then spread the tent on the ground; this would be my first time seeing a tent without poles set up in the bush. Ignorantly, I asked Gabe where the poles for the tent were. He looked at me puzzled and said, "In the bush." He grabbed his axe and walked into a stand of young spruce trees and started cutting. Once enough trees were cut, Gabe removed any branches and twigs, eventually turning them into poles. I followed suit and started to cut and trim a young spruce with my axe. By the time I finished my pole, Gabe had already cut all the poles needed to set the tent up. Feeling unsure, I gave my pole to Gabe; he looked at it and said, "Too short." I could sense a disappointment in his eyes. After feeling incompetent, I joined Mary and Phoebe, who had just finished collecting spruce boughs from nearby trees and intertwined them into a floor for the tent. The spruce boughs brought a sweet natural scent that was needed for a good night's sleep.

Once the tent was set up and the gear stored inside, we noticed a very large weather cell with heavy rain across the river. It was then that Gabe spotted a boat on the river coming in our direction. The wind had picked up, causing whitecaps to form on the river. Immediately, Gabe asked me to help collect large rocks along the shore; I didn't know the purpose until I saw him using them to secure the tent's wall. Soon, heavy rain with thunder and lightning targeted our location. I was thankful for Gabe's quick thinking, as the winds increased tremendously and would have blown away our tent, leaving us without shelter. The thunder above was deafening. I'm certain that a few strikes must have hit nearby. As such, and because of the closeness of the flash and sound, I tried to remember an old formula for determining the distance of a lightning flash from one's current location. (By counting seconds between the flash and sound; one second is 1.6 kilometers (1 mile). With this in mind, I counted the seconds between the flash and the sound; most were one second, meaning the lightning was right above us. We all sat in the tent waiting for the storm to pass; Mary, terrified, prayed out loud.

The boat seen earlier finally arrived at our campsite. It was a family from Jean-Marie River. If I remember correctly, their last name was Sanquez. They were an elderly couple with their grandson Ralph. Ralph was a couple of years older than Melvin, knew both boys and soon found themselves playing outside in the storm. Ralph, friendly and mature for his age, spoke Slavey and English fluently, often translating for his grandparents when needed. Melvin, inquisitive and smart, was always asking questions, whereas Allan liked to have fun, laugh, and play jokes. Regardless of their different personalities, and the weather, the three found a way to have fun and pass the time. The family had tried to cross the river but had to turn around because of the violent waves brought on by the storm. They stopped to say hello, and once the storm passed, they would head upriver. After forty minutes, the cell moved on, and within a short time, the rain stopped, the winds eased, and the sun shined.

Gabe, having lost time to the storm, wanted to set a fishnet nearby before going to bed. He wanted something to check first thing in the morning. Everything was soaked from the torrential rain. Grabbing his razor-sharp axe, Gabe looked for dry trees, primarily gray in color with no bark. He found a couple and started to make kindling. As he chiseled off the kindling, he told me that the inside of these types of trees is dry and makes great kindling. In no time, a big fire roared. Meanwhile, Mary prepared dough for Bannock and placed a pot of water on the fire for tea. Gabe walked over to the shore and picked up some small rocks. I asked him, "What was the purpose of the rocks?" He responded and pointed at the nets, "The rocks were for weight on the bottom line of the fishnet." I noticed the nets had small empty plastic containers attached to the top line of the net, which served as floats for the net.

Gabe and I took a short boat ride to where the fishnet was going to be set; he had set fishnets in this area in the past while living at the mouth of Trout River. I tried my best to help, but it soon became evident that I was green; I had never set or seen someone set a net. Fortunately, Gabe gave me directions. While setting the 50-meter (160 feet) long net, it is important to move the scow with a paddle in a specific pattern to ensure that the bottom line's attached rocks don't tangle with the top line's attached plastic bottles. I was not doing well, and at some point, felt that I was more a hindrance than help. After the net was set, we returned to camp. The day's events had made both of us hungry, and it was a blessing when we realized Mary had made some delicious Bannock on the open fire with tea. Furthermore, while in Jean-Marie River, Gabe was given a piece of moose meat, which Mary cut into small pieces and cooked in a frying pan on the open fire. This was a much-needed dinner, which I enjoyed very much.

Early the next morning, Gabe and I went to check the net. To my surprise, the net was full of fish, mostly whitefish and some pike. I watched Gabe with his strong hands remove the fish from the net; the pikes proved to be more work. He wanted to leave the net for two more nights.

Back at camp, Gabe built a rack for smoking and drying fish and an area to prepare the fish. Once built, Gabe, Mary, and Phoebe cleaned and prepared the fish for drying. Gabe made a small fire with dry willows and aspen. Placing them under the rack, and the fish above, allowed the smoke to dry the fish; this adds a smoky flavor to the fish and keeps the flies away. Mary demonstrated how to clean and prepare fish for drying; I had never cleaned fish or made dry fish. I did pretty well but needed more practice.

While prepping, we had some fresh fish boiled and cooked on an open fire. While fixing the pikes, Mary saved what she called fish balloons, which are the pike's intestines. She put them on a willow and cooked them by the open fire. It became obvious why she called them balloons; once cooked, the intestines looked like a small balloon. I sampled a couple; they tasted good, a bit chewy.

Later, we all took a walk along the shore. Decorated with small and large boulders, the beach was narrowed by willows that, at times, made it difficult to walk. We were looking for saskatoon bushes. I had never seen or eaten a saskatoon berry (there are no saskatoon bushes in Quebec). After a few minutes, Gabe spotted a large saskatoon bush at least four meters (13 feet) tall, full of juicy berries. Phoebe, who was four months pregnant with our son Danny, picked a handful and gave them to me. Like a hungry bear getting ready for winter, I stuffed the whole handful in my mouth; they were juicy and delicious. We all started picking berries and soon filled several plastic bowls (most of the ones I picked made it to my mouth. I couldn't get enough). Not long after, we returned to camp (we had fish drying, and needed to stay close to camp in case of bears).

The next morning, Gabe, with his cap firmly secured on his head, and I headed out to the net, and again there were more fish. I untangled a few fish from the net, mostly whitefish. After the fish were collected, and the net set, we returned to camp and made more dry fish. I attempted a couple, a much better job than yesterday. I was completely amazed at how fast and perfectly Mary made her dry fish.

On our final day, a beautiful sunny day, we checked the net for the last time and pulled it out. With another good catch, we made some more dry fish. Once the dry fish was packed in burlap sacks, we took the tent down and packed our gear. With the boat loaded, we headed to the mouth of the Trout River, where Phoebe was born. Once we got to the mouth, we stopped to dock the boat on the beach. We all disembarked, and Gabe led the way to his father's cabin built in the 1920s. When he was a young kid, Gabe lived there during the summer and spent most of the winter on the trap line. This was their base camp. After we explored the area, we got back into the boat and headed upriver. Gabe pointed across the mouth of the Trout River to a place he called Browning's Point. Gabe stated that he worked for Mr. Browning at his sawmill and farm back in the 1950s-1960s. Once there, Gabe explained that at one time there were large fields with potatoes, turnips, cabbage, and other vegetables spread out all over the area. At harvest time, the vegetables were placed into sacks and loaded onto barges. These produce-filled barges were delivered to communities along the Mackenzie River as far away as Inuvik. Gabe continued the history lesson by saying there was a local sawmill that milled the nearby White Spruce. At first, horses were used to move logs, until Browning purchased a small dozer. The lumber was used to build Browning's house and several other buildings. In the 1960s, the mill produced most of the wood used for the schools in Fort Simpson. After a short but informative time, we left Browning's Point and headed towards Jean Marie River. The trip back was shorter, as we did not have to fight the current. Once we arrived in Jean Marie River, we gave some dry fish to a few of the elders and then carried on to Fort Simpson.

In all, my first trip into the bush was an eye-opener. I had so much to learn and was truly a rookie. However, and fortunately, I was lucky to have a good mentor who taught me the ways of the land. I am always in awe of Gabe and Mary's traditional knowledge and skills. They know the land and how to use its resources. Sadly, a few days after returning from our trip, their son and Phoebe's younger brother Allan passed away in a tragic drowning accident in Fort Simpson on August 17th, 1974.

Chapter 11:
Setting a Rabbit Spring Pole Snare Line

Listening to Gabe's bush stories sparked a deep curiosity in me to learn the traditional Dene way of life. The thought of setting a spring pole snare to capture a rabbit using only the materials from the land was both thrilling and intriguing. However, the knowledge of making and setting a rabbit spring pole snare was reserved for those who lived a traditional lifestyle. I was fortunate to meet Gabe, and I was eager to learn from him the age-old techniques passed down through generations.

In the north, Snowshoe Hares are often referred to as rabbits. Gabe and I decided to head into the bush to find the perfect birch trees for making snowshoes, one pair for him and the other for me. Gabe, though a man of small stature, had enormous, strong hands. Shaking his hand was an experience in itself: a firm, dry, calloused grip that spoke of years of hard work and self-sufficiency. Known for his hunting and trapping expertise, Gabe was also a master snowshoe maker.

Snowshoes Hare Caught in Spring Pole Snare

It was the winter of 1974-75 when we set out on the highway in my car to find the perfect birch trees. Gabe suggested we head toward the main airport, where we might find the trees that were best suited for making snowshoes. After driving for a while, Gabe asked me to stop the car and pointed to a small stand of birch trees. We stepped out of the car, and Gabe spotted a large birch tree along the creek. "Let's check that one out," he said.

From a distance, the tree looked promising. As we approached, Gabe explained that the best birch tree for snowshoes should be free of knots from the base to about 1.2 to 1.5 meters (4 to 5 feet) high. The grain should run straight, without any twists.

We made our way toward the tree, carrying Gabe's old chainsaw (he was the only one who could start it), two axes, and a sledgehammer. Once we reached the tree, Gabe carefully inspected it, walking around it and scanning it from top to bottom. He was meticulous, wanting to ensure that we had the perfect resource for our project. Any knots would indicate twisted grain, which would make carving difficult. Gabe checked which way the tree was leaning, then asked me for the chainsaw.

The tree was about 45 centimeters (18 inches) in diameter at the base. Gabe made a notch on one side, then another on the opposite side. The tree cracked and fell exactly as he had intended. Choosing the best area for carving, he cut out a section about 1.8 meters (6 feet) long.

Next came the task of splitting the section in half. Using an axe as a wedge at one end of the 1.8 meters (6 foot) length, Gabe struck it with the sledgehammer while I held the axe in place. After one or two swings, the axe was wedged deep into the base, and a crack ran along the length of the birch.

271

A second axe was placed further along the crack, and Gabe struck it with the sledgehammer until the tree split in two. He smiled and looked at me. "The tree has straight grains. We should be able to make two pairs of snowshoes from this."

Gabe and I repeated the process, splitting the two halves into four pieces, then splitting them again to make a total of eight pieces. Each pair of snowshoes would require four pieces, two for each shoe.

After lighting a cigarette, Gabe grabbed his razor-sharp axe with his left hand to continue the process. It was then that I noticed he was left-handed, or at least he favored using his left hand for most tasks, even though I had previously seen him write with his right hand. Confused, I asked him about it. He recalled that while attending residential school in Fort Providence (1928-1936), which he called the Covenant, he was compelled by the nuns to write with his right hand. Oddly familiar, I also remembered attending an elementary school in Quebec run by the Grey Nuns, where left-handed students were obliged to write with their right hand. The Catholic Church believed back then that writing with the left hand was a sign of the devil. Gabe confirmed that the nuns at the Covenant had told the students the same tale.

Still puffing on his cigarette, Gabe rested one end of a split birch on his right shoulder while holding the rest with his right hand. He took his axe and carefully began shaping half of the section into dimensions of about 7 by 5 centimeters (3 by 2 inches). Once done, he turned the piece around and continued shaping it until the entire length matched those dimensions. In no time, Gabe had shaped all eight pieces the same way. I was dumbfounded by how quickly he worked and even more amazed by the consistency in size. He was pleased with the straightness of the grain and explained, "A straight grain is important for the strength and shaping of a snowshoe." He added, "The base of the birch tree, where the wood is strongest, is used in carving the head of the snowshoe."

Gabe used a pencil to mark a dot at the base of each piece. He then used strings to secure the eight pieces into two bundles of four. We each slung a bundle over our shoulders, freeing our hands to carry the tools back to the car.

The following day, after allowing the birch pieces to thaw, I arrived at Gabe's house to continue my learning. Once set up, Gabe used a handsaw to cut the eight pieces into four 1-meter (3.5 foot) lengths and the rest into 1.2 meters (4 foot) lengths. Gabe explained that the bigger the person, the longer the shoe needs to be, and that the 1.2 meters (4 footers) were mine. "A snowshoe of that length is called a Trail Snowshoe," he added.

Gabe grabbed his old Hudson Bay Store carving knife, which had been sharpened so many times that the blade was now half of its original width. This was Gabe's favorite knife. It was single-beveled for a left-handed carver (the blade was sharpened only on one side). With the knife in his left hand, and always carving toward himself, Gabe started to carve the snowshoe's frame. I use the word "carve" because making a pair of snowshoes is an art. The two-piece frames are carved by hand with an axe and a sharp knife. A wood chisel is used to notch the breaches to secure three crosspieces that are used in the lacing of the shoe with babiche.

As an experienced snowshoe maker, Gabe had engineered tools that had a specific purpose in the process. The first tool was made from a chainsaw file, which was heated by fire until red hot, then struck with a hammer to fashion the needed shape. He then cut the tool and sharpened both ends; one end was secured into a piece of moose antler (the handle), and the other end was further sharpened and used to bore holes into the inside of the frames. This allowed the babiche to be inserted to make the laces of the snowshoe. The second tool, a needle to lace the snowshoes, was made with a small piece of metal that was again heated until red hot, then struck with a hammer to flatten it. A hole large enough to string babiche through it was drilled into the middle of the tool.

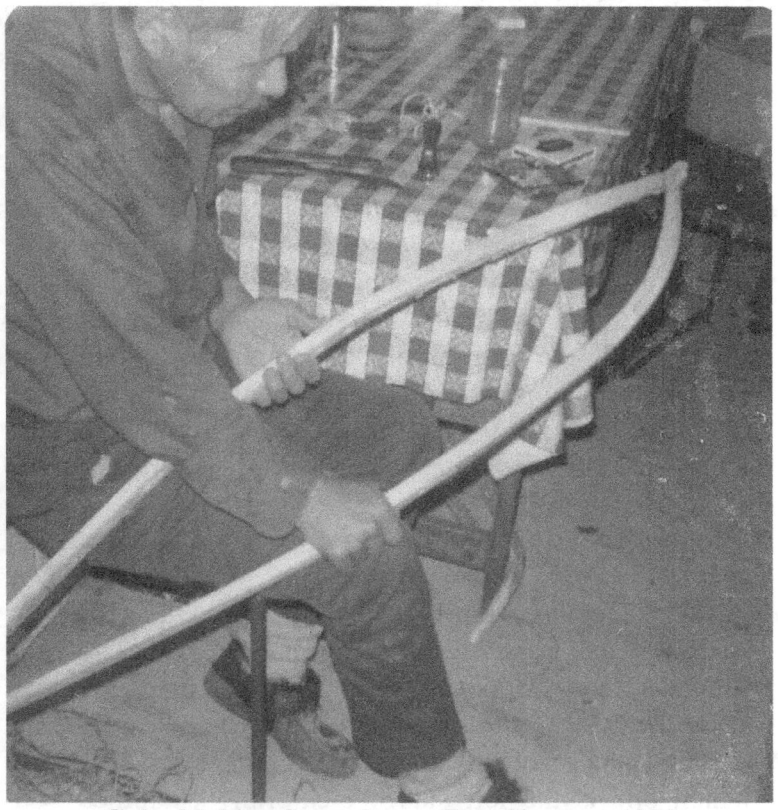

Gabe Making Snowshoes - Fort Simpson 1975

From the previous fall hunt, Mary had already prepared (fleshed and scraped) a caribou hide to cut into babiche. Before cutting the hide into strips, it had to be soaked in water. Once saturated, Gabe and Mary worked together to cut the babiche. Gabe held one side of the hide while Mary used a sharp knife to cut even widths, always pulling the knife toward her. Starting on the edge, Mary cut in a circular direction around the hide, eventually making her way to the middle. This allowed for longer strips of babiche, resulting in three to four long pieces. Once cut, the babiche was stretched between poles in Gabe's backyard and left to dry in the cold temperatures.

For several days, Gabe worked on bending, shaping, and lacing the snowshoe frames. Each frame consisted of two pieces carved as a matching pair. Gabe used warm water to soak the head of each snowshoe frame to facilitate the bending, which could be a challenging process. Breaking the head of the snowshoe while bending it would render the piece unusable. Each snowshoe head was carved thinner than the rest of the frame and soaked in warm water as needed during the bending process. Once the desired bend was achieved, Gabe would attach a string to a small notch made at the head and the other end to the frame, maintaining the shape of the bend. Each frame piece was formed in this way and left to dry for a few days.

Once dried, the frame pieces were put together. Gabe placed a piece of wood between the frames to maintain their shape. The pair of snowshoes was then tied back-to-back with their heads in opposite directions. The frames were tied together with strings to keep them in matching shape. It was then that Gabe grabbed one of the snowshoes and asked me, "Which one is the left side?" I carefully examined both snowshoes, and after a while, I said, "I'm not sure which one is which. How can you tell?" Gabe grabbed the snowshoes from my hands and smiled, holding his cigarette with the other corner of his mouth. With his index finger, he touched the side of the frame with a more pronounced curve and said, "This side of the snowshoe is for your right foot," turning the attached frames over. He continued, "The other side is for your left foot. This is why snowshoes are tied together back-to-back to dry." The snowshoe frames were left to dry until the head string became loose, indicating that the frames were dry and ready to be laced.

Gabe inserted three crosspieces into the breaches that he had previously carved. The crosspieces were cut from leftover birch. After the crosspieces were installed, Gabe began lacing the snowshoes with the babiche that Mary had prepared. Before lacing, the babiche was soaked in lukewarm water. Gabe and Mary took turns lacing the shoes. It had been a long time since Mary had laced snowshoes, so Gabe showed her how, just as he had done when they first got married in 1955. Once laced, the snowshoes were left to dry. For the final touch, Gabe made harnesses using a piece of moose hide left over from the material Mary had used for moccasins.

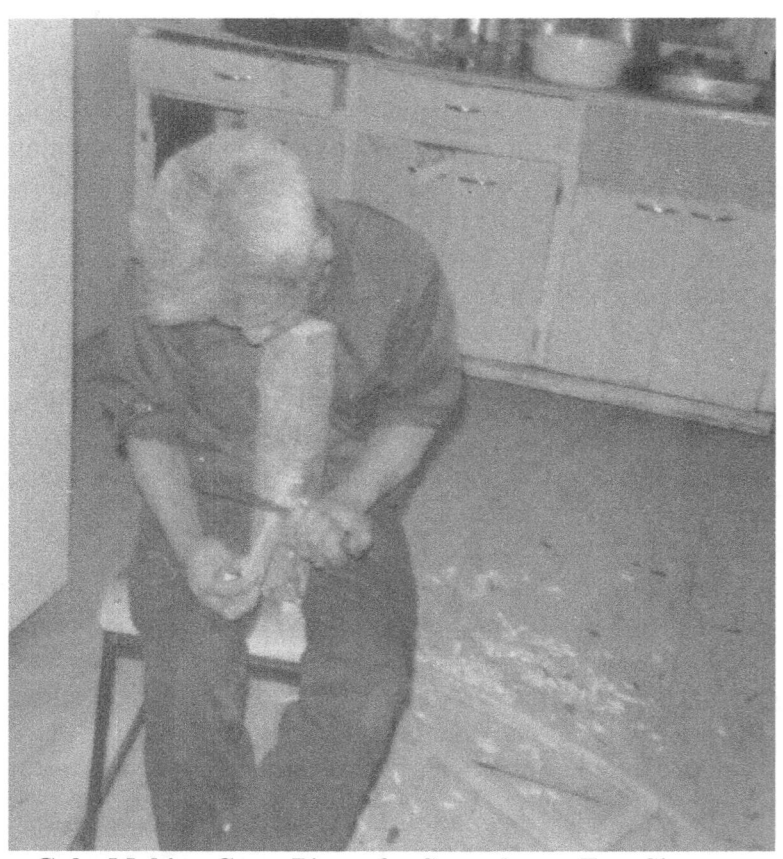

Gabe Making Cross Pieces for Snowshoes - Fort Simpson 1975

Gabe installed the harnesses for each snowshoe and demonstrated how to attach them to my feet. He put his foot into the harness, adjusted it to his foot, and tied it on the outside of his foot. Then, quickly, he removed his foot from the harness by twisting it and pulling it out. He then quickly put his foot back into the harness by twisting and sliding his foot in. "Once the harness is adjusted to your foot," Gabe said, "it's easy to remove your feet in and out of the harness." Gabe added, "If you were to go through the ice while walking with snowshoes, it would allow you to remove the shoes with your feet under the ice." The best footwear to use with snowshoes is canvas-top moccasins with duffle inserts to keep your feet warm. Mary and Phoebe had made a pair of *Jihke*, which is the Slavey name for canvas-top moccasins, for Gabe and me.

By early January (1975), a couple of weeks before the birth of our son Danny, the snowshoes were fully dried and ready for use. For my first experience setting snares, Gabe suggested an area where he had had success before, but access was remote and reachable only by walking. We left home early on a Sunday morning. There was no wind, but it was minus 30 Celsius (minus 22 Fahrenheit) and still dark. Our gear consisted of packsacks, axes, snowshoes, snare sticks, a teapot, and our .22 rifles. We walked up the ski hill located on the mainland across from Fort Simpson. Our objective was an area now called the Wrigley Highway's right-of-way (the Wrigley Highway had not been built yet). Once we reached the edge of the bush, we put on our snowshoes. With the bush being quite dense, Gabe led the way and started to cut a small trail through. I followed behind him, working on some of the trail. It wasn't long before we came across our first well-used rabbit trail. Gabe took off his backpack and said, "I'll set the first spring pole snare to show you how it's done. Once I am done, you'll set your snare."

He first cut a long pole. At the butt end, it was 5-7 centimeters (2-3 inches) diameter and approximately 3-4 meters (10-13 feet) in length. Using his axe, he removed the branches on the pole, saying, "You can also use a dry tree for a pole." After putting the pole aside, he cut a small dry tree about 45 centimeters (1.5 foot) in length and sharpened one end with his axe.

Next, he scanned a nearby bush for a small aspen tree with branches shaped like a fork. He found one, cut it, and

278

shaped the fork at the end of the small tree. After cutting the forked branch, he said, "You can also use nails to secure the pole to a tree instead of a forked tree."

Gabe then looked for a tree near the rabbit trail that was large enough to support the forked branch and the pole. He placed the branch leaning against the tree at a height of approximately 1.5 – 2.0 meters (5 – 6.5 foot), with the forks sticking out the other side. This would hold the pole in place.

Next to the rabbit trail, Gabe hammered the sharp stick into the ground with his axe, leaving approximately 30 centimeters (1 foot) sticking out (the stick must be strong enough to hold the weight of the poles). Once done, he cut down two young jack pines and placed them on either side of the rabbit trail, with both treetops facing each other, parallel to our snares. I asked him why he had placed the trees in that manner. He replied, "The rabbit likes to eat jack pine needles. The fresh-cut jack pines will attract them." Grabbing a handful of needles from the treetops, he rubbed them between his mitts and spread them over the rabbit trail. Before I had a chance to ask him why, he looked at me and smiled. "The needles on the trail will attract them to the snare."

From his backpack, Gabe pulled out a spring pole snare stick that he had carved out of birch. While the snowshoes were drying, Gabe had used leftover birch from the snowshoes to carve the spring pole snare stick. The spring pole stick is used to attach the snares and prevent them from tangling with each other. The spring pole snare is made with a piece of string, a willow stick, and a rabbit snare. The string and rabbit snare are both secured to the willow stick; the string is on one side of the willow stick, and the snare is on the other side. Gabe asked me to collect some willow the size of my little finger in diameter along the Mackenzie

Riverbank. As a measuring tool, we used our hand with the thumb up to measure the length of the stick. Once the sticks were cut, the bark was removed with a knife. The willow sticks were placed on a cookie sheet and put in an oven to dry out. I asked him, "Why do the sticks have to be dried?" He replied, "Rabbits do not chew on dry sticks." Once the sticks were dried out and cooled off, we bit into each end of the sticks and rotated them between our teeth. This created a groove at each end of the sticks, which is used to fasten the string and snare. Gabe's snare stick held 30 snares, 15 snares on each side.

Gabe pulled out a snare from the stick and attached the string to the end of the pole, which had to be lowered by grabbing the pole near the fork. Gabe lowered the pole and held it under one arm while attaching the string. The second step was to lower the end of the pole to the dry stick he had pounded into the ground, then secure the string with the attached willow around the dry stick. Once the string and willow were secured around the dry stick, the back of the pole stayed upright. The weight of the pole kept pressure on the string and willow, which was held inside the string. The rabbit snare was then set about 5 centimeters (2 inches) above the trail. A rabbit can be caught from either direction. Once the rabbit is caught in the snare, the pull exerted by the rabbit will release the pressure on the willow and make the pole go up, thereby lifting and choking the rabbit quickly. Gabe mentioned to me that I should never set the pole facing me, as this could cause injuries if the pole releases by accident. The setting of this snare took approximately 10-15 minutes.

We continued cutting the trail until we encountered numerous well-used rabbit trails. The area was an immature jack pine stand, prime rabbit habitat. Gabe handed me a couple of snares and asked me to set a snare where I was standing. He continued cutting the trail ahead of me while I set my first snare. I followed the same method he had used. My first snare took some time. The pole was a bit short, so I had to cut a longer one. I also had some trouble setting the string and willow stick, which slipped while I was trying to set it up. Thankfully, the pole wasn't facing me, or I would have been down for the count. It was amazing to see how clever the set was.

I moved on to the next rabbit trail, following Gabe's trail. I could hear him ahead of me, cutting trees for his snare. The second snare was quicker to set than the first one. I was starting to get the hang of it. Once done, I caught up with Gabe, who was setting another snare. The area we were in was full of rabbit trails. Gabe gave me a couple more snares and asked me to follow the jack pine stand. I continued cutting the trail and stopped at a well-used trail, not far from where Gabe was. Again, I cut my pole, forked a tree, dry stick, and two young jack pines, and set my snare, which was quicker than the second one. Before I finished, Gabe caught up with me and continued cutting the trail. We set a few more snares until we came across open wetlands, which weren't area for rabbit trails. Gabe scanned the area and pointed to a jack pine stand to the left of us, about 0.5 kilometer (0.3 miles) away. We headed in that direction, with Gabe leading the way.

Shortly after, a flock of grouse, which had been napping under the snow, took off, and some landed in nearby trees. I didn't know that grouse slept under the snow. They sure gave me a jolt. We managed to shoot a few grouse that had landed in the trees, but most of them flew a great distance. Gabe had a bit of a laugh at me for being jumpy. He said, "It's best to pluck the grouse while they're still warm." We put the plucked grouse in our backpack.

We reached the jack pine stand to find rabbit trails everywhere. We continued cutting the trail and setting snares until we ran out. In total, we had set thirty snares. We made a fire at the end of the trail and brewed some tea. While the snow melted in the teapot, the water was used for our tea. Gabe prepared two grouse to be cooked on a stick, bush-style. We had been breaking trail and setting snares for a few hours, and we were both thirsty and hungry. We had some tea and ate the delicious grouse cooked over an open fire, which gave them a nice smoky flavor. Going back, following our trail was quick. It was a cold day, and the trail had started to freeze, making walking easier. On the way back, Gabe looked at the snares I had set. He didn't make any comments, which I took as a sign that my snares were set correctly. We timed ourselves walking back to the Wrigley Highway's right-of-way. It took us just under one hour and forty minutes.

The following Saturday, I asked Gabe if he was going to check the snare line. I was eager to see how many rabbits we had caught. Gabe wasn't feeling well and asked me to check the snare line. The next day, I left before sunrise with my gear. As I walked down the street, a local fellow, who was inebriated, asked me, "Where are you going with those snowshoes?" I replied, "I'm going to check the snare line Gabe and I set last week." He responded, "You think you'll be catching any rabbits?" and laughed at me. I took offense to some of the other remarks he made, but decided to ignore him and headed to the Ski Hills. The air was cold and crisp. It must have been around minus 30 Celsius (minus 22 Fahrenheit). Soon, my mustache and eyelashes were icing up. I was looking forward to checking the snare line and wondering how many rabbits would be in the snares. I arrived at the beginning of the trail, put on my snowshoes, and took a few steps.

The trail was frozen solid, like walking on a sidewalk. It had snowed the previous week, enough to see fresh rabbit tracks, which were numerous. As I approached the first snare, I saw from a distance a rabbit hanging by the neck. I gently removed the snare from the rabbit. I remember Gabe telling me to be careful while removing a snare from a rabbit when it is very cold. A rabbit snare is made of brass wire, which can break in cold temperatures. I used my fingers to straighten out the snare, which had a few kinks from catching the rabbit. I reset the snare and shook the snow off the jack pines on both sides of the rabbit trail. For my final touch, I grabbed a handful of pine needles from the jack pine and rubbed them between my mitts, spreading them over the rabbit trail. This snare had been set by Gabe to show me how to set a spring pole snare.

The next snare was one that I had set. Coming around a bend on the trail, I saw from a short distance another rabbit hanging by the neck—my first rabbit! After resetting the snare, I put the frozen rabbit in my pack and continued checking the snare line. I could see lots of fresh rabbit tracks on our snowshoe trail. Again, from a distance, I saw another rabbit hanging by the neck, three rabbits in a row. The rabbits, like the other two, were frozen solid, and as a result of being hung by the neck, they were all stretched out, which took up a lot of room in my backpack. To avoid carrying all the rabbits to the end of the trail and back, I left some on the trail, attached to a small string that I hung in a tree. After reaching the end of the trail, we had caught a total of twenty-two rabbits out of thirty snares, which demonstrated that the snares were well set and that there were plenty of rabbits in the area. A few of the snares were either a miss or had no rabbits near them. I picked up the rabbits I had left on the trail on my way back and packed as many as I could fit in my backpack. The remaining rabbits were secured to the outside of my backpack. Gabe had mentioned that I should always carry extra string in my pack. You never know when you'll need a piece of string while in the bush.

I headed back to Fort Simpson with my gear and my backpack full of rabbits. Lo and behold, the same fellow who had laughed at me was outside his house splitting wood. He looked at me as I passed by, but didn't say anything. I stopped at Gabe's to drop off the rabbits. Gabe and Mary were delighted to see so many rabbits. Mary hung four behind the stove to thaw them out. Once thawed, she said, "I'll cook them and make rabbit soup." I checked the snare line three or four more times, then pulled out the snares. I had to return to work at River Between Two Mountains camp, north of Fort Simpson, a few days after our son Danny was born on January 26th, 1975.

While writing this story, I researched on the internet ways to set a spring pole snare for rabbits. I found several methods for setting the snare, but did not find any that depicted the way Gabe had taught me. This method must be unique to the north. Gabe mentioned that, before using brass wire, Dene people used the sinew from the backstrap of a moose or caribou to make a rabbit snare. This same sinew is also used to sew moose hide moccasins and mittens. I saw a spring pole snare using sinew set by a Jean-Marie River elder at Reid Lake, the location where I spent part of winter/spring 1975-1976 fishing with nets under the ice and beaver hunting. To properly hold the sinew snare, two small twigs are placed inside the base of the snare to help maintain its shape.

Chapter 12:
Fishing Under the Ice at Reid Lake
December 1975

WhiteFish Caught in fishnet under the Ice - Reid Lake- 1975

In July of 1974, I purchased a camp on the mainland near the syne, across from the campground in Fort Simpson, from a French fellow known as Tarzan. I never learned his real name. The camp consisted of a tent frame, fifteen wooden dog houses, a small shed, and an outhouse. The 1.2 meters by 30 centimeters (4-foot-high by 1-foot-wide) tent frame's walls were constructed with white spruce slabs from the local sawmill. The interior walls were lined with plastic and packed with sawdust. A 3.6 by 4.8 meters (12 by 16 foot) waterproof canvas tent was securely fastened to the walls. A wooden door and a floor made from 2.5 by 15 centimeters (1 by 6 inches) white spruce boards completed the tent frame. A large wood stove provided heat during the cold months. Inside the tent frame, there were two beds, a table, and chairs. The tent frame was warm and cozy.

Tarzan was a dog musher and worked as a bouncer at the local bar. He wasn't a big man, but nobody messed with him. I saw him in action a couple of times at the dances. He knew how to handle himself. No matter the season, you could always see Tarzan driving his dog team around town with a sleigh in the winter or a sleigh on wheels in the summer. He didn't own a vehicle, relying on his team of dogs to do his shopping, check his mail, or get to work. When Tarzan worked at the bar, his dog team would be parked outside, waiting for him. His dogs were well-trained. He left them outside while he had a drink or worked. His dogs never ran away or wandered off. People would walk by, and the dogs wouldn't bark, growl, or wag their tails. No matter how long Tarzan was inside, the team would just lie down and wait for him, like statues.

This reminds me of a story my maternal grandmother once told me about my great-grandfather, Laurent Rocheleau. He had a small farm near the village of Lesage in Quebec. On weekends, he would go to the local tavern for a few drinks. He didn't own a car or truck but had a horse with a sleigh for the winter and a farm cart for the summer. Come Friday night, he would hitch his horse and travel to the tavern, which was about 6 kilometers (3.7 miles) away. He would tell his horse to stay put, then go inside for several drinks. Back then, taverns in Quebec only closed for about one hour, usually around 6 a.m., just enough time to clean up and reopen. My great-grandfather was known to stay at the tavern for as much as two days in a row. After his drinking, he would climb into his farm cart or sleigh and tell his horse to go home. My great-grandfather would fall asleep in the cart while the horse made its way home.

In the summer of 1974, Baptiste Cazon (Phoebe's uncle) came to visit me at my camp with his son, Louie. At that time, Baptiste was the Chief of the Fort Simpson Dene Band. He was a burly man, nearly 182 centimeters (6 feet) tall, with a toothbrush mustache, which is a patch on the upper lip that's the same width as the nose or slightly wider. Charlie Chaplin had this style of mustache. Baptiste often had a twinkle in his eyes and smiled a lot. He was interested in purchasing some of the gear I had at the camp. We looked through the gear I had in the shed. I wasn't planning to sell anything, but Baptiste said he was planning to set up a camp in the bush and wanted to see what kind of bush gear I had. He saw a tent and other gear that he could use for his camp. We set the tent and gear aside. Then he looked at me and asked, "How much do you want for the tent and gear?" I told him, "One hundred and twenty dollars." Baptiste smiled and said, "It's a deal," reaching into his pocket and handing me six twenty-dollar bills, fresh from the bank. The bills looked like they had just been printed. One hundred and twenty dollars was a lot of money back then. I was working at a local sawmill, making four dollars per hour. That was big money at the time.

The camp was our home from July to September 1974. Phoebe was pregnant at the time, expecting our son Danny in late January. With Phoebe expecting, we decided that it would be best to move to the Mackenzie Manor, an apartment building where I worked, in the winter of 1973-1974. We shared the apartment with another couple who were also expecting a child.

287

In November of 1975, I purchased a used snowmobile from a resident. I didn't know anything about snowmobiles and had never driven one before. The snowmobile was yellow and about 3-4 years old. The body of the snowmobile was in good shape with no major indentations. From what I knew about snowmobile engines, which wasn't much, it seemed to be running well. The person who sold it to me showed me how to start it and what kind of mixed gas to use. I took the snowmobile for a ride at the syne to get a feel for it. Fort Simpson is located on an island near the mouth of the Liard River. The syne is a body of water partially surrounding the southerly portion of the island, adorned with willow flats and cattail plants. Depending on the water level, the syne is approximately 90 – 150 meters (300 to 500 feet) wide. I used to hunt ptarmigan in the willow flats on snowshoes during the winter months.

It was a sunny day with calm winds and not too cold. The syne was covered with snowmobile trails. I drove on one of the trails and squeezed the throttle. The snowmobile surged forward with power until I realized the throttle was jammed. The throttle cable was wide open and wouldn't go back in. I turned the key off, and shortly after, the snowmobile came to a stop. I inspected the throttle cable and was finally able to unjam it. Before starting the mobile again, I made sure the throttle was working properly. I started it up and gave a few squeezes on the throttle. It seemed to work fine.

I drove the snowmobile for another hour or so, breaking trails around the syne. I was enjoying the ride, feeling like a little kid who had just received a gift at Christmas. I drove to Phoebe's parents to show Gabe the snowmobile. He didn't seem impressed. He had never owned or driven one; he was a dog team guy. I asked him if he knew someone who might have a sleigh for sale. He told me that Mr. Nahanni might have one. Mr. Nahanni had a trapline in the McGill Lake area, south of Fort Simpson, and trapped using a dog team.

I drove to Mr. Nahanni's home, which was two doors down from Gabe's. He was outside cutting firewood with a large Swede saw. Mr. Nahanni was a man of small stature. I'd guess he was in his late seventies or early eighties. I wasn't sure if he spoke English. I introduced myself and asked him if he had a sleigh for sale. He replied in English and said he didn't trap anymore; his dogs were getting too old for pulling a sleigh on his trapline. Mr. Nahanni pointed to the back of his home where the sleigh was. It was 2.4 meters (8 feet) in length, with a canvas wrapper fastened to the sleigh and a backboard, just what I was looking for. I asked him, "How much do you want for your sleigh?" He said, "Give me fifty dollars." I told him, "I'll be right back," started my snowmobile, and headed to the bank. About half an hour later, I returned with a fifty-dollar bill. I shook his hand and gave him the money. He smiled back at me. I had some ropes with me, so I attached the sleigh to the back of the snowmobile and drove home.

Now and again, I would visit Baptiste at his home. I got along well with him and asked all kinds of questions about bush life. He would answer my questions and tell me stories from when he was a young man living in the bush. He knew I was interested in being in the bush and learning about life there. While visiting him at his home in November 1975, Baptiste asked if I would be interested in helping him and his son Peter set fishnets under the ice at Reid Lake. The lake is located southeast of Fort Simpson, about 80 meters (130 kilometers) away, as the crow flies. I had heard many stories from both Gabe and Baptiste about Reid Lake, which they referred to as Fish Lake. I was eager to learn how to set fishnets and experience the bush life at Reid Lake. Baptiste had acquired a commercial fishing license for Reid Lake and was planning to set a few nets before Christmas and sell the fish in Fort Simpson.

I asked Baptiste, "When are you planning to leave for Reid Lake?" He said that he was waiting for the ice crossing to open. The Liard River had frozen over at the ferry crossing and should open for light traffic in a few days. Baptiste planned to drive from Fort Simpson to the start of the Trout Lake Winter Road, where we would snowmobile to Reid Lake, about 28 kilometers (17.5 miles) away. I had just purchased a snowmobile and sleigh and was excited to put them to the test. Baptiste was working on building a sleigh for his snowmobile, which was a more powerful machine than mine. He had bought two curved boards, each 2.4 meters (8 feet long), from the Hudson Bay store in Fort Simpson and was working on assembling the sleigh. Alphonsine, Baptiste's wife, was sewing a large piece of canvas into a sleigh wrapper when I visited. Once the sleigh was assembled, Baptiste built a backboard for it, with handles for holding on while riding.

I asked Baptiste what kind of gear and food I should take for the trip. He had already made a list, which I copied down. The next day, I went to the Hudson Bay store and purchased the gear and food for the trip. In addition, I bought four jerry cans and oil to mix with the gas for my snowmobile. The plan was for Peter (Baptiste's son) and me to travel with Sam Ramson, the Game Warden in Fort Simpson, carrying Peter's gear and mine, along with my snowmobile and sleigh. Baptiste would travel with his son Alex, who was giving him a ride, carrying his gear and his snowmobile with the new sleigh.

On the morning of November 25th, the winter ice crossing at the Liard River officially opened. I hugged my Phoebe and our son Danny, who was 10 months old, and told her I would be back before Christmas. We didn't have an exact date for our return to Fort Simpson.

We loaded our snowmobiles, sleighs, and gear onto the two trucks and headed to the ice crossing. The drive on the ice was a bit bumpy due to the rough surface. The drive from the ice crossing to the Trout Lake Winter Road took about an hour and a half. The winter road wasn't officially open yet; however, there were Bombardier tracks on the road that appeared to be fresh. The morning air was cold and crisp, around minus 30 Celsius (minus 22 Fahrenheit). We unloaded our snowmobiles, sleighs, and gear from the trucks. Once my sleigh was unloaded, I started my snowmobile. Baptiste told us he was having trouble starting his snowmobile and asked us to go ahead, saying he would catch up.

I left with Peter holding on to the backboard handles, which we quickly realized were built too low. Mr. Nahanni was a short man, which is why the handles were low. Peter, who was a couple of years older than me and about 182 centimeters (6 feet) tall, was hunched over as he held on. The snow was deep for this time of year, making it difficult to break trail while pulling a heavy load. I tried following the Bombardier tracks, which were narrow and hard to stay on. This was my first time driving a snowmobile while pulling a sleigh. I felt like I was riding on a wire and quickly learned how to use my body weight to stay on the trail as much as possible.

We made good progress on the trail until my snowmobile began to lose speed and backfire. I wasn't sure what the problem was. Now and then, the snowmobile would speed up and run fine without backfiring, but then it would slow down and barely move. Peter and I stopped and opened the hood to inspect the engine. It seemed that we were running

291

only on one cylinder, which would explain the lack of power. I had extra spark plugs that came with the snowmobile when I bought it. I replaced the spark plugs, which looked new. I pulled on the starter cord, and the snowmobile started, but it still seemed to be running on one cylinder.

I turned off the snowmobile to check the spark plugs again, thinking one of them might not be firing. I disconnected the first plug and remembered watching Gabe work on his chainsaw, checking for spark by pulling on the starter cord. I learned my lesson quickly. I held the plug with my left bare hand and pulled on the starter cord. I felt an electric jolt from my hand to my elbow. That was a lesson I would never forget—I didn't like electric shocks.

Peter and I heard a snowmobile coming our way. A couple of minutes later, Baptiste pulled up next to my snowmobile. He asked, "Are you having problems with the Ski-Doo?" I replied, "Yes, I think the Ski-Doo is running on one cylinder." Baptiste said, "Let me have a look." He examined the spark plugs and coils and said, "The problem is a crack in the wire from the coil." Baptiste took some electrical tape and taped the wire. I started the snowmobile, and it sounded like music to my ears, purring like a cat.

About 1 kilometer (0.3 miles) before the junction of the Trout Lake Winter Road and the seismic line to Reid Lake, we saw a flock of sharp-tailed grouse take off from the winter road. One of the grouse landed at the top of a tall black spruce tree about 100 meters (300 feet) away. The grouse looked like a little black dot. Peter and I pulled out our .22 rifles from the sleigh and aimed at the grouse. We both took a few shots but missed. The grouse was still sitting at the top of the tree. I propped my rifle on a nearby tree for a steadier shot. I took my time, squeezed the trigger, and to my amazement, the grouse fell to the ground. I put on my snowshoes to retrieve the grouse while Baptiste and Peter made a fire. It was time for a tea break and to warm up.

It took me some time to find the grouse. The snow was deep, and the black spruce trees looked alike. I walked back to the winter road, took a bearing on the tall black spruce tree where I had seen the grouse, and then headed back. I finally found the grouse, which was under the snow. We had some tea and a bite to eat.

Upon arriving at the Reid Lake seismic line, we were surprised to see that the Bombardier's tracks were heading towards Reid Lake. We had assumed the tracks were from someone working on the winter road. We continued our trip and followed the tracks to Reid Lake, which was another 7 kilometers (4.3 miles) away. Baptiste took the lead, breaking trail with his more powerful snowmobile, which had a wider track. Following his trail was much easier than following the Bombardier tracks. The snow was like a book. Instead of letters and words, animal tracks adorned the fresh snow: hare, grouse, ptarmigan, marten, and lynx tracks told stories of animals and birds' eating and hunting activities.

We stopped halfway to Reid Lake to fuel up our snowmobiles and heard, at a distance, a Bombardier and a snowmobile. Once both snowmobiles were fueled up, we continued our trip to Reid Lake, arriving a couple of hours before sunset. There were two cabins along the north shore of Reid Lake, about 30 meters (100 feet) apart. The first cabin looked incomplete. The lack of insulation between the logs was visible from the outside, indicating it still needed work. Upon closer inspection, we found that there was no floor, and large rocks protruded from the frozen ground. Inside, there was some fishing gear for setting nets, two wooden beds, a sheet of plywood, and a bundle of insulation.

The second cabin was finished and in much better condition. There were blankets on the four beds, a large table with four chairs, dishes, pots, and pans, along with a large wood stove. Baptiste had brought a 3.6 by 4.2 meters (12-foot by 14-foot) tent, the same one I had sold him a year and a half earlier, along with a large airtight wood stove and stove pipes. Baptiste planned to set up the tent at Reid Lake to use as our shelter for the length of our stay.

However, Baptiste opted for the cabin instead. Peter and I unloaded the sleighs and moved our gear and food inside the cabin while Baptiste set up the wood stove and stove pipes. There was already a stovepipe hole installed in the cabin's roof.

About half an hour later, a Bombardier and a snowmobile arrived at the cabin. The passengers were from Jean-Marie River: Douglas Norwegian, Billy Norwegian, Ernest Hardisty, and Jimmy Sanguez. I had just turned 20 years old in November. Douglas, Billy, and Ernest were in their mid-thirties, and Jimmy was about the same age as Baptiste. Douglas and Billy were brothers. This was the first time I met them, although I knew their father, Louie. Louie was a smart man, well-respected by all, and spoke English well. I had several discussions and laughs with him when he visited Gabe in Fort Simpson. Ernest was friendly and interesting to talk to. He had a good sense of humor and liked to laugh. Jimmy was a good friend of Gabe's. He told me many stories about the two of them trapping and hunting in the bush.

All four of them had been setting nets at Reid Lake for the past week and had taken some fish back to Jean-Marie River. They planned to fish for a couple more days, then pull their nets and return to Jean-Marie River.

Douglas and Billy moved their fishing gear from our cabin. Fortunately, there was a bundle of insulation inside, which we used to fill the gaps between the logs that lacked insulation. We also found a small stack of firewood. Baptiste installed the pipe on the stove and started a much-needed fire. The inside of the cabin was as cold as outside. Peter and I grabbed our axes and went looking for dry trees. We managed to find some nearby and cut them down. The trees were small in diameter but very dry. We cut and transported them to a homemade sawhorse near the cabin. Peter and I took turns cutting the trees with the large Swede saw that Baptiste had brought with his gear, as we didn't have a chainsaw. While we were cutting firewood, Baptiste made some tea, warmed up some Bannock he had made in Fort Simpson, and boiled the grouse I shot. We cut and split enough firewood for the night and called it a day when it got too dark to continue. After supper, we fixed the cracks between the logs to ensure the cabin would stay warm. There were two wooden beds in the cabin and a piece of plywood. I volunteered to sleep on the plywood sheet on the ground while Baptiste and Peter took the beds. By the light of the gas lamp, I fixed my bed, which was on uneven ground. There were large rocks in the ground, frozen stiff, making it impossible to dig and remove them. The group from Jean-Marie River invited us to their cabin for tea and Bannock. Baptiste asked them, "Where are your nets set?" Douglas replied, "We've got four nets set south of the cabins." Baptiste also asked, "How was the fishing?" Douglas said, "The fishing was good. We caught enough fish to make a trip to Jean-Marie River."

We were all tired, called it a night, and returned to our cabins. Baptiste mentioned that once the group left, we would move to their cabin. I was looking forward to the move; the beds next door looked comfortable. Baptiste turned off the gas lamp and went to bed. We all slept soundly, and I was the first one to wake up. The fire had gone out in the middle of the night. My feet had been sticking out of my blanket for most of the night. I was so tired that I didn't notice my feet being cold. I stood up to make a fire and dropped to my knees. I couldn't feel my feet or stand up. I was afraid I had frozen my feet. I put my feet under the blanket and rubbed them until I could feel them warming up. I was relieved when I could feel my feet again. After that, I made a fire in the stove and went to the bathroom outside. I checked the thermometer, and it was minus 30 Celsius (minus 22 Fahrenheit), very cold indeed!

Once back in the cabin, I went back under my blanket and waited for the cabin to warm up. By then, Baptiste had gotten up, added more wood to the stove, and put the tea kettle on. The kettle contained the frozen snow water from last night. Once the cabin warmed up, I got up and moved my bed (plywood) against the wall, draping my blanket over the sheet. Baptiste made some tea, which he liked very strong. He used to say, "I like my tea strong enough so smoke comes out of my nose," and believe me, he wasn't kidding! He would keep the used tea bags in the teapot, add another five bags, and then boil the tea until the tea bags had ruptured. Drinking tea like that made my mouth pucker. I liked my tea not too strong and would add hot water or snow to dilute it.

After breakfast, Baptiste told us that we would be setting the five nets in front of the cabins, about 15 meters (50 feet) from the lakeshore. We gathered the nets, ice chisels, shovels, and a large roll of blue string and loaded them into Baptiste's sleigh. Peter started Baptiste's snowmobile, which took a few pulls to get going. Once it was warmed up, Peter drove the snowmobile to where the nets were to be set. The group from Jean-Marie River started their snowmobiles and drove to their nets, which were located to our left, not far from the cabins.

Baptiste walked along the lakeshore and cut two small birch trees and two willows, each about 1.5 meters (5 feet) in length. Just like his younger brother Gabe, Baptiste was in his element out on the land. Both Peter and I paid close attention as Baptiste explained that we would be setting the fishnets using two long sticks tied together and two willows, each fashioned with a hook, to set the line, which was the blue rope, under the ice. The line under the ice is used to pull the fishnet beneath and to check and reset the net. In addition, he cut four long poles to secure the nets.

We proceeded to make a hole in the ice with an ice chisel to begin setting the first net. We measured the water depth, which was about 5 meters (15 feet), and noted that the ice was about 30 centimeters (12 inches) thick. Baptiste asked us to help stretch the first net from the hole we had just made, heading toward the middle of the lake, to measure the length of the net and mark where the end of the net would be on the ice.

Baptiste tied the two birches together, creating one long piece, with a piece of the blue rope. He trimmed the branches from the birch trees. Once the birch sticks were tied, Baptiste laid one end of the birch stick next to the hole we had just made, facing the direction where we laid the net. Baptiste asked us to each use an ice chisel to make a hole at the end of the birch.

I started making a hole at the end of the birch pole while Baptiste moved the birch pole from the hole I was cutting to the next hole. Peter cut a hole with the ice chisel at the end of the birch pole while Baptiste moved the poles in the same direction as the net on the ice. Once I finished my hole, I moved to the next hole past Peter and started cutting. Baptiste moved the birch pole in that fashion two more times, and Peter and I cut two more holes. In total, we had cut 5 holes in the ice.

Baptiste cut a piece of blue rope twice the length of the net and tied it to one end of the birch stick at the last hole we cut. Baptiste asked us to each take a willow that he had fashioned with a hook at one end. The willow branch was left about 15 centimeters (6 inches) in length to form the hook. The willow was about 120 centimeters (4 feet) long. Baptiste submerged the birch pole under the ice toward the next hole. Using the willow with the hook, Peter grabbed the underside of the birch stick through the hole in the ice and slightly twisted the willow, pushing it as far as he could. He repeated this technique until I could see the end of the birch stick at the next hole. I did the same thing Peter did and pushed the birch pole to the following hole where Peter had moved. We repeated the technique until the last hole was reached and then pulled the long pole outside of the water.

Baptiste untied the blue rope from the birch pole and explained to us that the blue rope had to be at least twice the length of the fishnet, so the blue rope wouldn't fall back into the water when pulling the fishnet out to check it. If the rope fell back, we would have to start the process again with the birch stick. Once we had the blue rope under the water, we moved on to set the net.

The net was moved to the first hole that had been cut. Baptiste tied the end of the net to the blue rope that was under the water and asked me to start pulling the rope toward the middle of the lake. He instructed me to follow his command and not pull on the string too quickly. While I was pulling the net, Baptiste and Peter made sure the net was set correctly by ensuring that the bottom of the net did not twist or tangle with the top, with the weight line at the bottom and the float line at the top.

Once the entire net was under the water, Baptiste told me to stop pulling the blue rope. He tied the end of the fishnet to a pole he had cut earlier, using the attached string on the net, and secured the pole to the bottom of the lake. The net was set closer to the bottom of the lake, rather than the top, to ensure it would not freeze under the ice. Baptiste walked to the other end of the net and secured it to a long pole with a depth of about 6 meters (20 feet), in the same way as the first. Once the pole was secured to the bottom of the lake, Baptiste gave a few tugs on the pole to ensure the net was snug. If the fishnet didn't feel tight, the pole would be twisted by hand inward until the net was snug. A loose fishnet under the ice may rise and freeze under the ice.

A second net, located parallel to the first, was set using the same method as the first. The distance between the two nets was about 40 meters (120 feet).

After setting the second net, we returned to the cabins for a tea break and a bite to eat. This time of year, the daylight is short, so we had to make the best of it and manage our time accordingly. After lunch, Baptiste decided to stop setting nets for the day and focus on gathering firewood for the next few days. We didn't have enough firewood for the night, and the temperatures were cold. According to Baptiste, the next few days would be even colder. Baptiste and Peter went out cutting dry trees while I sawed the trees into pieces small enough to fit into the stove using Baptiste's Swede saw. We cut and sawed firewood until darkness fell. We had enough firewood for the next 3 or 4 days. Setting nets on the lake at minus 30 Celsius (minus 22 Fahrenheit) is cold on the body and the hands. Baptiste told us that if we wanted to warm up our hands while working on the fishnets, we should put them in the water, which was about 0 Celsius (32 Fahrenheit), much warmer than minus 30 Celsius.

Setting fishnets and untangling fish from the net sometimes requires working with bare hands.

Once the firewood was stacked in the cabin, we fed the stove and melted snow for tea. Baptiste wanted snow water for tea, rather than using lake water. We hung our mitts, hats, and duffels from our boots behind the stove on a string to dry them. Baptiste emphasized the importance of drying our clothes and boots overnight, particularly duffels and the inside of boots. If they weren't dried properly, moisture would transpire on the duffels and inside the boots, which would not keep our feet warm. Douglas gave Baptiste a jumbo whitefish that was caught that morning in their fishnet. Baptiste removed the scales of the fish with the back of his knife, gutted it, and washed it with lake water. The fish was then cut into pieces and boiled in a large pot on the stove. While the fish was cooking, we had some tea and Bannock. Baptiste commented on how tasty the whitefish from Reid Lake was. Once the fish was cooked, we all grabbed our plates and helped ourselves from the pot. Baptiste was smiling and enjoying the whitefish. In between bites, he said, "This is what we are here for." Peter uttered, "I hope that we catch a lot of fish tomorrow."

I was careful while eating my fish. A few months ago, I nearly choked on a whitefish bone that went right through one of my tonsils and hit the back of my throat. I was near panic. I went to the hospital in Fort Simpson after hours and rang the front bell. A nurse came to the door and asked me, "How can I help you?" I asked her if there was a doctor. She replied that the doctor was traveling in the smaller communities and would be back tomorrow. I told the nurse what had happened and asked her if she could remove the fish bone, which by now was hurting the back of my throat. She looked inside my mouth with a flashlight and saw the fish bone sticking out of one of my tonsils. She grabbed a tweezer and tried to pull the bone several times without success. I wasn't helping the situation; each time she put the tweezers in my mouth, I would nearly vomit. The nurse finally gave up and told me to come back tomorrow to see the doctor. In the meantime, she gave me a pill to calm me down. I cannot remember the name of the pill, but it sure calmed me down. Once back at the house, I asked Phoebe to try to pull the fish bone out with a pair of tweezers. I sat down and opened my mouth wide. Phoebe put the tweezers in my mouth. After a few attempts, she was able to grab the end of the fish bone and pull it out. The fish bone was long and sharp. Since that incident, I have been careful when eating fish.

After supper, Baptiste told us that in the old days, when people set up their camps near lakes known for their fish, they never went hungry when living near fish lakes, especially when wildlife in the bush was scarce. Baptiste's dad, Johnny, had told him that in the old days, many families, including his family, used to set camp during times when wildlife was scarce in the bush at Reid Lake to fish, which was known for its whitefish. Other lakes in the area, such as McEwan Lake (which Baptiste called Francis Lake in honor of his brother) and Lenoir Lake (where Baptiste's grandfather was buried), were also lakes known for their fish and used by Dene people. Baptiste, born in 1914, said that when he was a young boy, he remembered being carried on the back of his older sister Emily while his family traveled on foot in the bush with their belongings in backpacks carried by their dogs and on their backs, moving from camp to camp. Dene people back then, and before them, were nomads who moved around according to the seasons and where the wildlife inhabited.

He mentioned that his dad had told him about a year called the Year Without a Summer. I was told the same story by Gabe. That year, cold and cloudy conditions, along with heavy snowfall that didn't melt throughout the summer, killed a lot of wildlife in the bush, such as young rabbits, grouse, moose, and caribou, to name a few. Everyone was affected by this weather phenomenon, which caused hardship for everyone. Families moved to fish lakes to survive. I did some research on the internet years later about this weather phenomenon, which was caused by the eruption of Mount Tambora on April 1815, on Sumbawa Island, east of Java, in what is today Indonesia. Mount Tambora sent so much debris into the atmosphere that it blocked the sun, leading to what became known as the "Year Without a Summer" in 1816. This must have happened when Baptiste's dad's grandfather was alive.

Before we went to bed, Baptiste said that the plan for the next day was to set the remaining three nets, then check the two nets we set today. I made some kindling with my axe and set it aside by the stove on the ground. The kindling and some birch bark we had collected were to be used to make a fire in the morning. I set up my plywood sheet bed on the ground and went to bed. I made sure the zipper on my blanket was closed, wanting to ensure that my feet would stay warm.

The next morning, temperatures were in the minus 30s Celsius (minus 22 Fahrenheit). Baptiste was the first one up and made a fire to warm up the cabin, which was very cold. Once the fire got going, the cabin warmed up quickly. We had breakfast and got dressed. My duffels and mitts were warm and dry. Once outside, I could feel how cold it was. My mustache and eyelashes quickly iced up. Baptiste wanted to first set what he called the Japanese net. He had never used this type of net before. I believe that Sam Ramson, the Game Warden in Fort Simpson, gave him the net to try. We stretched out the Japanese net on the ice to measure it and proceeded, to set the net. We set the net again parallel to the one we set yesterday, at about a distance of 40 meters (120 feet).

Once the net was set, Baptiste said that he was told that this type of net, made of monofilament, which is similar to fishing line, is very strong and blends with the water, making it nearly invisible to the fish. This type of net does not freeze up like the twine nets we set when pulling out the fish. Peter and I tried to start the snowmobiles, but they wouldn't start due to the cold temperatures. The nets were not very far from the cabin, so we used one sleigh to haul the nets and our gear by pulling and pushing on the sleigh.

Once the Japanese net was set, we walked back to the cabin to warm up and have a cup of tea. After the tea break and a quick bite to eat, we returned to the lake to set the last two nets. Once the last two nets were set, we walked over to the two fishnets we had set the previous day. The ice was thick, over 30 centimeters (one foot) overnight, due to the cold temperatures. We cut the ice on the two holes where the first net was tied to the poles. Baptiste pulled out the pole farthest from the shore and untied the net from the pole, then tied one end of the long blue rope to the net. Baptiste and Peter walked to the pole closest to the shore and pulled the pole out of the water, leaving the net tied up to the pole. Peter dragged part of the net out of the water a short distance while holding the pole. He then put the pole on the ice and walked back to the hole to help his dad check the net. Both pulled the net out of the water and started checking the net. I walked toward them to see how many fish were caught in the fishnet. It's always exciting to see the results of setting the net.

At the first caught whitefish, Baptiste bit the fish on the mouth and used both hands to untangle it from the net. Once the fish was free, he would turn his head to one side, still holding the fish in his mouth, then move his head back quickly and let go of the fish, which fell on the ice away from the net. For each whitefish, Baptiste repeated the same process to free the fish from the net. Baptiste was good at it, and I could see that he had done these many times before. A couple of large pikes were caught in the net. Peter began untangling a pike, which tends to tangle in the net more than whitefish. Baptiste helped him free the two pikes, which were still kicking. Baptiste laughed when I asked him why he didn't bite the pike's mouth to untangle them. He said, "Pikes have sharp teeth."

Baptiste asked me to start pulling on the blue rope in order to reset the net under the water. I started pulling on the blue rope while Baptiste and Peter ensured that the fishnet didn't tangle, with the floats at the top and the weights at the bottom. Once the whole net was under the water, Baptiste grabbed the pole, put it in the hole, and then pushed it firmly to the bottom of the lake. He walked over to the other end of the fishnet, untied the blue rope, and tied the string of the net to the pole. Baptiste then put the pole back into the water and firmly pushed it to the bottom of the lake. In total, we caught about a dozen jumbo whitefish and two pikes in the first net. We checked the second net, which yielded about the same number of fish as the first net. Baptiste was happy with the catch.

We loaded the sleigh with the fish we caught and pulled and pushed it to the cabin. We kept the largest jumbo whitefish for supper and laid the other fish on the snow to freeze near the cabin. Baptiste told us that we would not gut the fish but leave them whole. Before I could ask him the question, Baptiste said, "The fish will keep fresh longer with the guts inside." Baptiste prepared the fish for supper and then boiled it on the stove. While the fish was boiling, Baptiste made some Bannock,

Freshly cooked Bannock with butter and boiled fish were on the menu that evening. We all enjoyed our supper and drank some tea while listening to Baptiste telling stories about his trapping days in the Reid Lake area. The cabin was nice and warm, making us all sleepy, especially after a big meal. I set up my sheet of plywood bed and blanket and crawled into my blanket. It wasn't long before I could hear Baptiste snoring softly.

Early the next morning, we heard the Bombardier and snowmobile running next door. The Jean-Marie River group had pulled out their nets the day before and were loading their gear into the Bombardier and snowmobile. It was very cold, about minus 35 Celsius (minus 31 Fahrenheit). Douglas and Billy used a torch, a stove pipe, an elbow, and a tarp to warm up the Bombardier before attempting to start it. We went outside to say our goodbyes and shake hands with Douglas, Billy, Ernest, and Jimmy. Douglas told Baptiste that they were finished with the fishing and would not be coming back to Reid Lake this winter. He also said that if we wanted, we could move into their cabin. After the group left, we moved all our gear to their cabin. There were four beds in the cabin, two beds apiece along the north and south walls. The cabin had a wooden floor, which looked to have been built recently, and a large table attached to the east wall. The stove was bigger than the one we had in the other cabin. The cabin was larger and cozier. The unfinished cabin we stayed in was mostly used for storage. I waited for Baptiste and Peter to select their bed before I selected mine, which ended up being near the stove. I guess I was the one who would be making the fire in the morning. I didn't mind. I was happy that I didn't have to sleep on a sheet of plywood anymore.

After breakfast, we walked to the nets, pulling a sleigh. Baptiste was curious and wanted to see how the Japanese net did. The net was set in the middle of the five nets. Peter and I cut the ice with the chisel on both holes. Baptiste and Peter walked to the pole closest to the shore. While pulling the pole, Peter noticed that the net was not budging. Both Baptiste and Peter pulled on the pole a few times, but the net still didn't budge. Baptiste announced that the net must be frozen to the bottom of the ice. He asked Peter and me to clear the snow on the ice that was above the net. Peter and I cleared all the snow with shovels, from one pole to the other pole. The ice was clear, making it possible to see the fishnet through the ice. Baptiste walked over, checking the net through the ice, and saw two sections of the net that were frozen to the ice. These were short sections.

Baptiste grabbed his axe and headed toward the shore. He returned quickly with a forked stick in hand. "Peter, you and Daniel help me clear the ice around the net," he said, his voice calm but firm.

Peter and I set to work, chipping away at the thick ice over the sections where the net had frozen solid. The ice was stubborn, but we moved with precision, careful not to damage the net beneath. Once the ice was cleared, Baptiste used the forked stick to push down on the trapped net, freeing it with a soft crack.

When the last section was free, Baptiste and Peter tugged on the pole to pull it out of the water. The net was heavy, teeming with whitefish. More than we had caught yesterday, by far. I could feel my heart race at the sight, the excitement building in my chest.

"Can I help?" I asked, my voice eager.

Baptiste's face softened into a grin. "Sure, you're here to learn."

I bit the mouth of one of the whitefish, gripping its slippery body with my bare hands. It wasn't easy, working the fish free from the tangled net. Baptiste did the same, turning his head to one side as he freed each fish. Peter joined in, and we worked together in a rhythm, pulling fish from the net, one by one. The weight of the whitefish felt satisfying in my hands, their sleek bodies a testament to the richness of the lake.

"No pikes this time," I said, a little surprised.

Baptiste chuckled. "Not this time, but we'll get plenty soon enough."

After the net was cleared, Baptiste eyed the floats and noted, "Too many floats on the top line. That's why it froze." He methodically removed every second float, ensuring the net would perform better on the next pull.

My hands were cold and covered in the slimy residue of fish. Remembering what Baptiste had told us earlier, I plunged my hands into the cold water to wash off the fish slime. The ice-cold liquid took me by surprise, but as I kept my hands submerged, they began to warm. I couldn't help but smile at the unexpected relief.

Once the net was reset and we had checked the other four, we loaded the fish into the sleigh. The sleigh was heavy, laden with fish that felt like they could sink it into the snow—but we moved as efficiently as we could. I pulled from the front while Peter pushed from the back. It was slow work, but it was necessary.

We set up a cache near the cabin in the snow, laying the fish out to freeze before bringing them inside. By the time we were done, we had caught about eighty whitefish and a handful of pikes. But despite the success, the cold was creeping into our bones, and hunger was setting in. We hadn't stopped for tea yet.

The fire in the stove was almost out, so we started a new one, throwing a few pieces of wood into the stove. Baptiste tossed five fresh tea bags into the kettle, over the five used ones from before. As the tea began to brew, I could already smell the strength of it.

"That's going to be some strong tea," I joked, shaking my head.

"You bet," Baptiste replied, a knowing look in his eye. "Tea strong enough to make you see smoke coming out of your nose."

Peter and I laughed, feeling the warmth of the cabin and the tea slowly chasing away the cold. It wasn't long before Baptiste had the fire crackling, the fish sizzling in the pot. The savory smell filled the cabin, mingling with the scent of the strong tea.

After supper, we cleaned our plates and sat down with our mugs of tea, letting the warmth sink into our tired muscles. My bed felt surprisingly comfortable, and the fire's crackling warmth made me drowsy. It had been a long day, but I could feel a sense of accomplishment settling in.

Baptiste, having his after-supper cigarette, looked over at me. "Tomorrow," he said, with a thoughtful pause, "we should set some rabbit snares across the lake. There's a good area for rabbits over there. Maybe we'll even set a few marten traps while we're at it."

I nodded, feeling the weight of the long day begin to lift. "I brought my spring pole snare stick," I said, "I can set the snares for rabbits."

Baptiste raised an eyebrow. "You know how to set spring pole snares?"

I grinned. "Gabe showed me how. We set a snare line in early January this year, and I even set one by myself near the Mexican Hat this past summer."

Baptiste smiled, impressed. "Well, then. I guess you're ready to put that knowledge to work."

Baptiste carefully set the trap and smiled at me, "This is how it's done," he said. I watched as he checked his work, making sure the trap was stable and would catch the mink if it came by. I was learning something new, and the method seemed so simple yet so effective.

Peter had been busy cutting the small spruce trees, now placed them on either side of the trap, as Baptiste had instructed, to create a protective roof. Once everything was set, Baptiste stood back and surveyed the trap.

We continued down the trail, Baptiste leading the way, pointing out areas where we could set more traps. Every so often, he would stop to check for tracks—mink, rabbit, marten or anything else that might be in the area. As we walked, I realized how much Baptiste knew about the land. Every detail, every track, every tree seemed to tell him a story, and I was eager to learn.

After setting several more traps and snares, we decided to break for lunch. The cold had started to bite, and we needed to warm up. We found a spot in the shelter of some tall trees, unpacked our thermos of tea, and ate the remaining Bannock. The hot tea helped ease the cold that had settled deep into my bones.

"Tomorrow, we check the traps," Baptiste said, taking a sip of his tea. "And then we can check on the beaver lodges by the lake."

I nodded, feeling a sense of accomplishment. The day had been long and tiring, but rewarding. We were learning new skills, things that I knew would serve me well in the future.

After lunch, we continued our work, setting a few more traps and snares along the way. The sun was beginning to dip, casting long shadows across the snow. By the time we made it back to the cabin, we were all tired but satisfied with our progress.

As we settled into the cabin for the night, the fire crackling in the stove, Baptiste mentioned once again that we would check the traps and snares in the morning. I couldn't wait to see what we would catch. The excitement of being out in the bush, learning from Baptiste, made the cold and the hard work worthwhile.

I set up my bed; I pulled my blanket tight around me. It wasn't long before I drifted off to sleep, the warmth from the fire keeping me comfortable as I dreamed of the adventures that awaited us the next day.

The next part of the trail was quieter, with fewer signs of animals, but the work continued. I could hear Baptiste and Peter chopping and moving ahead, and I was determined to keep up. As I followed, the peacefulness of the forest surrounded me, with only the occasional sound of snowshoes crunching and axes striking the wood. The air was crisp, and every breath I took seemed to cut through the cold like a knife, sharpening my senses.

As I approached them, I saw Baptiste crouching by a young tree. He had found another good spot, a location that looked promising for marten traps, and he was already preparing to set one. He and Peter had been moving methodically through the forest, cutting the trail as they went, and it was clear they knew this land well.

"We're getting close to some good spots," Baptiste called to me as I joined them. "The fresh rabbit tracks here tell us they're moving around; we need to make sure the snares are set just right."

This was what I had come for, the chance to learn, to be part of the land in a way I had never been before.

Baptiste worked with precision, setting the marten trap carefully in the snow. His hands moved with confidence, knowing exactly what to do. I watched intently, absorbing every movement, every piece of advice he offered. "Patience is key," he said, setting the trap with delicate care. "You'll be surprised at how quickly they come once you have the right setup."

Peter was nearby, already checking on the rabbit snares we had set earlier. The mix of anticipation and focus in his eyes was something I could relate to. We were all in this together, learning and working in the quiet rhythm of the bush. It was hard work, but there was a deep satisfaction in it, something that felt more real than anything I had done before.

We worked through the day, setting more snares, marking trails, and making adjustments as needed. As the sun started to dip lower in the sky, we began to head back toward the cabin, the day's efforts already starting to show signs of success. There was a quiet energy in the group, a shared feeling that our hard work would pay off.

By the time we returned to the cabin, we had set nearly all the snares and traps we needed. We settled in, tired but content, our bellies filled with tea and the promise of a good night's rest before another day in the bush. The land had given us much already, and we were ready to see what it would offer us the next day.

Baptiste looked at me curiously but didn't ask any more questions, trusting that I knew what I was doing. I set to work on the birch, carefully carving the handle for the axe. I used my knife to shape it into the right fit, remembering the time Gabe had shown me how to make an axe handle from a birch tree. The work required precision and patience, but the task felt familiar, almost instinctive. The birch was strong and pliable, and soon enough, I had fashioned a handle that looked promising.

While I worked, Peter continued with the sawing and splitting of the firewood, keeping the stove fueled with each load. The smell of the boiling whitefish and baking Bannock filled the cabin, making my stomach rumble. The cold, hard day in the bush had worked up an appetite, and soon we would sit down to a warm, satisfying meal.

I checked the birch handle against the axe head, making adjustments where needed. It took a few tries, but eventually, the new handle fit perfectly. Baptiste smiled at my handiwork, clearly impressed. "That's how it's done," he said, as he took the axe from me and tested its balance. The handle was sturdy and fit snugly in place. It was ready to be used.

With the axe fixed, I joined Peter by the stove, where we shared a hot meal. We ate in silence for a while, savoring the warmth of the food and the fire. The cold outside seemed a distant memory as we relaxed and refueled.

312

After supper, Baptiste took a deep breath, content. "Tomorrow, we'll finish cutting more wood for the fire. We still have plenty to do. But tonight, we rest."

We all agreed, and after cleaning up the plates and utensils, we sat back, the comfort of a full stomach and the warmth of the fire soothing our tired bodies. As the night settled in, I could hear Baptiste and Peter chatting softly. I listened, their voices mingling with the crackle of the fire, feeling the quiet peace of the bush settle around me.

Tomorrow, we will continue our work checking nets and completing the tasks that would keep us fed and safe. But for now, I was content to let the warmth of the cabin and the bond we had in the bush wrap around me like a blanket.

After we had cleared the ice and set everything up, Baptiste moved over to check the first net. The cold air made everything feel sharper, more intense, as we worked in the crisp, freezing temperatures. He pulled out the first pole from the water and carefully untied the net, testing it for any entanglements. I could see him glancing over the water, his eyes sharp even in the bitter cold. He gave me a nod to help pull the net.

Peter and I tugged carefully, working together to bring it up from the depths. The net slowly rose, the once-hidden fish starting to appear in the clear water. As the net came closer to the surface, I could make out the familiar shapes of whitefish and the occasional pike. The excitement of a good catch buzzed through me, reminding me of how satisfying it was to see the rewards of hard work come to fruition.

Once the net was fully out of the water, Baptiste used his quick hands to untangle the fish one by one, tossing them aside onto the ice. He looked at me with a grin and said, "You've got the hang of it now, keep at it."

The cold was biting at my hands as I helped with the fish. It was hard to focus on anything but the task at hand, but the feeling of satisfaction from setting the nets and pulling in fish made it all worth it. We quickly checked the rest of the nets and started pulling them in one by one, collecting the catch from each net.

With the nets checked, we headed back to the cabin, hauling the fish on a sleigh. The icy wind made the walk back feel longer, but the idea of getting back to the warmth of the cabin kept me going. When we arrived, we unloaded the fish and got to work preparing them for storage. The fire in the stove crackled, and I felt the heat creeping into my frozen bones. We were all hungry, the cold making our stomachs growl louder.

Baptiste immediately got to work boiling some of the fish while Peter and I chopped firewood for the evening. The smell of fish cooking on the stove mixed with the scent of fresh wood smoke. We settled in for another meal, all of us appreciating the comfort of warmth and food after a long, cold day.

As we ate, Baptiste shared more stories of his youth in the bush, his experiences with the land, and how things had changed over the years. I listened intently, absorbing everything. His stories were rich with the history of the area, lessons learned from years of living off the land. It wasn't just about survival; it was about a way of life, a connection to nature that few would ever understand. His words filled the cabin as we all relaxed, savoring the meal and the company.

Later, as we sat around the fire, Baptiste talked about the importance of being prepared for the harsher winter months ahead. We would need to set more traps, gather more firewood, and ensure we had enough provisions to last us through the cold. The days ahead would be challenging, but there was a sense of calm in knowing we were well-prepared, both mentally and physically, for whatever came next.

That night, as I lay in my bed, the warmth from the fire and the satisfaction of a productive day lulled me into a deep sleep. The crackling fire and the wind outside kept me grounded in the reality of where I was, but in that moment, I felt a peace I hadn't experienced before.

After supper, we sat around the stove in the cabin, warming ourselves and sharing stories. The heat from the fire was comforting after a long day spent working outside in the cold. Baptiste talked about his experiences hunting and trapping in the area, offering bits of wisdom about the land and its rhythms. Peter, chimed in now and then with his own stories from the bush, making the conversation flow easily.

As we sat there, the cabin filled with the comforting smell of the fish and freshly baked Bannock. The food gave us the energy we needed, and soon, everyone was in high spirits. The fire crackled, and the warmth slowly seeped into our bones, making it easy to forget about the cold temperatures outside.

Baptiste seemed pleased with the day's work, and after a bit, we all retired to our beds for the night. The cabin had a cozy feel now, with enough firewood to keep us warm. The days were short, but the nights felt long and restful.

The next morning, we woke up early, as usual, to face the day. It was a cold one once again, with the temperature hovering around minus 30 Celsius (minus 22 Fahrenheit). We quickly ate breakfast, fueled up with more tea and Bannock, and prepared ourselves for another day of setting traps and checking the nets. The air outside was sharp and biting, but we were used to it by now.

I knew that the day would be filled with more work, more learning, and the steady rhythm of life on the land. It was a pace I had come to enjoy, with its rewards of fish, firewood, and the satisfaction of living off the land, relying on skill and resourcefulness. As we walked out into the cold morning light, I felt a sense of connection to the place, to the work, and to the people I was learning from. It was a life I knew I would carry with me, one that would shape my understanding of nature and survival.

Baptiste carefully placed the curved stick into the hole Peter had made and pushed it into the water beneath the ice. He explained that this was the technique used to locate the beaver's entrance, as the beavers usually feed on the winter's stockpiled food just below the ice. The curved stick would allow us to confirming the location of the entrance.

Baptiste retrieved a trap from the sleigh. The trap was a number 4 leghold trap designed for catching beavers. He demonstrated how to set them in the hole under the ice, explaining the importance of setting the trap in a way that would trigger the beaver's movement when it passed by. Baptiste worked with the kind of precision that comes only with years of experience.

While he set the trap, I stood by, absorbing the process, keen to learn from his every move. Peter helped clear away the snow, keeping the area around the trap clean and clear.

Once the trap was set and hidden under the ice, Baptiste moved on to the second lodge, ready to repeat the process. The air was sharp, and the sun glistened off the frozen lake, making it both beautiful and brutal.

We worked quickly but efficiently, the ice was a constant reminder of how unforgiving nature could be, but with Baptiste's expertise, it felt like we had an advantage.

After setting the traps, we made our way back to the cabin, the cold now biting even deeper into our bones. The trail we had made earlier was now frozen solid, making the walk back easier. The sky was still clear, but the sun was beginning to dip lower, signaling that daylight was running short.

Back at the cabin, we warmed up by the fire, and Baptiste set to work preparing supper. The day had been long, and the cold had taken its toll. I was looking forward to some warmth and a hot meal, but I couldn't shake the excitement from setting those traps.

As the evening settled in the warmth of the cabin contrasting sharply with the frigid landscape outside. Baptiste shared more stories of his youth, of times spent trapping and hunting in the same woods. The quiet of the cabin, broken only by the crackling of the fire, felt like the perfect end to a day of hard work and learning.

The cold wind bit at my skin as I stepped outside, but the task at hand kept me focused. The sound of the axe striking wood was soothing, and I chopped and split the firewood with precision, determined to make sure we had enough for the coming nights. The scent of the cold air mixed with the smell of the burning wood in the stove, creating a comforting atmosphere in the cabin.

Once I had finished the firewood, I returned to the warmth inside. Peter came back shortly after, having checked his snares and traps. He looked satisfied with the catches, and we settled around the stove, letting the warmth seep into our bones.

Baptiste began preparing a simple but hearty meal, boiled rabbit with some of the fish we'd caught earlier. The aroma filled the cabin, making our stomachs growl in anticipation. We sat together, eating our meal in silence, each of us lost in thought, the crackling fire providing a steady rhythm in the background.

As the evening wore on, we chatted about the day's events and made plans for the next day. There was more work ahead, checking traps, snares and nets and preparing for the journey back. But for now, we were content, surrounded by the quiet beauty of the land.

The firelight flickered on the walls, casting long shadows that seemed to dance with the rhythm of the wind outside. I leaned back, taking a deep breath, feeling the weight of the day's work on my shoulders. There was something about this life, in the stillness and harshness of the bush, that felt grounding, like I was part of something timeless.

Baptiste made some tea and hung three rabbits behind the stove to thaw them out for supper. He said, "Supper will be late, we'll have to wait for the rabbits to thaw out a bit." Peter returned to the cabin with a marten that he had caught not far from the cabin. Not a bad day, six rabbits, one mink, and one marten.

Once thawed out, Baptiste cleaned the three rabbits and cut pieces of slab bacon. The rabbits and bacon were put in a big pot to boiled. Baptiste said, "I will make rabbit soup with the broth and add some rice." I had boiled rabbit and bacon and rabbit soup many times before at Gabe's house. The bacon and rabbit meat complemented each other. It was getting late, and we were all hungry. I devoured my rabbit and bacon and had two helpings of soup.

"We will be checking the nets tomorrow," Baptiste said. He added, "We caught about one hundred and sixty whitefish and a couple of dozen pikes. We will check the nets two more times before we call from the camp at Trout River for a plane on skis to pick up the fish." Baptiste wanted to sell the whitefish at the local stores in Fort Simpson. The temperature was minus 40 Celsius (minus 40 Fahrenheit), and it would be another cold day the next day. The frozen mink and marten were attached to a string and hung on the wall in the cabin to thaw out. "They will be thawed out enough to be skinned in the morning," said Baptiste. Throughout the night, I fed the stove a couple of times to keep the cabin warm.

Early the next morning, still dark, Baptiste confirmed that the mink and marten were ready to be skinned. From the light of the gas lamp, Baptiste explained to Peter and me how to remove the skin from the marten and mink, which is an identical method. He held the marten by one of the back legs and made a straight cut with his sharp knife on the inside of the legs, starting from near the paw to near the base of the tail. He then held the other leg and did the same method, cutting the skin until it met the other cut. Using his thumb, he pulled apart the skin from the leg until it was freed. He then used his knife to cut the skin near the top of the toes. He did the same method on the other leg.

Baptiste used two small sticks and placed them at the base of the tail, one stick over and one stick under the tail. Putting pressure on both sticks, he held the marten with his left hand

and pulled on both sticks with his right hand to free the fur tail from the bone tail. Baptiste then made a cut inside the front legs from the paw to the elbow. He held the marten by the back legs with his left hand and slowly pulled the skin with his right hand to the front legs. Baptiste used the same method that he used to pull the skin from the back legs to the front legs. Once the front legs were freed, he pulled on the skin until he reached the base of the ears. He then used his knife to cut the base of the ears and pulled the skin to the eyelids. Again, he used his knife to free the skin around the eyes and pulled it to the nose. He cut the base of the nose cartilage to free the skin from the body of the marten. This whole process took about 2 minutes.

Baptiste then grabbed the mink and removed the skin using the same method he used on the marten. He highlighted that the mink has a gland near the base of its tail and that we must be careful not to puncture it. The liquid in the gland is greenish and very smelly.

Peter discovered under his bed a couple of stretchers for drying the pelt of the marten or mink. A stretcher consists of a wooden board and a belly wedge, which is mainly crafted from white spruce or pine tree. The stretcher is shaped like the pelt of a marten or mink after the animal has been skinned. The pelt is stretched out on the stretcher, fur side in, leather out, and tacked on each back leg to the side of the stretcher. In addition, the tail is split on the inside of the tail so that it dries properly; the end of the tail is tacked onto the stretcher. A string is used to uniformly spread the back legs to the edges of the stretcher. The pelt should not be overstretched. The belly wedge, with the flat part against the stretcher, is inserted under the pelt's belly. The pelt is left on the stretcher for about 12 hours or overnight. Once partially dry, the pelt is removed from the stretcher and rolled fur out. The pelt is once again stretched and tacked onto the stretcher. The string is strung over the back legs, and the belly wedge is inserted back under the pelt's belly. The pelt is left on the stretcher until completely dry and then removed from the stretcher. The pelt is now ready to be sold.

Mink is dried fur in and leather out until completely dry. Mink is usually fat, which should be removed before drying the mink pelt. Baptiste and Peter stretched the marten and mink on the stretcher. "Do not dry the fur too close to the stove," said Baptiste. He added, "The fur should be dried slowly, not fast."

After the marten and mink were skinned and stretched, the sun had begun to rise to the east. The absence of clouds in the sky hinted at very cold temperatures overnight. The thermometer had plummeted from minus 40 Celsius (minus 40 Fahrenheit) to near minus 50 Celsius (minus 58 Fahrenheit) overnight. Remembering that day, as I'm writing this, I feed my fireplace with some dry firewood. Back in the 70s and 80s, it was foreseeable during the winter months to be afflicted with very cold temperatures of minus 40 Celsius or colder for weeks on end. Nowadays, temperatures of minus 40 Celsius, are sporadic and do not last for long.

I grabbed my sleigh and pulled it to the nets. On account of the cold temperatures, it felt like I was pulling the sleigh over sandpaper as opposed to snow. Peter and I grabbed an ice chisel each and began chipping the ice at each net's hole. The ice was well over 30 centimeters (1 foot) thick. Before setting the nets, Baptiste had installed a piece of blue rope at the top end of the ice chisel and fashioned it into a handle large enough to put one hand through. The purpose of the blue rope handle was to prevent the ice chisel from slipping right through our hands and getting lost in the lake.

The nets had not been checked for 2 nights; we were expecting a lot of fish in the nets. While chipping the ice, I took a break and blew my nose, which was constantly running due to the cold temperatures. Forgetting that I wasn't wearing my mittens, I grabbed the ice chisel, which was made of metal, with my bare hands. As soon as I touched the ice chisel, I let go and felt a burning sensation in my hands. I quickly put my mitts on and carried on chipping the ice.

The first net yielded a good catch of whitefish. We used Baptiste's technique to remove the fish from the net. Our hands were cold after checking the first net. We came to the decision that it was a good time for a tea break. The warmth of the cabin felt good. It must have been about 20 Celsius (68 Fahrenheit) inside the cabin as opposed to near minus 50 Celsius (minus 58 Fahrenheit), a noticeable difference in temperatures. After a short tea break, we returned to the nets and checked two more nets before taking another tea break, which was an excuse for warming up our bones. The two nets, which included the Japanese net, yielded more whitefish.

After we checked the last two nets, we loaded the fish into the sleigh. We caught well over eighty whitefish, bringing our total to about two hundred fifty whitefish and a couple of dozen pikes. Peter and I had to make two trips with the sleigh. We both struggled, pushing and pulling the sleigh to the cabin.

There was about one hour of daylight left in the day. After a quick warm-up, Peter and I grabbed our axes and headed to the stand of dead trees behind the cabin. Looking to the west, the sun was making its way below the horizon. It was another amazing sunset and winter scene painting. The wind was dead calm, as if it were too cold for the wind to be blowing. Looking at the cloudless sky, I told Peter that tonight may be a good night to look at the Northern Lights.

Peter and I cut and hauled two trees each to the sawhorse near the cabin. It would be dark soon. Using the Swede saw, I cut pieces of wood until it was unsafe to do so. I hauled some firewood into the cabin for the night. Baptiste had skinned the three remaining rabbits and had them boiling in the big pot with bacon. He boiled a whitefish for himself. We had a well-earned supper and relaxed on our beds. Baptiste and Peter had their usual after-supper cigarette.

"Tomorrow we will check the beaver traps and snare line," said Baptiste.

Before I went to bed, I went outside to see if the Northern Lights (Aurora Borealis) were out. To my surprise, the Northern lights were lighting up the sky in multiple shades of colors and appeared as curtains, rays, and spirals. The sky was dancing and on fire. I had seen the Northern Lights many times before, but this was one of the best I've seen. I called Baptiste and Peter and told them the Northern Lights were out. Both came outside to view the Northern Lights, which were amazing to see.

The next morning, Baptiste announced that the weather was warmer than yesterday. I checked the thermometer outside, and it was minus 25 Celsius (minus 13 Fahrenheit), a significant welcome increase in temperatures of nearly 25 degrees. After our breakfast, Peter said, "We should try to start the snowmobiles." Baptiste and I went to our respective snowmobiles and pulled a few times on the recoil. My snowmobile started after a few pulls. I was ecstatic, the snowmobile had woken up from its slumber. After a few more pulls, Baptiste's snowmobile came back to life. We both hooked up our sleighs to our snowmobiles and loaded our gear needed for the day. Peter rode in the back of his dad's sleigh, and I drove my snowmobile. We headed across the lake to the beaver lodges, Baptiste in the lead. In no time, we were at the first beaver lodge.

Baptiste parked and shut down his snowmobile about 30 meters (100 feet) from the feed piles. I parked my snowmobile behind him. "The ice near the beaver lodge is thinner than the ice on the lake," said Baptiste. He added that the snowmobiles might go through the ice if they are too close to the lodge. Peter started chipping the ice where the trap was set, and I used the shovel to clean the ice. Baptiste approached the trap set and slowly pulled the pole up until the end was resting on the ice. Baptiste announced that a beaver had come to the trap but did not get caught. The piece of green poplar he nailed above the trap had been chewed and taken away. He nailed another piece of green poplar above the trap, a little closer to the trap than before. The pole was set back into the water and secured to the cross stick. I shoveled some snow on top of the water hole. Baptiste had told us that the snow would freeze at the top of the hole and reduce the light from the sun and the moon from shining under the ice, which might scare the beaver from coming close to the trap.

We walked to the next beaver lodge, which was only about 90 meters (300 feet) away, with our gear. After the ice was chipped and cleaned from the hole, Baptiste pulled out the pole slowly and announced, "We got a beaver, and a big one." Once the stick was out of the water, Baptiste freed the beaver and, using his two hands, rubbed the beaver against the snow back and forth a few times. He then turned the beaver over and did the same thing. "The snow absorbs the water from the hide so it will not freeze," said Baptiste. He cut a piece of the beaver's chin and a small bone from both back feet. Baptiste then put the piece of chin and the two small bones in the water hole and said something in South Slavey. The only word I understood was "*Tsa*," which translates to "beaver." He nailed a fresh green piece of poplar and reset the trap, then set the pole back into the water. I shoveled some snow on top of the water hole and secured the blue rope to both dry sticks.

We put the beaver into a backpack and walked back to the snowmobiles. We then drove to the start of the snare line. We put on our snowshoes and checked the snare line and traps. Baptiste caught another mink in the same trap near the lakeshore. We walked to the end of the snare line and only caught one rabbit. "It was very cold these last few days; the rabbit does not travel very far when it is very cold," said Baptiste.

Peter grabbed the backpack with the beaver and brought it into the cabin. The sun would be setting in about one hour, enough time for me to finish sawing the wood Peter and I cut yesterday. Peter went to check his snares and traps on the trail behind the cabin with his dad's snowmobile and came back about fifteen minutes later with a rabbit that he had caught in his ground snare.

Baptiste lit the gas lamp in the cabin and used some cardboard that was in the cabin to fix an area to skin the beaver. He laid the beaver on it's his back and sharpened his knife. Peter and I sat on our bed and watched Baptiste skin the beaver. Baptiste cut the tail, back feet, and front feet and said, "Beaver tail is like bush bacon, and the back feet are also good to eat." He made a straight cut from the middle base of the tail to the chin, and using his knife, cut the fat and meat away from the skin, starting around the stomach section. He skinned half of the beaver hide off, then skinned the other half of the beaver hide. In no time, he had the hide off the carcass. Baptiste folded the hide and put it on a piece of cardboard.

He then removed the castor, which is a pair of anal glands located between the pelvis and the base of the tail. Baptiste said, "Castor is a good bait for trapping lynx."

Our source of heat was an airtight wood heater that we also used for frying or boiling our food by lifting the lid on top of the heater and laying our pot or frying pan directly on the open fire. The cast-iron frying pan that Baptiste used for cooking Bannock and frying bacon was the same size as the hole on top of the heater. The boiling pot was a bit larger but fit well on top of the heater. The airtight wood heater suited our needs for cooking and keeping the cabin nice and warm.

Baptiste used a willow stick that he had sharpened at one end and inserted the base of the tail onto the stick. He put the beaver tail inside the stove, directly on the flames, and turned it around a few times until the leathery skin started to blister. Once the leathery skin was removed from the tail, Baptiste cut the tail into smaller pieces. Next, he inserted the willow stick into one of the beaver's back feet and put it into the stove to singe the hair on the feet. Baptiste did the same for the other feet. Once the hair was singed, he used his knife like a scraper to remove the burnt hair and skin on the feet. Once tanned, the leather from the beaver tail can be made into watch straps, boots, wallets, and small knife sheaths. Baptiste and Gabe never mentioned this to me, but I did some research. On the internet on the use of leather from the beaver tail.

Baptiste put a pot of snow water on the air-tight heater to create water, then placed the beaver tail, feet, and about half of the beaver into the pot. Beaver meat was on the menu for the evening, and I had never eaten beaver meat before, so I was looking forward to it. After the beaver's tail and feet were cooked, Baptiste removed the pot from the heater. "It has been a while since I had beaver meat," said Baptiste. We all dug into the pot and filled our plates; Baptiste ate both feet. I enjoyed the beaver meat and tail. The meat had some fat on it, which complemented the taste. After eating my fill of beaver meat, my belly was full. There was little to no conversation while we were eating our supper; everyone was busy eating and enjoying their meal.

After supper, we cleaned our own plates. Each one of us had our plate, cup, and utensils. "Don't throw your beaver bones in the stove or outside," said Baptiste. He added, "We will save the bones and put them back in the water at the beaver lodge." Baptiste also mentioned, "Eating bush meat will keep you warm." Gabe had mentioned while telling me trapping stories. He explained that eating meat from the store while in the bush will not keep you warm in the winter. The heat from the stove and my full belly made me feel sleepy, and I soon fell asleep.

The next morning, still dark outside, Baptiste lit the gas lamp while Peter fed the stove with fire-killed wood. Peter checked the mink that was hanging on the wall to see if it had thawed. "The mink is ready to be skinned," said Peter. "You can skin the mink," said Baptiste.

After breakfast, Peter skinned the mink; It was his first time skinning a mink. He did well and did not puncture the mink's glands. Once skinned, Peter removed the fat from the skin and then stretched the mink pelt onto the stretcher. Across the lake, the sun was beginning to slowly rise, and the Northern Lights were still visible, giving their last performance before sunrise.

I pulled on the recoil of my snowmobile a couple of times, and the motor fired up, purring like a frozen cat. I loaded the gear required to check the net into the sleigh and drove the snowmobile along the lakeshore for a short distance to warm up the engine. We had a few jerry cans of mixed gas for our snowmobiles and needed to ensure that we had enough for our stay at the lake and return to the highway.

We checked all five nets and caught fewer fish than the last time we checked them. Peter and I stored the fish after they were frozen and took a count. We had approximately 280 whitefish and 25 pikes. "We'll go to the highway camp tomorrow and call for a plane," said Baptiste. I said, "I could stay behind, cut some firewood, and check the snare line across the lake." "That's a good idea," said Baptiste. "Peter and I will go to the highway camp." He asked me to make an airstrip on the lake for the plane by packing the snow with my snowmobile.

We ate the last of the beaver meat for supper and had some freshly cooked Bannock. "I cooked the Bannock with whitefish eggs," said Baptiste. The Bannock had an interesting, pleasant flavor. He added, "You can cook Bannock with bacon grease or bear grease. The Bannock won't dry up or get hard with bear grease."

Just before I went to bed, I went outside to check the thermometer. The temperatures had dipped to minus 30 Celsius (minus 22 Fahrenheit). The sky was clear, and the stars were bright, shining like diamonds. The Northern Lights were just as colorful as the previous evening. It was amazing to see such a display of colors dancing in the sky.

The next morning, Baptiste and Peter fueled their snowmobile and loaded the sleigh with their backpacks, axes, guns, and extra fuel. It was still dark, and the sun had not peeked over the horizon yet. Before they left, Baptiste said to me, "We should be back before dark. If we are not back by 5 p.m., come look for us." Baptiste drove the snowmobile while Peter rode in the back of the sleigh, holding on to the backboard's handles.

It was too dark for cutting trees, so I walked to my snowmobile and pulled off the tarp that I used to cover it. I turned on the choke and pulled on the recoil a couple of times. The snowmobile came to life. I went inside the cabin to get dressed and left the snowmobile running to warm it up. I drove on the lake, east of the nets, and drove back and forth, breaking trails north to south. The trails were about 460 meters (1,500 feet) in length and 20 meters (65 feet) in width. I drove back and forth on the trails until the snow on the bush airstrip was well packed.

Once done, I went back to the cabin to pick up my axe and my .22 rifle. The sun had risen above the horizon; it was now light enough to cut dry wood. All the dead dry trees in the stand behind the cabin had been cut, and it was time to find another source of dry trees. I drove on the trail in the direction of the highway camp, no more than 1 kilometer (0.6 mile) from the cabin. I located a good stand of dry trees. It was a good thing that I had a snowmobile and a sleigh to haul the dry wood; it would have been a long haul on my shoulders. I felled about eight good-sized dry trees and cut them in half with my axe. I lowered the backboard of the sleigh by untying the rope that held it and laid all the dry trees on the sleigh. The trees were longer than the 2.4 meters (8 foot) sleigh, so using a piece of blue rope, I secured the dry trees to the sleigh and drove back to the cabin. It was much easier hauling dry trees with a sleigh and snowmobile than carrying the dry trees on my shoulders.

Every day, the daylight hours were getting shorter and shorter, and time was of the essence in carrying out tasks such as cutting firewood, checking nets, snare and trap lines. The day's priority was to saw and split the trees I harvested. Having a good stockpile of firewood on hand is imperative in the bush to keep your cabin or tent warm and to cook food. Working outside in very cold temperatures for long hours, I learned how to appreciate the warmth of wood heat.

I was now alone at the camp for a few hours. Baptiste and Peter were on their way to the highway camp at Trout River and would not be back at the camp for several hours. I had to be vigilant while using an axe or saw, which can cause serious or even life-threatening injuries. Being alone at the camp, if I were to injure myself, there would be no one to help me. I was a person who worked at a fast pace, particularly when I was younger. I had turned twenty years old only one month earlier and was, for lack of a better word, a greenhorn who was new to bush life. Baptiste had stressed to Peter and me the importance of being cautious while working with an axe, knife, and saw. I had to be very careful and slow my work pace to minimize the risk of injuries. I took my time while sawing and splitting the dry trees I harvested that morning. I estimated that we should have enough firewood for a few days. I brought some firewood into the cabin and made some kindling for the morning.

The sun was just above the horizon and setting quickly. It would be dark soon. The snare line would have to wait until the next day. I gave myself one hour after the sun had set, and if Baptiste and Peter were not back at the camp, I would drive toward the Trout River camp to meet them. An hour had passed; I started my snowmobile and headed to the seismic line. From a distance, I could see a snowmobile light coming in my direction. I turned around and headed back to the camp. I had made some tea and cooked three rabbits, which I put back on the stove to warm up. Baptiste and Peter must be hungry and thirsty and would appreciate a meal and hot tea.

Once back in the cabin, they both took off their coats, mittens, and hats and warmed up by the wood stove. Baptiste poured himself some tea and added a couple of heaping teaspoons of sugar to his teacup. After he finished his tea, Baptiste poured himself a second cup. He walked over to the stove and looked in the pot then looked at me and smiled and said, "You did not cut the knee joints on the rabbit's back legs." I smiled back at him and said, "That would explain why the rabbit's back legs are sticking out of the pot." We both had a good laugh. We all took a rabbit each, along with pieces of bacon, and settled down for a well-deserved meal.

After supper, Baptiste said, "A plane on skis will be landing at the lake tomorrow afternoon around 1:00 pm." He added, "The foreman at the Trout River camp told me that the winter road should be open to the Reid Lake Junction in two days." I then said that, "I finished the airstrip. It should be long and wide enough for the ski plane". We'll move all of the fish we've caught so far near the airstrip tomorrow morning," said Baptiste.

Peter went outside and brought in two small pieces of green black spruce. Baptiste asked him to rest the pieces against the wall behind the stove to let them thaw out. "I'll make a beaver stretcher in the morning," said Baptiste. I checked the thermometer before I went to bed. It was minus 30 Celsius (minus 22 Fahrenheit). The airstrip should be frozen solid by morning. Before I returned inside the cabin, I took a deep breath of fresh, cold air and eavesdropped on the ice singing a melancholy song; ice expands and contracts as a result of temperatures rising and falling, producing creaking and groaning sounds. The sky was clear, and the moon was out, almost full. The Northern Lights were out, dancing to the ice's melancholy song. The only sound missing in the song would have been a wolf howling at the moon; that would have sent shivers down my spine. I counted my blessings to be so fortunate to have witnessed such a concert.

Early the next morning, Baptiste lit up the gas lamp and began working on the beaver stretcher. It was mesmerizing to watch Baptiste work on the stretcher. He had selected two young green black spruce trees to fashion the stretcher. Each piece was about 1.5 to 1.8 meters (5 to 6 feet) in length and 2 to 2.5 centimeters (3/4 to 1) inch in diameter. Both pieces were flattened on one side with a knife. The round side of the piece was the outside of the stretcher, while the flattened side was the inside. Flattening one side of the piece made it easier to bend into a semicircle. Both pieces were bent into a semicircle, then combined to form an oval shape. String was used to attach both overlying pieces. Once completed, Baptiste rested the stretcher against the wall behind the stove and said, "I'll let the stretcher dry a bit and use it this evening to stretch the beaver hide."

The sun was slowly rising over the horizon. Peter and I walked to our respective snowmobiles. After a few pulls on the recoil, the snowmobiles groaned and came to life. We let the snowmobile warm up and went inside the cabin to get dressed. Baptiste had a look at the airstrip and said, "We will need to add some small spruce trees along both sides of the airstrip so the pilot can see it." Peter and I grabbed our axes and headed to the airstrip. I walked a short distance on the airstrip; it was frozen solid. We both cut a few young spruce trees and stood them in the snow along each side of the airstrip, about 60 meters (200) feet apart.

Next, we drove to the cabin where the fish were stored and loaded our sleigh. Baptiste had instructed us to pile the fish like a cord of wood. He added that the pilot would have large bags, used to ship fur, with him to put the fish in.

Baptiste was eager to have the fish for sale in the stores in Fort Simpson. Alex, Baptiste's son, was tasked with meeting the plane in Fort Simpson and ensuring that the fish were delivered to the two food stores. In all, we had caught just over three hundred fish, mostly whitefish. We had a couple of hours before the plane's arrival. Baptiste wanted to send some fresh fish to his wife and his brother Gabe. We first checked the Japanese net, which had been the most productive net to date. The net produced a good catch of fresh whitefish, mostly jumbo in size. Once we reset the net, we heard a plane coming in our direction. We didn't have time to check another net; the plane was early.

Baptiste walked to one of the small spruce trees and tied a red flagging at the top end of the tree as a wind indicator for the pilot. The wind was light from the north, which had been blowing from that direction for the past week.

The plane circled our camp and made its approach into the wind. I was watching the plane carefully, wondering if it would stay on top of the trails and not sink into the snow. To my amazement, the plane stayed on top of the trails as if it landed on a paved airstrip. The pilot parked the plane next to our cord of fish. The pilot came out of the airplane and said, "This is a good airstrip, I should be able to take a heavy load of fish." It was the first time I saw this pilot; he must have been a new pilot in town. He was young, tall, and heavyset, not sure how he got in the airplane, which looked too small for him.

Peter asked the pilot, "Do you have a package for me?" "Yes, I do," said the pilot, while reaching for the package on the front seat. He gave Peter his package and then gave us the large bags. Peter and I began filling up the bags with as many fish as we could get in. Once the bags were filled, we gave them to the pilot, who stored them in the back of the Cessna 206 behind his seat.

The pilot asked us, "What is the estimated weight of the fish?" Baptiste replied, "Should be around 550 kilos (1,200 pounds)." "I removed the backseats, and I'm not too heavy with fuel, I should be able to take the whole load of fish," said the pilot. We gave the pilot the bag of freshly caught fish last, and Baptiste told the pilot, "Tell Alex, who will meet you at the airstrip, that this bag of fish is to be split between his mother and my brother." Baptiste added, "Tell Alex to meet Peter at the Reid Lake junction in two days; he will have my snowmobile and sleigh to take back to town." "Will do," said the pilot.

The pilot got into the plane and started the engine. After a few minutes, the pilot drove the airplane to the southern end of the airstrip, revving the engine a couple of times before taking off. All three of us watched the airplane take a run on the makeshift airstrip. The airplane labored for a short time and got off the ground before the end of the airstrip. Looking at the airplane's takeoff, you could tell that it had a heavy load.

Once the plane was off the ground, Peter opened the package the pilot gave him. It contained packs of cigarettes. He opened one of the packs, took a cigarette out, and quickly lit it up. I could tell that Peter was enjoying his cigarette; he had run out of cigarettes a couple of days ago. Baptiste was also a smoker but didn't care if he ran out of cigarettes.

"There were a few couple of hours of daylight left, we have enough time to check the beaver traps across the lake," Baptiste said. We loaded all our gear needed to check the beaver traps into our sleighs. Before we left, Baptiste grabbed a small bag from the cabin containing the beaver bones.

Once at the first beaver trap, Peter chiseled the ice around the trap's dry stick. Once done, I cleaned the ice chips with a shovel. Baptiste grabbed the dry stick and carefully pulled it out of the water. "We caught another beaver," he said. Baptiste took the beaver out of the trap and dragged it back and forth into the powdery snow to absorb the water in the fur to prevent it from freezing. He smiled and said, "We will have some beaver meat for supper."

Before resetting the trap, Baptiste put the beaver bones he had brought from the cabin into the water and spoke a couple of phrases in Slavey. The only word I understood was *"Tsa,"* which translates to beaver. Baptiste was raised in the traditional Dene ways by his father to respect all animals in the bush. Once back in Fort Simpson, I told Gabe about Baptiste putting the beaver bones back into the water and saying something in Slavey about the beaver. He explained to me that Baptiste and his father would always put back the beaver bones they hunted or trapped back into the water and praise the beaver, asking it to come back to them.

As he had done before, Baptiste cut a small piece of the beaver's chin and removed the small bones in the back feet of the beaver, putting them back into the water. Peter put the beaver into a backpack, and Baptiste added a fresh piece of poplar stick, then reset the trap. Thus far, we had caught one beaver at each lodge. The second beaver trap was a miss. Baptiste changed the piece of poplar and brought it a little closer above the trap. The beaver had taken a bite on the poplar piece but did not finish chewing on it. We returned to the cabin just as the sun was setting.

Once inside the cabin, Peter asked his father, "Can I skin the beaver?" "Yes, you can. That's why you're here, to learn the bush ways," said Baptiste. Peter prepared an area to skin the beaver while Baptiste lit up the gas lamp. I sat on my bed and observed Peter skinning the beaver; he took his time and did a very good job.

After the beaver was skinned, Baptiste cut the beaver meat into small pieces and put them into a pot of boiling water. "We'll keep the beaver tail and feet and will eat them with the rabbit meat," said Baptiste.

While the beaver meat was cooking, Baptiste started to stretch the first caught beaver hide on the wooden stretcher he had made the previous evening. He rested the stretcher against the cabin wall. Using a 10 centimeters (4 inches) triangular needle with a flat head and twine, Baptiste began by making a hole with the needle, about 0.6 centimeters (1/4 inch) from the edge of the hide, at the nose from the leather side. He looped the twine around the stretcher. Another hole was made with the needle about 2.5 centimeters (1 inch) apart, and the twine was looped again around the stretcher. "The twine should be loose at first and will be tightened after," said Baptiste. This process was repeated until the twine was about halfway down one side of the hide. The same process was done from near the nose to the opposite side of the hide.

Once both sides were completed, the stretcher was turned 180 degrees until the base of the hide was facing upward. Baptiste used the needle to make a hole in the middle of the base of the hide and used the same process as he had done for the top part of the hide. Once the twine was all around the hide, he began tightening it, starting at the nose and working his way along the side of the hide until he reached the middle, then tightened the opposite side of the hide until he reached the center. Baptiste then turned the stretcher 180 degrees and mimicked the same process, starting at the base of the hide. "Be careful not to overstretch the hide," said Baptiste. He added, "The hide should have an oval shape after the twine has been tightened."

After the twine was tightened all around the stretcher, Baptiste used his sharp knife to cut a small piece of the hide around the front and back feet. "The hide will look better after the small holes, where the front and back feet were, are stitched up with thread," said Baptiste. The beaver meat was cooked, and Baptiste stood up, announcing it was time to eat. We all took our turn and dug into the pot. I sat down on my bed, ate my beaver meat, and washed it down with a cup of tea.

After supper, Baptiste dug into his sewing kit for black thread and a needle. As he was threading his needle, Baptiste said, "On a good beaver hunt in the spring, I have skinned and stretched one hundred beavers, lots of work and not much sleep." He stitched the thread around the hole of each front and back leg and pulled the thread until the hole closed, then made a knot to ensure that the hole stayed closed.

As a kid and a teenager, I watched my mother sew countless times. She made all my clothes when I was a young child. I never saw this sewing technique before. It is a clever technique that I learned and used many times to repair holes in my furs while trapping.

Baptiste told Peter to store the beaver pelt he skinned in the cardboard box under his bed, where it was cool. "The beaver I stretched should be dry in a couple of days; you can

337

use the same stretcher to dry your beaver. If we trap a few more beavers, I'll make more stretchers," said Baptiste.

Relaxing on our beds, Baptiste said, "We'll check the nets in the morning, then check the snare line and traps across the lake." Baptiste wanted to catch a few more fish before Peter left for Fort Simpson. It had been three nights since we checked the snare line and traps across the lake. Hopefully, we will find a few rabbits in the snares. Baptiste added a few pieces of wood to the stove and turned off the gas lamp.

The next morning, while it was still dark outside, we had our breakfast of oatmeal, bacon, and tea. I had a peek outside and checked the thermometer; It was still at minus 30 Celsius (minus 22 Fahrenheit). We then started our snowmobile, loaded our fishing gear into the sleighs, and drove to the first net. The sun was starting to peek over the horizon, and the sky was cloudless with no wind to speak of. The ice had thickened to well over 30 centimeters (1 foot). Peter and I chiseled and cleaned the ice on our respective holes for all five nets before pulling and checking the nets.

"We will pull the two nets that produce the least fish and keep the best three nets in the water for a few more days," said Baptiste. The first net we checked only had a couple of fish in it. Baptiste said, "Let's pull this net out of the water." After further inspection of the net, Baptiste said, "There are a couple of big holes in the twine net. Must have caught a big pike that got away."

Gabe told me a story when he was at McEwan Lake with his wife and Baptiste's family hunting moose and building a cabin in the fall of 1976. The lake is located due south of Reid Lake. He was checking a net that he had set near their camp in the late part of September. Gabe was using a 4.8 meters (16 foot) canoe to check his net. While approaching the net, he noticed from a distance what appeared to be a log caught in the net.

Once at the net, he saw a huge pike, about half the length of his canoe, trying to swallow a jumbo whitefish. The pike made a quick splash, let go of the whitefish, and went right through the net, leaving a large hole. Gabe had heard stories from his dad and elders about huge pikes living in the waters of Reid Lake and McEwan Lake.

We then checked the second twine net, which produced about half a dozen whitefish, and reset it back under the ice. The third net (Japanese) yielded close to two dozen whitefish. This net was reset under the ice. The fourth net did not produce any whitefish, so we pulled the net out of the water. The fifth net produced about half a dozen whitefish and was reset under the ice. Overall, we caught about three dozen whitefish, which is considered a good catch.

We still had a couple of hours of daylight left, so we loaded our sleighs with the fish and two nets and stored them in the cabin. We then drove across the lake to check the snares and traps. Baptiste told me, "Check the snare line and traps. Peter and I will check if there are moose tracks at the end of the lake." I said, "Once I'm done checking the snare line, I will go to the cabin and cut some firewood." Baptiste and Peter headed to the southern end of the lake, and I picked up my backpack, axe, and .22 rifle from my sleigh.

The trail was frozen solid, so there was no need to use snowshoes to check the snare line. Hiking on the trail felt like walking on a sidewalk. There was a trace of fresh snow on the trail, enough to distinguish fresh animal tracks, reminiscent of a new page depicting the forest floor.

From a short distance, I saw a snared rabbit in the spring pole snare. I reset the snare and added some freshly cut young pine trees, as the rabbits had eaten most of the pine needles from the trees I had previously cut. A few minutes later, I reached the fence spring pole snares I had set. To my surprise, there were four snared rabbits hanging from the five snares I had set. Fence spring pole snares consist of a fence built from young pine trees laying on their sides with small openings left to set spring pole snares. Again, most of the pine needles from the fence I created were eaten. I grabbed my axe and cut enough young pine trees to restock the fence. I reset the four snares and continued checking the snare line.

Before I reached the end of the snare line, Peter had snared a couple of rabbits in his ground snares. In all, we had snared seven rabbits. I returned to the lake and headed back to the cabin.

The sun was setting to the southwest behind the horizon. It would be dark in about one hour, just enough time to cut a few dry trees. Once back at the cabin, I fed the wood stove and hung three rabbits behind the stove. The remaining four rabbits were hung outside on the cabin's wall. Baptiste and Peter had not returned yet from their hunting trip. I headed to the area where I had last cut firewood. I managed to cut four good-sized dry trees, which I cut in half before it got too dark.

When I returned to the cabin, Baptiste and Peter were inside, having a cup of tea. I left the dry wood in the sleigh and decided to unload it in the morning. Walking in the snow while cutting trees kept me warm. Swinging an axe is a good workout.

"I will cook the rest of the beaver meat for supper; we will have the rabbit soup in the morning for breakfast," said

Baptiste. I asked Baptiste, "If he had seen any moose tracks at the end of the lake?" "There were no moose tracks, but we found three beaver lodges," said Baptiste.

After supper, Baptiste said that tomorrow morning, after we check the nets, Peter will drive my snowmobile to the Reid Lake junction by the Trout Lake winter road to meet Alex. Peter had some personal business to attend to in Fort Simpson. "Daniel and I will follow you to the Reid Lake junction." Baptiste said to Peter. Baptiste then said to Peter, "Tell Alex to pick us up at the Reid Lake Junction in four days.".

The next morning, the temperatures had significantly plummeted to the low minus 30 Celsius (minus 22 Fahrenheit). There were no winds to speak of, but it felt colder than the previous days. It was challenging, but Peter and I were finally able to start our snowmobiles. The sun was rising above the horizon, promising a very cold day.

We checked the three nets, and our catch yielded two dozen whitefish. All three nets were reset, and the fish, minus one jumbo whitefish (which would be our supper that evening), were bagged into a leftover bag the pilot had given to us. Baptiste then told Peter, "Take the four rabbits hanging on the cabin's wall and give them to your mother."

Peter loaded the fish and rabbits we caught and his gear into the sleigh. The Trout Lake Winter Road had been open for a few days for light traffic. Baptiste and I followed Peter to the Reid Lake junction with my snowmobile. Baptiste's snowmobile was having some issues that required mechanical attention and parts.

Once Peter was at the Reid Lake junction, Baptiste and I returned to Reid Lake. There were still a few hours of daylight left. "Let's check the beaver traps and the creek at the north end of the lake for moose tracks and beaver lodges," said Baptiste. "The moose don't move around much this time of year, only when it's windy. If we see some fresh moose tracks, the moose should not be very far."

Before we headed across the lake, Baptiste added, "I will take the beaver bones with us to the trap."

We checked both beaver traps and caught another beaver in the second trap, the one that we had missed a couple of days ago. Baptiste took the beaver out of the trap and dragged it back and forth into the powdery snow to absorb the water in its fur. Before resetting the trap, Baptiste put the beaver bones in the water and spoke a couple of phrases in Slavey as he had done before. Baptiste cut a small piece of the beaver's chin and removed the small bones in the back feet of the beaver, placing them back into the water as well.

The winds had picked up in the last hour, making it much colder. We headed to the north end of the lake, where Reid Lake Creek flows into the Yellowknife Creek. While riding the backboard, I stumped my feet to keep them warm. I was getting the hang of riding the backboard, bending my knees, and absorbing the bouncing and movement of the sleigh.

Baptiste eased on the throttle and trailed the lakeshore to scan for moose tracks. Looking over his left shoulder, Baptiste brought the snowmobile to a halt. He turned off the snowmobile and grabbed his 30-30 rifle from the sleigh. I followed him into an open area adorned with tall willows.

"There are some old moose tracks; you can see where the moose was feeding on willow and lying down," said Baptiste. "This is a good area for hunting moose."

We walked back to the snowmobile and resumed our outing to the creek. From a distance, we could see two beaver lodges along the western lakeshore. Baptiste headed to the beaver lodges, breaking trail into the fresh snow. I held on tightly to the backboard's handles.

Once at the beaver lodges, Baptiste turned off the snowmobile. The only sound we could hear was the wind blowing in the bush. Baptiste confirmed that both lodges were occupied and inhabited by beavers. We continued to the creek. After a short ride on the creek, we spotted two beaver lodges in close proximity to each other. One of the lodges was the tallest and biggest lodge I had ever seen. I had seen numerous beaver lodges throughout my trapping days, but none came close in height and size. The smaller lodge looked like an added dwelling to the larger one.

"That is a big beaver lodge; there must be a lot of beavers in it," said Baptiste.

The sun was quickly setting behind the horizon. "We'd better return to the cabin; it will be dark soon," said Baptiste.

Back at the cabin, I checked the thermometer; it was near minus 40 Celsius (minus 40 Fahrenheit). The sun was behind the horizon as if it were hiding from the cold temperatures. I did not have much daylight left before darkness. I sawed a couple of dry trees with the Swede saw and brought the firewood into the cabin.

Baptiste had a roaring fire in the wood stove and had made some tea. The cabin was nice and warm. What a difference in temperatures from outside to inside! Baptiste had skinned the beaver and had the meat boiling in the large pot. He was making some Bannock, and I was looking forward to Baptiste's Bannock and beaver meat.

Baptiste asked me to remove the beaver hide from the stretcher. He demonstrated how to remove the piece of string around the hide without cutting the strings. "Save the strings, I will need them for the other beaver hides," said Baptiste. The hide had dried evenly, and it was ready to be stored. After I removed the hide from the stretcher, Baptiste asked me to roll the hide fur out and tie a string around it to keep it rolled.

After he checked the beaver meat, he announced that supper was ready. We both grabbed our plates and dug into the pot. I sat on my bed and wolfed down my supper; the cold temperatures had made me hungry. The cabin smelled of Bannock, the aroma reminded me how as a teenager the bakery near my home in Quebec would smell.

After supper, Baptiste stretched the beaver Peter had skinned. "I will make another beaver stretcher tomorrow," said Baptiste. While he was stretching the beaver hide, Baptiste told me a story about the beaver pelt trade that his dad, Johnny Cazon, had told him.

He said that, "Back in the old days, beaver hides were used as money to trade for store-bought goods, things like brass kettles, gunpowder, muzzle loaders, shot, knives, axes, blankets, sugar, matches, flour, tobacco, and tea. Those were the main things Dene people traded. It took about 100 beaver hides to trade for a muzzle loader. The beaver pelts were stacked on top of each other until the height of the pelts was the same as the muzzle loader. The Hudson Bay Company and the North West Company were the main traders. The traders paid the value of two beaver pelts for the cost of one muzzle loader. With one hundred beaver pelts, a trader could buy fifty muzzle loaders. The traders made a fortune trading with the Dene people."

Baptiste added, "My father spoke Slavey, Chippewa, French, and English. In the summer months, he was hired by the church in Hay River to transport the Nuns by canoe to Fort Providence and Fort Simpson. Back then, there was no kicker (outboard motor), just a canoe and paddles. The trip would take a few days to paddle the Mackenzie River and set up and take down the camps on the banks of the river. The Nuns wore nun clothes (a habit) the whole trip, even when they slept. While my dad paddled, the Nuns would pray or sing in French."

After he finished stretching the beaver pelt, Baptiste said, "We will check the nets and the snare line and traps across the lake in the morning." Before I went to bed, I glanced through the window and caught a glimpse of the Northern Lights. The spectacle was about to begin.

I stepped outside and heard the ice singing its song to the bright colors of the Northern Lights, reminiscent of a symphony. The winds had increased speed since this afternoon, making it even colder. The thermometer was hovering near minus 40 Celsius (minus 40 Fahrenheit). It would be a very cold night and day tomorrow. Baptiste turned off the gas lamp, and I fed the stove before getting into my blanket.

Throughout the night, I fed the stove to keep the cabin nice and warm. The stove was hastily consuming the firewood I had cut and sawed, and there were a few dry trees left that needed to be sawed. The winds had not let up all night. Using my flashlight, I checked the thermometer early in the morning, which indicated around minus 50 Celsius (minus 58 Fahrenheit).

Baptiste lit up the gas lamp and said, "I do not think that the snowmobile will start in this cold weather." "We will wait for daylight before checking the nets," said Baptiste. We had a breakfast of oatmeal and bacon and washed it down with a couple of cups of tea. The sun slowly peeked over the horizon. Baptiste and I got dressed and walked over to the nets. This was the coldest day we had had since our arrival at Reid Lake.

We both grabbed an ice chisel each and chipped and cleaned the ice at the first net. Baptiste asked me to tie the blue rope at the end of the net. Once done, Baptiste pulled the net out of the water and walked a short distance while pulling on the net. Whitefish caught in the net were flapping their tails. Baptiste and I pulled the fish out of the net using Baptiste's technique. After the fish were extracted from the net, I pulled on the blue rope while Baptiste fed the net back into the water.

The second and third nets were checked and reset under the ice. In all, we had caught roughly two dozen whitefish. We both returned to the cabin to warm up and left the fish on the ice to freeze. The warmth of the cabin felt good to our bones. "Let's have something to eat, then go across the lake on snowshoes to check the snares and traps," said Baptiste. The now frozen fish were hauled in the sleigh to the cabin by pulling and pushing the sleigh.

The walk across the lake took about fifteen minutes on snowshoes. Once in the bush, the trees protected us from the winds. It didn't feel as cold as walking across the lake. The fresh tracks were few due to the extreme temperatures. Only a couple of rabbits were caught in our snares.

The walk back to the cabin was just as cold. Once at the cabin, we warmed up our bones by the stove. There were only a couple of hours of daylight left before the sun went into hiding.

"I will look for some young black spruce and make another beaver stretcher," said Baptiste. "There were four good-sized dry trees left by the sawhorse to be sawed," I replied to Baptiste. I managed to saw the four remaining dry trees before darkness. Baptiste had a couple of young black spruce trees behind the stove, thawing out.

We had a large boiled whitefish for supper. "We only have enough flour for one more batch of Bannock. I will save it for tomorrow night," said Baptiste. The winds subsided in the evening; nevertheless, it was still very cold. Before bedtime, Baptiste fashioned the beaver stretcher with the young black spruce and tied the two pieces together with strings. "I will stretch the beaver hide tomorrow morning," said Baptiste.

The next morning, I checked the thermometer; the mercury looked as if it was frozen at minus 40 Celsius (minus 40 Fahrenheit). The Northern Lights were making their final appearance to the sounds of the ghostlike groaning ice. After breakfast, Baptiste stretched the beaver hide on the stretcher he had fashioned the previous evening.

"No point starting the snowmobile; it is still too cold," said Baptiste. He added, "We will check the nets tomorrow and pull them out. We will pull the beaver traps and cut firewood today." The sun slowly rose over the horizon; that was our signal. It was time to put on our snowshoes and head across the lake to the beaver lodges. I grabbed an ice chisel by the nets and used it as a walking stick. Our snowshoe trail on the lake had drifted due to yesterday's howling north winds.

The walk across the lake kept me warm, but my mustache and eyelashes were iced up. I had to clean the ice from my eyelashes from time to time so I could see where I was heading. We checked both beaver traps, but they were empty. None were caught. A beaver had nibbled on one of the poplar baits, as if it wasn't fond of the bait. Gabe used to say that beavers like poplar or aspen with thick bark.

We followed our snowshoe trail back to the cabin. Once back at the cabin, Baptiste was standing at the window looking to the west across the lake and said, "A change in the weather is coming; it will get warmer soon. We will have a Chinook tonight or tomorrow."

I asked Baptiste, "How can you tell?" With his right mitt, he pointed to the west and said, "I can see *Shíhnakah* at a distance, slightly above the horizon. *Shíhnakah* is the South Slavey name for the Redknife Hills, which translates to Porcupine Hills."

"A long time ago, when the world was new, *Shíhnakah* was a giant porcupine," said Baptiste. He added, "There is also *Shíhnakah aetséle*, which translates to Little Porcupine Hills."

A few years later, while trapping at Notana Lake, Gabe pointed out to me across the lake to *Shíhnakah*, which had a bluish mirage of the hills. "Most times, we couldn't see *Shíhnakah* from Notana Lake or Reid Lake", said Gabe. He also stated that *Shíhnakah* can be seen when warm weather was coming, such as *Chinook*, warm winds from the west.

Baptiste and I grabbed our axes and walked along the north shore of the lake to look for dry trees. Not far from the cabin, we found a couple of dead, standing tall trees. We each cut one tree down and then cut the tree into three pieces, making it easier to carry on our shoulders. The sun was setting; it would be dark soon. After the wood pieces were hauled to the sawhorse, I started sawing the wood with the

348

Swede saw while Baptiste went into the cabin to cook supper.

It was rabbit with the last piece of bacon, as well as Bannock, were on the menu for this evening. I sawed wood until it was too dark and unsafe to continue. We had burned a lot of wood these past few days, as the temperatures were very cold.

After supper, Baptiste told me a story of when he was a young man trapping by dog team to Shíhnakah. Baptiste said, "When I was young, before I was married, I lived with my dad and brothers at the mouth of the Trout River on the Mackenzie River. My dad, my brothers, and I built a house in the early 1930s at the mouth of the Trout River using a broad axe to square the logs for the walls and a two-man crosscut saw to cut planks for the floor and roof. A stage about 2.1 meters (7 feet) tall was built to hold the logs. One person was on the stage, and another person was under the stage. Both people would pull and push the two-man crosscut saw to cut planks. The person under the stage would get sawdust in their face." He added, "One time, I left our house to check my traps in *Shíhnakah* with my dog team. When I left Trout River, it was minus 40 Celsius minus 40 Fahrenheit). It took me about four days to travel to Shíhnakah, checking my traps and camping outside on my trail. When I arrived at Shíhnakah, the warm wind was blowing, the snow was melting, and it was very warm. Most winters, we would have warm winds called Chinook."

Early the next morning, I woke up to the sound of running water from the roof. Although the fire in the wood stove was out, the cabin was warm. I got up and opened the door of the cabin, and felt the warm wind blowing in my face. The wind was very strong, and the snow on the roof of the cabin was melting. I checked the thermometer, and it was +10 Celsius

(50 Fahrenheit). It felt like we went from winter to spring overnight. Baptiste got up and sat on his bed, putting on his socks. I made a fire and put the teapot on the wood stove. It was getting warm in the cabin, so I opened the door to cool the cabin a bit. Baptiste walked to the door, looked outside, and said, "The warm weather should last at least one more day."

We had rabbit soup and the last of the Bannock for breakfast. "We will pull the traps and snares across the lake first, then check and pull out the nets," said Baptiste. The snowmobile started on the first pull of the recoil. Baptiste drove, and I rode the sleigh across the lake to the snare line. The warm winds made the trail soft on the snare line. We had to use our snowshoes; my canvas-top moccasins *Jihke* were damp when we reached the end of the trail. We caught a few rabbits and pulled out our snares and traps.

Once back at the cabin, I took off my *Jihke* and put on my winter boots to check the nets. All three nets were checked and pulled out of the water. In total, we caught a couple of dozen whitefish in the nets. The nets were put away with the other nets in the cabin, along with the fish.

"I plan to come back to the lake in January to set traps and hunt for moose," said Baptiste. "We will load the sleigh with the fish and our gear tomorrow morning and meet Alex at the Reid Lake junction," said Baptiste.

After lunch, I sawed and split the firewood that Baptiste and I had cut the day before. A large boiled whitefish was for dinner. The winds had subsided in the evening; the temperatures were still above 0 Celsius (32 Fahrenheit). After supper, we cleaned the cabin and dishes and started packing our gear for the next morning. Baptiste wanted to have an early start. "Alex will be at the junction before noon," said Baptiste.

I packed the fish in the large bags the pilot had given us and told Baptiste that we would have a big load in the sleigh. I fueled my snowmobile before darkness. I stored one full mixed gas jerry can mixed gas in the second cabin for later use. "We will leave the tent, stove, gas lamp, and dishes in the cabin," said Baptiste.

The next morning, the thermometer indicated minus 2 Celsius (28 Fahrenheit). The Chinook winds were fading; the temperatures were becoming colder. After breakfast and a couple of cups of tea, we loaded the sleigh with the fish and our gear and headed to the junction. Baptiste stopped at the traps and rabbit snares Peter had set on the trail and pulled them out. When we arrived at the junction, Alex was waiting for us; he had arrived about twenty minutes before us. We loaded my snowmobile and sleigh into his truck and headed to Fort Simpson. The trip back to Fort Simpson took about two and a half hours. The temperatures in Fort Simpson felt much colder than Reid Lake. Alex dropped me off at Gabe's house. I was longing to see Phoebe and our son Danny; I had been away in the bush for nineteen days. We unloaded my snowmobile and sleigh from the truck, and Baptiste told me to "Take a bag of fish", said Baptiste. He thanked me for helping him at Reid Lake. I shook his hand and thanked him for allowing me to learn from him. Before I opened the door, Phoebe met me at the door and gave me a big hug; she was expecting me to be back today. Our son Danny was sleeping in his swing, which looked like a mini hammock.

Chapter 13:
Breaking Trail with Snowshoes
February 1976

After the Christmas holidays, I returned to work at Anderson Mills, where my job involved stripping the bark from white spruce trees using a drawknife. The cold temperatures, often dropping to minus 30 Celsius (minus 22 Fahrenheit) or colder, made the work slow and challenging. Anderson Mills had secured a contract to supply four hundred forty-foot-long power poles to Frobisher Bay, now known as Iqaluit, Nunavut. I had joined Anderson Mills in May 1975; my first task was to work the tailing saw. I was responsible for removing tree slabs and lumber from the mill's carriage after they were sawed. The job was physically demanding, and the constant noise from the saw made it difficult to concentrate. Being aware of my surroundings was crucial to avoid accidents, especially with the saw blade nearby. Most of the sawing happened in the warmer months, from spring to fall, as the winter months made operating the sawmill nearly impossible.

The mill operated with older equipment, so breakdowns were frequent. Spare parts were hard to come by, and shipping them was often a nightmare. I remember once when Mr. Anderson ordered a vital part for the sawmill, it took two months to reach Fort Simpson, and only to be returned because it was the wrong part. Back then, we didn't have fax machines or the internet, making the process even more cumbersome. Winter work at the sawmill was intermittent, but I was still well paid—four dollars an hour, with free room and board at the camp. Ms. Anderson was a fantastic cook and made delicious meals. I quickly became good friends with the Anderson family, and they treated me like one of their sons.

By early February, we had exhausted our supply of white spruce trees. The contract required more trees, and the skidder broke down, needing repairs. Due to the snow depth and challenging conditions, Mr. Anderson decided to shut down mill operations until spring. That winter, the Dehcho Region had an unusually heavy snowfall. The snow at the sawmill was over three feet (one meter) deep, making it difficult to fell trees by chainsaw.

There were three of us stripping bark from the trees: Lyn, Mr. Anderson's youngest son; Gilbert Cholo, a local Dene; and me. Between the three of us, we managed to strip the bark from around two hundred trees. The remaining two hundred trees would be harvested and stripped in May and June when the bark could be removed more easily.

Fortunately, Phoebe worked at the local hospital, in the laundry room, cleaning rooms, and translating for the elders. Between my irregular paychecks during the winter months and Phoebe's income, we managed to keep up with our bills. Our living expenses were modest compared to today, as we only needed enough money to make ends meet. Life was much simpler then.

We celebrated our son Danny's first birthday on January 26th. While Danny wasn't walking yet, he could stand and maneuver his way around by holding onto anything within reach. He was a happy baby, full of joy and curiosity, just as most babies are at that age. Danny was well-behaved, loved to laugh, and enjoyed having fun. His milk bottle, which he called "baboo," was one of his favorite things. He would crawl around the house, feeding on his bottle while playing with his toys. He must have inherited that trait from me. My mother told me that when I was a toddler, I loved my milk bottle so much that when it was empty, I would steal my sister's bottle. She was thirteen months younger than me.

I remember once, when Danny was about eighteen months old, he found our last twenty-dollar bill. At some point, he hid the money somewhere in the apartment. Our furniture was minimal: a bed, a crib, a small kitchen table with a couple of chairs, and a cardboard box that served as a TV stand for our small black-and-white fourteen-inch television. There were very few places to hide the twenty-dollar bill, so when Phoebe and I realized we needed groceries before the store closed that Sunday evening, we searched the apartment but couldn't find it. We looked at each other, puzzled, wondering where Danny had stashed it. We both asked him, but Danny couldn't speak yet. He could only mumble a few words, like "dadoo," which meant daddy. After a while, Danny walked over to the living room heating panel, pointed to it with his finger, and mumbled a few more baby words. I reached into the heating panel and, deep inside, felt the twenty-dollar bill. Danny had folded it repeatedly and pushed it into the panel. Although he couldn't speak, Danny understood exactly what we were asking him.

I rushed to the grocery store just in time and bought the much-needed groceries, including milk for Danny. We were down to his last "baboo."

After I was laid off from the mill, I visited Baptiste at his home and asked him when he would return to Reid Lake. I told him I wasn't working at the moment, so I was available to help him at Reid Lake. Baptiste was waiting for parts for his snowmobile before he could head back. The previous owner of my snowmobile had ordered a new coil before I bought it, and he contacted me to let me know it had arrived. I told Baptiste that I had already installed the new coil on my snowmobile and that we could use it for the trip to Reid Lake. Baptiste was eager to return to the lake, so we sat down and planned the trip with his son Peter. Baptiste made a list of the groceries and equipment we'd need.

A few days later, Baptiste learned that the parts for his snowmobile had arrived and should be in Fort Simpson within the week. He was eager to get back to Reid Lake. During my visit, he told me he missed the bush and was ready to return. Our plan was for Baptiste and me to be dropped off at the Reid Lake junction with our gear, my snowmobile, and sleigh, while Peter would wait for Baptiste's snowmobile to be repaired before joining us at Reid Lake.

After saying my goodbyes, hugs, and kisses to Phoebe and Danny, I headed to Baptiste's house with my snowmobile and sleigh loaded with my gear. Alex had already packed his dad's gear into his truck. We loaded my snowmobile and sleigh into the back of his truck and secured both with ropes. We started late and arrived at the junction a couple of hours before sunset. It was a nice, sunny day, but very cold, around minus 30 Celsius (minus 22 Fahrenheit). Our trail to Reid Lake was nonexistent; two months had passed since our last ride on the trail. Once the snowmobile and sleigh were unloaded, Alex returned to Fort Simpson.

After we started the snowmobile and loaded Baptiste's gear into my sleigh, I rode the backboard, and Baptiste drove my snowmobile. We barely made it over the Trout Lake winter road's snowbank and got stuck on the other side. The snow was powdery and deep, making it feel like swimming in the snow. Baptiste and I dug out the snowmobile with a shovel. I broke the trail by walking in front of the snowmobile; the snow was up to my waist. I stood in the back of the sleigh, gripping the handles of the backboard, waiting for Baptiste to squeeze the snowmobile's throttle. Once Baptiste squeezed the throttle, I pushed on the handles as hard as I could. The snowmobile barely moved and stopped after advancing about 15 meters (50 feet). It got stuck again and had to be dug out again.

Baptiste suggested we break the trail without the heavy sleigh loaded with gear. I unhooked the sleigh, started the snowmobile, and stood on the running board for better control as I squeezed the throttle. The snowmobile pushed snow, but I didn't go far, and once again, I was stuck. The snowmobile had only broken about 60 meters (200 feet) of trail in two or three attempts. At that rate, the snow would melt before we finished breaking the trail to Reid Lake.

Baptiste said, "We won't make it to the cabin today. It will be dark in about an hour. We'll make camp on the hill."

A small hill was on the right side of the seismic line near where the snowmobile was stuck. We had spent a lot of energy digging out the snowmobile and attempting to break the trail. I returned to the sleigh, grabbed the shovel, and started digging. I cleared an area large enough to manually turn the snowmobile around and headed back to the winter road, where I turned around and drove back to the sleigh. Once back at the sleigh, I hooked it up and drove to the end of the broken trail. Baptiste had his axe and started cutting down a sizable dry pine tree near the campsite. He asked me to clear an area for our camp with the shovel. While I was clearing the snow, Baptiste cut more dry trees for the night. After I finished clearing the snow, Baptiste asked me to cut some spruce boughs. I had learned from my trip up the Mackenzie River how to intertwine boughs into an area for the camp. While I laid the boughs on the ground, Baptiste made a fire midway against the large pine tree he had cut. He then added three pieces of dry trees at a 45-degree angle from the large pine, with the ends of the trees extending about 30 centimeters (1 foot) over the large pine. Baptiste repeated the process of laying three more dry trees on the opposite side, placing their ends on top of the first three pieces of dry trees. In no time, Baptiste had a roaring fire about 1 meter (3 feet) tall. Cutting the dry trees into short pieces would have been unnecessary and time-consuming.

My father-in-law, Gabe, had taught me how to make a fire for warming and cooking. As the fire burns, the long, dry pieces of wood are moved over the flames. The longer the pieces, the longer your fire will burn. Once a large pine tree burns into two pieces, they are moved over the fire from both ends. Pots can be placed on the dry trees to melt snow and make tea. Green trees can be added to the mix; the dry trees will burn quicker, causing the pots to fall into the fire. The green trees help delay this from happening. Coals from the fire can be moved aside in front of the fire, and a frying pan can be placed on top of the coals to cook meat, bacon, and even Bannock. Gabe used to call it a bush stove. Meat, such as ribs, beaver, fish, rabbit, and grouse, can also be cooked on a stick by the fire.

Baptiste made some tea and cooked a piece of moose meat by the fire. He also warmed up some Bannock he had cooked in Fort Simpson. After our meal and a few cups of tea, we laid our blankets on the spruce boughs by the fire. The fire produced a lot of heat, and although it was minus 30 Celsius (minus 22 Fahrenheit), it was warm enough to remove my wool sweater and sit by the fire in my long-sleeved thermal underwear shirt. I only had a summer sleeping bag; I wasn't expecting to spend the night under the stars. This was my first time camping under the stars in the winter. After supper, Baptiste said, "We'll use our snowshoes to break the trail to Reid Lake. There's too much snow for breaking the trail by snowmobile." He added, "We'll carry food, a pot, and our blankets in our backpacks." Before bed, I put on my sweater and toque, thinking it would be a cold night. Baptiste made some kindling and placed it under some boughs near his blanket. We were both exhausted and soon fell asleep.

As a result of drinking too many cups of tea before bedtime, I had to go to the bathroom in the middle of the night. Before getting back into my blanket, I moved some of the trees into the fire and warmed up my body for a few minutes. After a few hours, I felt warm in my blanket; the temperature had warmed up considerably overnight. Surprisingly, it had snowed about 15 centimeters (6 inches) in the early morning hours. As if we needed more snow! That explained why I was so warm in my blanket; snow is a good insulator. Baptiste and I got up at the same time and cleaned the snow off our blankets and around the fire. Baptiste grabbed the kindling he had made from under the boughs and started a fire. The skies had cleared up, and the snow had stopped. It was a cold morning. After breakfast and a good warm-up, Baptiste and I gathered the food and gear needed for our snowshoe trail-breaking trip. The food, pots, and blankets were packed into our backpacks, along with one axe each. Baptiste carried his 30-30 rifle, and I had my .22 rifle.

Baptiste's snowshoes were 1.5 meters (5 feet) long, while mine were 1.2 meters (4 feet) long. We put on our snowshoes and began the long walk to Reid Lake, about 7 kilometers (4.3 miles) one way. I looked at my watch; it was eight o'clock in the morning.

Baptiste said, "We should make the trail three snowshoes wide."

This meant that the person walking behind must walk one snowshoe on the trail and the other breaking the trail. I was walking behind Baptiste and soon found out that walking in this manner was difficult and tiring. The pace was slow, and the snow was intense and fluffy. The snowshoes sank deep into the snow, but following the trail was easier. I did my best to widen the trail by walking next to Baptiste's effort. After a while, he asked me to break the trail. The seismic line we were breaking trail on was straight as an arrow, which gave us the impression that we were moving at a snail's pace; it was misleading. It felt like we were at the end of a tunnel but couldn't see the light. We broke the trail for another hour and stopped to make a small fire to melt snow. We had taken a thermos filled with tea, but we had drunk it a while ago. We were both very thirsty and dehydrated. Baptiste filled the pot with snow and put it over the fire. Once there was water in the pot, he quickly drank it and filled it with more snow. We both drank the snow water and filled our thermos. After a short rest, we continued breaking the trail. We broke the trail walking side by side. We continued for a couple more hours until we stopped again to melt snow, drink water, and eat a piece of Bannock.

Baptiste was, at the time, sixty-one years old, and I twenty. I was impressed by his stamina; however, I could see that he was starting to get tired, and I was getting tired too. As the day went on, we made more stops to melt snow. The sun had set, and the full moon was out. I estimated we were about 1 kilometer (0.6 mile) from the cabin. Baptiste had stopped and was sitting, leaning against a tree.

Suddenly, I had a burst of energy, a second wind, and told Baptiste, "I'll break trail to the cabin and come back to meet you." I didn't feel tired anymore. I quickly reached the cabin, cleaned the drifting snow in front of the door, and left my backpack inside. I returned to the trail to meet Baptiste, who was slowly walking along the seismic line, one step at a time; he looked exhausted. I took his backpack and rifle.

He looked at me and said aloud, "You're a good man on snowshoes."

Baptiste made his way to the cabin. I split some kindling and made a fire in the cabin. It was good that we had cut some firewood before we left the cabin in December; we had enough firewood for the next couple of days. I filled the pot with snow and opened the stove lid to put the pot over the open flame to melt the snow faster. Baptiste sat on the bed for a while. After the cabin started to warm up, he got up and stood near the stove to warm himself. We had both sweated a great deal and were beginning to feel the chills. We kept warm as long as we walked, but the chills set in once we stopped. Baptiste and I had a change of clothes that we carried in our backpack. I changed my long underwear shirt and hung it behind the stove.

The thermometer outside indicated temperatures in minus 30 Celsius (minus 22 Fahrenheit). We had walked for a couple of hours after sunset. Thanks to the full moon, we had enough light and did not need to use our flashlights. We had some candles in the cabin and lit two of them. The fuel for the gas lamp was in the sleigh at the junction. Baptiste added some snow from the pail in the cabin that I had filled and put the pot back on the stove. Once the snow had melted, Baptiste poured water into a cup and drank it. I split a few pieces of firewood on a stump in the cabin. The cabin was now lovely and warm.

I looked at Baptiste and told him, "I guess we're done walking with snowshoes for the day."

He replied, "Yes, we are," with a slight laugh.

The heat in the cabin unwound me and helped me relax. We were both tired and hungry, so we had some Bannock and tea before going to bed. Stretching on the bed felt good, and I soon fell asleep.

Early the following day, I awoke to the sound of the stove's lid. Baptiste had put some wood in the stove and was making tea.

"My legs are sore; I can hardly walk," Baptiste moaned.

Not looking surprised, I replied, "You exerted yourself yesterday and should take it easy today. After breakfast, I'll walk back to the junction and bring the snowmobile back to the camp; the trail should be frozen solid."

I filled my thermos with hot tea and sugar, and put my axe, thermos, Bannocks, and survival bag (which contained a hunting knife, matches, first aid kit, chocolate, granola bars, .22 bullets, axe file, snares, haywire, strings, and ropes) in my backpack. I put on my snowshoes and headed to the junction. I checked my watch; it was 7:30 a.m., and the sun would be up soon. The trail was frozen solid, and walking was much easier. When walking on the trail alone, you have a lot of time to think. The day before, we had received 15 centimeters (6 inches) of fresh snow in the early morning hours, and I didn't see any animal tracks on the seismic line. The bush had turned to another page. As I walked, I saw a few fresh rabbit and marten tracks. I noticed a few areas that would be good for setting spring pole snares. I wasn't tired and didn't stop for a break. I arrived at the snowmobile around 10:00 a.m.

The night we camped, I laid a tarp on the snowmobile. After cleaning off the snow from the tarp, I turned the key, choked it, and hoped for the best. The recoil was stiff from the cold temperatures. I pulled slowly on the recoil a couple of times, and when I let go, the rope returned. I gave a couple more pulls, and the engine fired but didn't start. I didn't have a primer on my machine; I don't think any snowmobiles had primers in the seventies. A couple more pulls on the recoil, and to my delight, the old girl started. I cleared the snow off the sleigh, folded my tarp, and secured it on the sleigh. I lifted the back of the snowmobile and squeezed the throttle to run the track a couple of rotations. All was good. I sat on the machine, turned the throttle, and the sleigh started moving down the trail. The trail was frozen solid and narrow in some areas. I could see the trail we had made previously, and it was apparent that the heavy sleigh didn't help keep the snowmobile on the trail.

Back then, we used rope to tie the sleigh to the back of the snowmobile, which was not the best way to pull a sleigh. The ride was challenging without someone on the sled for weight and push when needed. Not very far, the sleigh pulled the machine to the left of the trail and abruptly stopped. It felt like I hit a ditch and got stuck. I got off the snowmobile and assessed the situation. Not having much experience breaking trails back then, I felt like I was walking a wire in a balancing act. After several attempts to drive it out, I grabbed the front of the snowmobile and lifted it back onto the trail. Next, I untied the sleigh, grabbed the rear of the machine, and lifted it back onto the trail. This was followed by recovering and attaching the sled back onto the snowmobile. Unfortunately, this workout started to make me sweat. Although dressed for the cold temperatures, I was unprepared for this workout. I caught my breath, climbed on my snowmobile, and turned the throttle. I drove about 2 kilometers (1.2 miles) before the machine once again pulled into the ditch.

With about 5 kilometers (3.1 miles) to camp, I repeated the same process of getting the snowmobile and sled out of the ditch. In doing so, I continued to sweat and get colder. My mitts were getting damp, and my hands were freezing. I climbed on the snowmobile and drove to a large open area about 3 kilometers (1.8 miles) from the camp. Again, the snowmobile went off the trail and came to a sudden stop. I got off and sank into the snow up to my armpits. It felt like swimming in a pool of snow, I was getting nowhere. It took me a long time to get out; once I was out and back on the trail, I was drenched in sweat and had the chills. My hands were getting colder and numb. I needed to make a fire to warm my hands. Driving across the open area, I entered a stand of mixed wood and stopped.

After retrieving some dry wood, I remembered Gabe telling me not to wait until my hands were too cold to strike a match to make a fire. I was close to that threshold. I struggled to light the dry kindling. It started slowly, but then I poured some mixed gas onto the wood pile once I had a flame. Boom! The fire got going, and I was able to warm up my cold hands. It was a close call and a lesson I will never forget.

After warming my hands, I started the snowmobile and headed to the cabin. I was happy to have made it to the cabin with all our gear. Baptiste was in the cabin resting; his legs were still sore from the day-before-yesterday's trail-breaking. I unloaded the sleigh and brought our gear inside the cabin. I changed into a fresh set of long underwear and put on a new top and bottom. While warming up by the stove, I drank some snow water. I was thirsty and dehydrated. Before I came north, I was surprised to learn that dehydration was common in cold temperatures. My first experience with winter dehydration occurred when I was setting up benchmarks on the Wrigley Highway. The frigid temperatures draw the moisture from your body. On most days, the temperatures were around minus 30 Celsius (minus 22 Fahrenheit). The winter snow was deep and powdery, making it difficult to break trail. I'd stop every five 150 meters (500 feet) and cut a benchmark with an axe, which expedited my dehydration. I had two thermoses: one with tea and sugar, the other with apple juice. Once my thermoses were empty, I'd stop and make a fire to melt snow, drink some water, and fill my thermoses with snow water again.

After my body warmed up, I check the pork chops and the slab of bacon I had bought with me. Both were frozen solid, so I put a couple of pieces of firewood by the stove and rested the pork chops and bacon on top of it.

"After the meat thaws out, I'll cook it for supper," said Baptiste.

"I've got enough time to set a few rabbit snares down the seismic line, not far from here, before dark.", I said.

I grabbed my spring pole snare stick, put it into my backpack, got dressed and left. I started the snowmobile and headed to the seismic line. Three rabbit trails crossed our trail not far from the cabin. I set a spring pole snare on each rabbit trail. I finished setting the snares as the sun set over the horizon. It would be another cold night with a full moon. Back at the cabin, the gas lamp was lit, and Baptiste was cooking the pork chops. The smell of the meat cooking made me hungrier. I had a long day with little food and needed to restock my energy. After supper, I went outside to check the thermometer, which hovered at minus 30 Celsius (minus Fahrenheit). The bright moon was shining, casting shadows on the trees in the bush. The sky, empty of its Northern Lights, was dark and starry. I listened for the ice song but heard nothing. It had snowed a lot since our last stay at the cabin in December. The amount of snow on the lake inhibited the ice from singing.

I returned inside to the warmth of the cabin, looked at the woodpile, and said to Baptiste, "I'll cut some wood tomorrow along the seismic line. I saw a good bunch of dry trees not too far from here." I poured myself a cup of tea and sat on my bed.

Baptiste announced that dinner was ready. We both took from the frypan each a large pork chop and a few slices of bacon. In no time, the chop and bacon were devoured.

"I'd like to come back in the spring to go beaver hunting at McEwan and Lenoir Lake. We could build canoes to drift down the Yellowknife Creek and Trout River to the Falls," said Baptiste.

I then asked, "Would the canoes be made of spruce bark?"

"The canoes would be made of canvas and spruce bark," he stated and added, "The canvas must be painted to make it waterproof."

That night, Baptiste told me a story passed down by his father when he was young. It was a harsh winter; the snow was so deep that a moose's belly would drag in the snow. Animals were few in the bush, and people had to travel long distances to trap and hunt. Three families and their dogs traveled together to Shíhnakah to trap marten. They had left that fall before the snow was deep. Shíhnakah was known to be a good area for trapping marten and hunting moose and caribou. The families set up camp for the winter near the foot of Shíhnakah, setting marten traps using deadfall traps. Leg hold traps were expensive and bulky to carry.

The men make trigger sticks (the length of a hand with the thumb up) the night before setting their traps. One end of the stick was sharpened to hold the bait, and the other end was flattened. The bait was left to freeze overnight on the stick.

Traplines were set away from the main camp. The men would check them and look for moose and boreal caribou tracks, but none were found. The women and children set rabbit snares, but few were caught. As the winter progressed, animal tracks became scarce, and snowfalls were substantial, hindering the movement of all animals on the land. Even whiskey jacks were rarely seen. The men had shot a moose in the fall and shared the meat between the families. However, by mid-winter, there was no more meat. The men hunted daily, hoping to return to camp with food for their families. A few martens were caught in the deadfall traps, but the meat from the marten was insufficient to feed everyone. One hunter had not eaten for many days and grew weaker with each passing day. He would give whatever he harvested to his wife and children. One day, he did not return from his daily hunt. The next day, two men went looking for him. He was found dead, plucking the feathers of a whiskey jack he had killed. Some small dry sticks had been put together to make a fire that was never lit. The dead man's body was brought back to his family at the camp.

A few days later, two men went out to look for moose tracks and told their families that they would not return until they had killed a moose. The men broke trail in deep snow with their hunting snowshoes until they found fresh moose tracks. They followed the tracks for two days and were eventually able to overtake and kill the moose. They returned to the camp the day after the kill with as much moose meat as they could carry. The meat was shared with all the families. Because the moose was a large bull, the meat that could not be taken was cached at the kill site. The families agreed to move their camp to the kill site. The hunters' trail made it easy for the group to reach the cached meat.

After Baptiste finished the story, I asked him, "Was the body buried at the camp? Yes, back then, when people lived in the bush, they were buried where they died."

He added, "My grandfather died at Lenoir Lake. He was buried there."

I was intrigued now, I pushed further, "How did people bury their dead when the ground is frozen?" I asked.

"They would make a big fire to thaw out the ground for digging," he replied.

Being more inquisitive, I asked, "Do you know what year this story happened?"

"Don't know, that was before my time. It must have been when my dad was young, in the late 1800s," said Baptiste.

"What kind of gun did they use back then?" I inquired again.

"Muzzleloader," he said bluntly.

Baptiste's story instilled in me respect for the Dene people's resilience and adaptability in their way of life. I was fortunate to have had the opportunity to experience firsthand the Dene way of life in the bush. I genuinely cherish the spring hunt, trapping, fishing, hunting excursions, and spending time in the bush with Gabe and Mary Cazon, along with Baptiste Cazon, Gabe's older brother.

The following morning, after breakfast, I got dressed and started the snowmobile. It had warmed up a tad, to the minus 20 Celsius (minus 4 Fahrenheit) range, which felt warmer. I told Baptiste I would cut some dry trees on the trail about 1 kilometer (0.6 mile) from the cabin and set a few more rabbit snares. Baptiste was still having pain in his legs.

"Peter should be at the camp today or tomorrow," said Baptiste, before I left.

I headed toward the seismic line. The trail was frozen solid and easy to drive on, a stark contrast to breaking trail with snowshoes in deep, powdery snow. From a distance, I could see two rabbits hanging in the spring pole snares I had set yesterday. I retrieved the animals, reset the snares, and continued on to the dry trees site. Before I reached the site, I noticed fresh rabbit trails. I turned off the snowmobile, put on my snowshoes, and broke trail to where I had set the rabbit snares. There were three good trails nearby. I grabbed my new axe (I had purchased it before the trip, keeping my axe with a birch handle I craved as a spare) and cut the required poles for setting the snares, along with some succulent young pines. After setting the snares, I continued to the dry trees site, which was nearby.

There was a good cluster of tall, dry trees near the edge of the seismic line, and there was enough dry wood for a while. I put on my snowshoes and broke the trail by walking over it a couple of times to ensure it was well-packed (the next time I return to this site, the trail will be frozen solid). I cut down half a dozen tall, dry trees, cutting each into three sections. I turned the snowmobile around, facing the camp's direction, and lowered the backboard. After loading the trees onto the sleigh, I secured them with a blue rope. The day was still young, and the trip to the cabin was short, leaving me time to section and split most of the trees when I got back. I felt content and enjoyed cutting firewood, finding it very rewarding. Once done and loaded, I returned to the cabin and had a bite to eat with a cup of tea. Baptiste made fresh

Bannock, which was just what the doctor recommended. I gave him the two rabbits.

"I'll cook them for supper and make some rabbit soup with rice," Baptiste said, smiling.

I took off my parka and wool sweater to chop the wood, so I wouldn't sweat too much. I split enough firewood for the night and made some kindling. I heard a snowmobile approaching while I was carrying the firewood into the cabin. Peter arrived with his dad's snowmobile and sleigh a few minutes later. He entered the cabin and took off his parka.

"The trail is good; I saw where you guys got stuck," said Peter.

"Did you guys' camp at the junction?" he continued.

Baptiste explained, "We couldn't break trail with the snowmobile due to the snow being deep. We camped at the junction and broke the trail with snowshoes the next day. Daniel went back to pick up the snowmobile."

"The snowmobile parts came in yesterday," Peter told his father.

Baptiste was still walking with a limp.

Peter, looking puzzled, asked, "What happened to your legs?"

"My legs are sore since we broke trail to the camp," Baptiste responded.

Peter unloaded the sleigh and brought his gear inside the cabin. That evening, we had rabbits and bacon, finishing the meal with fresh Bannock and strawberry jam.

"If you don't feel better in a couple of days, we should go back to town to see a doctor," Peter said, directing his concern to his dad.

"I'm starting to feel a little better," Baptiste muttered.

Peter sat on his bed and stated, "We should set some beaver traps tomorrow!"

"The beavers are easier to trap in February. It's their mating season," answered Baptiste.

It was getting late, so Peter turned off the gas lamp. The cabin's warmth was a blanket of comfort for our sore bodies, and I soon fell asleep.

Next morning, I checked the thermometer after breakfast, and the temperature was hovering at minus 20 Celsius (minus 4 Fahrenheit). The winds were calm, the sun shone, and it was a beautiful February day. Peter wanted to break trail on the lake and set beaver traps. We started our snowmobiles and headed across the lake to the two beaver lodges where Baptiste had set traps. The snowmobile began to bog down just a short distance from the cabin. Slush flew from the tracks. We both ran into an overflow (water from the lake seeping through cracks in the ice and rising above the ice layer, causing a layer of slush under the snow). The deeper the snow, the deeper the overflow. We quickly returned to the cabin before getting stuck deeper in the overflow. However, the overflow on the snowmobiles and sleighs froze quickly, slowing our journey.

I remembered, Baptiste saying to turn the sleigh over, bottom facing up, and use the axe blade to scrape the ice off. Using both hands, I held the head of the axe and scraped the bottom of the sleigh until all the ice was removed. (Frozen overflow left on the sleigh would make it more challenging to pull on the trail.) Then we attended to the ice on the tracks of the snowmobile. Using a chisel, I chipped off the frozen pieces of ice between the bogey wheels (snowmobiles did not have sliders back then).

After the sleighs and snowmobiles were freed of ice, we arrived at the cabin in time for a cup of tea.

"I'll set some traps on the trail towards the junction. I saw a few fresh marten tracks," said Peter.

"I'll check my snares and set a few more," I replied.

A few moments later, Peter and I were headed on the trail with our de-iced snowmobiles. Not long on the trail, I saw from a distance that one rabbit was hanging in the snare. The once-pure, snow-covered forest floor had turned another page; there were signs of rabbit tracks everywhere. The warmer temperatures had enticed the rabbits to travel up and down their trails. I stopped at the first three snares, removed the rabbit, and reset the snare. I grabbed a handful of pine needles with my mitts and rubbed them over the rabbit trail. Continuing on to the other snare, near the site where I had cut the dry trees, I found another rabbit hanging from the snare. It must have been caught not long ago, as it was not completely frozen. I then reset the snare and continued on the trail. Peter was ahead of me; I could see from a distance that he was setting a trap. I soon saw some rabbit tracks crossing our trail. Stopping, I took my axe from the back of the sleigh and cut a half dozen young pine trees. Given the snow was abnormally deep, the rabbits lingered on their trail.

I pieced together a small fence of young green pines on both sides of three well-used rabbit trails and set the snares. Continuing on the trail, I observed numerous rabbit tracks overlapping, indicating that the rabbit cycle was trending upward. I set three more snares and then returned to the cabin with my catch.

Once back at the cabin, I hung the rabbits behind the stove and split the remaining firewood from yesterday. Peter returned to the cabin shortly after sunset.

"I set a dozen traps to the junction; there are quite a few signs of marten and many rabbit tracks," said Peter.

Baptiste boiled the two rabbits with bacon and made rabbit soup with the broth. We ate and then relaxed in our beds.

The following morning, Baptiste said that his legs were still sore. It had been five days since we broke trail with our snowshoes.

"We should go back to town to see a doctor about your legs," Peter stated with concern.

"We'll see how I feel tomorrow," Baptiste sighed and rubbed his legs.

After breakfast, Peter and I headed to the junction to check the traps and snares. The temperature was in the mid minus 20 Celsius (mid minus 4 Fahrenheit) range, with calm winds and a beautiful sunny sky. The light snowfall from the previous night exposed new tracks, showing renewed rabbit activity near my snares. The ground-up pine needles I had placed on both sides of the trails were almost all eaten. I cut several young pine trees and laid them on both sides of the trails. Yesterday's work had yielded four rabbits caught in the snares. I fixed and reset them, then headed back to the cabin. When I arrived, Baptiste was cooking Bannock. I hung the four rabbits behind the stove and poured myself a cup of tea.

"I'll cut some firewood along the lakeshore; there's a good stand of dead-standing trees not far from the cabin," I said.

Baptiste inquired, "There's no overflow along the lakeshore?"

I broke trail with my snowmobile along the lakeshore to the stand of trees. With snowshoes, I continued breaking trail to the stand and walked on it several times to ensure it was well-packed.

When I returned to the snowmobile, I spotted something white moving out of the corner of my left eye. I looked in that direction and saw half a dozen ptarmigans eating willow tips along the lakeshore. Camouflaged in their white feathered suits, they didn't notice my presence and continued feeding. I grabbed my .22 rifle and steadied it on the snowmobile's handlebar. The birds were about 30 meters (100 hundred) feet away. I aimed at the one furthest to the right and squeezed the trigger. The ptarmigan collapsed onto its side. I repeated the process, aimed at the next ptarmigan, and squeezed the trigger. It flew a short distance before tumbling to the ground. The remaining birds flew away, following the lakeshore. I collected the carcasses and plucked them while they were still warm. I remembered Gabe saying that grouse and ptarmigan should be plucked while still warm. It's easier, and the feathers provide warmth when shoved inside your mitts. I put a few plucked feathers inside both mitts, and before long, I could feel my hands warming up.

After cutting down six good-sized dry trees, I sectioned them into three pieces each. I loaded them onto the sleigh and secured the blue rope to the snowmobile. I returned to the cabin and unloaded the pieces of dry wood next to the sawhorse.

I singed the ptarmigan inside the stove. The purpose of singeing is to remove any leftover small feathers. Once clean of feathers, I removed the guts and saved the gizzards, hearts, and livers.

Peter returned with two martens caught in his traps and two spruce grouse he had shot on the trail. The grouse were added to the pot with the ptarmigan.

"I'll make a broth soup with rice," said Baptiste.

We all enjoyed a tasty meal. After cleaning the dishes, we sat on our beds to relax. Baptiste and Peter enjoyed their after-supper cigarette.

"If my legs are still sore tomorrow, we'll go back to town," Baptiste said between exhales of smoke.

Peter responded quickly, "I think that is a good idea, for you to see a doctor."

Baptiste changed the subject, "We should go to Reid Lake in the spring. It has been a long time since I've hunted beaver."

"When should we come back to the lake?" asked Peter.

"In early April, when the ice is still safe to sit for beaver," said Baptiste. He continued, "I want to use my snowmobile to bring my factory-made canoe to the lake and use it to paddle from Reid Lake Creek down the Yellowknife Creek and then down Trout River to the Falls."

"I'd like Donald to come with us on the beaver hunt; it would be a good experience for him," Baptiste proposed.

Donald was Baptiste's youngest son, a tall, slim fourteen-year-old. He combed his hair to one side and gave the impression of confidence.

"We would travel from Reid Lake to McEwan Lake and Lenoir Lake by following the sun," said Baptiste.

"Is there a trail between the lakes?" I asked.

Baptiste grinned and uttered, "No, we would walk cross-country by following the sun. We can sit for beaver at Reid, McEwan, and Lenoir Lakes when the ice is safe."

I was excited and couldn't wait for the trip to start. What an experience that would be! I felt honored to be invited to a beaver hunt with Baptiste and his two sons. I'd heard many of Gabe and Baptiste's stories about beaver hunts. Beaver hunts is a tradition in the Dene Elder's way of life. After listening to Baptiste's stories, I turned off the gas lamp. With the cabin warm and cozy, I crawled into bed and thought about the upcoming beaver hunt.

The next morning, Baptiste's condition had not improved; his legs were still sore, and he had severe pain when walking. Peter and I packed the gear and loaded it all onto Baptiste's sleigh. Peter's martens were thawed and ready to be skinned. He packed his martens into the sleigh.

"I'll skin the martens in town," said Peter.

Baptiste rode in my sleigh with a blanket for warmth.

"We'll drive to the highway camp and use their mobile phone to call Alex and ask him to pick us up," Baptiste's voice demanded.

We left the remaining food in a wooden box back at the cabin and loaded the four rabbits caught the day before into the sleigh. I checked the thermometer before leaving; it had warmed up to the low minus 10 Celsius (low 14 Fahrenheit) under overcast conditions. With the snowmobiles fueled the day before, we headed to the highway camp. Peter drove his dad's snow mobile while I rode mine. On the way to the junction, we stopped to pull out the traps and snares Peter and I had set.

We arrived at the Trout River highway camp around noon. The foreman led us into his trailer to use his mobile phone. Baptiste called Alex and asked him to pick us up at the highway camp. Alex arrived two and a half hours later. Baptiste's snow mobile and gear were loaded into Alex's truck, but there was no room for my snowmobile and sleigh.

The foreman let me park my equipment on the edge of the camp's clearing. I promised to return in a few days to pick up my snowmobile and sleigh.

Chapter 14:
Spring Hunt
1976

After supper, Baptiste laid out the spring hunt he had in mind. It would begin at Reid Lake in early April. There were nine beaver lodges on the lake, along with a few muskrat push-ups where we could set traps. Later in the month, we'd sit for beavers once the ice near their lodges began to thaw.

From Reid Lake, we'd travel cross-country to McEwan Lake, where we'd stay for a few days to sit for beavers, then continue on to Yellowknife Creek near the mouth of Lenoir Lake. After the ice broke up along the Yellowknife Creek, we would build two canoes using black spruce, spruce bark from large white spruce trees, and canvas. The canvas would be painted to make the canoes waterproof. We'd then paddle along Yellowknife Creek to the mouth of Reid Lake Creek, making our way back to the cabin for a few days of rest. From there, we'd paddle down Yellowknife Creek to the Trout River falls, portage to Highway #1, and return to Fort Simpson.

It was February of 1976 when Baptiste, Peter, and I were at Reid Lake. That's when Baptiste told me he wanted to do a spring hunt. He asked, "Would you be interested in coming along on the hunt?"

I answered, "When are we leaving?"

I felt honored that Baptiste wanted me to be part of the spring hunt. The group included Baptiste, his two sons Peter and Donald, and me.

"It would be a good experience for Donald to come with us," Baptiste said.

Donald was fourteen at the time. He was tall for his age, with dark brown hair combed back. He bore a strong resemblance to James Dean, the actor who was hugely popular in the fifties.

Gabe and Baptiste had told me many stories about their spring hunts. Baptiste had followed this same route several times with his father and brothers. Back then, the spring hunt was an annual tradition. Once the trapping season for land fur bearers ended in March, trappers would begin setting traps under the ice for beaver and muskrat. After the ice broke up on the rivers and creeks or melted off the lakes, beaver and muskrat were hunted or trapped in open water.

At the time, I was working for John Moreau at his garage and taxi dispatch. I pumped gas, fixed tires, and dispatched taxi calls to the drivers. John was at least a decade older than me. He stood 182 centimeters (six feet) tall, slim, with not an ounce of fat on him, and had wavy brown hair combed back.

I asked John if I could take some time off for the spring hunt. I wasn't sure how long we would be gone or how much time I'd need.

"When you're back in town, you can come back to work if you want," John said.

I told him I'd work until March 31st and start my time off on April 1st. Baptiste and his sons left for Reid Lake on March 30th. Baptiste had given me a list of items and groceries I'd need for the hunt, and I purchased everything before he left for the lake.

The engine on Baptiste's snowmobile had seized after our February trip to Reid Lake. I offered him my snowmobile and sleigh to transport the groceries and supplies. Alex drove

378

Baptiste and his two sons, along with everything we had packed, to the start of the seismic line leading to Reid Lake. The seismic line was located 16 kilometers (10 miles) up the Trout Lake winter road. Once they arrived, they loaded the sleigh. Baptiste and Donald rode the snowmobile, while Peter sat on the backboard.

The winter road had closed around mid-March. A sign posted at the entrance read, "Use at your own risk."

At that time of year, temperatures from mid-morning to late evening were well above freezing. The safest time to travel the winter road was at night or early morning. The plan was for me to be dropped off at the seismic line early on April 1st. Alex didn't want to risk driving back on the deteriorating road. Over the last two days, afternoon temperatures had reached the mid-20 in Celsius (68 Fahrenheit). The snow was melting quickly, exposing thawing bare ground and worsening the road conditions.

I didn't own a vehicle at the time. The car I had bought from Louis, Baptiste's son, back in 1975 had kicked the bucket. The engine burned more oil than gas. I asked around town if anyone was willing to give me a ride, but no one wanted to chance it on the winter road.

Someone suggested I ask Captain Crunch. I didn't know his real name, only that he was one of two captains who worked the Johnny Berens Ferry at the Liard crossing. I had spoken to him a few times while riding the ferry. He was tall and slim, with a dark mustache, probably in his late thirties or early forties. No matter the season, he always wore the same cap, which looked like it was made for a captain. I never learned how he got the nickname, but Captain Crunch was the only name I knew.

By chance, I ran into him at the Bay store the day before I was to leave. I asked, "Would you be willing to give me a ride to a seismic line 16 kilometers (10 miles) up the Trout Lake winter road tomorrow morning?"

He looked surprised. "Why do you want a ride to the middle of nowhere?"

"I'm going spring hunting at Reid Lake with Baptiste Cazon and two of his sons," I said.

He paused for a few seconds, thinking it over. "I don't want to drive up the winter road this time of year, but I can give you a ride to the winter road."

The distance between the highway and Reid Lake was 27 kilometers (16 miles), at least a nine-hour walk with a heavy pack.

"I guess you're the only one willing to give me a ride. I don't have any other choice," I told him.

"I'll pick you up at the Borealis apartment at 4 a.m. tomorrow morning. If you're not ready, the deal is off."

"How much for the ride?" I asked.

"Fifty dollars. I only take cash," said the captain.

I handed him the fifty and told him I'd be ready and waiting at my apartment.

I didn't sleep much that night. I was worried I might miss my ride. I had spoken with Gabe about going on the spring hunt with his brother Baptiste.

"There was a lot of snow this winter. The water on the Trout River will be high. The river is dangerous when the water is high. You don't have any experience paddling a canoe on a dangerous river," Gabe said.

He was right. Up to that point, I had never been inside a canoe, let alone paddled one. He didn't tell me not to go, but in his own way, he tried to talk me out of it.

Phoebe had asked me not to go either. She said it was too dangerous. She must have spoken to her dad about it. But I was determined. Phoebe saw that in me and eventually stopped trying to convince me otherwise.

Early the next morning, Captain Crunch was outside our apartment right on time. He gave one quick beep to let me know he was there. I hugged Phoebe. She hugged me back and held on tight, as if she didn't want to let go. I told her to kiss Danny for me and that I would be alright. She said, "Take care of yourself and be careful."

I grabbed my heavy backpack, my axe, and my .22 rifle, then made my way to Captain Crunch's one-ton flat deck truck. It looked like a beast. I saw Phoebe watching me from the window. I waved to her, and she waved back.

The morning air was cold. I could see my breath when I said good morning to Captain Crunch. As I climbed into the truck, I said, "The winter road should be frozen," trying to hint that he might drive me all the way to the Reid Lake seismic line.

The Liard ice crossing was solid, with no sign of water. Even though the last few days had been warm, with temperatures nearing the low 20 Celsius (68 Fahrenheit), the crossing was still frozen.

The drive to the start of the Trout Lake winter road took about two hours. It was still early when we arrived. Captain Crunch pulled up to the entrance and stopped. I opened the door, ready to hop out.

"I'll drive you to the seismic line. If the road starts getting soft, I'll drop you off and turn around," he said.

I closed the door and thanked him. He stepped out, locked his front wheel hubs into four-wheel drive, and got back in. We drove about 1.6 kilometers (1 mile) up the winter road before the captain said, "The road's frozen. We should be good all the way to the seismic line."

I smiled at him, relieved. I wouldn't have to walk the full distance, which would have taken most of the day.

The road was bumpy from the ruts left by vehicles that had traveled over it while the temperature was still above 0 Celsius (32 Fahrenheit). We reached the seismic line around 7 a.m. The sky was clear, not a single cloud, and it looked like another warm day ahead.

"That's as far as I go. From here, you're walking," the captain said.

I grabbed my backpack, axe, and rifle from the back of the truck. I shook his hand and thanked him for the ride. As he turned the truck around on the narrow road, he rolled down the window and called out, "Better get going before it gets warm. Good luck with your hunt."

I waved as he closed the window and drove away.

I put my backpack on my shoulders, with my axe in my right hand and my rifle slung over my left shoulder. I started walking along the snowmobile trail on the seismic line. The trail was frozen solid. I wore rubber boots with thick wool socks on my feet and had to be careful walking on the frozen trail, as it was very slippery.

I passed the camp where Baptiste and I had spent a night under the stars during a brutally cold evening back in February. The snow had been waist deep then. We couldn't break the trail with the snowmobile and had to walk to Reid Lake on snowshoes to break a path first. The snow had melted a bit since then, but there was still plenty left in the bush.

I was making good time, following the trail and remembering where Baptiste and I had stopped to take breaks and build fires to melt snow and quench our thirst. We did that several times, not to warm up, but just to rest and get water.

The day was warming up fast. There was no wind at all, and the silence in the bush was deafening. The sun was shining, and its rays bounced off the snow, creating a harsh glare across the frozen surface.

A few days before I left, Gabe had told me a story from when he was young. He had been on a spring hunt and developed snow blindness from the glare off the frozen snow.

"We were sitting for beaver at a lake," Gabe said. "That evening at the camp, my eyes were burning. Felt like something was in them. My dad told me to put Vaseline on them. I stayed back at camp the next day to rest while my dad and older brothers went to sit for beaver. By the day after, my eyes were okay."

He added, "I used sunglasses on spring hunts from then on. You should take a pair with you."

I reached into my jacket pocket and pulled out my sunglasses, then slid them on.

About 1 kilometer (0.6 mile) from the camp, a couple of grouse spruce hens flew up into a jack pine tree. I took off my backpack, aimed, and shot. Both birds fell to the ground. I plucked them and tucked them into my pack.

I arrived at Reid Lake around 11:30 a.m. Baptiste, Peter, and Donald were inside the cabin having lunch. I dropped my backpack on the bed I'd be using and joined them.

Peter and Donald had also shot some grouse on the seismic line near the camp. With the two I had just taken down, we had enough for supper that evening.

After lunch, Peter, Donald, and I used my snowmobile and sleigh to cut firewood along the seismic line leading to the winter road. Meanwhile, Baptiste worked on his fishnets. He wanted to set two nets where we had previously placed five back in December. He laid out the five nets on the ice in front of the camp to inspect them for damage.

We had caught plenty of whitefish and a few large pike that December. Some of the larger pike had caused damage by twisting themselves up in the nets, tearing holes, some worse than others.

From the five, Baptiste picked the best two. He repaired the floats and sink lines where needed, then folded the nets and set them aside, ready to go.

The area where we cut firewood was in a burnt patch, evidence of a past forest fire. The burn zone was small. It looked like the fire had been sparked by lightning and had scorched about 10 hectares (24 acres). It seemed to have burned with some intensity, enough to fire-kill the standing jack pine trees.

We felled trees with an axe and cut them into short pieces that would fit in the sleigh. While Peter and I brought down the trees, Donald hauled the wood back to camp using the snowmobile. He made several trips, hauling enough firewood to last us a couple of weeks. With the warmer April temperatures, we didn't need to keep the stove burning all day and night. Fires in the cabin were mostly for cooking, making tea, and warming up the place and ourselves in the morning.

The next morning, we hauled the nets and tools for setting them out onto the lake using the snowmobile. Baptiste had bought a jigger to help run the line under the ice. The jigger was built from a wooden plank with an iron lever hanging from it. That lever operated an arm that moved through a slot in the plank. It moved forward under the ice using a sharp metal point that stuck into the underside of the ice each time the string was pulled, propelling it forward.

A blue nylon line, twice the length of the net, was tied to the jigger. The jigger was then pushed under the ice through the first hole we chipped. Only two holes were needed to set the net. It was aimed toward the location of the second hole. Once we could either see or hear the jigger near that second hole, we pulled it out of the water. Then we untied the line from the jigger and used it to pull the net beneath the ice.

Baptiste had measured the length of the net when it was stretched out on the ice where he planned to set it. The ice was nearly 1 meter (3 feet) thick. We spent a longtime taking turns chipping through it with two ice chisels that Baptiste had sharpened ahead of time. We worked both holes simultaneously. After the holes were finished, we pushed the jigger in at the hole closest to shore. Once it emerged at the second hole, we set the net.

The second net was placed parallel to the first, about 100 meters (300 hundred feet) apart. The jigger made the process much faster and easier. Unlike our December method, which required six holes, we only needed to chip two.

Back in December, when we set and checked the nets, the temperature had been in the minus 30 and 40 Celsius (minus 22 and 40 Fahrenheit). In April, afternoons usually hovered just above freezing.

Baptiste wanted to set beaver traps at the far end of the lake. There were a couple of large beaver lodges that would soon be unreachable once the ice became unsafe to cross. It was still too early to sit for beaver, as they hadn't chewed a hole through the ice near the entrance of their lodge. The temperatures weren't yet warm enough to start melting the ice.

"When the temperatures warm up around the middle of April and the beavers chew through the ice in front of their lodge, they come out in search of fresh food. That is the time to sit for beaver," Baptiste said.

Smoking Split Whitefishes Reid Lake Spring 1976

"You have to check the winds when you get close to the lodge to make sure the beaver cannot smell you. You must be very quiet and not make any noise. Look at the water near the hole to see if the beaver is coming out. You will see a small wave before the beaver pokes his nose out to smell for danger. If the beaver smells danger, he will dive back to the lodge. If there is no danger, the beaver will show his head and start swimming slowly. Have your rifle loaded before the beaver comes out and aim at the head, taking your shot when the beaver is sideways. If the beaver is dead, use your hook tied to a long pole to pull it out of the water. Try not to make any noise. You can sit and wait for another beaver to come out," said Baptiste.

He added, "Before we leave Reid Lake to walk to Yellowknife Creek, we will have time to sit for beaver at the lakes."

After the nets were set, I told Baptiste I would set some spring pole snares along the seismic line heading to the winter road. I walked to the seismic line and set the snares where I had placed them in February. The spring poles were still intact, so I only needed to attach the snare to the trigger pole and cut a few young jack pine trees to lure the rabbits in.

The snow was still deep. Baptiste had told me to buy a pair of hip waders for the spring hunt, which I used to set the snares. I had left my snowshoes in Fort Simpson. As the snow melted in the spring, they were no longer needed. By the time we were hunting by canoe, there was hardly any snow left in the bush.

While I was setting snares, Baptiste, Peter, and Donald went to set beaver traps at the far end of the lake. I returned to camp after placing a dozen snares. Baptiste and his sons hadn't returned yet. I spent the rest of the day sawing firewood with the Swede saw for the stove until supper.

Baptiste cooked the grouse Peter and Donald had shot in the morning near camp. He boiled them, using the broth to make soup by adding rice. Throughout the spring hunt, grouse became one of our main food sources.

Baptiste also made Bannock for supper in a frying pan, since we didn't have an oven. He made delicious Bannock. We brought three 11 kilos (25 pound) bags of flour for the spring hunt. Back then, flour came in canvas sacks instead of paper bags. We also brought enough baking powder and lard for the making of the Bannock.

Three 11 kilos (25 pound) sacks of sugar were packed as well. The canvas sacks were more durable and better suited for carrying flour and sugar in our backpacks. Once empty, they had many uses, such as storing Bannock, dry meat, or rice.

At the start of the trip, I believed the amount of flour and sugar we purchased for the spring hunt would be more than enough. However, after the first week at camp, it became clear we would run out of both before the end of the trip. Sugar was used in tea, and we used a generous amount, at least two heaping teaspoons or more per cup. I didn't keep track of how many cups we each drank daily, but I wouldn't be exaggerating to say that each person including me had between six and eight cups of tea every day.

The flour lasted only a few days longer than the sugar. We used five tea bags per kettle, and once our supply began to run low, we started recycling them. Baptiste would say, "I like my tea to be strong and see the fumes coming out of my nose." He wasn't joking. I often had to add water to mine because it was too strong for me.

The next day, we checked the two nets. Neither had yielded a single fish. The nets were reset under the ice.

"It's only been one night since we set the nets. We'll check them in two days," said Baptiste.

Peter and Donald went hunting for grouse along the seismic line near camp while I went to check my rabbit snares. We had only a few gallons of gas left for the snowmobile, which was needed to set and check beaver traps on the lake and to haul firewood. So, I walked, wearing my rubber boots. The trail was slippery and frozen solid. The sky the night before had been perfectly clear, not a single cloud. The morning air was cold and refreshing. A light breeze from the north reminded me that winter wasn't over just yet.

From my dozen snares, I caught one rabbit and a ruffed grouse. I reset the two snares and made my way back to camp. The ruffed grouse has white meat, similar in color to farm-raised chicken. In the spring, the male drums on a log lying on the ground. The sound could be heard from far away. This drumming gives away their location and makes them easier to hunt by sound. They hadn't started drumming yet, but they would start within the next couple of weeks.

Peter and Donald managed to shoot a couple of grouse on the seismic line. Grouse were abundant and became a blessing, providing many meals during our spring hunt.

The following day, the weather turned miserably cold and windy, with blowing snow that created near whiteout conditions. It was a good thing we weren't walking cross-country in that weather. Baptiste wanted to check the beaver traps with his sons, so I stayed at camp and sawed and split firewood to keep the cabin warm.

They returned later with a large beaver, the first of our spring hunt. Baptiste skinned it and had the meat cooking on the stove in no time. He singed the beaver tail in the stove to remove the leathery skin, then cut the tail into pieces and added it to the pot. Just over forty minutes later, our plates were full of steaming beaver meat. No one spoke. We were all too busy eating and enjoying the meal.

The next couple of days brought more of the same, windy and snowy conditions that felt like winter had returned. We spent our time splitting wood, feeding the stove, and listening to Baptiste share what to expect on the rest of our spring hunt.

"We will travel cross-country to McEwan Lake by heading south and following the sun. We'll take turns breaking trail, one behind the other. The snow is still deep, and it will take about two days to walk to McEwan Lake. We'll find a good spot to camp and stay at the lake for a few days, depending on how many beaver lodges there are. Peter and Daniel will sit for beaver at their own lodge, and Donald will sit with me. We'll make a list of what we need for the trip. When the weather clears up, I'll show you how to make your own paddle from a spruce tree," said Baptiste.

After the weather cleared up, we checked the nets, hoping to catch a few whitefish. We waited until the sun had risen and warmed the cold air. It looked like the fresh snow we had received would start melting by the afternoon. The nets yielded two large whitefish.

"We will leave the nets set for another three nights," said Baptiste. He was hoping to catch a few more whitefish and make split smoked fish for our trip to Yellowknife Creek. The smoked fish would be handy in case of a food shortage.

As we reset the nets, Baptiste pointed to the south and said, "If we do not catch any whitefish the next time we check the nets, we will pull them out and reset them at the point south of the cabin."

Reid Lake is a large, deep lake known for its abundant and high-quality whitefish. The Cazon family and other families in the area have fished its waters for many generations.

After we had our lunch and tea, Baptiste said, "Each one of you grab an axe and follow me."

With Baptiste in the lead, we followed him along an animal trail by the lake. As he walked, he scanned the forest for a couple of young white spruce trees about 17 to 20 centimeters (7 to 8 inches) in diameter.

"It's best to use a straight grain tree with no knots to make a paddle. You'll know the tree has straight grain when you split it in two pieces. The tree should split evenly. There should be no large branches from the base up to about 1.8 meters (6 feet). We can make two paddles from one tree," said Baptiste.

Straight grain in a tree runs in a single direction, parallel to the trunk. Baptiste located two young white spruce trees he believed were straight grain. Peter and I each cut down one of the trees at the base. Once we had pieces about 1.8 meters (6 feet) long, we carried them on our shoulders back to the sawhorse at camp.

We used the Swede saw to square off both ends. Baptiste laid the first piece on the ground and wedged an axe into the middle at the base. He struck the axe with another to drive it deeper until a crack formed along the length of the tree.

"Looking at the crack, this looks like a straight grain tree," said Baptiste.

He inserted an axe into the middle of the crack and gave it a few hard hits. The tree split into two equal pieces. Baptiste smiled and said, "That is a good straight grain tree. Hopefully the other one is too."

"Let me split the other tree," said Peter.

Baptiste stepped aside and handed him the axes. Peter followed the same steps. The tree split cleanly and evenly. Baptiste used his sharp axe to rough out the shape of a paddle, starting at the handle and then flattening both sides of the blade.

"The paddle should be about 15 centimeters (6 inches) wide and shaped like a V at the end. This shape and width make less noise in the water when hunting beaver. A wider paddle makes too much noise and scares them off," said Baptiste.

He grabbed the second piece of wood and began shaping a paddle for Donald.

"You don't have to finish your paddle today. You can work on it when you have time. We still have a few days before we leave for our walk to Yellowknife Creek," he said.

I started shaping my paddle, beginning with the handle. Working with straight grain made all the difference. It was much easier to carve. After about an hour, I had a rough paddle formed.

The next step would be to use a carving knife, then a small planer, the same one we used for making marten stretchers, to finish the paddle. It felt heavy, since it was made from green wood.

Baptiste had said, "A paddle made from a green tree will be stronger than one made from dry wood. It'll dry and get lighter over time. We'll use the paddles as walking sticks on our way to Yellowknife Creek. They'll help us walk through the deep snow."

Baptiste cooked both whitefish for supper and made Bannock using the fish eggs from one of the fish. The fish egg Bannock was very good, unique in its taste. There was hardly any boiled whitefish left in the pot. The fish was fat and delicious. We each had a large piece of freshly cooked Bannock with a hefty smear of butter.

After supper, I took out my knife and started carving the handle of my paddle. I took my time, trying to do my best. I carved until I could comfortably fit my hand around it. At the end of the paddle, I shaped a knob about 5 centimeters (2 inches) in diameter and 5 centimeters (2 inches) in length, then flattened both sides with my knife. The knob fit nicely in the palm of my hand. I wanted to take my time and do the best job I could. The handle still needed some finishing work with my knife and the planer.

The weather was beginning to warm up each day. The snow, still abundant in the bush and on the lake, was slowly melting in the sun. It was starting to feel like spring.

Baptiste and his two sons had trapped a few beavers under the ice. They skinned them and stretched the hides on beaver stretchers made from young black spruce trees bent into semi-circles and tied together with string.

The carcasses were sliced into what Baptiste called "*Tsá lǫ*" which is the deboning of the beaver and cutting the meat into one continuous piece, similar to a large sheet of dry meat. An incision was made along one side of the backbone, from the base of the tail to the neck. The meat was then cut along the backbone, ribcage, and neck, all around the carcass, until it became one large piece. The bones from the front and back legs were removed, and the stomach and intestines were taken out without cutting into the belly.

This large piece of meat was hung over a pole, about 1.2 to 1.5 meters (4 to 5 feet) above the ground, over a smoldering fire made from dry aspen and poplar. These dry woods gave a pleasant flavor to the meat. The smoking and drying helped cure the meat and delayed spoilage. The meat was smoked from morning to evening, with the fire fed throughout the day. A small tarp was laid over the meat to help trap the smoke.

A good sign that the beaver meat is properly smoked is when the fat turns a yellowish color. After a couple of days of smoking, the meat took on a delicious smoky flavor. It was then cut into strips about 5 to 7 centimeters (2 to 3 inches) wide and 15 to 17 centimeters (6 to 7 inches) long. The meat could be boiled in a large pot or cooked over an open fire, which was my favorite way to eat smoked beaver.

To cook it by the fire, two or three small willows were inserted into the meat to keep it spread open so it would cook evenly. A tripod was set up near the fireside to hold the open piece of meat, tied with string to hang over the heat. Baptiste and Gabe would use a stick to gently tap one side of the meat, causing it to twist and rotate as the string unwound and spun back in the opposite direction. The meat was gently turned from time to time until it was fully cooked.

"Always cook the meat by the fireside, not directly over the flames," said Baptiste.

A few days before we left for Yellowknife Creek, Baptiste made three hooks from used chainsaw files he found in the cabin. Using a pair of old leather gloves, he heated the larger end of a file in the coals of an open fire until it was red hot. He used an axe wedged into a stump as an anvil, and with a hammer, he began shaping and flattening the end of the file.

The heated file was laid across the axe head while Baptiste pounded and flattened the end. It was returned to the fire several times to reheat until it glowed red. Once flattened, he shaped the end into a hook. After forming the desired shape, he placed the file in a tub of cold water to cool it off.

Then he heated the opposite end of the file, the one typically used to secure a handle, until it was red hot. Baptiste rested that end on the axe head and gently pounded about 6 millimeters (1/4 inch) of it into a ninety-degree angle, aligned with the direction of the hook. Once complete, it was cooled in water.

Baptiste handed the finished hook to Peter and said, "Use an axe file to sharpen the end of the hook." Then he worked on the second hook and passed it to me to sharpen after it had cooled off. Peter sharpened his hook while Baptiste sat back with a cigarette and a cup of tea.

After Baptiste finished his tea, he handed me the hook I had sharpened and said, "That is your hook for sitting for beaver. Do not lose it. Cut a dry pole about 3 meters (10 feet) long and flatten one side of the small end with an axe. I will show you how to attach the hook to the pole."

I brought Baptiste my pole, he secured the hook by pounding its bent end into the flat part of the pole, about 10 centimeters (4 inches) from the end. Then he wrapped a white string tightly around the hook and pole to secure it.

"Put your hook in this old leather mitt to protect your backpack when we're travelling, make a pole for the hook when you sit for beaver," said Baptiste.

It was an eye-opener watching Baptiste work like a blacksmith with only basic tools. It had been at least a couple of decades since he had gone on a spring hunt, I could see how happy he was. He looked forward to it, enjoying every moment spent sharing his knowledge and stories with his sons and with me. I was like a sponge, soaking in everything he shared and asking question after question.

Afternoon temperatures had been warming into the low 20 Celsius (70 Fahrenheit), dropping slightly below 0 Celsius (32 Fahrenheit) at night. We heard geese flying over the lake, a sure sign of spring. Ducks would likely be showing up in the next few days.

A pair of bald eagles arrived at the lake a few days earlier, returning to their nest south of the cabin. The nest sat near the top of a large dead white spruce, overlooking the lake. It was massive and looked like it had been used for many years.

After lunch, we checked the two nets. Neither had caught a single fish. We pulled the nets and the blue rope out of the water.

"We will set both nets at the point tomorrow," said Baptiste.

The nets were folded and packed into the sleigh along with the jigger, rope, and chisels. Baptiste and his sons pulled the beaver trap from the far end of the lake and reset it at a lodge located at the southern end of the lake.

I went to check my spring pole snares for rabbits. While I was out there, I decided to build a fence of young jack pine trees between the snares. Gabe had once told me that during this time of year, when the snow is frozen solid, rabbits tend not to follow their usual winter trails. The frozen crust allows them to move freely anywhere.

Building a small jack pine fence helps guide the rabbits toward the snares. I spent the better part of an hour cutting trees and laying them out between the snares. In total, I built two fences connecting my twelve snares.

One rabbit was caught in a snare, when I arrived. Rabbit and rice would make a good soup for supper.

Early the next morning, we had breakfast and tea. The sun was shining with the promise of a beautiful day and warm temperatures. All four of us caught a ride to the point south of the cabin using my snowmobile and sleigh. Baptiste wanted to set the nets and then check the beaver traps he had set with his sons the day before.

We used a snow shovel to clear the snow where the two holes would be chiseled. Armed with our chisels, we took turns chipping at the ice until air trapped underneath made a swooshing sound, followed by water gushing from the holes. The jigger was pushed under the ice in the direction of the second hole. The ice was approximately 1 meter (3 feet) thick. After a few minutes, we were able to locate the jigger under the ice near the second hole.

Baptiste took one of the hooks he had fashioned from a file and attached it to a long, dry curved pole. He used it to locate the blue rope tied to the jigger. Once hooked, the rope was pulled out from under the ice.

Baptiste had decided to set only one net for now to test whether this was a good location for whitefish. Looking at the holes in the ice, he said, "There are a lot of water bugs in the water. Whitefish eat these water bugs. I think this is a good spot to set the net."

After the net was set, we drove across the lake to a beaver lodge not far away. As we neared the beaver set, Baptiste said, "The pole in the water has moved." It was leaning at an angle instead of standing upright. The trap had been set on that pole. The ice around it was about 5 centimeters (2 inches) thick. Peter chiseled through the ice while Baptiste began pulling the pole out. I could see how heavy it was by the way Baptiste strained to lift it. A large beaver had been caught.

"The beaver must have been caught not long after we set the trap," said Peter.

The trap was reset. Baptiste tied a dry pole flat across the top of the ice to secure the trap pole in place.

Before heading back to the cabin, we drove to the south end of the lake to check on two more beaver lodges. The recent warm temperatures had melted some of the snow on the lake. At the first lodge, Baptiste used his chisel to check the ice thickness between the lodge and the feed pile.

"The ice should be thin by the entrance of the lodge and the runway," said Baptiste.

We saw bubbles of air trapped under the ice, indicating the beavers' underwater path from the lodge to the feed pile. Baptiste struck the ice a few times with the chisel, and suddenly air rushed out with a whooshing sound. The ice was only a couple of inches thick.

"You have to be careful around the beaver lodge. The ice is usually thin over the runway. Never drive a skidoo over the entrance of a lodge. It may fall through the ice," Baptiste warned.

He enlarged the hole with the chisel. "The beavers should be starting to come out in a few days. We will be able to sit for them," Baptiste said.

We then drove to the second lodge, about 1 kilometer (0.6 mile) away. As we neared it, a flock of geese flew in formation overhead. We all raised our heads to the sky. What a sight. Spring had finally arrived.

At the second lodge, we noticed a small hole in the ice in front of the entrance.

"Looks like the beavers are starting to chew through the ice to come out," said Baptiste. He added, "We will sit at these two lodges on the first day of our trip to Yellowknife Creek."

The temperatures had warmed considerably. I wore my sunglasses, as the glare on the lake was hard on my eyes. It was a beautiful day. With spring at our door, the bush was beginning to awaken. I looked forward to sitting for beaver and walking to Yellowknife Creek.

We headed back to camp, cruising across the lake and scanning the sky for more geese. The bald eagle pair were hard at work cleaning and restoring their nest. Perched nearby, they watched us calmly as we passed by.

Back at the cabin, Peter brought the beaver inside to skin it. Baptiste made a fire and put the tea kettle on the stove.

"I will check my snares by the seismic line," I said.

I grabbed my backpack, axe, and rifle and walked out to my snares. The snow on the trail was slushy and wet. Walking in my rubber boots, I had to be careful, as the trail was slippery. I was curious to see if the rabbits had been enticed by the jack pine fence I built the day before. From a distance, I could see four rabbits hanging in the snares. Not bad for just one night, I though.

As I got closer, I noticed where the rabbits had been eating the needles off the young jack pine I had cut. Gabe had once told me that rabbits will eat jack pine needles along a fence and often follow it to the entrance of a snare. Sometimes they go straight through and get caught. Other times, they follow along the fence a bit longer before getting snared.

This fence-style setup is typically used in the spring, since rabbits no longer follow their winter trails once the snow crusts over. This was my first time using spring pole snares with the fence technique. Gabe had also said that his father told him, when there are lots of rabbits around, cut jack pine trees where you see heavy tracks. Then wait two or three nights before setting snares. The rabbits will come to feed on the pine and create their own trails. They fatten up nicely on the jack pine.

I was both thirsty and hungry. The smell of fresh Bannock coming from the cabin made my stomach growl.

"There is some beaver meat left in the pot for you," said Baptiste.

I gulped down a couple of cups of cold snow water to quench my thirst and hung the four rabbits on the wall of the cabin to thaw.

"I'll cook them tomorrow and make soup with rice," Baptiste said.

The cooked beaver meat and tail were tasty. By the time we finished supper, we had eaten the entire beaver and tail. I sat on my bed, relaxing with a cup of tea.

That evening, I worked on my paddle, smoothing the handle with my knife and the small planer. Once I was done, I held the paddle in my hands, pretending to paddle. The handle and knob felt just right. I turned the blade toward me and began carving one side of it. I worked at it until one side was nearly finished. I wasn't used to carving, and my hands started to ache.

"We'll check the net after two nights and make a list of the gear we'll need for our trip to Yellowknife Creek tomorrow," said Baptiste.

The next day, I woke to the sound of wind blowing through the trees. I stepped outside to check the thermometer. It was above 0 Celsius (32 Fahrenheit). The trees were swaying as if they were dancing with one another. Every now and then, one would squeak, like it was singing while it danced. The wind was from the south, bringing in warm air.

Baptiste cooked the rabbits and made soup with rice for breakfast. The plan for the day was to cut firewood and make a list of the gear we needed for the trip.

Peter had started sewing a green tarp into the shape of a canoe. The tarp had been acquired at the last minute before Baptiste and his sons left for camp. Using a needle and thread, Peter stitched the tarp by hand. It took him a few evenings to complete.

The canvas I had bought for my canoe was sewn ahead of time with a hand-crank sewing machine by Baptiste's wife, Alphonsine, before we left for Reid Lake.

By evening, the winds had settled. It was still warm outside, and the sky was completely clear.

The rabbits were eaten for supper, one rabbit each, just the right amount for a meal. In the evening, I finished smoothing out the side of the paddle's blade I had worked on. I was pleased with the work I had done so far.

I remembered watching my mother's father make paddles when I was a kid. He worked in the shed behind his house using a homemade cardboard pattern. He'd trace the paddle outline with a carpenter's pencil onto a 2.5 by 25 centimeters (1 inch by 10 inches) rough pine board milled at a local sawmill. Once the lines were drawn, he used a small table saw to cut close to the outline. Then, he'd use a planer and sandpaper to finish the paddle. Afterward, he applied a couple of coats of varnish, letting each coat dry. The finished paddle looked like it had come straight from a factory.

Back in the present, I began working on the opposite side of my paddle blade. Using the same method, I held my knife blade facing me and carved by pulling it toward me. I took my time, careful not to remove too much wood. Eventually, I carved and planed the blade to match the shape and thickness of the other side. After a little more work, which I completed the following evening, the blade was smooth and finished. I was proud of it. It didn't look factory-made, but it was ready for the paddling trip.

Baptiste, Peter, and Donald also had their paddles near completion. Peter had finished sewing the tarp for the canoe, and he did a great job. Our gear list was complete. Baptiste estimated it would take us six days to walk from Reid Lake to Yellowknife Creek. That included two nights or more at McEwan Lake, depending on the number of beaver lodges. Then, we'd need at least two days to build the two canoes, followed by another two days to paddle back to Reid Lake. Altogether, the trip would take a minimum of ten days, depending on ice conditions on the Yellowknife Creek.

Our supplies of flour, sugar, lard, rice, and oatmeal were running low.

"We should leave some flour, sugar, lard, and rice at the cabin. Our backpacks will be heavy enough as it is," said Baptiste.

"I'll leave a couple of packs of cigarettes at the cabin," said Peter.

"I don't mind running out of cigarettes. It doesn't bother me," Baptiste added. "We'll leave all our fur in the cabin and store the skidoo and sleigh in the other cabin. By the time we get back, the bears will be out of their den."

The following morning, it was time to check the net near the bald-headed eagle nest. All four of us rode on my snowmobile and sleigh. The day was warm and windless, with only a few clouds in the sky. The eagles were busy refurbishing their nest, but they paused to watch us pass by.

We chiseled both ice holes. The ice was only about 1 inch (2.5 centimeters) thick. Baptiste pulled the end of the net and attached the blue rope to it. Peter pulled the opposite end, which was still tied to the pole, and began dragging it onto the ice. He struggled, so I walked over to help. The net felt frozen under the ice. Together, we gave it a strong pull—and to our surprise, dozens of whitefish burst through the hole, caught in the mesh.

Baptiste came over and started pulling fish from the net with his mouth. Peter, Donald, and I did the same. I couldn't believe how many whitefish we had caught.

"That's more than I expected. We've got enough fish. We'll pull the net out," said Baptiste.

There were between thirty and forty whitefish in the net. We pulled them out and loaded them into the sleigh.

"Let's leave some fish on the ice for the eagles. They'll appreciate it," said Baptiste.

We left a couple of whitefish on the ice before leaving.

"Donald, drive the skidoo to the camp and unload the fish. Then come back and pick us up," said Baptiste.

While Donald was gone, we folded the net and tucked the poles into the bush. The eagles had already spotted the fish we left. Their nest, high above the lake, gave them a perfect view. With a steady supply of fish to feed themselves and their young, it was no wonder they had built their nest in such a prime location.

As we waited for Donald to return, Baptiste said, "We'll make split fish and smoke them for our trip."

Once back at camp, I walked to my spring pole snares and pulled them out. I had caught three rabbits. It was clear they had been feeding on the pine needles from the trees I had cut.

Baptiste and Peter, with the help of Donald, built a rack made of dry poles between four large trees near the cabin. Two good-sized dry poles were nailed between the four trees. Poles strong enough to hold the weight of the fish were laid parallel to each other on the top of the two poles, which were about 1.5 meters (5 feet) up from the ground. There were enough poles to hang the fish we had caught. A small smoldering fire was lit under the rack with dry aspen and poplar.

The heads of the whitefish were removed along with the scales, which were scraped off using the back edge of our hunting knives. Lastly, the fish were gutted and then split along the backbone up until the beginning of the tail. The split fish were washed with water from the lake and then hung on the poles with the two sections of the split fish hanging on both sides. A small tarp was laid over the split fish to keep the rain or snow off, and to keep the smoke under the tarp to speed up the smoking and curing process.

For the next few days, we ate boiled and fire-cooked smoked whitefish. Baptiste had brought a metal fish grilling basket that could hold a large whitefish between the two grills. The basket could stand upright next to an open fire. Smoked fish cooked this way is my favorite way to eat whitefish or any fish. The flavor was incredible.

The fish heads and guts were laid on the ice where the net had been set. Donald and I brought the leftovers by snowmobile. The eagles had already snatched the whitefish we had left. We could see them in their nest enjoying their meal.

The next two days were spent getting our gear ready for the walk to Yellowknife Creek. Near the end of the afternoon, we drove the snowmobile to the north end of the lake and parked it back from the lodges. We didn't want to get too close and alert the beavers. We split into two hunting parties: Baptiste and Donald went to the larger lodge, and Peter and I went to the nearby lodge.

Temperatures had been warming the past three days, reaching near 20 Celsius (68 Fahrenheit). It was beautiful out. The sun's rays were intense, reflecting on the ice. I was glad I had brought sunglasses. The wind was from the west, which worked in our favor. Baptiste and Donald walked directly across the lake to the large lodge while Peter and I headed to the other one.

As we got closer, we saw a small area of open water between the lodge and feed pile. It wasn't a big opening, but it was wide enough for a beaver. We crept toward it, paying close attention to the wind and staying quiet. My heartbeat quickened.

Peter and I had brought our backpacks with small foam pads to sit on. We sat down on the ice about 4 meters (14 feet) from the opening. I had my beaver hook, which was tied to a dry pole about 4.8 meters (16 feet) long. Both of our .22 rifles were loaded, safety on.

This was Peter and my first time sitting for beaver. I had waited a long time for this moment. I heard many stories about sitting for beaver from Baptiste and Gabe. While we sat, I recalled what both had said to anticipate from the beaver. Peter and I stayed motionless on our foam pads without saying a word. The wind stayed in a westerly direction. The bush was quiet apart from the occasional creaking of a tree.

It's amazing how much noise our bodies make when we try to be quiet. I could hear Peter's and my stomachs gurgling, our heartbeats, and our breathing. I was trying my best not to cough or sneeze. "You have to be patient while sitting for beaver," Gabe had told me several times.

Two hours later, Peter and I heard noises coming from inside the lodge that sounded like whining from more than one individual. We both turned our ears toward the sound. I remembered Gabe and Baptiste telling me that kit beavers make whining sounds when they want to be fed. The matriarch beaver, the oldest breeding female, oversees the lodge and hands out food to the kits when they are hungry.

Not long after the whining sounds, we saw a gentle wave in the open water by the ice. Slowly but surely, a beaver's nose rose above the water, sniffing the air for threats. I was sitting on the edge of my pad, heart pounding. We both switched off our safeties and aimed our rifles at the beaver, waiting for its head to rise.

It seemed like forever before the beaver finally nudged its head above the surface and started to swim slowly, nose up, sniffing. Almost at once, we both pulled our triggers within a fraction of a second of each other. The beaver stopped moving, its head down in the water.

I quickly got up and used my pole to hook it out, thinking it might sink or had just been knocked out. Gabe had told me in his stories that if you shoot a beaver head-on, there's a chance the bullet could ricochet off the skull, especially in older ones with thicker heads.

A week later, while sitting at McEwan Lake, I shot at a beaver thinking I had killed it. It floated still for a few seconds, but by the time I reached for my pole, it came back to life and dove underwater in the blink of an eye. That one didn't give in to a frontal shot. It swam toward me, stopped, and stood still as if it had seen me. Before it had a chance to dive, I took my shot.

The beaver was pulled onto the ice up to our sitting area. We both looked at it to confirm that it was dead. In the excitement of recovering the beaver, we had made some noise on the ice. We sat for another two hours, but no other beavers dared to come out of the lodge. We decided to call it a night and put the beaver into my pack. We walked back to the snowmobile and waited for Baptiste and Donald. We hadn't heard any shots from their direction and soon saw them walking back toward us.

"No beavers came out of the lodge. Let's go back to the cabin," said Baptiste.

The sun had set below the horizon. It would be dark soon. We drove back to the cabin. Baptiste made a fire, and Peter lit the gas lamp. We were all hungry and thirsty for a cup of tea. Peter skinned the beaver, and once done, Baptiste cut the carcass into pieces and boiled it for our supper. The beaver was fat and of fair size. The hide was put aside, and Baptiste said, "I'll stretch the beaver hide tomorrow. Once it's dried, we'll leave for Yellowknife Creek. The beavers should all be out in the next couple of days."

We were getting close to the end of the second week of April. Baptiste wanted to build the canoes at Yellowknife Creek near the end of the month to ensure the creek would be open and safe for travel by canoe. Baptiste, Peter, and Donald completed their paddles the following day.

The gear for our trip was divided between the four of us, which included our clothing, sleeping bags, and rubber boots. We also packed store-bought food like flour, sugar, baking powder, lard, rice, salt, tea, small first aid kit, two canvas tarps sewn into canoe shapes, small nails, a roll of white string, blue rope, a plastic tarp for shelter, one gallon of paint with two paintbrushes for waterproofing the canoes, spare ammunition, matches, hunting knives, axes, small pieces of canvas with thread and needles for canoe repairs, hooks for recovering beavers, pots and pans, a fish grilling basket, smoked split whitefish, *Tsá lǫ* and my Kodak C110 camera (35mm).

A few days before I left Fort Simpson, I bought a large, heavy-duty canvas backpack with leather straps and a leather tumpline at the Bay store. The tumpline is a strap that crosses the head or chest and is used to carry heavy loads over long distances.

The following day, the sky was as blue as it gets, not a single cloud to be seen. Temperatures were well above 0 Celsius (32 Fahrenheit) and were sure to hit the low 20 Celsius (low 60s Fahrenheit) by the afternoon. The forest was still, and a woodpecker could be heard tapping loudly on a tree trunk in the distance.

We headed out by snowmobile and sleigh to check the trap where Baptiste had caught a beaver. We stopped by the bald eagle nest to get a look. One eagle was in the nest, and the other flew high above, scanning the area. They looked in our direction as if waiting to see if we had brought more fish.

The trap was empty, most likely sprung by a beaver. Baptiste pulled it from the dry pole and placed it in the sleigh. We continued to the two lodges at the south end of the lake. Baptiste wanted to check for open water in front of the lodges. He used a chisel to widen the holes in the ice at each location. Once done, we headed back to the cabin.

While we had tea, Baptiste said, "We'll leave for McEwan Lake the day after tomorrow. The first night we'll camp at the end of Reid Lake and sit at the two lodges. There's a good camp spot not far from them."

He added, "Tomorrow we'll pack our gear and make sure we have everything. We'll take it easy and stay at camp to rest. It's going to be a long, hard walk with heavy backpacks."

There was still a lot of snow in the bush. On average, snow depth was about waist to knee deep. I loaded my backpack with all the gear I was to carry to Yellowknife Creek. My backpack must have weighed well over 45 kilos (100 pounds). In addition to our gear, we brought some split smoked whitefish and one Tsá ló which was the beaver Baptiste had trapped. Since we had caught whitefish in the net and made them into smoked split fish, we ate as many as we could, just like bears putting on as much fat as possible before the long walk to Yellowknife Creek.

The day before we left the cabin, we made a cache for the smoked split fish that were to stay behind. The cache was built about 60 meters (200 feet) north of the cabin. The poles that had been used to smoke the fish were salvaged and reused in the new cache. The leftover fish were hung over the dry poles. They were semi-dry and nearly cured. We spent the day going over our backpacks to ensure we had all the gear needed for the trip and the canoe building. The one gallon of paint and two brushes were in my backpack, along with flour, sugar, rice, my clothes, sleeping bag, rubber boots, axe, hunting knife, hook, and as many smoked split fish as I could fit into the remaining space, which wasn't much.

We set off around April 20th. After breakfast, we loaded our backpacks and paddles into the sleigh. The temperature was around 0 Celsius (32 Fahrenheit) with a broken sky and a slight breeze blowing from the west.

"We'll use the snowmobile to move our backpacks to the camp at the south end of the lake, and Peter will drive the snowmobile back to the camp. Daniel will stay behind to help Peter put the snowmobile and sleigh inside the old cabin and board up the doors and windows on both cabins," said Baptiste.

Once we were done with the snowmobile, sleigh, and cabins, Peter and I walked with our rifles to the camp at the south end of the lake, about 5 kilometers (3 miles) walk. We both wore our hip waders for the walk on the lake. We followed the frozen snowmobile trail, and it took us about two hours to reach the camp. Baptiste and Donald had already set it up along the east shore of the lake, in an area stocked with dead standing trees.

Baptiste had cooked fresh Bannock and brewed a pot of strong tea. I was hungry and thirsty. The Bannock was still warm. I had a piece and a cup of sweet tea. Smoked fish were grilling in the fish basket and boiling in a large pot. We all sat on spruce boughs near the fireplace and had lunch. The smoked fish was delicious and hit the spot.

"We'll sit for beaver around 4 p.m. Donald and I will sit at the lodge south of camp, and Peter and Daniel will sit at the lodge north of camp," said Baptiste.

For the next couple of hours, we relaxed by the fire, enjoying its warmth.

"Our spring hunt has begun. We'll sit for beaver every afternoon after 4 p.m. until after sunset. By the time we return to Reid Lake, the bears will be out of their dens for sure," said Baptiste.

The sky began to clear in the early afternoon, and the temperature rose until the snow started to turn into slush. Wearing hip waders kept our pants dry from the melting snow and open water. However, the heat generated from walking in deep wet snow and water caused moisture to build up inside the hip waders, soaking our pant legs and socks. In colder temperatures, this made the inside of the waders cold and uncomfortable.

I asked Baptiste, "Before hip waders were available, what kind of footwear did hunters use?"

He replied, "I remember my father wearing canvas-top moccasins, or *Jihke* when he went spring hunting. He'd wear one pair for the whole day and change into a dry pair in the evening, along with wool socks. He'd carry a few pairs of *Jihke* and dry them by the fire at camp. My father would walk in water and wet snow with his *Jihke*.

412

When hip waders became available, most old-timers didn't like using them for spring hunting and continued using their *Jihke*. Hip waders were already in use up north before World War II. I remember my brothers and I using them for spring hunting, while my father stuck to his traditional *Jihke"*.

Walking all day in hip waders tired out our legs. The strain from trudging through deep wet snow while carrying a heavy backpack took its toll by the end of each day. Once at camp, we'd switch to our rubber boots or moccasins with rubber overshoes to rest our feet. I always looked forward to slipping into my moccasins with overshoes in the evenings. The snow depth would have been too much for regular rubber boots. They would have filled with wet snow in no time.

Peter cut a dry pole for his hook and secured it to the pole. The walk to the lodge was less than 1 kilometer (0.6 miles) from the camp. The winds were still coming from the west, blowing lightly.

"Approach the beaver lodge from the bush side, not from the ice side. The beaver will smell you from the ice side. Donald and I will do the same," said Baptiste.

The lodge to the south of the camp was located about half a kilometer (0.3 miles) from the camp.

"We will keep an eye on the camp while sitting for beaver. The snow is still deep in the bush. I do not think the bears are out yet," said Baptiste.

We hung our smoked split fish and *"Tsá lǫ"* near the fireplace to smoke and cure. The smell of the fish and beaver meat might attract bears if they were out and in the area.

413

Peter and I grabbed our axes and rifles and headed to the lodge north of the camp. We could see the lodge from a distance, protruding along the shoreline. The sun was shining, and the snow on the ice was slushy. About 60 meters (200 feet) from the lodge, we walked along the shoreline until we reached the beaver lodge. We located a good spot to sit for beaver; an overturned large spruce tree provided us with a gun rest for our rifles. The snow along the exposed shoreline had mostly melted, so we had a dry location to sit for beaver, and the gun rest made it easier to take our shot. We made ourselves comfortable and patiently waited for a beaver to surface. From a distance, we could hear geese flying over the lake and a ruffed grouse drumming not far from the lodge.

A couple of hours later, we saw a small wave in the open water at the front of the lodge. Both Peter and I had a bullet in the chamber of our rifles and the safety off. I could hear the beating of my heart in the silence. With our rifles resting on the overturned tree and our index fingers on the trigger, we patiently waited for the beaver to surface.

A few seconds later, the nose of the beaver appeared above the water, smelling for danger. Slowly, the beaver's head rose above the water. It started swimming in the open water, its head facing across the lake into the westerly winds. We both took a shot. The beaver lay still in the water.

Peter carefully approached the open water and hooked the beaver out of the water. About half an hour later, we heard a shot in the direction of the lodge where Baptiste and Donald were. We sat for another couple of hours, but no other beaver surfaced.

Peter attached a piece of blue rope to the front and back feet of the beaver and slung it over one of his shoulders, resting the back of the beaver against his back. He carried the beaver back to the camp.

Before we left camp to sit for beaver, Baptiste told us, "No need to empty out your backpack. If you shoot a beaver, use a piece of blue rope to pack the beaver back to the camp." When we got back to camp, Baptiste and Donald were sitting by the fire, drinking tea. Baptiste had skinned the beaver he shot and made *Tsá lǫ* from the carcass. The slab of beaver meat was hanging next to the other *Tsá lǫ*. A smoked split fish was cooking by the fire on the grill, and another fish was boiling in the large pot.

"We shot a beaver at the lodge. It was the only beaver that came up," said Peter.

"Sometimes, only one beaver comes up when you sit for beaver, or sometimes more than one beaver comes up," said Baptiste. He added, "The smoked fish should be cooked."

I helped myself to the fish cooked by the open fire and a piece of Bannock. The evening was beautiful, our first night camping and sleeping under the stars by an open fire. The smoked fish cooked by the open fire tasted excellent. This meal would fetch top dollar in a fancy restaurant down south. Being in the bush in the winter and then in the spring made me appreciate what the seasons had to offer. Listening to the birds, squirrels, and even the mosquitoes made the bush come alive.

After supper, Peter skinned the beaver we shot while Baptiste fixed the beaver tails and back feet by burning off the leather from the tails and singeing the hair on the feet.

"We will have beaver tails, feet, heart, and liver for breakfast tomorrow morning. Beaver tail is our bush bacon," said Baptiste.

I liked the taste of the beaver liver and tail. The boiling pot was emptied, and the broth was drunk with the last of the Bannock.

We had an early start. Baptiste estimated that it would take us a couple of days to walk to McEwan Lake. We loaded the two *"Tsá lǫ"* and smoked split fish into our backpacks. Using our paddles as walking sticks, we crossed the lake with our backpacks and rifles. I used the tumpline on my backpack across my forehead, which helped balance the heavy load and relieve some of the weight off my shoulders. In that position, I found it best to walk slightly bent forward. The walk on the lake was easy as most of the snow had melted. Once we reached the shoreline, buried with deep snowdrifts up to my waist, it was another story. The northeast shoreline, where we camped, had a southwest aspect, which translated into early snowmelt. The camp area and where we sat for beaver were almost snow-free. On the other hand, the southwest shoreline across the lake from where we camped had a northeast aspect, hence the deep snowdrifts.

I volunteered to be the lead in breaking the trail to McEwan Lake, or at least to be the first one to break the trail. Before I started, Baptiste told us, "Use *Shíhnakah* (Redknife Hills) as your bearing. Going in that direction, you will not miss McEwan Lake". The distance between Reid Lake and McEwan Lake, as the crow flies, is 8 kilometers (5 miles). Our single-file line had me in the lead, followed by Peter, Baptiste, and Donald at the rear.

I struggled to break trail through the snowdrift along the shoreline and the edge of the bush along the lake. The snow was crusty and frozen, as it was still early in the morning. The snow was waist-deep and difficult to break through. I understood then why Baptiste had us carve our paddles at the cabin instead of at Yellowknife Creek. As a walking stick, my paddle was very helpful in balancing and pulling myself out of the deep snow. I took my time in breaking the trail; if one hurries, an accident could undoubtedly happen. The going was slow at the beginning; I had to break trail through dense bush and deep snow near the lake. Once we reached open areas like muskeg, the snow was knee-deep.

I had been breaking trail for about half an hour when Baptiste said, "Let's stop for a break and some tea." That sounded good to me. I put my backpack on the ground and felt like I could fly like a bird. In the open areas, we could see *Shíhnakah*, but in the dense bush, we couldn't see it as the hills were hidden. "Use your bearing of *Shíhnakah* with the sun," said Baptiste.

Later in the day, while I was breaking trail in the dense bush, Baptiste said, "Keep the sun to your right cheek and walk straight ahead." We didn't have maps or a compass to navigate. GPS didn't exist back then. While traveling cross-country, Baptiste and his brother Gabe used the sun, winds, and landmarks to navigate in the bush. They knew the land well, where they trapped and hunted. Landmarks such as hills, ridges, stands of trees, creeks, and rivers were used to navigate. "When it's cloudy or foggy and you cannot see the sun, it is easy to get lost. You have to be careful not to get lost," said Baptiste.

We made a small fire to melt snow and made tea; we then laid spruce boughs near the fireplace. I rested against a small tree and drank some snow water to quench my thirst. It was nice to rest my back and shoulders. We rested for another twenty minutes after we had tea, then Baptiste said, "Let's continue breaking trail." The snow was melting in the sun. I put my backpack against the tree I was resting against and sat on the ground. Once I put the straps over my shoulders, I used my paddle and the tree to stand up with my backpack on my shoulders. I learned this trick from Gabe.

"I will break trail from here," said Peter. I followed pulling my tumpline over my forehead. We walked for about an hour and then stopped for another break and tea. The temperatures felt like they were in the low 20s Celsius (68 Fahrenheit). There were little to no winds, and the sun was quickly melting the snow. As we walked and broke trail, we could hear the slushy snow against our hip waders. We made another fire, melted snow to drink, and made tea.

"We should have something to eat before we continue," said Baptiste.

We cooked two smoked split fish by the open fire, which were devoured once cooked.

We continued our walk for a couple of hours with a few breaks in between. The further we walked, the more frequently we stopped to rest our backs and shoulders. Walking in the deep, wet snow took its toll on our legs. The hip waders made our feet and legs perspire. My back was sweating from carrying the heavy backpack. Peter, Baptiste, and I took turns breaking trail until we reached a small lake.

"Let's make our camp on the shoreline. There are a lot of dry wood and a good spot to camp," said Baptiste. We all took our backpacks off our shoulders and sat against a tree to rest our backs. It was still early; the sun would not be setting for at least three hours.

"We walked about halfway to McEwan Lake. We'll have a good rest and an early start tomorrow morning," said Baptiste.

418

"I will take a walk around the lake to hunt grouse," said Peter.

We made a fire to melt snow for water and tea. I was dehydrated from sweating so much. I had a small jar of instant Taster's Choice coffee. I'm not usually a coffee drinker, but I enjoyed it back then. My jar had enough coffee for about three or four more cups. Once the water was hot, I made myself a cup of coffee and sweetened it with a teaspoon of sugar. That was the best cup of coffee I ever had. I sat against a black spruce tree and watched Peter across the lake, while enjoying my coffee. The rays of the sun reflecting off the ice was blinding. I couldn't look at the lake for very long without my sunglasses; I would have surely gone snow blind without them. The area where we camped was mostly snow-free. The lakeshore faced a southern aspect, catching the heat of the day.

We cooked the last of the smoked split fish by the open fire and boiled a whole *"Tsá lǫ."*

"We'll have the leftovers for breakfast tomorrow morning. We should arrive at McEwan Lake sometime tomorrow. We can see *Shíhnakah*, and it will be easy to follow our bearing to the lake," said Baptiste.

It felt good to remove my hip waders and put my moccasins and rubbers on. I changed my pants and socks and hung them near the fire to dry.

Overnight, the temperatures had dipped well below 0 Celsius (32 Fahrenheit). We ate the leftovers, packed our gear, and set off early in the morning. The snow had frozen overnight. The second day of walking was much like the first, with us taking turns breaking trail and making stops to rest. Our walk that day was mostly through open black

419

spruce stands. The snow was melting fast each day, and I noticed the variations in snow depth as I led in breaking the trail. In the open areas, the snow was below knee-deep, while in the dense bush areas, the snow depth ranged from waist-deep to knee-deep.

We reached a large, dense stand of mixed wood.

"We're getting close to McEwan Lake. It should be straight ahead of us," said Baptiste. He pointed his finger in a southerly direction and said, "This way."

A short distance away, we saw fresh bear tracks crossing our path. Baptiste pointed with his finger and said, "The bear came from this direction." We followed the bear tracks a short distance and spotted its den under a large uprooted white spruce, with numerous fallen trees near the entrance. Baptiste poked the tracks with the butt end of his rifle and said, "The tracks are fresh, a few hours old."

We laid our backpacks on the ground and walked over the fallen trees to the entrance of the den. We approached the den cautiously, rifles ready. Inside the den, the bear had laid a bed of spruce boughs and dead leaves on the ground.

"The bear came out of his den earlier. There were old tracks going in the other direction," said Baptiste.

This was the first time I saw a bear den. The warm temperatures had woken the bear from its hibernation.

After a short break, we continued our walk toward the lake until we reached the crest of a small hill.

"The lake is at the bottom of the hill," said Baptiste.

I was happy to hear that we were almost at the lake. It was mid-afternoon, and the sun was still high in the sky. Perhaps we would be able to sit for beaver this evening. We walked down the hill, and shortly after, we reached the lakeshore. The lake wasn't wide but was very long.

"We're at the halfway point of the lake. Last time I was here hunting beaver, none of you were born yet," said Baptiste.

We walked along the north shore of the lake, heading in a southeast direction. Baptiste found a good camp spot with a lot of dry standing trees. Most of the snow had melted along the north shore of the lake, so there was no need to clear snow for our camp. The snow on the lake had all melted, leaving only clear ice. We felled a few dry trees for firewood with our axes and made a fire. The last of our *"Tsá lǫ"* was hung over a dry pole to smoke over a small fire of dry aspen and willows. Spruce boughs were laid on the ground for our bedding.

"Let's set our tarp over the camp in case it snows or rains," said Baptiste.

We had tea and fresh Bannock that Baptiste had cooked on the open fire in a frying pan.

After supper, Baptiste walked on the lake to look for beaver lodges. He spotted a large lodge across the lake, about 1 kilometer (0.6 mile) from camp, and another lodge on the same side of the lake as the camp. The winds were light, and the temperatures were still warm. Baptiste asked me to sit for beaver across the lake while he and Peter sat at the other lodge. Donald was tasked with staying at camp to keep an eye on it. The bears were now out of hibernation, and our

421

camp could attract them, so we needed someone at the camp. Donald had bad blisters on his feet from wearing hip waders.

I was excited to sit for beaver by myself for the first time. I cut a dry pole and secured my hook to it. I walked across the lake; the ice was still solid and safe, and followed the shore to the beaver lodge. As I approached the lodge, I noticed a large open water hole between the food piles and the lodge. Carefully, I walked behind the lodge and made my way near the water opening. The winds were light, blowing from across the lake. I sat on a log and made myself as comfortable as possible.

Less than half an hour after I reached the lodge, without warning, a beaver popped its head up above the water, looking at me as if to say, "What are you doing there?" and quickly dove. I was taken by surprise and was not ready. I told myself that maybe the beaver, or another one, might come up. I readied my rifle and stayed motionless, waiting for the next beaver.

Less than a minute later, a beaver popped its head above the water. This time I was ready. I squeezed the trigger of my rifle, and the beaver's head dropped face down into the water. I grabbed my pole with the hook and pulled the beaver out of the water. As I was pulling the beaver with my hook, I noticed that it had a long, narrow furry tail. Once the beaver was out of the water, I realized that I had shot a large otter, not a beaver.

About half an hour later, I heard several shots, at least six to eight, coming from Baptiste and Peter's direction. I was surprised to hear so many shots. From the stories I'd heard from Baptiste and Gabe about sitting for beaver, only one or two shots would usually be fired for shooting a beaver. The first shot would result in the killing of the beaver or a miss, and the second shot would ensure that the beaver was dead.

The sun had set, and it would be another cold, clear night. I stayed at the lodge, hoping a beaver would surface. None came up. I tied the otter's front and back feet with a blue rope and slung it over one shoulder. When I came back to camp, Peter and Baptiste were sitting by the fire, having tea. I was proud that I didn't come back empty-handed. I removed the otter from my shoulder and laid it on the ground. It was getting dark; by this time.

"You shot a beaver," said Peter.

I replied, "No, I shot an otter."

Baptiste stood up and came over to look at the otter. "It's a large otter. I'll skin it tomorrow morning and make a stretcher to dry it," said Baptiste.

"Did you hear our shots?" asked Peter.

I replied, "Yes, I did". "We saw a big wolverine across the lake, walking along the lakeshore towards you. We shot a few times above its head to scare it away from you." said Peter

Peter continued, "Looks like the wolverine is hunting the beavers. A wolverine will sit for beaver, waiting at the open water until a beaver comes up, then jump on the beaver to kill it."

Baptiste added, "After we took the shot, no beavers came up. We must have scared them."

"Maybe there are no more beavers at the lodge you were at. The wolverine and otter may have killed them all," said Baptiste.

Baptiste cooked the last of our *"Tsá lǫ"* for supper.

The night was cold, well below 0 Celsius (32 Fahrenheit). Early the next morning, a wolverine was walking across the lake, once again heading to the beaver lodge where I sat. Peter and I both fired our rifles above the wolverine's head to scare it away. The wolverine stood defiant, looking in our direction as if to say, "This is my hunting ground, I dare you." Finally, the wolverine got the message and retreated back into the safety of the bush. Sightings of wolverines in the wild are rare. In my twenty-plus years of trapping and hunting, I came across about twenty or so wolverines in my traps or on my trail. Once, while driving my snowmobile on my trapline, I encountered both a snowy owl and a wolverine within ten seconds. The snowy owl flew over my trail first, and then the wolverine quickly ran across it, both heading in the same direction.

Baptiste skinned the fat otter with his sharp knife. I recalled Gabe telling me that skinning an otter involves removing all fat, including the tail fat, which holds most of the fat on the otter's hide. After the otter was skinned, Baptiste took a piece of dry tree we had cut for firewood and shaped it with his axe and knife into two similar pieces, one for the left, the other for the right. The pieces were about 1.6 meters (5.5 feet) in length, 1 centimeter (3/8 of an inch) thick, and 9 centimeters (3.5 inches) wide at the head of the stretcher. The two pieces were shaped like a butter knife, with the curved section of the blade at the head of the stretcher and the handle of the knife at the base. The two pieces were positioned with the top of the blade of the butter knife against each other. The otter hide, leather out and fur inside, is positioned over both pieces until the otter's head fit snugly at the top end of the stretcher. The bottom of the two pieces was then spread until the otter hide was fully stretched. A small flat piece of wood about 30 centimeters (12 inches) in length was nailed across the base of the stretcher to hold the tension of the hide until it dried.

The next day, Baptiste and Peter walked on the lake ice toward the southeast end of the lake to look for beaver lodges. I stayed at the camp with Donald, felling more dry standing trees for firewood. Donald's feet were still hurting from the blisters.

Baptiste and Peter returned to camp about an hour later, "we saw two lodges from a distance. We should move our camp tomorrow morning near the lodges. We will sit at the same lodges that we sat at yesterday," said Baptiste.

Freshly cooked Bannock on the open fire was on the menu for lunch. We rested by the fire, enjoying our Bannock and tea, waiting for 4 p.m. The day was beautiful; the sun was out, warming us up. The wind was light, coming from the same direction as yesterday. I wondered if the wolverine would make another appearance across the lake.

Baptiste & Daniel

At 4 p.m., I stood up, picked up my rifle and hook, and started walking across the lake. The walk was easy, with no heavy backpack on my shoulders and no deep snow to break trail through. I sat on the same log I had sat on before. I put a shell into the chamber of my rifle and turned the safety on, waiting for a beaver to come up. I sat by the lodge until well after the sun had set. A couple of hours earlier, I heard one shot being fired in the direction where Baptiste and Peter were sitting for beaver. The whole time I sat by the lodge, I didn't hear any sounds from the lodge or see any little waves in the open water. Maybe the wolverine and otter had killed all the beavers in the lodge.

I took the shell out of the chamber of my rifle, picked up my hook, and headed back to the camp. Walking toward the camp, I could see everyone sitting by the fire, relaxing and drinking tea.

"Any beavers come up at the lodge?" asked Baptiste.

I replied, "None, not even a sound from the lodge."

"The wolverine and otters must have killed all the beavers in the lodge," said Baptiste.

"We shot a beaver at the lodge. It was the only beaver that came up," said Peter.

The big pot was boiling over the open fire with fresh beaver meat and tail.

"The meat should be cooked in a few minutes," said Baptiste.

Sitting by the fire eating beaver meat, we could hear a ruffed grouse drumming up the hill behind our camp.

"I will go up the hill tomorrow morning to look for the grouse," said Peter.

"After breakfast, we will take down the camp and walk to the beaver lodges to look for a campsite," said Baptiste.

Early that evening, the sky was clear with stars winking at us. It would be another cold night below 0 Celsius (32 Fahrenheit). I had a good sleep; dreams of the bush and hunting beavers played like a movie throughout the night. Some of the best sleeps I had were while trapping, hunting moose, or spring hunting. I rarely had unpleasant sleeps while in the bush.

Peter was up before sunrise and walked up the hill behind our camp. About five minutes later, we heard a single shot. Shortly after, Peter returned with a plucked ruffed grouse in his hand. We ate the remainder of the Bannock along with the leftover beaver meat for breakfast. We packed our gear and put on our hip waders. The walk would be a short distance on the ice. My backpack felt a little lighter since I didn't have any smoked split whitefish or *"Tsá lǫ"* in it. Donald's feet were much better; the two days of rest had helped with the healing of his blisters. We all walked side by side on the bare ice, occasionally looking up to see geese or ducks flying overhead.

We followed the northeast shore of the lake, not far from the shoreline, to see if any grouse were along the shore gathering small stones and grit. Along the way, we heard a flock of spruce grouse taking flight and landing. If both sounds of the grouse taking flight and landing are heard close together, it indicates that the grouse landed in a nearby tree. If only the taking flight sound is heard, the grouse have flown away, to who knows where. We took our backpacks off and carefully walked in the direction of the sounds where the grouse landed.

On the way to our new camp, we shot a few grouses, enough for a meal. The sun had risen above the tree line across the lake and reflected off the bare ice. The glare on the ice made me squint and hurt my eyes. I reached into my jacket pocket and put on my sunglasses. I was glad I had followed Gabe's advice to purchase a pair.

Baptiste stopped and pointed his finger to a stand of white spruce trees to our left.

"We will set up camp under the spruce trees," he said.

The area was snow-free and faced the rising sun to the east. There were a few dead-standing trees nearby to feed our campfire and warm our bones in the morning. From the campsite, we could see two beaver lodges protruding along the shoreline. Both lodges were about a kilometer (0.6 miles) apart.

Baptiste looked at the sky and said,

"Looks like the weather will be good for the next couple of days. We will sleep under the stars."

Spruce boughs were laid on the ground, large enough for the four of us. A few large dead-standing trees were felled with our sharp axes, and a fire was lit.

"Let's chop some ice from the lake to melt for water," said Baptiste.

Small chunks of ice were melted in two pots, one for tea and the other to cook the grouse. I used my backpack as a backrest and sat on the spruce boughs, relaxing with a cup of tea, waiting for my meal of boiled grouse and soup. Baptiste did all the cooking and Bannock making.

"We're getting low on flour. I have enough to make a couple batches of Bannock," said Baptiste.

"Bannock and grouse soup sound good for lunch," said Donald.

We sat by the fire, eating our lunch, and waited for 4 p.m.

"I will take Donald with me and sit at the lodge closest to the camp. Peter and Daniel will sit at the other lodge. We will pack up tomorrow and walk to Yellowknife Creek. We should be able to get there on the same day," said Baptiste.

I cut a dry pole and attached my hook to it. I was looking forward sitting for beaver, wishing we had shot a large one. The sky was cloudless with little wind, and the day had been warm, surely near the 20 Celsius (68 Fahrenheit) marks. The snow in the bush was rapidly melting. The winter had been long and cold, but the bush was quickly turning into spring.

Peter and I headed to our lodge while Baptiste and Donald went to theirs. From our lodge, we could barely see Baptiste and Donald sitting near their lodge. Peter and I sat motionless, facing the water opening, waiting for a beaver to come up. A few hours went by, and then, suddenly, a beaver poked its nose above the water, smelling for danger. I could feel my heart pounding in my chest. I aimed my rifle at the beaver's nose, waiting for its head to show. Peter and I fired our rifles at the same time. The beaver, looking as though it were dead, laid motionless in the water. I grabbed my pole and pulled the beaver out of the water. Peter and I looked at each other and smiled. The beaver was a large one, enough for two meals.

About half an hour later, we heard a shot in the direction where Baptiste and Donald were. The sun had set, and the temperatures were getting colder. My feet were getting cold from sitting motionless and wearing hip waders. We decided to head back to camp. Peter attached a blue rope to one of the beaver's front and back feet and rested it over his left shoulder.

When we arrived at camp, Baptiste had skinned the beaver he and Donald had shot. The pot full of beaver meat was near boiling.

"Donald shot his first beaver," said Baptiste. Donald was all smiles. "We will stretch and dry the two beaver hides at Yellowknife Creek while we are building the canoes," said Baptiste. It was apparent that Baptiste was happy to see his youngest son shoot his first beaver. Several times, while we were at Reid Lake during the winter months, he had told me he missed being in the bush in the springtime.

Early the next morning, I got up and warmed my bones by the fire. Baptiste had made a fire, tea, and breakfast. I could tell he was eager to hit the trail. It was still a bit dark, and the night had been cold. The stars were shining in the sky like diamonds, and the windless morning and cloudless sky looked as if we would have another sunny, warm day. Peter and Donald were still sleeping. Baptiste and I sat by the fire, drinking our tea and staring at the flames.

"I used to camp at this site when I spring-hunted with my dad and brothers. I can still see the stumps from the trees we cut down for firewood and the poles we used for our camp. This place reminds me of my brother Francis. We called the lake Francis Lake," said Baptiste.

Both Peter and Donald got up a few minutes later. Donald was cold. He stood by the fire warming his backside and said, "It was cold last night. I was freezing."

"You should sleep with your socks on. It will keep you warm," said Baptiste.

We split the leftovers Bannock from the day before in equal shares and ate the rest of the beaver meat and drank the broth. I understood now why Dene elders boiled most of their meat. It's nutritious and revitalizing. Gabe had told me many stories about when he ran his trapline by dog team from the mouth of Trout River to *Shíhnakah*. He would spend ten to fourteen days by himself, checking his trapline, making camp at the end of each day, and sleeping under the stars in very cold temperatures. While on the trapline and in the bush, he would eat wild meat such as moose, caribou, beaver, rabbit, grouse, and fish, as opposed to store-bought meat. Gabe said that wild meat kept him warm and gave him energy.

In the mid-sixties, Gabe moved from the bush up the Mackenzie River to Fort Simpson when his children started school. His diet, to some extent, changed from wild meat to store-bought meat.

"After living on store-bought food, I couldn't stay outside in the cold all day like I used to," said Gabe.

With our hip waders on, we left our camp as the sun was rising. The beautiful blue sky above our heads was enticing. Now and then, I looked up at the sky while walking across the lake. Eleven kilometers (6.8 miles) in length and averaging 350 meters (0.2 mile) in width, the lake is one of the largest in the area. Once across the lake, Baptiste said, "Follow the sun, walk towards it." We walked in a single file, taking our time while breaking trail through the frozen top layer of snow with the help of our paddles.

"At this time of the year, moose and caribou sometimes cut their shins walking through the frozen top layer of snow," said Baptiste. He added, "The wolves can stay on top of the frozen snow when chasing a moose or caribou."

Breaking trail, I could feel the sharp edge of the frozen snow rubbing against my hip waders. The snow had melted considerably since we left Reid Lake six days ago. At its deepest, the snow was about knee-deep. Our backpacks were much lighter, and we didn't have to take as many breaks to rest. As the day progressed, the snow began to soften, which made our walk much easier. In some open areas, the ground was almost snow-free. We stopped in one of those areas to take a break.

As I sat down on the ground with my backpack against a black spruce tree, I noticed small bright red berries growing on a single stem. I picked a few berries and put them in my mouth. Wow, did they taste delicious—a perfect blend of tanginess and sweetness.

"What kind of berries are these?" I asked Baptiste.

"They are crane berries. The crane eats them in the spring when they arrive in the north," said Baptiste. He added, "The berries don't fall from the stem in the fall. They stay frozen under the snow all winter." I couldn't get enough of the berries. I picked as many as I could and put a handful in my mouth, enjoying their juice. The ground in the open muskeg was frozen solid, making the walk easy.

Near noon, Baptiste said, "Keep the sun on your right cheek and walk straight ahead." I followed his advice and kept the sun on my right cheek. We walked for about another hour and reached a stand of tall white spruce trees. From a distance, we could hear what sounded like a waterfall with trees crashing into the water. Baptiste stopped to listen, looked at us with his trademark smile, and said, "We are close to Yellowknife Creek; it's just ahead, down the big hill."

As we walked toward the sound of the water and crashing trees, it became louder and louder. What a contrast from hearing the odd sounds of birds flying by or drumming to the sounds of water and crashing trees. We reached the crest of the hill and could see the creek down below.

"The ice on the creek must have broken a couple of days ago," said Baptiste.

It was an incredible sight and feeling to hear the running water and trees crashing into each other. In the past six days, we had undergone a sudden shift from winter to spring to open water. We walked down the steep hill until we reached the creek. Along the shoreline stood large white spruce trees, similar in girth to the ones we harvested at the sawmill where I worked before; close to the Liard River.

The creek was about 20 to 30 meters (65 to 100 feet) in width, with towering white spruce trees standing guard along the banks. The sheer volume of ice, trees, and water coming down the creek was impressive and very loud. I sat down by the creek, resting my backpack against a large white spruce, and marveled at the sounds and sights of the creek. The noise was deafening; we had to raise our voices to be heard.

"Let's walk up the Lenoir Creek, where we will make camp," said Baptiste. The shoreline was virtually snow-free. Baptiste led the way, and we followed him in single file until we reached the confluence of Lenoir Creek and Yellowknife Creek. Baptiste stopped, took his backpack off, and said, "Let's make camp. We will build the two canoes here. There are some good-sized spruce trees for the floor of the canoe."

I took my backpack off my shoulders, thinking that from now on, I would be drifting down the creek in a canoe, not packing a heavy load through the bush and snow. The sun was high in the sky, shining on us and felt good on the body.

"We will start building the canoes tomorrow. First, we have to cut down two big spruce trees and take the bark off," said Baptiste.

We made camp and started a fire to cook our remaining *"Tsá lǫ."* I was hungry and thirsty. The water from Yellowknife Creek had a lot of debris and silt in it. I walked a little way up Lenoir Creek, dipped my cup in the water, and drank several cups of ice-cold water. I filled the teapot with water and walked back to camp. Baptiste was preparing a batch of Bannock with the last of our flour we had packed from Reid Lake. Our sugar supply was quickly running out, maybe enough for one more day. The smell of Bannock cooking in the frying pan on the coals by the fire made me hungrier.

While the Bannock was cooking, Baptiste set up a small tripod by the fire to cook the slab of smoked beaver meat. Small sticks were poked through the meat to keep the slab from folding into itself. The slab of meat was attached to the tripod with white string to cook by the side of the fire. Now and then, Baptiste lightly pushed one side of the slab with a small willow to make it spin. The fat of the beaver meat was yellowish from the smoking by the fire. Baptiste had saved two smoked beaver tails that were extra smoked. The tails were also cooked by the open fire. The Bannock was laid on its side on two green sticks by the fire, away from the ashes, to brown the top and bottom of the frying pan-shaped Bannock.

I sat by the fire, drinking a cup of tea, and breathing in the smell of the cooked Bannock and smoked beaver meat.

Baptiste cut the beaver meat and Bannock into equal parts and told us, "Save a piece of Bannock for breakfast." The smoked beaver meat was quickly devoured by all; it was delicious. After supper, we sat by the fire, drinking a cup of sweet tea boiled with Lenoir Creek's water.

"This is where my dad, my brothers, and I built spruce bark canoes for hunting beaver and paddled back to our house at the mouth of Trout River. In the spring, we would walk with pack dogs, following our trapline from the mouth of Trout River to Yellowknife Creek," said Baptiste.

"Did the pack dogs ride in the canoes?" I asked.

Baptiste looked at me with a grin on his face and said, "The pack dogs followed the canoes along the shores." He added, "We would camp at Reid Lake, McEwan Lake, and Lenoir Lake for a few days, sitting for beaver when the ice was still safe."

"When did you spring hunt?" I asked.

"Before I got married, in the thirties and forties. We built our canoes by Yellowknife Creek because there are good-sized spruce trees along the creek. Before I was born, my dad traveled all over the area. He took my brothers and me on spring hunts when we were young. My grandfather was buried not far from here, on the other side of Lenoir Lake, close to the shore, up a small hill by a big spruce. I used to know where his grave was, but the bush around Lenoir Lake doesn't look the same after a big forest fire."

Baptiste asked Donald and me to stay at the camp while Peter and he set out to look for beaver lodges at Lenoir Lake. "Bears travel along the creeks at this time of the year, looking for food. Someone will have to stay at the camp to look after our backpacks."

The sun was still high in the sky around 4 p.m. I had a watch at the start of the spring hunt, but the battery died while we were at Reid Lake. Donald and I sat by the fire talking. That gave me a chance to get to know him better. I was seven years older than him and already a father to a toddler. Donald was a fourteen-year-old teenager on his first spring hunt, which was also my first spring hunt.

"What do we do if a bear comes to our camp?" Donald asked.

I replied, "We'll scare him away from the camp."

Our camp was located a short distance up the mouth of Lenoir Creek from Yellowknife Creek. We could hear the water and trees crashing in the water from our camp. A squirrel came by to investigate us, likely wondering what kind of animals we were. The squirrels climbed up a tree, stood still looking at us, and then run up the tree, screeching and alerting other squirrels of our presence.

"The squirrel had never seen a human being before; they're curious," I said to Donald.

"I wonder if squirrel is good to eat," said Donald.

I replied, "I heard that squirrel is good to eat."

Donald stood up and walked to a big spruce where the squirrel ran up the tree. He took a small stick from the ground and threw it in the direction of the squirrel. The squirrel went up the tree, screeching, then stopped to look at us as if saying, "Come and get me." Donald gave up on the squirrel and sat by the fire, staring at the flames.

A few hours later, the sun gradually began to disappear under the horizon. The sunset was beautiful and peaceful. It was nice to be relaxing by the fire.

"I hope my dad comes back with a beaver," said Donald.

I replied, "I hope they come back with two beavers." The four of us could eat a large beaver in one sitting.

As the last light of the evening faded away, Baptiste and Peter returned to camp empty-handed.

"Looks like a wolverine or bear got the beavers in the fall. There are a couple of lodges on our side of the lake, but no sign of beavers," said Baptiste.

Another pot of tea was made before bedtime. The fire was fed, and our sleeping bags were laid on the spruce boughs near the campfire. Aside from a small piece of Bannock we set aside for tomorrow's breakfast, there was nothing left for supper. We went to bed without having our supper.

The next morning, we woke up to a beautiful sunrise looming above the horizon. We had our small piece of Bannock and the last cup of sweet tea for breakfast. Today was the day we were going to start building the canoes. I had been looking forward to this day for a long time and was excited to begin. I had heard so many stories from Gabe and Baptiste about spring hunts and canoe building. Now, I would have the opportunity to see canoes being built and ride in one.

Baptiste explained to us that he was looking for two trees with minimal branches from the bottom up to a length of 4.8 meters (16 feet). I asked Baptiste, "Can you use a tree with many branches?" He replied, "The more branches on the tree, the more holes in the bark." Baptiste pointed to a large spruce tree nearby the camp and said, "That's a good one. Let's cut that tree."

The tree was leaning slightly away from our camp. Baptiste started to cut the notch with his axe. Peter and I took turns with our axes, cutting into the notch. Once the notch was cut about one-third of the way, Baptiste said, "That's enough. We'll start cutting the back cut," which is on the opposite side of the notch. Peter and I took turns cutting down the tree until we heard the tree creaking and starting to fall in the direction Baptiste had intended. The tree made a loud bang when it hit the ground.

While we were cutting the tree, Baptiste located a second tree with very few branches along the creek. The second large tree was cut down parallel to the creek. Both trees were cut to a length of about 4.8 meters (16 feet).

"Be careful when removing the branches to avoid damaging the bark," said Baptiste.

Peter and I were sweating from chopping with the axes and needed something to drink. We had some cold water from the creek and took a quick rest by the fire. We only had a small piece of Bannock each for breakfast, and our last meal had been nearly twenty-four hours ago. Our energy levels were low, and we were in need of a good meal. This was my first time cutting a tree of that size with an axe. Resting by the fire, I couldn't help but think about my ancestors, the Allaire, who arrived in New France, now called Quebec, on the Island of Orleans in August of 1652 to clear land for farming.

Daniel & Peter

My 9th great-grandfather and great-granduncle, Jean and Charles respectively, were contracted for three years to clear land for the Seigneurs who granted land to settlers. All the clearing was done with an axe and crosscut saw. The stumps were pulled out of the ground by hand with an axe and pick, as no oxen were used in the first days of New France. Thinking of my ancestors' hard work and contributions to the founding of New France made me proud to be a descendant of the Allaire family.

The next step was to remove the bark from the two large trees. I had a lot of experience at Anderson Sawmill, where I worked removing the bark from large white spruce trees with a drawknife, which were then turned into power and telephone poles. Baptiste cut two dry poles from a small white spruce tree about 5 to 7.5 centimeters (2 to 3 inches) in diameter and 1 meter (3 feet) in length. All branches were removed from the poles. One end of each pole was cut with an axe at a forty-five-degree angle on both sides of the pole.

Baptiste used his sharp axe to cut through the bark in a straight line from the bottom to the top of the log. He demonstrated how to use the pole to remove the bark in one piece.

"Do not push too hard with the pole, follow along the tree to remove the bark from one end to the other," said Baptiste.

Peter and I used the poles to carefully remove the bark from the log in one piece. While we were removing the bark, Baptiste walked a short distance from the camp to look for young spruce trees. Donald followed him to help carry the young spruce trees.

Removing bark from a tree with a drawknife or a dry wooden pole is not the same. Using a drawknife removes the bark in small pieces, while using a dry pole, when done properly, will remove the bark in one piece. This technique is done in the spring when the cambium is creating new wood, which results in a slippery layer beneath the bark.

The two canvas canoes were shaped and tied to two poles hammered into the ground at each end of the canoes. The canvas was stretched between the poles, with the bottom of the canvas resting on the ground. The top sections of both canvases were sewn to accommodate poles inside the overlapping edge of the canvas along both sides, forming the sides of the canoes. The poles were made of young spruce, which were flattened with a knife on one side to facilitate the outward bending of the poles. The two poles were inserted inside the overlapping edge of the canvas on both sides and tied together at the bow and stern with a piece of blue rope.

A pole made of spruce was cut to length and inserted between the two poles at the mid-point of the canoes to hold the shape. The spruce bark was cut to size and laid inside the canoes, bark side up. The keel of the canoes was fashioned from a young spruce, about 5 centimeters (2 inches) in diameter, which was flattened on both sides with a knife. The bow and stern of the canoe were made from young spruce, about 5 centimeters (2 inches) in diameter, which were also flattened with a knife on one side. These three pieces were attached together with white string to form one solid piece, which was then inserted inside the canoe, with the bow and stern fitting tightly.

Ribs for the canoe were fashioned from young spruce trees about 2.5 centimeters (1 inch) in diameter. The ribs were flattened on one side with a knife, cut to size, and then inserted inside the canoe, fitting tightly between the top two poles inserted into the overlapping edge of the canvas. The ribs were spaced about 25 centimeters (10 inches) apart. Once the ribs and keel were installed inside the canoe, the canvas stretched tightly against them, giving the canoe its shape. Two additional poles were added along each side of the inserted poles to strengthen the sides of the canoe. The poles were flattened on one side to facilitate their outward bending. These poles were secured at each end of the canoe with blue rope.

Baptiste & Peter installing ribs in canoe

The canoes were built without a measuring tape or tools, apart from an axe and knife. Everything used to build the canoes was harvested from the bush, apart from the canvas, blue rope, white string, and paint to waterproof the canoes. I was mesmerized by Baptiste's knowledge and skills; the bush was his hardware store. Building the canoes took the whole day.

At the end of the day, we were all tired and hungry. We hadn't eaten a meal or had sweet tea in nearly a day and a half. We had expended a lot of energy cutting the trees for the bark and the required pieces to build the canoes, not to mention the time spent building them. Baptiste and Peter built the canoes, while Donald and I helped by gathering the necessary pieces.

In the evening, we sat by the fire drinking a cup of tea without sugar and with no meat to fill our bellies. Peter and Baptiste had run out of cigarettes while building the canoes. Being without cigarettes didn't bother Baptiste, but it was a different story for Peter, who couldn't stop talking about the cigarettes he had left at Reid Lake.

Baptiste installing ribs in canoe

"After the paint is dry on the canoes, we should return to Reid Lake," said Peter.

"There are still a lot of trees and ice to come down the creek. We'll leave the day after the canoes are dry," Baptiste replied.

The sun had just set behind the hill across the creek when suddenly a grouse near our camp flew up into a tree. Peter

443

was the first to grab his rifle. He walked in the direction of the sound where the grouse had landed and looked up the tree. He raised his rifle, aimed, and pulled the trigger. Down came the grouse, making a soft sound when it hit the ground. The grouse was plucked and prepared for our supper.

Donald and I grabbed our rifles and went for a short walk along the creek where the grouse had come from to see if there were any more. To our disappointment, there were no other grouse in the area.

We then boiled the grouse and divided into four pieces. There was no more rice, so grouse soup was out of the question. "We'll save the broth for breakfast," said Baptiste. The small piece of grouse was delicious but not enough to curb my appetite. I went to bed listening to my growling stomach saying, "Feed me! Feed me!"

The following morning, before sunrise, we shared the broth for breakfast, I followed the current down the creek to hunt grouse. Peter and Donald headed up the creek in the direction of Lenoir Lake. Baptiste stayed at the camp to make final touches on the canoes before they were painted. It was a beautiful morning, windless and warm for that time of year. The water level in the creek had dropped slightly, and the creek was almost free of trees, sticks, and ice. I walked for about half an hour and returned to camp empty-handed.

Peter and Donald returned to camp about an hour after I did.

"We didn't see any grouse, but we saw a few ducks at the end of Lenoir Lake," said Peter.

Baptiste & Peter building canoe at Yellowknife Creek

"We took a few shots at the ducks but didn't get any," said Donald.

After a cup of sugarless tea, the canoes were given two coats of paint to waterproof the canvas. I packed two paintbrushes in my backpack, one for Peter and one for myself. The gallon of paint I had carried in my backpack from Reid Lake to Yellowknife Creek, a walk of about 25 kilometers (15 miles) was not enough to cover the entire canoes.

"Start painting on the keel and work your way up to the side of the canoe, about halfway up. After the paint is dry, give it another coat until you run out of paint," said Baptiste to Peter and me.

I carefully brushed the canoe, ensuring that I didn't waste any paint. The canvas soaked in the paint as if it were thirsty.

We managed to paint half of the canvas on the canoes that would be in direct contact with the water.

While painting the canoes, I said to Baptiste, "If I were to tell my friends back in Quebec that I carried a gallon of paint in my backpack for 25 kilometers (15 miles), they would have told me that I was crazy. Baptiste quickly replied, smiling, "After this long walk and all this packing, you'll be happy to put your butt in a canoe and drift down the creek."

I painted the white canvas canoe, which I used for the trip to the Trout River Falls, now known as Sambaa Deh Falls, near Highway #1. I baptized the canoe "Bathtub." As I sat on the canoe's floor with my arms resting on the sides, that's why I called it the "bathtub." The canoe treated me well and brought me back home safely.

Painted canoes at Yellowknife Creek.

It was amazing to think that I had carried the canvas and paint for the canoe in my backpack, and that I would soon be drifting down the Yellowknife Creek and Trout River. I had never been in a canoe in my life, and I was a bit nervous; the current of the creek was swift, and the water ice-cold.

446

After we finished the first coat of paint, we heard a loud crack up the creek. We all stood up and listened in the direction of the sound.

"What was that sound?" Peter asked his dad.

"There are more sticks and ice coming down," said Baptiste.

We could hear the sound getting louder as it came down the creek like a freight train. The sounds of trees and sticks creaking and crashing in the water grew louder and louder.

"Will the water come over the banks of the creek?" I asked Baptiste.

He calmly replied, "We are okay where we are."

Trees, sticks, and ice came around the bend of the creek at a good speed. It was spectacular to see and hear, the trees and ice singing in unison. Trees, sticks, and ice floated by our camp like a parade on the first of July.

Peter looked at his dad and said, "It's a good thing we didn't put the canoes in the water."

Baptiste looked at Peter and didn't say anything. His body language said it all.

About an hour later, the trees, sticks, and ice started to scatter until the creek was flowing with just water. The water had risen about 30 centimeters (1 foot) but was still below the banks of the creek. By mid-afternoon, the paint had dried, and Peter and I gave the canoes a second coat of paint, ensuring that we divided the paint equally.

"I'll go up the creek to Lenoir Lake to check for beaver," said Baptiste.

"I'll go down the creek to hunt grouse," said Peter.

"I'll stay at camp with Donald," I said.

Baptiste had a cup of tea and headed to Lenoir Lake. Peter left shortly after his dad. Donald and I sat by the fire, talking about food. We were both hungry, and we were torturing each other, talking about what kind of food we'd like to eat at that moment.

"I want two big fat burgers with lots of French fries and a Coke," said Donald.

I replied, "I want an extra-large pepperoni pizza with extra cheese and pepperoni."

We went on and on about the food we were craving. It's amazing when you're hungry, all you can think about is food. We didn't starve, but we went hungry for about two days during the trip. Baptiste was counting on Lenoir Lake having a few beaver lodges. It had warmed up quickly in the past few days, and the ice at Lenoir Lake was no longer safe to walk on. There were a couple of lodges at the lake, but it seemed that either a bear or a wolverine had gotten into the lodge and killed the beavers, most likely in the fall after the lake had frozen. Baptiste mentioned that a lodge near Lenoir Creek had been ripped apart. Gabe had told me stories of wolverines tearing their way into beaver lodges when the lakes or creeks are frozen and killing all the beavers inside the lodge. The wolverine would make its way inside the lodge and wait for the beavers to return. The beavers would have to come up for air and return to their lodge, as the lake or creek was frozen.

Gabe once shared a story his father had told him when he was young. "Back in the old days, before guns and metal traps, people would sometimes dig into beaver lodges, spearing the beavers for food and using their hides for clothing. One time, an old man dug into a beaver lodge and found a lynx inside. It was late fall, so the lynx must have been waiting for a beaver by the lodge when the water was still open, then jumped on one. The lynx held onto the beaver and was carried back inside the lodge. Over time, the lynx killed all the beavers one by one. The old man killed the lynx and said it was fat from feeding on the beavers," Gabe said.

While we were talking about food, a squirrel ran up a tree near our camp. Donald quickly stood up and reached for his rifle. The squirrel looked at Donald from the safety of the tree and made a high-pitched chirp. Donald raised his rifle, aimed, and fired. The squirrel fell to the ground. Donald picked it up, took a close look at it, then dropped it on the ground, saying, "It's full of lice." He checked his hands and clothes, worried the lice had transferred to him.

I walked over, picked up the squirrel with two sticks like chopsticks, and asked, "Do you want to eat it?" Donald looked at me, surprised. "It's full of lice," he replied. "I'll singe it over the fire," I said. I poked a stick through the squirrel and held it over the flames until the hide singed off. I pulled out the guts and washed the carcass in the cold water.

"Let's cook it by the fire," I said. I poked a sharp willow stick through the squirrel and placed it by the flames. We both sat by the fire, watching it cooking, our eyes glued to the meat. The smell of the roasting squirrel made my stomach growl. I turned it over to cook the other side, letting it sit for a few more minutes. Once it was ready, I placed it on a plate and cut it in half with my knife, giving one half to Donald.

449

I pulled a small piece of meat from the squirrel's backstrap and tasted it. The meat was surprisingly delicious. Donald glanced at me, took a piece, and put it in his mouth. "The squirrel tastes good," he said. Before long, the squirrel was completely devoured. Donald and I kept picking at the bones even after the meat was gone.

"I wish we had a dozen of these," I said. Donald nodded. "That was good. We should shoot more," he agreed.

We took a short walk, keeping an eye on the two canoes, hoping to find more squirrels. But none were in sight.

We sat by the fire, brewing another pot of tea with recycled tea bags that were growing weaker with each brew. Shortly after sunset, Peter returned to camp empty-handed. "I didn't see any grouse," he said. We waited by the fire for Baptiste. As it got later, Peter grew worried about his dad; the sky was darkening. A few minutes later, Peter and I decided to head toward Lenoir Lake.

Soon, we met Baptiste walking back to camp, a pair of mallard ducks and a mid-sized pike slung over his shoulder on a blue rope. The three of us made our way back to camp together. Donald was sitting by the fire, relieved to see us return.

Peter asked, "Where did you get the ducks and pike?"

"At Lenoir Lake, there's open water at the mouth of the creek," Baptiste explained. "I saw a few mallards swimming in the open water. I took my time, crawled closer, and waited for two ducks to line up for a shot. I got both of them with one shot to the head. The rest of the ducks flew off. As I walked to retrieve them, knee-deep in water, I saw a pike swimming. I aimed just below its head and shot it."

Baptiste went on to explain that when you shoot in water, you need to aim slightly below the target. We cleaned the ducks and fish, placing the ducks in the pot to boil and the fish on the grill by the fire. Once, the ducks and fish were cooked we all ate.

I have to admit, it was the best duck I'd ever tasted, probably because I was so hungry. I made sure to get every bit of meat, leaving only bones behind.

The next morning, we had the duck broth for breakfast. We warmed it over the fire, drinking it hot like tea. Overnight, the creek had risen, and a few trees and sticks floated by the camp. Baptiste walked to the bank of the creek, and said, "We'll leave tomorrow morning, down the creek. There are still trees and sticks coming down."

Peter wanted to leave. "How many days to get to Reid Lake?" he asked.

"Two days down the creek, with a one-night camp," Baptiste replied.

"That's not too far," Peter said.

Baptiste stayed at camp to guard the canoes, and the three of us went hunting for grouse. Peter and Donald headed to Lenoir Lake, while I made my way down the creek. I followed the shore, looking for grouse and occasionally scanning the water for beavers, with my hook in hand.

As I walked along the creek, I noticed a muskrat swimming downstream in the swift current. I crept closer to the bank and saw the muskrat near the shore. Aiming at its head, I took a shot with my .22 rifle. I hit it squarely in the head and rested my rifle against a tree. Using my hook, I tried to pull the muskrat to shore. To my surprise, the muskrat swam towards the bank, climbed onto land, and charged at my feet, trying to bite me. I quickly stepped back to avoid its bite and used the hook to strike it on the head. It was a good-sized muskrat.

A couple of years ago, while working at Anderson Mills, my co-worker Gilbert Cholo had shot a few muskrats in a large wetland near the Mill site. Mr. Anderson had cooked them by dipping them in flour, seasoning with salt and pepper, and frying them in a pan. That was my first time eating muskrat, and I found the meat surprisingly delicious.

I walked back to camp, pleased with my catch. The day was warming up as the sun rose above the horizon. The creek was close to overflowing its banks, and the water appeared to be running downhill. Peter and Donald were still out hunting, while Baptiste was relaxing by the fire, sipping tea. When he saw the muskrat, he said, "That's a big muskrat. It must be fat. Muskrat is good to eat."

I replied, "It tried to bite my hip waders after I shot it."

"Was it in the water?" Baptiste asked.

"No, it swam to the bank and came on land, heading straight for my boots," I explained.

"On land, muskrats can be aggressive," Baptiste said.

I grabbed a cup of tea and sat by the fire. Baptiste warned, "Be careful in the canoe. They're light and can tip easily if you're not cautious. Take your time; don't make sudden moves. This creek is running high, the current's fast now, but once we hit McEwan Creek, it slows down. You won't need to paddle much; just stir the canoe to keep it on track."

Baptiste sharpened his knife and placed the muskrat on some spruce boughs. In no time, he had removed the hide. The muskrat was very fat. Baptiste hung it by the tail above the fire's smoke and said, "I'll cook it for supper and save the broth for breakfast."

Peter and Donald returned to camp mid-afternoon, empty-handed. Baptiste spoke up, "We'll leave early tomorrow morning, heading down the creek to hunt beavers. Donald and I will use the green canoe, and Peter and Daniel will use the white canoe."

Baptiste boiled the muskrat and cut it into four equal pieces. Peter didn't want any, but Donald and I gladly ate our share. The meat, slightly smoked, was tasty. Baptiste ate his portion and told Peter to eat his. Peter hesitated but eventually gave in and ate his share.

The night was cloudless, the stars twinkling above us. It was cold, and only a few embers were left glowing when I woke up in the early morning darkness. I added some wood to the fire and warmed my backside by the flames. The teapot had ice in it; it must have been at least -5°Celsius (23 Fahrenheit). A few minutes later, Baptiste woke up.

I walked to the creek with my bar of Irish Spring soap to wash my face and hands. The water was ice-cold, numbing my hands, but it woke me up. My stomach growled, reminding me it was time for food. Baptiste heated the muskrat broth, steaming it until it was hot but not boiling. A layer of fat floated on top. I poured myself a cup and drank it as if it was tea. The broth had a rich, smoky flavor.

Peter and Donald woke up and warmed themselves by the fire. Peter didn't want any broth, but Donald had a small cup. The broth was nourishing, giving me the energy I needed for

453

the day ahead. I was excited to finally get into the canoe and drift down the creek.

Baptiste asked me if I wanted more broth, I told him no and that he could have the rest. Baptiste grabbed the pot and finished the last of the broth. I could tell he enjoyed it. I packed my gear into my backpack, which felt much lighter than it had when we left Reid Lake.

This was the test. I had wondered over the past two days how the canoes would float and handle the water. In my mind, it was hard to imagine that a piece of spruce bark, pieces of spruce trees shaped in several sizes and lengths, and a piece of canvas painted with a gallon of paint to waterproof it could float us and our gear down a fast-flowing creek and river. The heavy snow of the winter of 1975-1976, combined with the quick melting of snow over the past three weeks, had produced copious amounts of water in the creek.

"This is the highest water level I've seen on Yellowknife Creek," said Baptiste.

Baptiste and Donald carefully embarked into their green canvas canoe, loaded with their gear and paddles. Baptiste gave a slight push with his paddle against the creek's bank. The canoe caught the current and started heading downstream at a good pace. I glanced at Baptiste's canoe and was reassured when I saw it floating smoothly.

Peter sat at the front of our canoe while I sat at the back. We both sat on the floor, with our legs crossed since there were no seats. Our gear was stored between us. As Baptiste had done, I gave a slight push with my paddle. The swift current quickly took us downstream. Baptiste had told us, "Just steer the canoe with your paddle; the current will do the rest." I was happy and amazed to see the canoe float and handle the current.

Baptiste was right when he said, "After packing a heavy backpack in deep snow, you'll be happy to have your behind in a canoe." I chuckled to myself, while steering the canoe and looking downstream. I could see Baptiste and Donald ahead of us, their canoe appeared to be going downhill at a fast pace. The canoe ride felt like we were on an oversized water slide.

The water was well over the creek banks, and large driftwood trees were stacked in crisscross piles in the bush. The canoe handled the waves and the swift current well. Peter kept a lookout for beavers, his .22 rifle loaded and ready. A beaver swam out of the bush to our left and dove into the swift water. Peter didn't have a chance to shoot at it.

The creek had many sharp bends and twists, like the back of a snake. We were traveling at a fast pace, and the current kept me busy steering the canoe. Paddling upstream was out of the question, the current was too swift. We drifted for a few hours, seeing many beavers either coming out of the bush or swimming in the current. Peter took a few shots but wasn't able to hit a beaver. The day had warmed up considerably, and the sun was shining directly in my face.

I reached for my sunglasses in the chest pocket of my jean jacket, it was not there, they must have fallen out while I was loading the canoe.

After a few hours of drifting and steering in the swift water, the current gradually slowed down until we reached peaceful, calm water. When we came around a bend, Baptiste was gesturing for us to stay put. Peter and I paddled lightly backward, trying our best not to make any noise with

455

our paddles. I could hear Baptiste calling a beaver with his mouth, sticking the tip of his tongue out and pulling it back and forth quickly between his lips. The sound mimicked a beaver eating.

From a short distance, I saw a beaver swimming toward Baptiste's canoe. With his rifle aimed at the beaver, Baptiste continued calling as the beaver headed straight for him. I sat motionless in the canoe, waiting for Baptiste to take a shot. The beaver kept getting closer. I held my breath, expecting the beaver to slap its tail and dive as soon as Baptiste squeezed the trigger. The sound of the rifle broke the silence.

I heaved a sigh of relief and took in a deep breath of air. Baptiste grabbed his paddle and told Donald, "Grab the beaver by the tail." Donald looked at his dad as if he had been told to put his hands in the fire. Baptiste made a couple of strokes with his paddle toward the beaver and said louder, "Grab the beaver by the tail!" Donald shrugged once and finally grabbed the beaver by the tail.

Baptiste paddled to the shore while Donald held the dead beaver by the tail. Once close to shore, Baptiste told Peter and me, "Put your canoe next to ours." We positioned our canoe beside theirs. "Hold on to our canoe with one hand each," said Baptiste to Peter and me. We used our right hands to hold the left side of their canoe while Baptiste pulled the very large beaver onto his right side and into his canoe. He struggled a bit but was able to slide the beaver into the canoe.

Baptiste looked downstream and said, "There's a good spot to set up camp ahead." Peter and I followed Baptiste's canoe to the camp location. It was early evening, and the sun was still high in the sky.

"I will skin the beaver while you guys cut firewood and make a fire," Baptiste said. Donald and I cut a few dry trees and made a fire. "I will go hunting for grouse," Peter replied.

"Put some water in the big pot and put it on the fire," Baptiste instructed.

"That's a big female beaver. I didn't want it to sink. At this time of the year, female beavers can sink after you shoot them," said Baptiste. He added, "We should set up the tarp over our camp, it may rain tonight."

Donald and I cut some spruce boughs and laid them on the ground near the fire. We then cut some poles and set up the tarp, which was large enough to keep us dry from rain or snow. Baptiste had the beaver skinned and cooked in under an hour. We sat by the fire with our plates in hand, waiting for our share of the beaver meat. Shortly after, our plates were loaded and we were ready to eat.

Peter returned to camp empty-handed. "I didn't see any grouse. I followed the shore of the creek for a while and came back the same way," Peter said.

I sat on my sleeping bag and ate the beaver meat, which tasted so good. I was hungry, my last fulfilling meal had been three days ago. The beaver meat was fat and nourishing. I felt energized. By the end of the evening, we had eaten the whole beaver, including the tail and back feet, along with a few cups of sugarless tea.

While we were eating, Baptist told us, "When I was spring hunting with my dad and brothers, we used to mix Labrador tea with regular tea to make it last longer. He added, "Labrador tea is used to make medicine for sore throats, coughs, and colds".

During the night, I woke to the sound of freezing rain landing on our tarp. The freezing rain was light but steady, it rained for a few hours. It was a good thing we had set up the tarp.

The next morning was cold; it must have been a few degrees below 0 Celsius (32 Fahrenheit). My sleeping bag was only rated for summer temperatures and packing a winter sleeping bag would have been too bulky to add to my heavy load. I slept with my clothes on and a pair of wool socks to keep warm. The teapot and the pot with the beaver broth were iced up. The sun was rising above the horizon.

We could hear songbirds singing and calling to their mates. While listening to the birds singing, we made a big fire with the remaining dry wood that Donald and I had cut. In no time, all four of us were warming our backsides and fronts. "We're not too far from the mouth of Reid Lake Creek. We'll be at the cabin by the afternoon," said Baptiste while warming up his backside.

We shared the beaver broth for breakfast. I drank my broth like it was a cup of steaming hot tea, warming up my insides. "The current on the creek won't be as fast as yesterday. There should be a few beaver lodges along the creek. The beavers are up early. They rest in the afternoon and are out around from 4 p.m. until dark," said Baptiste. He added, "Donald and I will leave first, and you two should leave about half an hour behind us."

Baptiste and Donald loaded and launched their canoe into the cold, icy water of the creek. Peter and I extinguished our fire and loaded our canoe, taking our time. Out of nowhere, like a squadron of jet fighters, a flock of mallard ducks flew low to the ground by our camp. As they flew by, they noticed us standing along the creek. The flock, in unison, made a sudden sharp left turn. The ducks flew close to us, and I could hear the wings steering into the wind. We didn't have time to retrieve our guns.

We launched our canoe into the creek about half an hour later. It was exciting to be in the canoe again. I kept the canoe a short distance from the shore and gave a stroke of my paddle from time to time. The sun was behind us, and the sky was near cloudless with a slight breeze from the south. It was relaxing to steer the canoe in the slow-moving current, as opposed to the fast current with choppy waves. We didn't wear any life jackets; back in those days, very few people wore life jackets. Of all the people I had seen traveling in boats or canoes, other than tourists, no one wore life jackets.

We drifted down the creek for about three to four hours, then just around a bend we saw Baptiste and Donald stopped at the mouth of a creek, pulling their canoe out of the water. Peter and I followed and did the same. "We're at the mouth of the creek leading to Reid Lake. We'll cache the canoes here," said Baptiste.

The water level on Yellowknife Creek was very high. While paddling down the creek, we saw several beavers hiding under the trees in the bush. By the time we spotted the beavers, they flapped their tails against the water, making a loud sound and diving into the deep water of the creek. The first time I heard a beaver flapping its tail, so close to our canoe, I almost jumped out of my skin. I sat at the back of the canoe, steering it, while Peter sat at the front, looking out for beavers holding his .22 rifle. We saw many beavers but had few chances to take a shot. The beavers would be swimming in the bushes, hiding from us. Once they had our scent, they would flap their tails or dive before we had a chance to shoot.

Between the mouth of the creek at McEwan Lake and the creek at Reid Lake, Peter shot a large beaver around a bend. Baptiste told us to drift with the current and only steer the canoe so we wouldn't make any noise. We loaded the beaver into the canoe, with me holding onto my paddle, I pushed into the mud by the shore to balance the canoe, while Peter lifted the beaver in.

I was enjoying myself paddling and steering the canoe. It was so peaceful and relaxing until a beaver nearby flapped its tail to remind us that we were hunting them. It was such a contrast after carrying a backpack on my shoulders that weighed over 45 kilos (100 pounds) and breaking trail in waist-deep snow.

Baptiste located four standing trees near the mouth of the creek in the shape of a rectangle. "We will make our cache for the canoes in these four trees," he said. Peter and I cut two long poles from young spruce trees, removing the branches and boughs. Baptiste cut four pieces of blue string to attach the poles to the standing trees. I asked Donald to climb onto my shoulders to gain more height and secure the two poles on the standing trees. Baptiste and Peter gave the poles to Donald while I stood near the trees, where Donald tied the poles. Baptiste had shown Donald how to tie the string around the poles and trees.

"Before we put up the canoes, we will wash the inside with water," said Baptiste. Both Baptiste and Peter had shot a beaver each, and there was a bit of blood inside both canoes that could attract a bear or other animals. The canoes were dunked into the creek and rinsed out by flipping them on the beach. The canoes were then stored on the poles using a long pole to move them into place. It was early afternoon when we finished caching the canoes.

The sun was shining, and it was warm enough for a few mosquitoes to harass us. It was the last day of April. We had been on the creek for the past five days, including building the canoes. Baptiste and Peter had run out of cigarettes and waiting for the ice and debris to clear on Yellowknife Creek. Baptiste didn't mind being without cigarettes, but Peter longed for one. He had left a couple of packs at the cabin and couldn't wait to get to them.

My backpack was now much lighter. I put the beaver Baptiste had shot inside my backpack.

"Let's follow the animal trail along the creek and lake to the cabin," said Baptiste.

As a result of the warm temperatures and sunshine, most of the snow had melted very quickly. Peter took the lead, followed by Donald, me, and Baptiste. The distance to the cabin was about 3.5 kilometers (2.1 miles). The mouth of the creek was decked with tall, imposing white spruce trees, standing as if on guard. The large sloughs along both sides of the creek leading to the mouth of the lake were nearly all open water. A few ducks were swimming. Peter took a few shots with his .22 rifle at the swimming ducks, but none were hit.

The animal trail was well-defined, with only a few patches of snow here and there. I couldn't see Peter or Donald ahead of me. I told myself Peter must be walking fast to the cabin, eager for his cigarettes. Unexpectedly, I noticed Donald facing me up the trail. He dropped his backpack to the ground and ran by me without saying a word, like he was a world-class sprinter in a 100-meter race.

I looked ahead on the trail and saw Peter standing tall, looking towards the animal trail, with his buck knife in his

461

right hand. I followed the direction Peter was looking and saw a very large black bear, its hair standing on its back. I dropped my backpack to the ground and, for a second, considered running like hell, just like Donald had. I quickly came to my senses, my mind racing and my heart pounding out of my chest. Talk about an adrenaline rush!

I aimed at the bear with my .22 rifle, considering whether or not to take a shot. The bear was very close to Peter, only about 1.8 meters (6 feet) away from where he was standing. My inner self told me not to shoot; the bear was too close to Peter. If I wounded the bear, Peter could have been mauled.

I fired a few shots above the bear's head and let out multiple screams to scare it. The bear finally turned its head toward me, realizing that Peter wasn't alone. It turned around and ran up a small hill about 15 meters (50 feet) away, then suddenly stopped as if it had forgotten something. The bear stood up on its hind legs for a better look at me. Its jet-black fur shone in the sunlight. It looked very fat and must have weighed over 136 kilos (300 pounds).

I raised my hands above my head to make myself appear bigger. The bear was looking down at me as it stood on the hill. I fired a few more shots above its head and screamed like I had never screamed before. The bear stood still for a few seconds, staring at me, then quickly dropped to its front legs and charged at me full speed. My instincts and adrenaline took over. Without hesitation, I walked toward the bear, hands still raised above my head, my rifle in my left hand, and screaming my head off.

The bear stopped about 3 meters (10 feet) from me, turned around, and ran into the bush, disappearing from view. Seeing it vanish was such a relief. I quickly reloaded my .22 rifle. If I had had a high-powered rifle, I wouldn't have hesitated to shoot the bear. But I didn't want to take a chance with a .22, given how close it was.

I turned around and saw Donald walking slowly toward me. He asked, "Are you okay?"

I replied, "Yes, I'm fine."

"When I heard you screaming, I thought the bear was attacking and killing you," Donald said.

Peter walked toward us, looking shaken, and said, "The bear came out of nowhere and chased me around a tree. I took a shot at it with my .22, but the rifle was empty."

We were only about 60 meters (200 feet) from the cabin. Baptiste had heard the commotion from quite a distance and arrived shortly thereafter "Are you guys, okay?" He asked.

We replied, "We're okay."

Peter began to describe what had happened, but Baptiste quickly told him to stop talking about the bear. The incident was over, and no one had been hurt.

About 60 meters (200 feet) from the cabin, we had made a small cache of whitefish that we had caught before leaving for Yellowknife Creek. We had forgotten about the cache. The fish nets had been moved and set at the point south of the lake. The nets were checked the next day and were loaded with more whitefish than we could use or pack for our trip. The nets were pulled out of the lake, and we ate as many fish as we could before leaving. We carried some split smoked whitefish in our backpacks, which were heavy. The remaining fish were hung on a small cache.

The bear found the cache and was feeding on it. The bear was protecting the fish it had claimed. Peter stood his ground and faced the bear with courage. His actions inspired me to do my best to scare the bear away and stand my ground. Running away from the bear, as if we were prey, could have been the wrong move and may have resulted in an attack.

We all walked to the cabin and removed the plywood pieces from the door and windows. Judging by the claw marks on the plywood, the bear had attempted to break into the cabin. However, the smell of the fish hanging nearby must have distracted the bear, keeping it away from the cabin.

It was good to be back at the cabin. There were some flour and sugar left in the grub box, so fresh Bannock and sugar in our tea were back on the menu. Peter sat on his bed, looking at the wall with his hands shaking. I had expected him to reach for his cigarettes as soon as he walked into the cabin. A few minutes later, I asked him, "Have you forgotten about your cigarettes?"

He looked at me, as if he had just come back to life, he quickly got up, and reached into the grub box for his cigarettes. He smoked two back-to-back, which seemed to calm him down and stop the shaking in his hands.

Baptiste and Peter skinned the two beavers. The beaver carcasses were sliced into *"Tsá ḷǫ"* and hung over an open fire outside near the cabin. The beaver hides were stretched and put outside to dry. In the evening, before we went to bed, both *Tsá ḷǫ* and hides were stored inside the cabin, close to our sleeping area. The bears were now out of their dens and would certainly lay claim to our meat and hides.

The day after our return to the cabin, five large black bears were seen by the fish cache. The bears were taking turns eating the leftover whitefish one by one. One bear would slowly make its way to the cache while the others were busy eating their fish between their paws. Once a bear finished eating its fish, it would return to the cache and take another.

I saw two bears fighting over the fish. They stood up, facing each other like wrestlers, taking a few swipes at each other until one backed out of the match. The winning bear would reach for a fish, then lay on the ground about 9 meters (30 feet) from the cache, eating its prize, while the loser bear quickly grabbed a fish and laid down about 30 meters (100 feet) away, eating its own. It was quite a sight to see that many bears sharing food and, to some extent, getting along with each other.

By the end of the day, all the fish had been eaten. Most of the bears left the area, except for one large bear, which may have been the one that charged us. We had to be careful with our beaver meat hanging and smoking, and with the hides drying on the stretchers. One of us had to be on guard at all times. The bear had become habituated to us and was no longer afraid. It hung around our camp day and night, looking for food. We tried to scare it by shouting, but the bear kept getting closer to the cabin, attempting to steal our meat and hides right in front of us.

While at Reid Lake, Peter shot an otter not far from the cabin. The otter was swimming along the shore of the lake where the open water was. Baptiste skinned the otter and laid the carcass in the water. A large bear came out from the edge of the bush and made a beeline for the carcass. Baptiste screamed at the bear and tried to chase it away, to no avail. The bear kept coming, trying to get at the otter carcass.

Baptiste was determined to scare the bear off once and for all. He aimed at the ground below the bear's front legs with his 30-30 rifle, thinking that the bear would feel the shot near its legs and run away. Baptiste fired at very close range, and suddenly, the bear dropped to the ground. Baptiste looked at me and said, "I didn't want to shoot him."

We slowly walked toward the bear. "Be careful, the bear may be playing dead," Baptiste warned. Baptiste aimed his rifle at the bear while walking forward. The bear was lying on his right side, facing away from us, looking as if he were dead. As we got closer, the bear let out a low growl without moving. Baptiste aimed at the bear and took another shot behind its head. The bear didn't make any sounds or movements. He waited a minute, then walked slowly toward the bear with his rifle cocked and ready. Baptiste poked the bear near its head with his rifle. The bear was dead.

He asked us to cut some spruce boughs and lay them near the bear. Baptiste was surprised that he had actually hit the bear. He only meant to scare it away from camp. Upon inspecting the bear, Baptiste noticed that the first shot had hit the bear in the head. He spotted a rock protruding from the ground where he had aimed. Baptiste had not noticed the rock when he took the shot. Judging from the streak on the rock, he concluded that the bullet had ricochet off the rock and hit the bear in the head.

The bear carcass was rolled over onto the spruce boughs. Baptiste and Peter skinned the bear while Donald and I held the front and back legs, helping to stabilize it while they made their incisions to remove the hide. After the bear was skinned, I asked Baptiste, "Can I make dry meat from the bear?"

Baptiste looked surprised and said, "Are you sure you can make dry meat from the bear?"

I replied, "I learned how to make dry meat from Phoebe's mother". During our walk to Yellowknife Creek, we experienced a food shortage and went hungry for a couple of days. We still had a few weeks left before our spring hunt ended. In my mind, the dry meat would ensure we had food in case of another shortage. In the last three weeks of our spring hunt, we lived off the land, meaning if we didn't harvest any birds, fish, or game, we wouldn't have anything to eat."

I made a rack from poles for smoking the dry meat. I cut the bear into pieces and made dry meat from nearly all of the bear meat, which was fat and healthy-looking. Making dry meat from a bear is different than from a moose. With moose, large pieces of dry meat can be made, but with bear, the pieces are smaller. The dry meat was smoked and cured for a few days. Once done, I tried a few pieces. It was tasty, well smoked and cured. I stored the dry meat in a large burlap sack, which was nearly full.

Baptiste, Peter, and Donald weren't interested in trying my dry meat, maybe because it was bear meat, not moose. We made a large stretcher to dry the bear hide, using dry poles and crosspieces at each corner to strengthen it. A string and a large needle were used to stretch the bear hide; the same large needle was used to stretch beaver hides. Fat and leftover meat on the leather side of the bear hide were scraped off with a knife.

After a couple of days of drying, the string holding the bear hide on the stretcher was tightened to further stretch it. Once the bear hide was deemed dry enough to remove from the stretcher, it was rolled up with the leather side inside and tied with string to keep it tightly rolled. After the bear was shot, no other bears came to our camp looking for food.

I managed to shoot a beaver near the cabin along the open water by the shore. I had been sitting on a rock, soaking in the sunset and the warm temperatures, when I spotted a beaver swimming towards our camp. Without hesitation, I grabbed my .22 rifle, which was resting on the exterior wall of the cabin, and made my way back to the shore. The beaver dove beneath the surface, disappearing from view. Just as I thought it was gone, the beaver resurfaced right in front of me. I aimed carefully and fired. The beaver was hit and began kicking close to the edge of the ice. Worried it might slip under the ice, I knew I couldn't let it get away.

Without a hook to pull it in, I waded into the freezing water, the cold seeping through my boots as I walked in to my waist. Grabbing the beaver by the tail, I felt a sigh of relief as it had stopped kicking and was now lifeless. I hauled it out of the water and laid it on the shore. Soaked and chilled to the bone, I quickly changed into dry clothes and warmed myself by the fire.

We had run out of beaver meat, and with four of us, one large beaver provided a single meal, including the tail and back feet.

Baptiste had brought a 17-foot fiberglass canoe to Reid Lake by snowmobile at the end of March. The plan was to use it for the final leg of our spring hunt, from Reid Lake to Coral Falls on the Trout River, known as "Sambaa Deh." By then, the ice on Reid Lake had melted enough that the only open water was along the eastern shore, just wide enough for a canoe. There were no beaver lodges on our side, only on the western shore and the north end of the lake, far out of reach.

Grouse hunting near the camp provided the protein we desperately needed. Ruffed grouse are commonly found in deciduous and mixed forest areas, and this time of year marked the beginning of their annual spring ritual. The male grouse would perform a drumming display, signaling his territory. Perched on a log, the drumming sound could be heard from far away, especially on calm, windless mornings or evenings.

We would head out early, straining our ears for the distinctive drumming sounds. It took me a while to learn how to locate the grouse without scaring it off. The drumming sounded like a small motor starting up. At first, I struggled to judge how far away the grouse was. But with time, I grew better at pinpointing its location just by the sound.

The grouse would always return to the same log, drumming from its perch. If it flew off, I would wait patiently, hiding until it came back. I spent countless hours listening to the sounds of its wings fluttering as it drummed. You know you're close when you hear the soft fluttering at the end of the drumming. At this point, it's best to stay still and move carefully, as any noise could send the grouse flying. The bird usually remained hidden, blending with its surroundings. After some time, I learned to spot the grouse by its shape as I scanned the ground slowly, making sure not to make any sudden movements.

If I managed to shoot the grouse, another grouse would often take over the territory and drum from the same log. But shooting or missing meant either having food or going without that day.

Spruce grouse were abundant in the area where we hunted. The males were striking, with their dark brown and black plumage adorned with white spots, and an intense red comb above their eyes during the mating season. Females, on the other hand, had a more subtle speckled mix of brown, gray, gold, black, and white, with the males being noticeably darker in color. These grouse were typically found in conifer-dominated forests of spruce and pine. We'd hunt them along seismic lines and lake or creek shores, where they would often gather grit or small stones to aid their gizzards in breaking down food. In the early hours, these areas were frequented by grouse, all eager to consume the grit.

One morning, while hunting near Reid Lake, a male spruce grouse came charging towards me with its chest puffed up and feathers fluffed, before abruptly stopping just 1.8 meters (6 feet) away. He fanned his tail open in full display. It was an astonishing sight; one I had only witnessed once. Needless to say, the grouse ended up in our pot for supper that night.

We stayed at Reid Lake for about a week. Baptiste wanted to wait for the water level to drop, hoping the beavers would start swimming in the creek rather than hiding in the brush. Our collection of furs, including beaver pelts, two otter pelts, a few muskrats, and a bear hide, had all been dried. It was time to continue our spring hunt along Yellowknife Creek and the Trout River. The snow had nearly melted, and the daytime temperatures had been hovering around 20 degrees Celsius (68 Fahrenheit).

I was eager to get back into my fourteen-foot canoe, which I had affectionately named "bathtub." When I sat in it, the sides came up to my armpits, giving me the feeling of sitting in a bathtub. Before we left the cabin, we boarded up the windows and doors with plywood. My snowmobile and sleigh were stored in the unfinished cabin where Baptiste,

Peter, and I had stayed during our ice fishing trip in December.

We made our way to the mouth of Reid Lake Creek, where we had left our two canoes a week earlier. Baptiste paddled the seventeen-foot fiberglass canoe along the shore to the creek's mouth. The ice had finally broken up, and Baptiste had checked the creek a few days earlier but wasn't able to paddle all the way through. Our backpacks were lighter now, containing mainly clothes, blankets, dishes, pots and pans, a large waterproof tarp for shelter if we had to camp in the rain or snow, and the furs we had harvested during the spring hunt. I also carried my burlap sack filled with dried bear meat.

Peter, Donald, and I walked the same path we had taken a week before. When we arrived at the creek's mouth, I was shocked to see that the water level in Yellowknife Creek had dropped by at least 2.4 meters (8 feet). The creek, which had once been well above its banks, was now well below them. Fortunately, the canoes and paddles were still at the cache, undisturbed. It was a challenge to walk down the muddy bank to put the canoes in the water and pack our gear into them, but we were relieved to find everything intact.

It was midday when the beavers were swimming, exploring new grounds in search of mates and fresh food. "Each spring, the matriarch beaver kicks the two-year-olds out of the lodge," Baptiste explained. "The two-year-olds leave to find a mate and build a new lodge."

Baptiste had set up our canoe hunting schedule, beginning at 7:00 a.m. and ending around 11:00 a.m. During this time, we'd stop to make a fire, have tea, and eat a quick bite. Any beavers we harvested were skinned, and the carcasses were made into Tsá lǫ. The hunt resumed at 4:00

p.m., and before darkness fell, we'd select and set up a campsite for the night. The beavers harvested in the evening were skinned and processed in the same way.

From the mouth of Reid Lake Creek to Yellowknife Creek at the Trout River, the creek twisted through a series of bends and turns, passing through seven portages. Baptiste and Gabe often mentioned in their spring hunt stories how log jams and sharp bends had led to the creation of these portages, which had remained in the same locations since their hunts, dating back to the 1930s or earlier.

"Wait half an hour before drifting down the creek," Baptiste advised. The reason for having the three canoes travel half an hour apart was to maximize our chances of spotting beavers and muskrats. If the first canoe missed a beaver foraging on land, the second or third could have a better shot. Similarly, if the second canoe missed a swimming beaver, the third might get a chance at it.

Baptiste and Donald launched the factory canoe down Yellowknife Creek with their backpacks and rifles. Half an hour later, Peter set off in the canoe Baptiste and Donald had used at the beginning of our trip, with his own backpack and rifle. A half-hour after Peter, I launched the canoe that Peter and I had shared, with my backpack, rifle, bear hide taking up a lot of space and my burlap sack of dried bear meat. I also had the hides we harvested and the *Tsá lǫ*.

Baptiste insisted that I load the bear hide and dry meat behind me in the canoe, leaving the beaver hides and meat at the front. "You should never mix bear hide and meat with beaver hide and meat," he said. "Never put these two together."

Before we left the mouth of Reid Lake Creek, Baptiste said he'd start looking for a campsite around 9:00 p.m. The day was warm, the sun was shining with a light breeze, and it felt great to be back in the canoe, drifting down the creek. The water level had dropped, slowing the current significantly.

As I drifted down the creek, I heard Peter take a shot from across the water. Shortly after, I rounded a sharp bend and realized that Peter had indeed taken the shot from the opposite side. The creek's winding turns had made it difficult to see exactly where he was, but the shot clearly came from across the creek.

From a distance, I saw a beaver swimming in my direction. I was downwind from it. I pointed my canoe towards the beaver and started calling it by quickly sticking my tongue out and pulling it back and forth between my lips, mimicking the sound of a beaver eating. I had seen Baptiste use this technique to call a beaver to his canoe before. Once the beaver heard my call, it started heading towards me. I aimed my rifle at its head and waited for the right moment to take a shot. When the beaver's head was exposed to the side, I squeezed the trigger. I saw the beaver drop its head into the water and floated motionless, drifting with the current.

I paddled towards the beaver and lightly tapped it with my paddle to ensure it was dead. Then I used a piece of blue rope with a knot fashioned into a noose and tied it to the beaver's tail. The rope was secured to the canoe. I then paddled to the shore, which was about 45 meters (150 feet) wide. Grabbing hold of some willows on the shore with my left hand, I pulled on the blue rope with my right hand until I could reach the beaver's tail. The beaver was large, and I struggled a bit but managed to lift it into the canoe, balancing myself with the willows on the shore.

The beaver was heavy, and Baptiste's warning echoed in my mind. "Be careful when pulling a beaver into the canoe. The spruce bark/canvas canoes are light and easily tipped over if you're not careful." This was my first beaver shot alone in a canoe, and I knew I had to be cautious not to tip it into the ice-cold water of the creek. I had all our fur, dried bear meat, and beaver meat on board.

Things were looking good. We had about six or seven days left in our spring hunt, and with the couple of *"Tsá lǫ"* we had already harvested, not counting the beaver I shot, we were in good shape. I was confident that between our three canoes, we would harvest more beavers and not face a food shortage. However, we had been completely out of flour, sugar, and other store-bought food for the last three days, relying only on birds and game from the land.

Throughout the evening, I saw a few more beavers swimming in the creek, but they slapped their tails on the water and dove, disappearing from sight. One beaver was foraging on land. As I drifted near the bank, it suddenly ran out and dove behind my canoe. I was startled when it made a loud splash diving into the water. I was amazed by how fast the beaver could run on land.

The evening was windless and warm, with only a few mosquitoes buzzing around my head. Ducks were quacking and flying overhead, sounding like bombers on a mission. I was really enjoying myself, drifting with the current, only steering the canoe when necessary.

As I came around a sharp bend, I saw smoke rising above the tree line. Closer to the camp, I saw Baptiste and Peter skinning a beaver each, with Donald sitting beside his dad, watching him work.

I pulled my canoe to the shore with Donald's help and unloaded it. I took the beaver I had shot to Baptiste, who smiled at me and said, "I'll cook some fresh beaver meat for supper." There was no more tea, and I wished I could have a cup of tea with sugar and fresh Bannock. The sugar, flour, and tea left in the grub box at the Reid Lake cabin had been consumed quickly, like there was no tomorrow.

Baptiste had selected a nice location, with plenty of firewood and a dry, level beach to set up our camp. The creek water was cold and refreshing, almost too cold. Baptiste skinned the beaver I shot. He had the beaver he shot boiling in a large pot. Peters and my beavers were cut into *"Tsá lǫ"*. I hung the two *"Tsá lǫ"* that I had in my canoe over a small smoldering fire. Once the two beavers were cut into *"Tsá lǫ"*, they were also hung over the smoldering fire.

"The portages are not very far from here. The last time I was here was about twenty-five years ago. The bush looks different; I can see that there was a forest fire," said Baptiste. We sat by the fire and ate the whole beaver in one sitting. "We will have the broth for breakfast," said Baptiste. Before we went to bed, Baptiste said, "I did not see any signs along the Yellowknife Creek where someone camped or made canoes. I think the last people who hunted beavers on Yellowknife Creek were in the late fifties or early sixties. The last time I came hunting beavers on Yellowknife Creek was in the late forties or early fifties." He added, "The portage trails have not been used in a long time. Before we portage the canoes and gear, we will have to check the trails and fix them. We should be at the first portage before 11 a.m. tomorrow."

`The sun stayed up above the horizon a little longer every day. The nights were cold, the temperatures were at their lowest, well below 0 Celsius (32 Fahrenheit), in the early morning hours. By mid-afternoon, the temperatures hovered around 20 Celsius (68 Fahrenheit). I remember one morning leaving our camp on Yellowknife Creek at 6 a.m., noticing a thin coat of ice on my paddle.

Our daily routine while hunting on Yellowknife Creek was to drift in our canoes from early morning until 11 a.m. We would then find a good camping spot, make a fire, and eat something. I would catch a snooze lying in the warmth of the sun and the heat from the fire. By 4 p.m., we would load our canoes and drift down the creek, half an hour apart, until the sun had set. I was the last one to make it to camp. By then, the camp was set, and dinner was cooked.

We arrived at the first portage at around 11 a.m., just as Baptiste had estimated. We unloaded our canoes and pulled them out of the water. Baptiste asked Donald to stay behind with our canoes and gear. "If you see a bear, take a shot in the air with your rifle to let us know. We will come right back to camp," said Baptiste to Donald.

All three of us, in single file, walked the overgrown trail, cleared and widened it, and marked it with our axes, one blaze on one side, the other on the opposite side. "This way you will see the trail from both directions," said Baptiste. To my left, I could see years of large trees and debris jamming the creek. The portage trail was about 400 meters (0.2 Miles) in length. We walked back to the camp and portaged our canoes and gear. I made two trips: one for my canoe and backpack, and the other for the rest of my gear. Whatever was in my canoe, I portaged at each portage. It took us about two hours to make the first portage.

We were on alert for bears. The smell of smoked beaver meat and hides would surely entice them to investigate. At this time of year, bears had been out of their den winter slumber for at least a couple of weeks and were on the lookout for food to replenish their fat reserves. A bear could, with one swipe of its paws, destroy our canoes. The spruce bark/canvas canoes were light to carry on our shoulders. I learned quickly that it was important to have the canoe well-balanced on my shoulders. The factory canoe was heavier and bulkier to carry over the portages. Baptiste carried the factory seventeen-foot canoe on all seven portages. He used two paddles, his and Donald's, to attach them to the sides and seat of the canoe. Once secured to the canoe, the paddles' blades would rest on his shoulders and be used to portage the canoe. My bark/canvas canoe was cautiously portaged and balanced on my shoulders. Caution had to be exercised not to damage the fragile skin of the canoe.

At the first portage, while portaging his canoe, Peter bumped into a broken tree branch on a fire-killed large tree that caused a gash along the side of his canoe. We made a fire at the end of the first portage, where Baptiste collected spruce gum to repair the canoe. The spruce gum was melted in a frying pan and mixed with beaver fat until it had an adhesive texture that would stick to the skin of the canoe. We had brought with us leftover small pieces of canvas to be used as patches to repair holes and gashes, along with needles and thread. Peter sewed a small piece of canvas over the gash while Baptiste heated the mixture of spruce gum and beaver fat until it boiled, which was then smeared on the small piece of canvas with a flattened dried piece of wood.

"Spruce gum alone will crack in cold water and leak. The mixture of beaver fat and spruce gum will not crack in cold water," said Baptiste. He added, "The smell of the beaver fat on the canoe will attract the bears, we cannot leave the canoes unattended." We took a break and had some smoked beaver meat cooked on the open fire. The *"Tsá lǫ"* was smoked to my liking. The beaver fat, yellowish in color from the smoke, added a smoky flavor to the beaver meat. While we were eating, the patch had cooled off and dried very well over the gash, giving the canoe a *"je ne sais quoi"* appearance and character.

"Let's paddle to the next portage. It's a couple of hours from here. We will camp there and fix the trail," said Baptiste. We all departed half an hour apart. I was the last canoe to leave. While waiting for my departure time, I doused the campfire with water from the creek to ensure that it was completely extinguished. I looked down the creek to see Peter's canoe disappearing around the bend of the creek. It was mid-afternoon. The beavers should be out soon, swimming and foraging for food and looking for mates. The two-year-old beavers venture into little-known waters away from their birth lodge and colony, searching for a new home and mate.

I untied my canoe and used my paddle by laying it across the top sides of the canoe to balance myself and sat on the floor of the canoe. Using my paddle, I propelled the canoe away from the bank of the creek. I gave a few strokes with my paddle to aim the canoe towards the middle of the creek. From there, I steered the canoe with my paddle and let the current do the rest. It was peaceful and relaxing drifting down the creek. The sun was shining with no breeze. Songbirds were singing in unison, calling to each other or trying to out-sing one another. My .22 rifle was loaded with the safety on next to me. I scanned the creek ahead for signs of beavers and muskrats.

As I rounded the bend, I saw a muskrat swimming ahead. I closed my lips tight and blew air through them to call the muskrat. At the sound of my call, the muskrat made a ninety-degree turn and beelined toward my canoe. I grabbed my rifle and clicked the safety off. I kept calling the muskrat until it was about six meters (20 feet) away and squeezed the trigger. The muskrat lay still in the water. I paddled towards the muskrat and picked it up by the tail. A few days ago, Baptiste had carved a couple of muskrat stretchers made from a dry tree where we built the canoes. As muskrats were harvested, we skinned and dried them on those stretchers.

The creek drains into the Trout River along a multitude of small tributaries, straight channels, and winding channels curving back and forth. The distance from where we built the canoes by way of Yellowknife Creek and Trout River to Coral Falls, where we ended our spring hunt, is 82 kilometers (51 miles). The distance, as the crow flies, between where we built the canoes and Coral Falls is 42 kilometers (26 miles), which is nearly half the distance.

I drifted down the creek for another hour and a half and noticed smoke from a campfire. I headed towards the smoke, paddling and steering my canoe. Three muskrats were harvested. Baptiste and Peter each harvested a beaver. When I arrived, beaver meat was cooking in the large pot and was almost ready. I unloaded and pulled my canoe out of the water and turned it upside down. I skinned the three muskrats I shot and smoked the carcasses. Peter and Donald helped me put the hides on the stretchers.

After dinner, Baptiste said, "Let's fix the portage trail this evening. Tomorrow we will have an early start." Donald will stay behind at the camp to watch over our canoes and gear. Three *"Tsá lǫ"* and three muskrats were being smoked by the fire, with ample scent to entice a bear or two to our camp. The trail was overgrown with vegetation, along with a few fallen trees across the trail. The distance of the trail was about half of the first portage. The trail was cleaned and widened with our axes.

At one time, Baptiste had said, "We will build a cabin at McEwan Lake next fall and set a trapline to "*Shíhnakah*". I would like to cut the trees jammed at the seven portages with a chainsaw next winter. We would cut the trees that are jammed into the banks of the creek so the high water in the spring can free them up. I want to do the spring hunt again next year. I used to do the spring hunt on the Yellowknife Creek every year with my father and brothers until I got married."

As I lay on my sleeping bag, I could see the shining stars and very few clouds in the sky. The night would be cold again. I put on a pair of cleaned wool socks and my grey wool tuque on my head before going to sleep. We slept with our rifles close at hand in case of an unwelcome visit from a bear.

Early the next morning, we boiled the smoked muskrat for breakfast. Peter did not want any. Baptiste, Donald, and I each had a muskrat. We portaged our canoes and gear without incident. The morning's air was cold on the skin; it must have been well below 0 Celsius (32 Fahrenheit). "The next five portages are within close distance from each other. It will take us about one and a half days to get through the portages. After the portages, we won't be far from Trout River," said Baptiste. From the second to the last portage, we traveled together. After drifting for about half an hour, we arrived at the third portage. Baptiste led the way on the portage trail while Peter and I followed him with our axes. The trail was restored in less than an hour. All four of us portaged the canoes and our gear to the end of the third portage. We loaded our canoes and carried on to the fourth portage, which was only about fifteen minutes away.

Baptiste led the way with his axe, swinging at a fallen tree across the beginning of the old trail. "The last time I was on this trail, we fixed the trail. It must have been about twenty-five years ago or more," said Baptiste. The trail was re-blazed and widened. It was the shortest portage distance thus far. We were back to our canoes in less than forty-five minutes.

The old portage trail followed a sharp bend in the creek. I could see years of large trees jamming the creek from bank to bank. It would take a great deal of work with chainsaws to cut through the trees to release the decades of trees clogging the creek's bend. The work would have to be done in the winter months when the creek is frozen. The congestion of trees and debris flowing downstream every spring has surely extended the clogging over the years. Canoes and gear were portaged to the end of the trail, where the canoes were loaded and launched in the direction of the fifth portage. Once again, the distance was only fifteen minutes drifting down the creek.

"We will camp at the portage and fix the trail before supper," said Baptiste.

The old trail followed the length of two sharp bends. The creek twisted back and forth like a snake's back, creating an impressive congestion of logs and debris. I stopped by the creek's bank to have a closer look. The trees and debris were stacked up to the banks. I could not see the water flowing but could hear it rushing underneath the huge pile of logs and debris. Clearing the old trail proved to be challenging and a great deal of work due to the abundant fallen trees across the path. Signs of a recent forest fire burning through the area were evident. Roots of large white spruce trees were overturned, several of them blocking the trail.

"Let's cut the trail around the roots," said Baptiste. Some of the white spruce trees lying across the trail were large in diameter and would take a great number of axe swings to cut through. Baptiste decided to clear the branches from the fallen trees to widen the trail.

"We will step over the trees," said Baptiste.

Hungry and tired, we returned to where we had left our canoes, gear, and Donald. On the way back, we did some touch-up work on the trail.

"You guys took a long time to cut the trail. I was getting worried," said Donald, who had stayed behind guarding our canoes and gear. Donald had made a fire, and we boiled a whole "*Tsá lǫ*", cut into strips about 4 centimeters (1.5 inches) wide. We had run out of tea a few days ago, so I drank the ice-cold water from the creek and the broth from our boiling beaver and muskrat meat. The meat and broth provided us with much-needed vitamins, fats, and protein.

The following morning, I woke up early, it was still dark. Mother nature was calling. The morning was cold and humid. I pushed the remaining trees from the campfire into the leftover coals that were still red-hot. Shortly after, the fire came back to life, displaying welcoming flames and the sounds of crackling burning wood. I stood by the fire, warming the front of my body and then my back until I felt nice and warm. Baptiste, Peter, and Donald woke up and followed suit. After breakfast, we would portage to the end of the trail and continue to the sixth portage. "It's not very far from here," said Baptiste.

While portaging his canoe, Peter rubbed it against sharp, dry broken branches. I was behind Peter and heard the ripping of canvas. Peter laid his canoe on the ground to inspect the damage. I also laid my canoe down to check. The canoe had a large tear about 30 centimeters (1 foot) long, halfway between the bottom and top. The canoe would require intensive repairs to make it seaworthy again. We were close to the end of the trail. Baptiste had portaged his canoe to the end of the trail and was returning for the second trip of this portage. He inspected the damage and said, "We can fix the canoe, but it would require a lot of sewing and spruce gum with fat." Baptiste paused for a moment, looking as if he was thinking. A few seconds later, he said, "Peter can come with us in our canoe. Peter's backpack will have to go in Daniel's canoe." We left Peter's canoe by the trail and continued with the portage.

As Baptiste had said, the seventh portage was only a ten-minute drift and paddle by canoe to reach. The old trail was cleared and widened, and the canoes and gear were portaged to the end of the trail.

"This is the last portage. We are not too far from Trout River. We will camp at the mouth of Yellowknife Creek for a couple of nights to dry the beaver hides we have left," said Baptiste. True to his words, the seventh portage was, in fact, the last portage on Yellowknife Creek. Before we reached the mouth of the creek, Peter shot a beaver. He sat at the front of the canoe while Baptiste steered the canoe and Donald sat in the middle.

My canoe was loaded with gear, and I did not have much space left. I was the last canoe to reach the mouth of Yellowknife Creek.

Viewing the width and fast waters of Trout River, I was a tad intimidated by the river. Trout River seemed to me as a hazardous river with its fast current and rolling water. I was asking myself, "Would my canoe or I be able to handle the river?" I was not convinced if I could graduate yet from a creek to a river. Trout River seemed so wide from bank to bank compared to Yellowknife Creek. I felt comfortable paddling and steering my canoe down Yellowknife Creek once I got used to being in a canoe. The creek was narrow enough that I knew I could swim to the shore in the event my canoe capsized. I am not a good swimmer and was unsure if I could swim to the shore of the river. At this time of the year, the water was ice-cold. Capsizing my canoe in the river and being in the river's ice-cold water would have given rise to hypothermia.

Since the time we left the location where we built the canoes, I hid a few strike-anywhere matches in my beard, which was long and thick enough to hold a few matches in the event my canoe capsized. If I lost all my gear and canoe, I had at least a few matches to make a fire to warm up and dry my clothes, along with using the fire to signal for assistance. We had no means of communicating with the outside world by radio or mobile telephone. Satellite phones and InReach devices did not exist back then. A large bonfire, fed with spruce boughs and generating heavy black smoke, was our only way to communicate with the outside world.

At the mouth of Yellowknife Creek near Trout River, signs such as camps, tripods, beaver stretchers, and stumps, most likely trees for firewood and building camps, were evident. "We used to camp for a few nights at the mouth of the creek, drying our beaver hides that we shot coming down the creek. We would hunt the beavers coming down to the mouth of the creek," said Baptiste.

He added, "From the mouth, we would paddle down Trout River, hunting beavers to the Falls, and portage to below the falls. From there, we would paddle back to our house at the mouth of Trout River near the Mackenzie River.

After we finished drying our beavers, we would use our boat to drift down the Mackenzie River to Fort Simpson to sell our beaver hides at the Hudson Bay store. We bought supplies and stayed in Fort Simpson for a few days and then made our way with our boat back up the Mackenzie to Trout River."

"How many days would it take by boat to Fort Simpson and back to Trout River?" I asked.

"One day to Fort Simpson and two to three days going back. That was before we had a kicker (outboard motor) for our boat," said Baptiste.

"When did you start using a kicker?" I asked

"The first kicker I bought was in the early forties during the war," said Baptiste.

We set up camp on the north side of the creek. The sky looked as if it would rain soon. We set up the large orange tarp over our camp where we laid a bedding of spruce boughs. We had fresh beaver meat and a *"Tsá lǫ"*.

Baptiste and Peter made a few beaver stretchers while Donald and I cut firewood for our campfire. It was in the early evening as we were eating, when a light rain began. The rain continued until the early hours of the morning. Fortunately, the beaver hides were all on the stretchers before we went to bed. The sounds of the rain on the tarp reminded me of the sound of the rain on the tin roof of my mother's house in Quebec. On rainy days, I would open my window so I could fall asleep to the sounds of the rain on the tin roof. I had some of the best sleeps and rest of my life falling asleep to the sounds of the rain. I had a restful sleep that night, and the sound of the flowing river nearby intensified the moment.

When I woke up; it was still dark. The sky was cloudless, with stars shining and winking at me. It was much warmer than the previous few mornings. It looked like we would have a sunny, warm day. We spent the next couple of days repacking our gear, smoking our *Tsá lǫ*, drying the beaver hides, and resting, enjoying the nice weather. In the late afternoon, Baptiste and Peter paddled up the creek to hunt for beavers. A few hours later, they drifted back to camp with two beavers in their canoe. The factory-made seventeen-foot canoe could easily make its way against the current up Yellowknife Creek with two people paddling. It would have been possible but difficult to paddle up the creek by myself with my spruce bark and canvas canoe.

On the last evening at camp, Baptiste said, "It will take us about four to five hours to get to the falls. From the falls, we will portage our gear to the highway and hitchhike a ride to Fort Simpson." Baptiste looked at me and said, "You will have to stay on the left side of the river for most of the way. Just follow us and do exactly as we do. There will be what we call a beaver dam about halfway to the falls where the river drops about 1 meter (3 feet). Make sure you are on the far-left side of the river when you go down the beaver dam. There are cliffs along the river in the area of the dam. The cliffs are about 15 meters (50 feet) straight up. The water is very high this year, the dam is at its worst in high and low water. You will have to be careful that the canoe is not sideways when you go down the dam. The canoe will flip and capsize. When you get close to the Falls, make sure you are on the left side of the river; otherwise, you will go down the Falls."

"Is the dam all the way across the river?" I asked. Baptiste said, "Yes, it is all the way across the river. You will see the dam from a distance. It's on a straight stretch of the river.

486

The far-left side of the river is the safest way to go down the dam."

I went to bed a bit stressed and had a hard time falling asleep. I kept thinking about the instructions Baptiste had given me and running them through my head until I fell asleep. For most of the night, I dreamt about the dam, which was stressing me out. I recalled Gabe telling me stories about going down the Trout River in the springtime, hunting for beavers in a spruce bark canoe in low and high water. He stated that the dam was at its worst in low water due to the height of the dam. The lower the water, the higher the height of the dam. Baptiste knew the journey like the back of his hand, and I trusted him.

Early the next morning, we had breakfast and loaded our canoes. The sun had not fully risen above the horizon as we launched the canoes. I followed Baptiste's canoe, heading to the other side of the Trout River. The current was strong, and I had to paddle with all my might to cross the river. Baptiste's canoe was ahead of mine by quite a distance. Once across the river, I stayed a short distance from the shore and steered my canoe with my paddle, following Baptiste's canoe. The current on the Trout River was much stronger and faster than Yellowknife Creek. The sun was at my back, the sky was blue with the odd cloud here and there, and there was no wind. There were a few rolling waves, which are found where there are generally flat shorelines. Most of the shorelines were underwater due to the high-water level.

From a distance, Baptiste's canoe veered towards the middle of the river. After a while, I heard a .22 rifle shot. Baptiste's canoe veered in the direction of the current, and shortly thereafter, Peter picked up a beaver and pulled it into the canoe. Baptiste's canoe headed back to the left side of the river. I was not far behind their canoe. I kept my focus on steering the canoe and looking ahead for the dam. I had a big load in my fourteen-foot canoe and did not want to take a chance chasing beavers on the river, as paddling upstream was out of the question.

About half an hour later, Baptiste's canoe took a turn and headed to the right side of the river. I steered my canoe in the direction of their canoe. Again, I heard a .22 rifle shot, and soon after, a second one. A second beaver was pulled into the canoe. Baptiste's canoe headed back towards the left side of the river while I steered my canoe back to the left side.

A quarter of an hour later, the river took a sharp turn to the left, and I could no longer see Baptiste's canoe. I kept my canoe on the left side of the river and kept an eye out for Baptiste's canoe. I was expecting to see his canoe on the right side of the river. Once at the bend, the river took a sharp turn to the right. I looked ahead and still could not see Baptiste's canoe. I was unsure which side of the river the canoe was on. I kept my canoe on the left side of the river. I saw a beaver to the right of my canoe, about 60 meters (200 feet) away. The beaver appeared to be swimming upstream, away from me. I kept drifting down the river at a good pace.

After the sharp bend, I could see from a distance Baptiste's canoe following the left side of the river. I could see the cliffs Baptiste had spoken about. The dam was coming up soon, so I steered my canoe closer to the left side of the river. The current speed had picked up some. The river was starting to narrow in width, which is why the current speed increased. About ten minutes later, tall cliffs were on both sides of the river. Just as Baptiste described them, the cliffs were at least 15 meters (50 feet) or more straight up, with no shorelines and nowhere to swim to in the event of a capsize. The cliffs were beautiful and majestic, yet scary and unclimbable.

Looking ahead, Baptiste's canoe was fast approaching the dam. From my viewpoint, I could see a roll of waves from shore to shore. Baptiste's canoe was hugging the cliffs along the left side of the river and vanished for a few seconds before reappearing below the dam. I was happy that they had made it without a mishap. My turn was next. As I approached the dam, I ensure that the bow of my canoe took the plunge first over the dam. The current was strong, and the water spilling over the dam was loud and impressive. I kept steering my canoe with my paddle to keep it straight ahead. The cliffs were so close that I could touch them.

I took a quick look to my right to examine the dam and immediately saw why Baptiste and Gabe had said the safest way down the dam was on the left side. If I had taken the dam in the middle of the river or anywhere else apart from the left side, I would have most likely capsized the canoe and injured or killed myself on the rocks below the dam. Just as I reached the top of the dam, the bow of the canoe dropped at about a forty-five-degree angle and slid down the dam about 1.2 meters (4 feet). The canoe landed below the dam without tipping. I was ecstatic; what an adrenaline rush that was!

I could see Baptiste's canoe down the river paddling against the current and looking in my direction. They saw that I was okay, and they veered their canoe down the river. We drifted down the river for about another two hours. Around a bend, I lost sight of Baptiste's canoe. I was expecting that we would be arriving at the Falls soon. Far off down the river, I saw someone standing on the shore of the river, waving their paddle. I steered my canoe in that direction. As I approached, I saw Baptiste making a sign with his arm to come to shore.

"We are done with our canoe trip, we are at the Falls," said Baptiste. I paddled my canoe to the shore and pulled it out of the water. Peter and Donald were making their way down the portage trail with their first load.

"Will we portage the canoes to the highway?" I asked.

"No, I'll come back in a couple of days with Louie to pick up my canoe," said Baptiste.

"How about my canoe?" I asked.

"We'll leave it here," said Baptiste.

I was a bit disappointed. I wanted to take my canoe back to Fort Simpson.

"Louie and I fixed the portage trail to the highway last fall," said Baptiste.

I unloaded my canoe and put it in the bush. I was thankful that the canoe took me down Yellowknife Creek and Trout River without any mishaps.

"Peter shot another beaver near the Falls," said Baptiste. In total, three medium-sized beavers were shot on Trout River. Two beavers were still left at the portage. I took both in my backpack and portaged them to the highway. On the way to the highway, a fallen tree across the trail, about 60 centimeters (2 feet) above the ground, blocked my way. I did not have my axe with me and decided to step over the tree. As I stepped over the tree, the weight of the beavers in my backpack made me lose my balance. I fell backward and landed on my back. In the process, I split my jeans from my crotch to the back of my jeans. I did not hurt myself, as the beavers in my backpack cushioned my fall.

I met Peter and Donald on the trail. They were returning to portage the last of their gear. We all made two trips each on the portage trail. It was early afternoon, and we were unsure if the ferry at the Liard River had opened for the season yet. Shortly after, we had our gear at the highway. A single-cab pickup truck heading towards Fort Simpson stopped next to our gear laying in the ditch. The driver was a highway maintenance employee I did not know. He was in his early thirties with short greasy hair and an unshaved face.

"Is the ferry at the Liard River open?" asked Baptiste.

"Yes, it opened a couple of days ago. Do you guys need a ride to Fort Simpson?" asked the driver.

"Yes, we do, please," said Baptiste.

We loaded our gear in the box of the truck. There was room for only two passengers. Baptiste and Donald climbed into the pickup while Peter and I rode in the box of the truck. The ride took about two hours to Fort Simpson. We were all dropped off at Baptiste's house, and I walked to Gabe's house with my backpack, burlap sack of dry bear meat, axe, and rifle. I felt happy to be back in Simpson and could not wait to see Phoebe and our son Danny. I had been gone for 42 days without any communication with Phoebe.

I walked into Gabe's house unannounced in the middle of the afternoon. It was a very warm day for this time of the year, and the door was wide open to let in the warmth and sunshine. As I walked inside the house with my backpack on my shoulders and my burlap bag, Phoebe came out of the front bedroom. In shock, she looked at me as if I were a revenant. She took two quick steps towards me and put her arms around my neck, sobbing like a baby. She was trying to talk, but I could not make out the words she was saying. At last, she said, "I didn't think that you would make it, I thought I would never see you again." She kept holding on to me tightly. I had my arms around her, and that was when the words she said hit me; I shed a few tears.

Gabe was sitting at the kitchen table having a cup of tea and a cigarette. He looked as shocked as Phoebe. Gabe stood up and walked towards us, throwing his cap at me. His cap hit me in the head. I was surprised that he had done this and did not know the meaning of it. Gabe was a man who seldom displayed his emotions. He came close to hug me or shed a tear or two with us. I could tell by the tone of his voice that he was emotional and very happy to see me, relieved that I had made it home in one piece.

Our son Danny came out of the bedroom, walking with his baboo in his mouth. I was surprised to see him walk on his own. When I left six weeks ago, he could not walk yet on his own. Danny looked at me shyly, as if I were a stranger. Phoebe turned around and told him, "That is Dadoo." He looked at me, still drinking from his baboo, and smiled from the corner of his mouth. I picked him up and gave him a big hug.

I looked like a *"Nahgáa"* (bushman). My hair was unwashed, and, in a mess, my jean jacket was in shreds, and my jeans were split from the crotch to the back of my pants. I wore my jean jacket around my waist to hide the split in my pants. "I need to take a shower and wash my hair," I said. Gabe did not have running water at his house. "Let's go to the Simpson Hotel for a shower," said Phoebe. Back then, the hotel would charge five dollars for a shower at one of their rooms.

492

During the forty-two-day spring hunt, I lost a total of 16 kilos (35 pounds). I was a bit overweight before the spring hunt. The weight loss did me some good; I felt strong and in good shape. At the hotel, Phoebe told me that her dad had told her that he did not think I would make it back. The water on Trout River was very high this spring, and I did not have any experience traveling in a canoe. Gabe had made this trip several times and knew how dangerous the river would be in high water. I asked Phoebe why her dad threw his cap at me. She said that it was a sign of respect.

Later in the day, Baptiste's son Louie picked us up at Gabe's house with his car. He drove us to his dad's house. Baptiste and Peter had skinned the beavers they had shot on Trout River. Baptiste gave a beaver with a few smoked tails and *"Tsá lǫ"* to his younger brother. Baptiste said, "When the beaver hides are dried, I will go to the Hudson Bay Store to sell the fur from the trip."

"How much money would you like?" asked Baptiste.

I replied, "Nothing, I went on this trip for the experience and to learn from you. I thank you for inviting me on the spring hunt." I shook Baptiste's hand as we both smiled at each other.

A few days later, I saw Baptiste at the Hudson Bay Store in Fort Simpson talking with the manager of the store. I knew the manager; he was well-liked in the community. He was of average height and weight, in his late thirties or early forties, with curly, wavy, light brown hair near shoulder length. The fur we had harvested on the spring hunt was being graded by the manager at the back of the store where the fur was purchased from the trappers. I was curious to see how fur was graded and valued. The manager was using a measuring tape to determine the size of the twenty-three beaver hides we had trapped or shot. Once measured, each beaver hide was stacked into piles according to its size. The manager checked for damages by examining the leather side of the hides. Next, the two otters were measured and examined for damages.

"The otters are extra-large and good quality," said the manager. He added, "I will give you thirty-five dollars for each." Baptiste smiled at the manager and said, "That is a good price." The bear hide was measured and inspected for damages. "I will give you fifty dollars for the bear. I will buy it for myself and get it tanned to make a carpet," said the manager. Baptiste looked at me and the manager and said, "I'm okay with that." The dozen muskrats were measured and examined for damages. "Muskrat prices are not too good this year. I can only give you two dollars for each," said the manager. Baptiste asked, "How much for the beavers?" The manager looked at Baptiste for a few seconds and said, "Thirty-five for the extra-large, thirty for the large, and twenty-five for the medium size." The manager counted the hides in the three piles and used his adding machine to tally the total price for the beaver hides. Once he was done, he looked at Baptiste and said, "How about six hundred and ninety dollars?" Baptiste replied, "Make it seven hundred and fifty and we have a deal." The manager was not expecting this. He had the look of a deer caught in the headlights. The manager looked at Baptiste and said, "Your beaver hides are good quality with no damages." He hesitated for a few seconds and said, "We have a deal."

"How much for all the fur?" asked Baptiste. I quickly calculated in my head the total of the fur and came up with eight hundred and ninety-four dollars. The manager used a sheet of paper and a pencil and said, "Eight hundred and ninety-four dollars." Baptiste looked at the manager in the eyes, smiling, and said, "Make it nine hundred dollars and we have a deal." The manager chuckled and said, "We have a deal." The manager gave Baptiste eighteen crispy fifty-dollar bills and counted each one as he laid them on the table. Baptiste grabbed the money and asked me if I wanted some. I told him, "I went on the spring hunt to learn from you, not to make money, but thanks anyway."

I gave the burlap bag of bear dry meat to Gabe and Mary. A few days later, the dry meat had been all eaten by Gabe, Mary, Phoebe and me. We all enjoyed the smokiness and flavor of the dry meat.

As I write this story, I was transported back in time and lived through a memorable spring hunt again. That trip was an experience of a lifetime. Before that trip, I had never been in a canoe, let alone made my own paddle and drifted down a creek and river in high water with a canoe made from spruce, spruce bark, canvas, and paint. This story brought back many fond memories and tears.

Acknowlegments

I am deeply grateful to the following individuals, whose contributions have been invaluable in bringing this book to life:

Danita Allaire: For her meticulous scanning of photos, ensuring the images preserved the essence of our history.

Phoebe Allaire Cazon: For providing the photos and sharing her story, which added depth and emotion to this work.

Pauline Allaire: For the beautiful photo that helped illustrate our family's journey.

Dan Brown: For his expertise in editing, refining my words and helping me present this story with clarity and precision.

Elizabeth Stock: For capturing the breathtaking Aurora Borealis photos that evoke the beauty of the North.

Mary Cazon: For her quiet strength, her kindness, and the wisdom she shared with me. Her love and guidance continue to shape my life in the North.

Michael Cazon: For his thoughtful contributions to the story and his skillful scanning of photos, enriching this book with his perspective.

Mary-Jane & Gilbert Cazon: For their valuable assistance with South Slavey pronunciation and spelling, and for the support from K'iyeli Tourism Services.

Gabriel (Gabe) Cazon: For generously sharing his wisdom and elder stories, which shaped the soul of this narrative.

Baptiste Cazon: For his insight and storytelling, which connect us to the traditions and teachings of our ancestors.

Gordon Seymour: For the detailed maps that guide the reader through the land that has shaped our lives.

Brenda Allaire: For her careful editing and her dedication to making this book a true reflection of our family's history.

Tonya Makletzoff: For her beautiful painting photo, which added an artistic touch to the story.

Without each of your contributions, this book would not have been possible. Thank you for sharing your talents and your time, and for helping me preserve our story for future generations.